MW00905954

Bridging the Gap

The 7th Day

Who Was Early Man

Age of Phenomenal
Accomplishments

H. Donald Daae P. Geol.

Volume Two

WestBow
P R E S S
A DIVISION OF THOMAS NELSON

WestBow Press books may be ordered through booksellers or by contacting:

WestBow Press
A Division of Thomas Nelson
1663 Liberty Drive
Bloomington, IN 47403
www.westbowpress.com
1-(866) 928-1240

ISBN: 978-1-4497-1363-8 (sc)
ISBN: 978-1-4497-1364-5 (hc)
ISBN: 978-1-4497-1362-1 (e)

Library of Congress Control Number: 2011924986

Printed in the United States of America

WestBow Press rev. date: 4/14/2011

Scripture quotations used in this book are from the Holy Bible, the New International Version
(NIV) and the New King James Version (NKJV) and sometimes from other versions as indicated,

This manuscript has capitalized all references to Earth & Heaven in view of the fact that they are
proper nouns describing a real geographical place. They are in the same category as other proper
names like Canada, Calgary, London, Jerusalem, Paris or Rome. However, they are not capitalized
when quoted in the NIV, NKJV or other Bible references.

There are many Figures and Photos to illustrate different historical and geological events and
places. In the context of this manuscript a figure or a photo can often speak one thousand words.

Several original illustrations and figures were done by Elaine Daae and Bette Davies.

Table of Contents

APPENDICES

List of Figures

Origin of the GIRA Interpretation

The GIRA Interpretation is presented in several places within this manuscript. The question arises, what is the GIRA Interpretation?

This interpretation had its beginning in November of 1970, when I was asked to give a lecture series on, "Geology, Archaeology and the Bible" at the First Alliance Church, Calgary, Alberta, Canada. This series of lectures has been repeated many times at First Alliance Church and at many other churches, study groups, summer camps, conferences, colleges in Alberta and Saskatchewan and other places over the past years. This series has always been well received. Many would comment, *"We have often wondered how the whole creation model fits together and this is the first time it has really made sense"* or *"You are answering my questions with respect to how the Bible Record relates to the sciences of geology, archaeology, anthropology and to Early Man. They would also say, "You are answering my questions with respect to Creation and Evolution."*

Over the past years, I have conducted intensive literature research into the earth sciences, particularly geology, archaeology, anthropology and pre-history. The term paleo means old or ancient. Thus, it was in the areas of paleo-archaeology and paleo-anthropology that I was primarily interested. This led to an exhaustive study of analyzing evidences that relate directly to ancient or to Pre-Flood Early Man.

Genesis International Research Association

Genesis International Research Association (GIRA) became a reality through a group of interested professional men who supported me to start an organization. We became a registered association through the Federal Government of Canada on March 22, 1989.

My first book, **Bridging The Gap: The First 6 Days** was published in August of 1989. It is now being revised and updated. Our first Newsletter, **Bridging The Gap** was published in January of 1990. Our website is at www.gira.ca.

The GIRA Interpretation is mentioned several times in the text of this book which describes the mysterious origin & accomplishments of Early Man. This interpretation is a result of the many years of research and lecturing that I have done with respect to this particular topic of Early Man. This research has been done under the umbrella of Genesis International Research Association in consultation and co-operation with my Board Members.

This book is dedicated to my loving wife Evelyn and to my two daughters Elaine and Connie and to their family members.

Introduction

Why did God Create the Earth?

We may ask the question, why did God create the Earth? The Bible states that the primary reason why God planned, created, formed and made the Earth was that it would be **a place of habitation**. We read, "*Thus says the Lord who created the heavens, Who is God who formed the earth and made it, who has established it, Who did not create it in vain, Who formed it to be inhabited, I am the Lord and there is no other*" (Isaiah 45:18, NKJV). In the beginning, God created, formed and made the Earth so that its inhabitants would honor and glorify Him. We read in "Isaiah 43:7, "*All who claim me as their God will come, for I have made them for my glory. It was I who created them.*" NKJV

God's original purpose and plan for the Earth was that it would be inhabited and that all the inhabitants would give honor and glory to Him. We may ask the question, who are the inhabitants of the Earth today? The answer appears to be very simple in that Man is the present inhabitant of our Earth. This leads to a second question, was Man the first inhabitant of our Earth? According to the Bible Man was not the first inhabitant upon the Earth, but was the second.

This opens up a host of questions, if Man was not the first inhabitant, then who could have been on the Earth prior to human beings? The Bible states very clearly to us that the first inhabitants upon this Earth were LUCIFER AND HIS ANGELS. They arrived during the early part of the First Day of Creation. God placed them in a beautiful Garden called Eden. This garden was decked with beautiful gemstones. At this early period of time, the Earth was a most beautiful, magnificent place. From a distance it would have appeared like a beautiful, sparkling gemstone.

It is, herein, believed that this first Garden of Eden encompassed the entire Earth. It was a place where Lucifer and his angels served and worshipped Almighty God. However, something went tragically wrong. **The question arises: What went wrong and what Happened to Lucifer?**

Maybe the most important question is: what is the origin of Lucifer?
What do we know about Lucifer and the hosts of angels under his jurisdiction? How long have they been on this Earth? Do we know anything about his origin?

The Origin of Lucifer

We read in Ezekiel 28:15, "*You were blameless in your ways from the day you were created till wickedness was found in you.*" There was a day or a point in time, in the immeasurable past when Lucifer was created. This event took place prior to the creation of the Earth and the galaxies of stars. The Hebrew word create is "bara." It means God has the power to create something or some form of life out of no previous existing materials by the power of His Word. See Figure 8-2. Lucifer was created blameless, that is without sin.

Secondly, Lucifer was a guardian cherub upon God's Holy Mount Zion in God's Heaven. We read in Ezekiel 28:14, "*You were anointed as a guardian cherub, for so I ordained you. You were on the holy mount of God.*" The Holy Mountain of God is located on Mount Zion within God's Third Heaven. Lucifer was one of many Cherubim in God's Heaven. Cherubim are described in the Bible as having four wings (Ezekiel 10: 20-22). The fact that Lucifer was anointed by God as a guardian cherub may indicate that he was chief among the other cherubim. He certainly was chief among all

2

the other angelic beings that were present in this mysterious Primordial Garden called Eden.

Another big question arises, where was this First Primordial Garden called Eden located?

What is the Origin of Early Man?

The sciences of archaeology and anthropology have much to say about the origin of Early Man. The big question arises: how long has Man been on this Earth? Is there a conflict between the sciences of geology, archaeology, anthropology and the Bible record? According to the Bible record, the origin of Adam and Eve would have appeared to have taken place much later than what archaeologists say about Early Man. How is it possible to unravel this apparent dilemma?

How Long Has Life been on this Earth?

It is now possible to realize that life in one form or other has been present on the Earth from the time a solid crystalline crust began to form to the present day. According to the Bible record, the Earth will never cease to be a place of habitation except for a short interval of time in the future. After that short interval of time, the Earth will continue to be a place of habitation forever and ever. We read in Revelation 21:1, *"Then I saw a new heaven and a new earth, for the first heaven and the first earth had passed away, and there was no longer any sea."* We also read in Revelation 22:5, *"There will be no more night. They will not need the light of a lamp or the light of the sun, for the Lord God will give them light. And they will reign for ever and ever."*

How is it possible to relate the record of the Bible with the record of geology, archaeology and anthropology? There is an amazing compatibility between these two records? Let us now look into some of the mysterious happenings that have taken place in the past. Also what is taking place today and what will continue to take place in the future.

Chapter 1

The Primordial Garden of Eden

In the beginning, God in His great love created and formed the Earth in a most detailed manner in preparation for the first inhabitants. He fashioned a magnificent Garden called Eden that was garnished with all kinds of precious gemstones. Lucifer and his angels were brought by God to this beautiful, primordial, ancient Garden of Eden from the Third Heaven. It was here that they were able to enjoy the magnificent beauty of this Primordial Garden.

This Garden is described as follows: "*You (Lucifer) were in Eden, the garden of God; every precious stone was your covering, the sardius, the topaz, and the diamond, the beryl, the onyx, and jasper, the sapphire, the emerald with gold. The workmanship of your timbrels and pipes was prepared in you in the day that you were created. You were the anointed cherub that covers, and I established you. You were upon the Holy Mountain of God; You walked back and forth in the **midst of the fiery stones.** You were perfect in your ways from the day you were created, till iniquity was found in you.*" (Ezekiel 28:13-15) NKJV

Ezekiel 28:1-12 descibes the glory of the King of Tyre. It relates how this earthly king started out with great glory, but ended tragically. He even believed that he was a god. In a similar way Lucifer began with great glory until one tragic day this all came to a sudden end. He also believed that he was a god. Just as The King of Tyre came under the judgment of God, likewise Lucifer also came under the judgment of God. Who was Lucifer and what led to his demise?

Who Was Lucifer?

Lucifer was a being of great beauty as the scripture relates, "*You were the seal of perfection, full of wisdom and perfect in beauty*" (Ezekiel 28;12b, NKJV). This verse reflects the inner beauty and character of Lucifer before His Fall. It also reflects the beauty and serenity within this beautiful Garden called Eden. It was a place of perfect peace, beauty and safety. It was a place of worship, because all of God's angelic beings worship and glorify Him. It was a place of music and singing for we read, "*The workmanship of your timbrels and pipes were prepared for you on the day that you were created.*" (Ezekiel 28:13b, NKJV) This verse is full of meaning. First, Lucifer, a cherub, was created by God. This verifies that the scripture is not referring to any human being, because only Adam & Eve were created by God. All other humans were born into this world. Secondly, God created Lucifer and all angelic beings in the immeasureable past with the ability to sing, to play music and to serve their Maker. Timbrels and pipes are types of musical instruments. The pipes that were prepared for Lucifer at the time he was created may also relate to his ability to sing.

Ezekiel 28:12-15 gives a brief insight into the grandeur and beauty of this ancient Primordial Garden of Eden and also into the appearance and character of Lucifer. Lucifer was a Cherub for we read in Ezekiel 28:14a, "*You were the anointed cherub that covers.*" (NKJV) Cherubim are a group of the second highest order of angelic beings in the Third Heaven. They are described in the Bible as having wings (Exodus 25:20, NKJV). Ezekiel describes the cherubim in Ezekiel 10:19 as follows, "*And the cherubim lifted their wings and mounted up from the earth in my sight.*" In verse 21 we read, "*Each one had four wings and the likeness of the hands of a man under their wings.*" Lucifer was created by God and was perfect in his ways, implying that he was without sin. He was adorned with precious gemstones, such as the sardius, the topaz and the diamond etc, In other words these gemstones were adornments for him.

In this magnificent Primordial Garden of Eden, Lucifer walked on stones of fire. Gemologists tell us that gemstones of great value appear as stones of fire. They have an inert or inner fiery brilliance within them. In other words this garden was garnished and adorned by these beautiful precious gemstones. The grandeur and beauty is beyond our very imagination. This was the home of Lucifer and his angels.

The Earth at this time was a most beautiful magnificent place. From a distance, it would have appeared like a brilliant diamond. It would have been a most enticing and wonderful place to visit.

The science of Geology confirms that all the gemstones mentioned above are present within the crystalline rocks of the Archean Age on this Earth. Geology also confirms that there were no oceans present on the Earth during the Archean Age. This would have been during the early part of the First Day of Creation (see Figures 3-1 & 3-5). However, there would have been water in lesser amounts and an atmosphere and hydrosphere suitable for life.

The Earth at this time was a foretaste of what it will be like in the future as was revealed to John in Revelation 21:1 NKJV, *"And I saw a new heaven and a new earth, for the first heaven and the first earth had passed away. Also there was no more sea (oceans)."* The future rejuvenated Earth will not have any sea or oceans. It will also be a place without sin, evil, death or darkness. It may be similar to what the Earth was like in the beginning prior to the Fall of Lucifer. More likely, its future beauty and magnificence will be beyond what we could ever imagine or think.

A Joyous Celebration in the Third Heaven

No wonder there was great joy, singing and celebration among the angels of God because the Earth had just been prepared for habitation. This joyous event took place within the Third Heaven. God the Father through His Son the Lord Jesus Christ, the Creator of all things, had just prepared a most magnificent place called Eden, the Garden of God. It was a place of habitation for Lucifer and the angels under his jurisdiction. A brief glimpse into this joyous occasion is recorded in the book of Job as follows: *"When the morning stars sang together and all the sons of God shouted for joy."* (Job 38:7 NKJV)

This amazing verse of jubilation is tucked between the time when God laid the cornerstone and foundations of the Earth in Job 38:4-7 and when he brought about the Birth of the Oceans in Job 38:8-11. See Figures 3-1 & 3-5'. Two groups of created angelic beings are referred to as follows:

1) The morning stars sang together.
2) All the sons of God shouted for joy.

The question arises who could the morning stars have been? Is it possible that the clue is to be found in the name Lucifer which means Morning Star? Isaiah 14:12 informs us that Lucifer was the Son of the Morning for we read, *"How are you fallen from heaven, O Lucifer, son of the morning!"* (NKJV) Is it possible that Lucifer was one of these Morning Stars that sang together in that time of great jubilation? Being that Lucifer was a Cherub, it is possible that the morning stars were the Cherubim of Heaven that were singing together and rejoicing that the Most High God of Heaven and Earth had just prepared the Earth as a place of habitation for Lucifer and his angels? I believe this to be true.

Second, who were the Sons of God who shouted with joy? Bible scholars generally agree that they were the multi millions of angels in God's Third Heaven. They were filled with joy and gladness because God had just prepared the Earth for habitation. Now, they were celebrating the fact that they were going to inhabit this most beautiful, magnificent place called Eden on Earth. It was called the Garden of God. It was indeed a time of great rejoicing and jubilee.

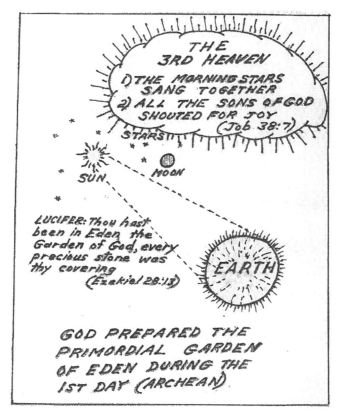

Figure 1-1: The Primordial Garden of Eden was planned, created & formed by God during the early part of the First Day of Creation. From space the Earth would have appeared as a beautiful gemstone. Figure by Don Daae

Earth's Golden Age

The dramatic moment came when the Earth's first inhabitants arrived on planet Earth from the Third Heaven. This took place immediately after this joyous and jubilant celebration in the Third Heaven and after God had laid the Earth's cornerstone and foundations. Geologically, it would have been during the early part of the Archean Age. See Figure 3-1. The Earth at this moment in time was a most beautiful and hospitable place. See Figure 1-1.

Lucifer and a host of angels under his jurisdiction began to occupy this beautiful, majestic place called Eden, the Garden of God. This beautiful primordial Garden of Eden was indeed a place of matchless beauty. It was a place of joy and gladness. There was no such thing as evil, sin, or death anywhere throughout the universe. The Earth during this time was a most hospitable place. Truly, this was "Earth's Golden Age."

The Bible says that Lucifer was able to walk up and down on the stones of fire in the Garden and he was also able to sit in the assembly places of the north that is before God's Throne on Mount Zion in the Third Heaven. We read in Ezekiel 28:14, *"You were on the Holy Mountain of God."* (NKJV) In other words, Lucifer and the angels were able to commute back and forth from Earth to the Third Heaven just as God's angelic beings are able to do today. They had the best of both worlds. The Earth was indeed a beautiful paradise.

On the basis of geology, The Earth would have continued to be a place of exquisite beauty throughout the entire Archean Age. This age is believed to equate to about 0.8 billion years in duration based upon geological radiometric dating methods. See Figures 1-1 & 3-1.

Something Tragic happened?

Indeed the Earth was a most beautiful, magnificent place. It was a place of worship, singing and music to the most High God until one tragic day, sin was found in the heart of Lucifer. This, indeed, became the blackest, darkest day that the First, Second and Third Heavens had ever experienced. In other words, what happened to Lucifer? See Figure 3-4.

Before we begin to examine the seriousness of what took place and what happened to Lucifer, it is important to clearly understand the differences between the First, Second and the Third Heaven.

Chapter 2

The Three Heavens?

The concept of Heaven is entrenched in our literature, our culture and our thinking. Every person has a deep inner desire to go to Heaven, but the question arises, where is Heaven located? What is Heaven like? How do I get There?

The Bible has much to say about Heaven and we are told in Genesis 1:8 that, *"God called the firmament heaven."*(NKJV) Is Heaven no greater than the firmament, which is the hydrosphere? Is this the same heaven found in Genesis 1:1 which says, *"In the beginning God created the heavens and the earth."* Could there possibly be more than one Heaven? Paul speaks about being taken up to the Third Heaven for we read in 2 Corinthians 12:2 (NKJV), *"God knows--such a one was caught up to the third heaven."* It becomes evident upon analyzing and comparing the various passages of scripture that the Bible is describing three separate Heavens (see Figure 2-1).

The Hebrew word for Heaven is **Shomayim**. It is a noun that is always in the plural. It is used to describe each of the three Heavens. They are in reality one Heaven with three distinct component parts.

The First Heaven

From the vantage point of Man standing on the Earth, the First Heaven that one observes is the firmament. Genesis 1:8 says, *"God called the firmament Heaven (Shomayim)."*

We read in Psalm 19:1b (NKJV), "And *the firmament shows His handiwork.*" When one observes the beautiful mountains, the sweeping prairies, the vast desert areas, the lush, beautiful vegetation throughout the world, one is beholding what the Bible is referring to as the "First Heaven." It is literally teeming with plant and animal life of all descriptions. It is that portion of our Earth that is able to sustain life. It encompasses the oceans with all its aquatic life, and the biosphere where you and I dwell. Every breath of air that we breathe is a gift from the First Heaven. It is a beautiful place that is very much alive.

The Second Heaven

The Second Heaven is the physical universe of galaxies and stars. The very first verse of the Bible says, *"In the beginning God created the heavens (Shomayim) and the earth"* (Genesis 1:1 NKJV). From the vantage point of the Earth looking out into space, all the heavenly bodies including the sun, moon and stars are included with this Heaven. The psalmist briefly describes this Heaven in Psalm 8:3-4a (NKJV), *"When I consider Your heavens, the work of Your fingers, the moon and the stars that You have ordained, what is man that you are mindful of Him?"* The Second Heaven includes the millions of galaxies, quasars, pulsars, solar systems and spheres of all descriptions and sizes in this vast area called the universe.

The fact that God is present throughout the universe makes it very much alive. The Bible is very clear that God's holy angels are continually commuting back and forth from the Third Heaven to the Earth and always for a specific purpose. It is also possible that God's holy angelic beings are being delegated by God to various parts of the universe for specific purposes. For instance, when Jesus was born in Bethlehem 2000 years ago, an angel appeared to the Shepherds announcing the good news that a Savior had been born who is Christ the Lord. This was followed by a great company of the heavenly host of angels who were praising God and saying, *"Glory to God in the highest, and on earth peace to men on whom His favor rests."* (Luke 2: 8 -14) NIV

The Third Heaven

The Bible describes the Third Heaven as God's home. Paul tells about an experience of having been caught up into the Third Heaven, "*I know a man in Christ who fourteen years ago—whether in the body I do not know, or whether out of the body I do not know, God knows—such a one was caught up to the third heaven.* (2 Corinthians 12:2 NKJV) In the context of this chapter, we realize Paul was literally taken up into the Third Heaven. He was taken to Paradise. This is where the Heavenly Mount Zion is located. This is where our prayers ascend. This is where God the Son, the Lord Jesus Christ is seated at the right hand of God the Father, continually interceding on our behalf. This is the Mission Control Centre of the universe. God has complete control over the entire universe and over all creation from the Third Heaven. He knows exactly what is taking place at every place at all times.

The Third Heaven is God's home and is very much alive. The Bible gives many references to the beauty, splendor and grandeur of this Heaven. In Psalm 48: 1-3 we read, "*Great is the Lord and most worthy of praise, in the city of our God, his holy mountain. It is beautiful in its loftiness, the joy of the whole earth. Like the utmost heights of Zaphon is Mount Zion, the city of the Great King. God is in her citadels.*"(NIVUK) Then we read in Hebrews 12:22-24, "*You have come to Mount Zion, to the heavenly Jerusalem, the city of the living God. You have come to thousands of angels in joyful assembly, to the church of the firstborn, whose names are written in heaven. You have come to God, the judge of all men, to the spirits of righteous men made perfect, to Jesus the mediator of the new covenant and to the sprinkled blood that speaks a better word than the blood of Abel.*" (NIV)

The only part of reality that is detectable by our five senses is the physical universe. We as finite human beings are able to see and observe the First and Second Heavens. We are unable to see or discern the Highest Heaven, because it resides within the realm of the invisible. It is within a different frequency or dimension. According to the Bible, reality consists of both the visible and the invisible for we read, *"For by him (the Lord Jesus Christ) all things were created that are in heaven and on earth, visible and invisible, whether thrones or rulers or authorities. All things were created by him and for him. He is before all things and in him all things hold together"* (Colossians 1:16 &17, NIVUK).

The Third Heaven, where God dwells, is often referred to as the Highest Heaven or the Heaven of Heavens. We read in Nehemiah 9:6, *"You alone are the LORD. You made the heavens [second heaven], even the highest heavens [third heaven] and all their starry host, the earth [first heaven] and all that is on it, the seas and all that is in them. You give life to everything, and the multitudes of heaven worship you." (NIV)* The multitudes of Heaven refer to all of God's holy angelic beings and to all human beings who have and will receive Jesus Christ as their personal Savior and Lord. Thus, we see that the First Heaven includes the oceans as well as the land areas with its great variety of life. It becomes apparent that the First and Third Heavens are very much alive.

Is it possible that the Second Heaven may also be very much alive? The omnipresence of the Triune God throughout the vast universe makes it very much alive. It is also highly possible that God's holy angels commute back and forth from the Third Heaven to various parts of the universe.

The Three Heavens are One

The main point to bear in mind is that the three Heavens (Shomayim) are one Heaven having three component parts. The three-in-one relationship of the Triune God is revealed in and through the Heavens and throughout all of God's creation. There is a finger print of our Triune God in all Creation. For example, atoms are the building blocks of all creation. Each atom is a trinity consisting of three primary parts which are a nucleus, protons and electrons.

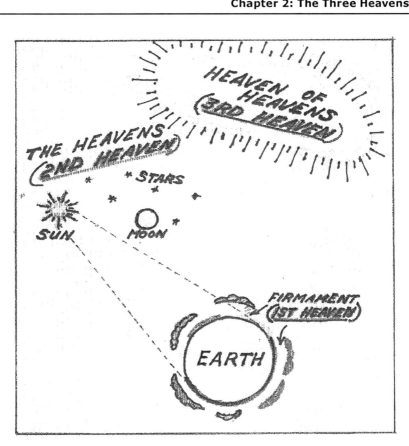

Figure 2-1: The Biblical Three Heavens by Don Daae.

Man is a trinity consisting of a body, soul and spirit. The Earth is a trinity with an inner core, a middle mantle and an outer crust. An egg has an inner yoke, a middle white and an outer shell, yet one egg. An apple has an inner core, a middle edible part and an outer peel. Light rays from the sun consist of three basic components, infra red, white and ultraviolet rays. We could go on and on with our illustrations to show how each one of God's creations reveals a three-in-one relationship.

God has Ownership of the Earth and All Creation

The Bible acknowledges God as the sole owner of the three Heavens. We read in Deuteronomy 10:14, *"To the LORD your*

God belong the heavens (second heaven), even the highest heavens (third heaven), the earth (first heaven) and everything in it." (NIV) God has total ownership of His creation by the mere fact that He is the Creator of all things. The Bible says, *"For every animal of the forest is mine, and the cattle on a thousand hills. I know every bird in the mountains and the creatures of the field are mine. If I were hungry I would not tell you, for the world is mine and all that is in it"* (Psalm 50:10-11 NIV). In other words, He owns every species and variety of animal, plant and microscopic (bacteria) forms of life on the Earth. He has placed man on the Earth to look after and to be a good steward of all that He has made. We read, *"Let us make man in our image, in our likeness, and let them rule over the fish of the sea and the birds of the air, over the livestock, over all the creatures that move along the ground."* (Genesis 1:26 NIV)

We may stand in awe at the wonders, beauty, and magnificence of God's creation as revealed in the First and Second Heavens. However, this is only a glimpse of a far surpassing beauty, magnificence, vastness, glory and awesomeness of the Third Heaven which is God's home and will also be our future home if we are willing to receive Him into our hearts and life.

If the Third Heaven appears great and glorious, how much greater, bigger, more glorious, beautiful, majestic and awesome must God be. Even reason and logic say to us that the Creator must always be greater than what He has created for we read, *"The Lord is exalted over all the nations and His glory is above the Heavens"* (Psalm 113:4 NIV). The Bible reveals that God is Omnipotent (all powerful), Omniscient (all knowing), and Omnipresent (everywhere present).

Who is God?

According to the Bible, God is infinite and the time prior to the creation of the universe is infinite. God has always been. He is from everlasting to everlasting as is recorded in Psalm 90:2 (NKJV), *"Before the mountains were brought forth, or ever You had formed the earth and the world, even from everlasting to everlasting, You are God."* How long is everlasting?

Our finite minds demand a beginning and an end, but with God there is no beginning and no end. God is the great timeless One, as He stated to Moses, *"I AM WHO I AM"* (Exodus 3:14 NKJV). God is always in the eternal present, as the great "I AM" of the universe. He is the High and Lofty One who inhabits eternity (Isaiah 57:15). He is the all powerful, all knowing, everywhere present God. He is the supreme intelligence behind all Creation. He never changes. He is the same yesterday, today and forever (Hebrews 13:8). However, all creation is in a continual state of change, but God will always be the same throughout all time and eternity. There is no beginning or end with God. However, when it comes to all that He has made within the universe, then the following verse applies, *"I am the Alpha and Omega, the Beginning and the End, says the Lord."* (Revelations 1:8, NKJV). He is the one who has brought all things within the universe into being and will one day bring about their demise.

Where is the Third Heaven Located?

Dr. Irwin Moon,[2] Producer of the Moody Institute of Science Films, had the following interview about heaven with a famous physicist who had won the Nobel Prize for his achievement in the Porosity of Matter. The conversation is as follows:

Dr. Moon: Do you believe in God?

Scientist: Oh yes, in fact all scientists I know believe in God. The closer you get to the basic construction of matter, the more you know there has to be a God. But don't get me wrong, I don't believe in God the way you do.

Dr. Moon: What is the difference?

Scientist: Let me ask you a question. Where is heaven located?

Dr. Moon: We used to say "up", but now that we know the world is round, we say it is "out" instead of "up".

17

Scientist: How far is out?

Dr. Moon: I don't know?

Scientist: Is Abel in heaven?

Dr. Moon: Yes, Abel is in heaven.

Scientist: How did he get there?

Dr. Moon: I don't know.

Scientist: If heaven is located just beyond the range of my telescope and Abel has been traveling at the speed of light for 6,000 years, he is only a tiny portion of the distance that I have seen with my telescope. So, assuming that heaven is just beyond the range of my telescope, he has literally thousands of years yet to go before he reaches heaven.

Dr. Moon: Doctor, you have received the Nobel prize for your work in physics. You have done more than any other person to popularize the idea of the porosity of matter. Now, if your research is true, is this wall mostly space?

Scientist: yes, it's about as porous as a breath of fresh air.

Dr. Moon: If this wall is porous and this chair is porous, why can't I push the chair through the wall the same way I can push my fingers in between one another?

Scientist: I don't know why you can't push the chair through the wall. I have tried it and it won't go through. But this I know, it is not because there is a collision of the solid particles. We assume that between the solid particles there is an electrical flux operating on opposing frequencies. To illustrate this, take two horseshoe magnets and try pushing them together, like poles against like poles. You will discover that there is a strong electrical force that keeps you from doing it. This is what the scientist is saying about opposing frequencies.

Dr. Moon: If your theory is true, would it be possible then for two earths to occupy the same space at the same time and neither be conscious of the others existence if they were perfectly synchronized by frequency so that there are no collisions?

Scientist: (after thinking a moment): Yes, not only two, but hundred's of thousands of earths could occupy the very same space.

Dr. Moon: I think I have learned something very valuable from this conversation. Just this morning I was reading Ephesians 2:6, which says, *"We are seated in heavenly places in Christ Jesus."* **To get to Heaven I may not have to move an inch.** All I have to do is to change to a different frequency or dimension and enter into a new and wonderful place. [2]

According to the Bible the Third Heaven is closer than we realize. **There is a thin veil that separates you and I from the Third Heaven.** As an example, when Stephen was stoned as a martyr, the Bible reports, *"But Stephen, full of the Holy Spirit, looked up to heaven and saw the glory of God, and Jesus standing at the right hand of God. `Look' he said, `I see Heaven open and the Son of Man standing at the right hand of God"* (Acts 7:55-56 NIV). Stephen was given a glimpse into the Third Heaven, or in other words into the throne room of the universe just prior to his death. **This makes us aware that the Third Heaven is near at all times.**

Dr. Moon presents a Biblical example when Israel and Syria were engaged in battle. the Syrian King was told that the Israeli prophet Elisha somehow knew all their battle plans. He even knew what the King had dreamed in his sleep, so they set out to capture Elisha. The next morning Elisha and his servant realized they were completely surrounded by a great host of Syrian soldiers with horses and chariots. The servant was afraid. Elisha consoled his servant and said to him, *"Do not fear, for those who are with us are more than they that be with them."* (2 Kings 6:16 NKJV) Elisha prayed to the Lord and said, *"LORD, I pray, open his eyes that he may see. Then the Lord opened the eyes of the young man, and he saw. And behold, the mountain was full of horses and chariots of fire around Elisha"* (11 Kings 6:17, NKJV). If we could translate this as follows, *"Change his frequency so that he can see what is out there."* **God lifted the veil**

so that the servant could see that God's army was greater and more powerful than that of the Syrians.

When Jesus Christ was born in Bethlehem an angel of the Lord suddenly appeared to the shepherds that were keeping watch over their flocks by night. The angel announced the birth of the Christ child. This is followed by a dramatic scene, *"And suddenly there was with the angel a multitude of the heavenly host praising God and saying, Glory to God in the highest and on earth peace, good will toward men"* (Luke 2:13-14 NKJV). **Once again God lifted the veil, so that the lowly shepherds could see the angels that normally would be in the realm of the Third Heaven.**

How close are we to the Third Heaven? Two thousand years ago when Jesus ascended into Heaven we read, *"After this, He was taken up before their very eyes, and a cloud hid him from their sight. They were looking intently up into the sky as He was going, when suddenly two men dressed in white stood beside them. `Men of Galilee,' they said, `why do you stand here looking up into the sky? This same Jesus, who has been taken from you into Heaven, will come back in the same way you have seen him go into Heaven"* (Acts 1:9-11, NIV). The two angels announced Jesus entry into Heaven. **Jesus entered into the Third Heaven immediately after the cloud received him out of their sight.** It was at this moment in time that He passed from the First Heaven into the Third Heaven.

In other words, to get to the Third Heaven I may not have to move an inch. All I have to do is to change to a different frequency or dimension. This will enable me to enter into a new and wonderful place called the Third Heaven. For example, If I were freezing to death in a blinding snowstorm, instantly, the Lord would take me into a new country of beauty, splendor and warmth where I would be in this beautiful place called the Third Heaven. However, this will only happen if you have connected with the God of Heaven and Earth. Otherwise, you are headed towards a lost eternity.

References for Chapter 2

1. DeHaan M.R., "The Primordial Garden of Eden." This booklet was written by Dr. DeHaan in the 1950's or early 1960's. I have written to the Radio Bible Class to get a copy of this booklet. Obviously it is long out of print.
2. This was an article describing a conversation between Dr. Irwin Moon, who was a Producer of the Moody Institute of Science Films and a Nobel Prize winning scientist. It was printed in one of "The Navigators Newsletters."

Chapter 3

The Origin of Sin & Death

Through the science of Geology, we are now able to determine the approximate time when the Earth was created in the distant past. It also identifies when and where the First primordial Garden of Eden was created, formed and made by God. It also identifies the length of time that this Garden was in existence. It also identifes when this beautiful Garden came to an abrupt termination.

Through the science of geology, the "Fossil Record" is now able to determine the approximate time when the Fall of Lucifer took place and when the first evidence of sin and death are found. The geological fossil record is a record of life and death. In other words, each species of animal and plant life that has ever lived on Earth have also experienced death. Thus, the presence of evil that resulted from the Fall of Lucifer had to precede the first appearance of life and death in the fossil record.

By tracing death back from the time of Man through the geological fossil record one arrives at a period of time called the Lower Proterozoic Age (see Figures 3-1 & 3-5). The first fossils on Earth are found in the form of bacteria and blue-green chlorophyl generating algae (sea weeds & plankton) in water laid sediments of Lower Proterozoic Age. **THIS MARKS THE BEGINNING OF THE FOSSIL RECORD.** It was also a time of "**A New Beginning on Earth.**"

Species are found within the Lower Proterozoic sediments that represent the bacteria and the marine algal plant kingdoms. This narrows the geological window when God prepared this most beautiful Primordial Garden called Eden to the preceding Archean Age.

The Geological Column
during the
The First Day of Creation

Earth's Golden Age|		Age of New Beginnings	
Hadean Age	Archean Age	Proterozoic Age	Cambrian Age
4.7 b.yrs	4.5 b.yrs 3.8 b.yrs		544-510 mm yrs
	The Fall of		Explosion
	1st Inhabitants Arrive Lucifer	Birth of the Oceans A Sin Cursed Earth	of
	1st Garden of Eden		Animal Life

Figure 3-1: Illustrates the entire Geological First Day of Creation. The Cambrian Age is now considered to be about 34 miilion years in length. The Proterozoic is about 3.6 billion years. The Archean is about 0.8 billion years and the age of the Hadean Age is unknown. These dates are based upon radiometric dating methods. See Figure 3-5 and the quote by Dr. Roger C. Wiens.[3] This Figure was prepared by Don Daae. It was computer generated by Mike Gilders.

Figure 3-1 reveals the Geological Histoy of the Earth from the beginning of the Hadean Age to the end of the Cambrian Age. It shows the approximate time the First Garden of Eden came into existence. This was truly Earth's Golden Age. It shows when the First Inhabitants, that is Lucifer and the angels under his supervision, arrived on Earth at the beginning of the Archean Age. It also shows when the Fall of Lucifer took place at the end of the Archean Age and when ocean waters first appeared on Earth. Compare with Figure 3-5.

The Hadean Age

In geology, the earliest stage of Earth's history is referred to as the Hadean. At the moment of creation, the Earth was in an extremely hot, gaseous state. As time progressed the Earth began to cool and to convert to a liquid and semi-liquid state.

The geological term Hadean is described by Preston Cloud[1] as follows, "*An interval (Hadean) for which no certain record has been discovered on earth, though it has on the moon - ended 3.6 to 3.5 aeons ago by a world-wide thermal event, possibly cosmic as the moon may also affected.*" The present author would re-define the Hadean period as follow: "*An interval (Hadean) which began with the creation of the Earth in an extremely hot gaseous state, and continued as the earth cooled to a liquid state and ended when a solid crystalline crust began to form which relates to the beginning of the Archean Age.*" [2]

The Bible record gives additional information that relates directly to the Hadean Age. We read in Genesis 1:1-2a, "*[1]In the beginning God created the heavens and the earth. [2] Now the earth was formless and empty.*" (NIV) What does formless mean? We are in reality talking about the very moment of creation when the Earth was created by God. It was in an extremely hot, gaseous and formless state. We are in essence talking about atoms, minerals and rocks. For instance a granite rock at normal temperatures is in a solid state, but if it is heated to its melting point it will revert to a hot liquid state. If it is heated to a higher temperature it will revert to an extremely hot gaseous state which is formless. Every rock, mineral or substance on Earth can exist in one of three states, a solid, liquid or gaseous state.

The Bible then gives additional information about what took place during the Hadean Age. We read in Job 38:4-6 NKJV, "*Where were you when I laid the foundations of the earth? Tell Me, if you have understanding. [5] Who determined its measurements? Surely you know! Or who stretched the (plum) line upon it? [6] To what were its foundations fastened? Or who laid its cornerstone?"*

In describing the Earth to Job in this way, God is stressing the significance of the creative process associated with the formation of the Earth. He asks rhetorical questions as to when the foundations of the Earth were laid, who determined the measurements of the interior of the Earth, and who stretched the plumb line upon it. The latter two questions indicate that planning was involved to determine the dimensions and the constructive accuracy of the Earth's interior. The science of geology and geophysics has provided great insight into the general make-up of the Earth's interior structure.

God asks a further question in Job 38:6 (NKJV) *"To what were its foundations fastened? Or who laid its cornerstone?"* The answer is obvious from the context: that the foundations are fastened to the cornerstone and secondly, this was all accomplished by the amazing Creator of the universe who created the Earth according to a pre-conceived plan. This plan was conceived by the Amazing Architect of the Universe. See Figure 8-1.

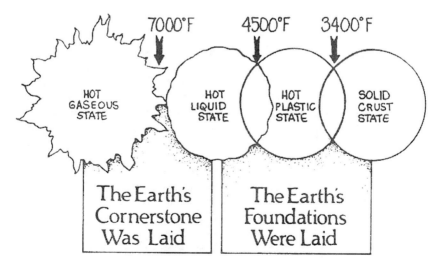

Figure 3-2: A diagram illustrating the time when the Earth's Cornerstone and Foundations were laid.

During the Hadean Age, the Earth was in a very hot gaseous / liquid state. This was the time when God laid the Earth's Cornerstone and Foundations. The crystalline crust began to form at the termination of the Hadean Age.

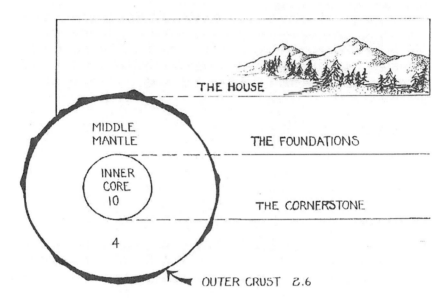

Figure 3-3: An Illustration of the Earth's Cornerstone, Foundations and House.

The Archean Age

All of the precious gemstones that are named in this Garden called Eden are found in the crystalline rocks of the Archean Age. According to geology, the Archean Age began the moment the Earth had cooled sufficiently for a solid crystalline crust to form.

The Archean Age spans a period of time of about 0.8+ billion years based upon radioactive methods of dating. This may give an insight into the length of time that this Garden was inhabited prior to Lucifer's Fall. It also give an insight into the immeasurable past. All the millions and billions of angelic beings were created by God in the immeasurable past. They have always been a part of God's Third Heaven from eternity past. They were created prior to the creation of the physical universe and the Earth which are in reality the First & Second Heavens.

On the basis of geology, the logical time for God to have prepared this beautiful Primordial Garden called Eden was at the beginning of the Archean Age, just after the crystalline crust had formed.

Why did Lucifer rebel against God?

The Bible tells us that it was pride that caused Lucifer to rebel against Almighty God. He was a created being of great physical and spiritual beauty. We read in Ezekiel 28:17(NKJV), "*Your heart was lifted up because of your beauty; you corrupted your wisdom for the sake of your splendor.*" Because of his beauty and the splendor of his surroundings, his heart was lifted up in pride. There is an old axiom which says: "*pride comes before the fall*". Sin always begins as a thought, which is later translated into action. Sin always evolves and becomes progressively more evil. This is how it was with Lucifer.

Lucifer after the Fall

The sin of pride that was conceived in Lucifer's heart began to grow. His sin was soon translated into evil, violent action. Sin corrupted Lucifer's entire being, his body, soul and spirit. He was no longer a creature full of wisdom, but now his wisdom was corrupted and became as foolishness. When he realized the great material wealth that he possessed within this beautiful Primordial Garden called Eden, it went to his head and he commenced a life of sinful pride against Almighty God. Sin always evolves. He, thus, became filled with violence which is recorded as follows: "*By the abundance of your trading, you became filled with violence within and you have sinned.*" (Ezekiel 28:16, NKJV) The multitude of your trading implies that a sophisticated paradigm was present on Earth based upon a trading and a transfer of goods and services among each other.

He was no longer the loving, considerate, mild cherub, but now he became as a roaring lion. He was no longer willing to submit his will to the Most High God, but now began to exert his own will and to begin a life of sin in an opposite direction to what he had known before. He wanted everyone to become like himself and wasn't satisfied until he had caused many of the angels in his realm to likewise commit sin as the following record testifies, "*You have defiled your sanctuaries by the multitude of your iniquities, by the iniquity of your trading*" (Ezekie1:28:18, NKJV).

There were sanctuaries in this magnificent Primordial Garden of Eden. This is where Lucifer and the hosts of angels under his care and direction would come to worship Almighty God. It was originally a place of worship, joy, music, and singing. In other words it was a place of paradise, sweet fellowship, reverence and praise to the Most High God. Now his sanctuaries were becoming defiled with the darkness and the blackness of sin. His iniquities became multiplied over and over again as one after another of his angels were deceitfully lured into a life of sin, wickedness, violence and evil against Almighty God. It is believed that possibly a third of the angels under his jurisdiction were deceived and began living a life of sin and evil. From this moment and onward, the Earth became very dark, black, sin cursed planet.

The demonic web that surrounded the Earth at this time became Satan's home. It is also the home of all the fallen angels that the Bible describes as evil spirits, demons, and unclean spirits. It has become a place of spiritual darkness, hatred, discord, jealousy, witchcraft and all kinds of evil.

The Origin of Sin, Evil, Violence & Death

The Bible associates the Origin of Evil with the Fall of Lucifer. Evil is a direct result of sin and death. We read in Romans 6:23, "*The wages of sin is death.*" (NKJV) We also read, "*The sting of death is sin*" (1 Cor. 15:56, NKJV). The Bible says, "The *last enemy that will be destroyed is death.*" (1 Cor. 15:26, NKJV). The origin of sin had to precede the first evidence of death on Earth. The place to look for the evidence of death on Earth is within the science of geology, which is a study of the history of the Earth.

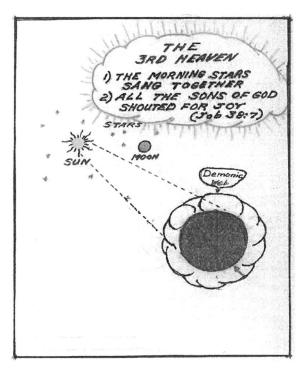

Figure 3-4: The Earth became a Dark Sin Cursed Planet as a result of the Fall of Lucifer. This is referred to as the Edenic Curse. See Chapter 4. Generated by Don Daae

The Bible refers to Lucifer after his Fall as Satan (Matthew 4:10, Luke 10:18), as the Devil (Matthew 4:1), as the god of this world (II Corinthians 4:4), as a murderer and the father of lies (John 8:44). Jesus said, *"He was a murderer from the beginning, not holding to the truth, for there is no truth in him. When he lies, he speaks his native language, for he is a liar and the father of lies"* (John 8:44, NIV). The beginning in the above verse refers to the moment in time that sin was conceived in his heart.

All persons who habitually lie are following their Father the Devil. If you want to get an insight into the character of Satan, then you will see him in the eyes of serial killers, murderers and liars. These persons have entered into the realm of wickedness.

The Bible also says that Satan is an unclean spirit (Matthew 12:43), our adversary (I Peter 12:10), prince of devils (Matthew 12:24), prince of the power of the air (Ephesians 2:2), prince of the air (John 14:30), ruler of darkness (Ephesians 6:12), serpent (Genesis 3:4), dragon (Rev. 12:9), tempter (Matthew 4:3), wicked one (Matthew 13:19). According to the Bible a demonic web of evil now surrounds our Earth. See Figure 3-4.

His angels that sinned are called demons, fallen angels, evil spirits. They are all very much alive in the world today. Satan is described in Ephesians 6:12 as the prince and power of the air. Jesus referred to Satan as the ruler of this world who will be cast out at a future day (John 12:31). The Bible admonishes us, *"Be sober, be vigilant; because your adversary the devil walks about like a roaring lion, seeking whom he may devour."* (I Peter 5:8 NKJV) Today, he is luring men and women, boys and girls away from the true and living God to a life of sin, wickedness, evil and violence. He wants all humans to be like himself.

It is important that men and women are aware who their real enemy is. If we want to see the results of the sinister forces of Satan and his fallen angels which are today called demons all we have to do is read the newspaper to get a glimpse of the murder, crime, violence, hatred, envy, strife, wars, rumours of wars, breakup of homes, separation, divorce and sufferings of all nature. This tragic picture can be multiplied over and over again. This is the result of a sinister, evil force working behind the scenes for *"For we do not wrestle against flesh and blood, but against principalities, against powers, against the rulers of the darkness of this age, against spiritual hosts of wickedness in the heavenly places."* (Ephesians 6:12, NKJV) Truly the darkest and blackest day in the history of our Earth and the Universe took place when Lucifer sinned and wilfully decided to challenge Almighty God.

Against this background of despair we have the bright shining news of the Gospel which states time and time again that it is possible for Man and Woman to have complete victory and power over sin and the Devil. The answer is given as follows:

"Finally, my brethren, be strong in the Lord and in the power of His might. Put on the whole armour of God that you may be able to stand against the wiles of the devil. For we do not wrestle against flesh and blood, but against principalities, against powers, against the rulers of the darkness of this age, against spiritual hosts of wickedness in the heavenly places. Therefore take up the whole armor of God, that you may be able to withstand in the evil day, and having done all, to stand." Ephesians 6:10-13, NKJV) Jesus said in John 10:10 NIV, *"The thief comes only to steal and kill and destroy; I have come that they may have life, and have it to the full."*

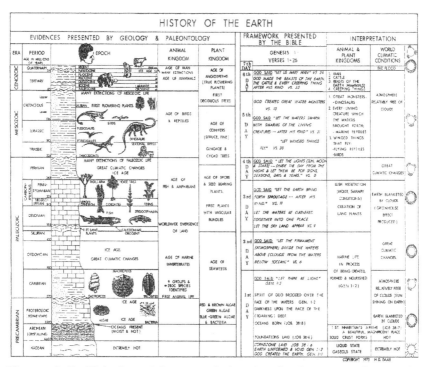

Figure 3-5: This is a history of the Earth chart. It shows the remarkable compatibility that exists between the Bible Record on the right with the Geological Record on the left. Figure generated by Don Daae. P.Geol. Also see www.gira.ca

Can the long Geological Dates be Trusted?

These geological dates can be trusted. I would like to quote Dr. Roger C. Wiens[3] who says, *"Radiometric dating -- the process of determining the age of rocks from the decay of their radioactive elements—has been in widespread use for over half a century. There are over forty such techniques, each having a different way of measuring them. It has become increasingly clear that these radiometric dating techniques agree with each other and as a whole, present a coherent picture in which the earth was created a very long time ago. Many Christians are completely unaware of the great number of laboratory measurements that have shown these methods to be consistent, and they are also unaware that Bible-believing Christians are among those actively involved in radioactive dating."*

There are only two basic ways to interpret the Geological History of the Earth. It can be interpreted as a carefully pre-planned work of an intelligent, all powerful creative God or as a result of a non intelligent, evolutionary process.

One can trust the science of geology and one can trust the Bible record as it relates to geology. See Don Daae's[4] book, *"Bridging the Gap: The First 6 Days*, Volume One" Also visit our website at www.gira.ca.

What Happened to the Primordial Garden of Eden?

The Bible is silent as to the method God may have used to destroy all traces of this beautiful and magnificeint Garden of Eden that probably occupied most of the Earth. The science of geology confirms that water laid sedimentary rocks of the Archean age are not present because ocean waters were absent.

I had the privilege of spending four months in northern Saskatchewan on a Geological Field Party in the vicinity of the Reindeer and the Churchill River region. We mapped and described the different Archean rock types and places of mineralization on the great Canadian Shield. About 75% of the Archean rocks were granite related. However, these crystalline rocks had been cut, deformed and intruded by many later basic and acidic batholitic intrusives, dikes and volcanics that were obviously of Archean Age. It was often remarked that this Archean Age had experienced tremendous amounts of intense heat, metamorphism, faulting and folding.

It is obvious that the Archean age was terminated by great heat and orogenic forces. I believe that the First Primordial Garden called Eden was completely destroyed by God with fire and great heat.

References for Chapter 3

1. Preston Cloud, Phd. "A working Model of the Primitive Earth," American Journal of Science, Vol.272 (June 1972).
2. Daae H. D., P.Geol., "Bridging the Gap: The First 6 Days." Genesis International Research Publishers, Calgary, Alberta Canada, 1989, p.31.
3. Dr. Roger C Wiens, "Radiometric Dating A Christian Perspective." See rwiens@prodigy.net.
4. Daae H. D. as above. p.17.

Note: There are two groups of persons who will be greatly distressed & offended by this interpretation and by Figure 3-5. They are the Darwinists & the Creation Science / Young Earth / Flood Geology persons.

The Darwinists completely deny the presence of Almighty God. They would agree with the Geologic Column and the age of the Earth, but they foolishly deny the existence of God. My intention is that this will be a wakeup call to all Darwinists. My prayer is that they will be willing to read this manuscript with an open heart. I trust that they will respond positively and not negatively. Please read Appendex D.

Creation Science (Flood Geology) persons believe the Earth to be about 6,000+ years old. They believe Noah's Flood is responsible for all of the great thicknesses of water laid sediments that contain fossil life. Thus, they foolishly view the traditional geological column as being false and evolutionary based. My prayer is that these people will be willing to read this manuscript with an open heart. I trust that they will respond positively and not negatively. Please read Appendices B & C.

Chapter 4

A New Age Begins under The Edenic Curse

The science of geology reveals the plan that Almighty God foresaw after He had passed judgment upon Lucifer and his fallen angels about three billion years ago. It was at this moment in time that God looked forward through the corridors of time and came forth with a new plan for the Earth. He foresaw all of the many future geological ages. It all began with the dramatic Birth of the Oceans.

The Birth of the Oceans

The birth of the oceans terminated the Archean Age and initiated the Proterozoic Age (see figure 3-5'). It was at this moment in time that God washed and cleansed the Earth with water.

Figure 4-1: This is an illustration of the dramatic Birth of the Oceans.

The Bible describes the Birth of the Oceans as follows in Job 38:8-11 NKJV, "*Who shut up the sea behind doors when it burst forth from the womb, [9]when I made the clouds its garment and wrapped it in thick darkness, [10]when I fixed limits for it and set its doors and bars in place, [11]when I said, 'This far you may come and no farther; here is where your proud waves halt?*" The youthful Earth's crust is here described as a door capable of holding the waters within the Earth. When the doors were opened, the waters that were present below the Earth's crust broke forth as if it issued out of the womb. The sudden appearance of the waters from below the Earth's crust are described as a birth and is likened to a woman in travail.

During the birth of the oceans, hydrothermal vents would have been opened through the thin, shifting, crystalline crust, allowing great fountains of molten rock and water to rise to the Earth's surface. The new waters would likely have been in the form of extremely hot water vapour that would have enveloped the Earth as a blanket.

The Earth Sciences of geology and geophysics have revealed amazing information with respect to the dynamics of the Earth's interior. A special edition of Scientific American entitled, "**Our Ever Changing Earth**," [2] gives a revealing insight into the powerful dynamics within the Earth that are continually changing, shaping and shaking our Earth.

There are those who do not realize the great amount of water that still exists below the Earth's thin crust. A paper presented by Enrico Bonatti [1] in a special edition of Scientific American says, "***The water in earth's mantle could equal the amount contained in several oceans***." He goes on to say, "*Much of this water is probably primordial, captured in Earth's mantle at the time of its formation over four billion years ago.*" In other words there are still great volumes of water remaining within the Earth's interior. This water would be more mobile and readily moveable below the Earth's crust than molten rock called lava.

The New King James Version gives a greater insight into this passage for we read in Job 38:8-11, NKJV, "*8Or who shut in the sea with doors, When it burst forth and issued from the womb; 9 When I made the clouds its garment, And thick darkness its swaddling band; 10 When I fixed My limit for it, And set bars and doors; 11 When I said, This far you may come, but no farther, And here your proud waves must stop*!" The reference to the cloud coverage as a garment with thick darkness as a swaddling band is a further reference to the condensate water and clouds that enveloped the Earth as a thick blanket. It was like a swaddling garment surrounding the earth obscuring the light of the sun from reaching the surface of the Earth. It is analogous to a baby that is wrapped with swaddling garments. The layer between the baby's tender body and the garment is sometimes referred to as a dark swaddling band.

God set a limit as to the amount of water that should cover this baby Earth, which is described in the book of Proverbs 8:27-29 KJV, "*When he prepared the heavens, I was there: when he set a compass upon the face of the depth. When he established the clouds above: when he strengthened the fountains of the deep. When he gave to the sea his decree, that the waters should not pass his commandment.*"

This passage also contains the idea that God placed a limit on the amount of water that would cover the Earth. The Hebrew word for "deep," as translated above, means "great abyss." In this context, it implies that the source of the waters was below the Earth's crust. Abyss is generally used to mean "the lowest depths" of something. In this case the lowest depth would be at the base of the thin Earth's crystalline crust. God strengthened the fountains of the deep, implying that these fountains of water were strong and powerful.

Additional insight into the emergence of the oceans is found in Genesis 1:2 (NIV), which states "*And darkness was over the surface of the deep.*" An alternate reading is, "*And darkness was on the face of the roaring deep (KJV).*" Once again, "deep" refers to the great abyss. The roaring deep can be taken to mean the traumatic events within the deep depths of the Earth, or the opening of the abyss and the roar of molten rock and water emerging on the surface of the Earth. As with the earlier reference in Job, the described "darkness" can be interpreted as analogous to the "dark swaddling band" of water vapor and other gases blanketing the earth. Darkness can also refer to the darkness of sin and the presence of the Fallen Lucifer who was now present on the Earth. From this moment onward our Earth became a dark, sin cursed planet.

This word "deep" is the Hebrew word for "abyss". It means the lowest part of anything. Now the lowest part of the Earth's crust is from beneath the crust. This portion of scripture is referring to the darkness of sin that was present when the "**Birth of the Oceans**" took place. Here we have roaring fountains of juvenile water, volcanic ash and igneous lavas flowing through the broken fractures of the Earth's crust bringing the hot juvenile waters from below the crust to the Earth's surface. In this dramatic and catastophic process all the evidences of the First Primordial Garden of Eden were removed and destroyed.

By the end of Genesis 1:2b NKJV, we read this most beautiful picture of the Earth, "*and the Spirit of God was hovering over the face of the waters.*" This is the first mention of ocean water on the Earth. This is also the most beautiful first mention of God the Holy Spirit hovering or brooding as a mother dove over the ocean waters of the Earth nurturing the new life that was now being created and formed by the Creator, the Lord Jesus Christ.

From the science of geology, we are now able to identify this new life that geologists call fossil life. These fossils are first found within the Lower water laid sediments of Proterozoic Age. This new life has been identified as new species of bacteria and chlorophyl generating blue-green algae. See Figures 3-1 & 3-5.

The question arises: how did the different species of bacteria and algae arise? Were they created by God or did they evolve? The answer is clear, Almighty God was in complete control of every event that the Earth has ever experienced past, present and future. He is the one who planned, formed and created every new species of bacteria and algae as well as all the later forms of algae, plant and animal life that are found in the succeeding layers of sedimentary rock throughout geological time.

The Devil who is the prince of the air would want us to believe the "BIG LIE" that all life on Earth came into existence by a naturalistic, evolutionary process. Satan's aim from this point in time was to prove that God does not exist and has never existed. It is sad to see that modern secular science people are wanting to believe "The Lie."

In spite of the fact that the darkness of sin was now present on the Earth, God was in control. He was now in the process of carrying out His new creative sovereign plan for the Earth. Since then, He has been preparing the Earth step by step in a most detailed way for the eventual and future arrival of Man.

The First Appearance of Sedimentary Rocks

The first water lain sedimentary rocks throughout the Earth are found within the rocks of Proterozoic Age. See Figures 3-5.

Water laid sediments of Proterozoic Age have been preserved in the great basin areas throughout the Earth. Their thicknesses often range up to 20,000 to 30,000+ feet (6,096 to 9,144 m). Where ever these sediments have not been exposed to later great heat and pressure, they contain preserved life in the form of bacteria and algae from bottom to top. During this early age God was establishing a food chain for future animal life. Elso Barghoorn[2], who is a specialist in Proterozoic life, implied that by the end of the Proterozoic Age the oceans were essentially modern. He says, *"Many living species [today] are almost indistinguishable in structure from species that flourished a billion or more years ago."* In the very latter part of the Proterozoic Age traces of three animal species have been found representing a sponge, jelly

fish, traces of worm burrowing and traces of shelly fragments that may represent a fourth animal species.

It wasn't till the Lower Cambrian Age that God initiated the
dramatic "Cambrian Explosion of Animal Life" that changed
our planet over night. This event took place within 525 to
530 million years ago. See Figures 3-1 & 3-5. In this geological moment, geologists are saying that 40+ new animal
body plans or phyla suddenly came into existence. There
were one or more species and in some cases several species
that belonged to each body plan or Phyla.

At the end of the Cambrian Age, these animal body plans
(phyla) were reduced to about 35. This was the first big
extinction of Animal Life recorded in the fossil record. From
this point onward to the present God has created multi
thousands of new species of animal life large, small and
microscopic. Each new species was created to fit into one
of the above 35+ body plans (phyla) that survived the
Cambrian Age. For instance, when God created man and
woman, He placed them into the chordate body plan. This
plan is characterized by having a vertebral column with a
notochord.

Each of the geological ages following the Cambrian Period
have great thicknesses of water laid sediments. They all
contain different species of animal and plant life as shown
on Figure 3-5. Varying amounts of oil and gas have been
found in sediments representing all of these ages from the
Cambrian Age to the Present. Commercial coal is found in
sediments of Pennsylvanian Age and younger. Truly, God
was in the process of meticulously preparing the Earth for
the future advent of Man and Woman.

My book, "Bridging the Gap: the First 6 Days" gives a more
detailed insight into the various species that characterize each geological age from the time of the "Cambrian
Explosion of Animal Life" to the present. It also reveals the
amazing compatibility that exists between the record of
geology and the record of the Bible.

The climate of the Earth fluctuated throughout geological time from cool to warm. During the Age of the Dinosaurs and to the end of the Tertiary Period the climate remained relatively warm with no indications of ice conditions. However there were five distinct periods when the Earth experienced cooler, glacial or ice age conditions.

The science of geology has confirmed that the Earth has experienced five major Ice Ages or Glaciations as follows:
1. The Lower Proterozoic Gowganda Ice Age.
2. The Upper Proterozoic Ice Age.
3. The Upper Ordovician Ice Age.
4. The Lower Permian Ice Age.
5. The Pleistocene Ice Age.

The above Ice Ages are identified on Figure 3-5. These Ice Ages are briefly described in my book, "Bridging the Gap: the First 6 Days."[1]

In spite of the fact that the darkness of sin was now present on the Earth, God was in control. He was now in the process of carrying out His new creative sovereign plan for the Earth. Since then, He has been preparing the Earth step by step in a most detailed way for the eventual and future arrival of Man.

The Edenic Curse

The Edenic Curse can be traced back to the moment Lucifer sinned. From that moment onward, the Earth became a dark sin cursed planet. We read in Romans 8:20-21, "*For the creation was subjected to frustration, not by its own choice, but by the will of the one who subjected it, in hope that the creation itself will be liberated from its bondage to decay and brought into the freedom and glory of the children of God.*" (NIV) God subjected the entire Earth and all created life on the Earth to the bondage of decay, hardship and death. Since that moment all creation has been groaning as a result of violent storms, earthquakes and other natural disasters. All life that relates to the bacteria, plant and animal kingdoms have all experienced hardship, constant trouble, suffering, pain, ageing and death as a result of the

Edenic Curse. See Figure 3-4. God subjected all creation to frustration knowing that the day would come when the total creation would one day be liberated and set free once again. This is still in the future.

We read in Romans 8:22-23 that the "whole creation" has been affected by the Edenic Curse as follows, "*We know that the whole creation has been groaning as in the pains of childbirth right up to the present time. Not only so, but we ourselves, who have the first fruits of the Spirit, groan inwardly as we wait eagerly for our adoption, the redemption of our bodies.*" **What is meant by the whole creation?** Does it also refer to the Second Heaven which is the universe of stars and galaxies?

To find a possible answer, we must return to the initial record in Genesis. In Genesis 1:1 (NIV) we read, "*In the beginning God created the heavens and the earth.*" This verse could be written, "*In the beginning God created the Universe (the Heavens and the Earth),*" This verse would imply that the whole creation would encompass the Earth and would also include the Universe of stars and galaxies. Is it reasonable to even dare to think that the entire Universe also came under the Edenic Curse?

Theologians apply the law of First Reference which says that the first time a word or phrase is found in the book of Genesis or any where else in the Bible, that it gives a clue to its meaning later on when its meaning may not be not too clear. We find the first mention of the word "**darkness**" in Genesis 1:2 (NKJV), "*And darkness was upon the face of the (roaring) deep.*" In this text, the word darkness is synonymous with evil and the Edenic curse.

The Origin of Darkness

What is the origin of Darkness? Has darkness always been present throughout the first and Second Heavens?

As a result of Lucifers Fall, the Edenic curse fell upon the whole Creation, the First and Second Heavens. From this point in time to the present the Earth has been experiencing day and night. The Earth is light on one side and **darkness** is on the other side. This type of 24 hour day began at the moment in time Lucifer sinned. The Earth will continue to experience light and darkness to the end of the future Millennial Age at which time the Earth will be destroyed by fire and rejuvinated to the place it was in the beginning.

Is it possible to believe that prior to the Fall of Lucifer there was no darkness, but only endless day throughout the First and Second Heavens? The answer is yes.

After the future Great White Throne Judgement Seat of Christ, God will once again create a New Heaven and a New Earth where there will be no darkness. In the future, the Earth will be experiencing endless day in the First, Second and Third Heavens as it was prior to Lucifers Fall.

According to the Bible there is a future day coming when God is going to create a new Heaven and a new Earth, We read in Revelation 21:1 NKJV, "*Now I saw a new heaven and a new earth, for the first heaven and the first earth had passed away. Also there was no more sea.*" This future rejuvenation of the Earth and the Heavens (the universe) will take place after the Great White Throne Judgement. It will also take place after God has eradicated all evidence of sin and death upon the earth by fire. We read in 2 Peter 3:10-13 NKJV, "*But the day of the Lord will come as a thief in the night, in which the heavens will pass away with a great noise, and the elements will melt with fervent heat; both the earth and the works that are in it will be burned up. Therefore, since all these things will be dissolved, what manner of persons ought you to be in holy conduct and godliness, looking for and hastening the coming of the day of God, because of which the heavens will be dissolved, being on fire, and the elements will melt with fervent heat? Nevertheless we, according to His promise, look for new heavens and a new earth in which righteousness dwells.*"

In the future new Earth and throughout the new Universe there will be endless day. The Three Heaven's will once again

43

become as one, just as it was prior to the Fall of Lucifer. We read in Revelation 22:1-5 NIV, "*Then the angel showed me the river of the water of life, as clear as crystal, flowing from the throne of God and of the Lamb down the middle of the great street of the city. On each side of the river stood the tree of life, bearing twelve crops of fruit, yielding its fruit every month. And the leaves of the tree are for the healing of the nations. **No longer will there be any curse**. The throne of God and of the Lamb will be in the city, and his servants will serve him. They will see his face, and his name will be on their foreheads. **There will be no more night. They will not need the light of a lamp or the light of the sun, for the Lord God will give them light**. And they will reign for ever and ever.*" When we get to Heaven, we will experience endless day. This does not only refer to the Third Heaven where there has always been endless day. The implication is, that endless day will also characterize the First and Second Heavens as well.

NOTE: See Appendix B & C to see how Creation Science persons explain the Edenic Curse & the Adamic curse.

References to Chapter 4

1. Enrico Bonatti, PhD. "Earth's Mantle Below the Oceans." This paper is published in the Special Edition of Scientific American, September 26, 2005 edition , "Our Ever Changing Earth." Pages 65-73.

Chapter 5

God's Pronouncements Upon Lucifer

God pronounced three judgments and three predictions upon Lucifer just after his Fall in the Primordial Garden of Eden as follows:

First Judgement: God's first Judgement upon Lucifer is found in Ezekiel 28:16a, NIV *"Through your widespread trade you were filled with violence, and you sinned. So I drove you in disgrace from the Mount of God."* The reason Lucifer was driven in disgrace from the Mount of God was because he had sinned. Sin is not allowed in God's home which is the Third Heaven. The door to the Third Heaven was shut the instant Lucifer sinned.

Prior to Lucifer's Fall, he was able to commute freely from the Earth to the Third Heaven and to sit in the assembly places of the north before the Mount of God. On this basis Lucifer was driven back in disgrace never to return to the Third Heaven ever again.

In other words, Lucifer was no longer free to access the Holy Mount of God in the Third Heaven. This is the Mission Control Centre of all Creation. This is where Almighty God is seated on a Royal Throne high and lifted up on Mount Zion as Isaiah & Ezekiel had the privilege of observing in Isaiah 6:1-15. and Ezekiel 1:27-28.

Second Judgement: Lucifer was cast out of the Primordial Garden of Eden, never to return. No longer could he walk up and down in the midst of the beautiful stones of fire. We read, *"I expelled you, O guardian cherub, from among the fiery stones"* (Ezekiel 28:16, NIV). This Primordial Garden of Eden at this point in time was completely destroyed. Geologists who have studied the Archean rocks, which I have had the privilege of doing, will verify that the Archean Age ended with intense heat and trauma. In other words this beautiful place called Eden was destroyed by fire.

Third Judgement: Lucifer was cast upon the surface of a desolate Earth where the Primordial Garden of Eden had now been removed by fire. We read in Ezekiel 28:17c, NIV *"I threw you to the Earth."* Then Isaiah 14:12, NIV says, *"How you have fallen from heaven, O morning star, son of the dawn! You have been cast down to the earth."* The NKJV says, *"How are you fallen from heaven, O'Lucifer, son of the morning! How are you cut down to the ground?"* At this point in time there would have been no oceans as yet. The Earth's surface would have been rocky and desolate as a result of the destruction of the primordial Garden called Eden that possibly encompassed the entire Earth.

God Looked Forward through the Corridors of Time

It was at this point in time that God looked forward through the corridors of time and He foresaw the following three events:

First: He foresaw the entire geological history of the Earth from the Beginning of the Proterozoic to the present and beyond. He foresaw the millions of species that would some day belong to the bacteria, plant and animal kingdoms. These are the species that he would plan, form and create. These are the species that would be able to survive and propagate offspring within a dark, sin cursed Earth. See Figure 3-5.

Second: He foresaw the Second Garden of Eden and the time when He would form and create Adam & Eve. He would give them the freedom of choice to either receive Him or to reject Him. He would give the same choice to all their descendents which includes you and I.

Thirdly: He foresaw the Cross. He knew that the only way that He could deal with the sin issue was for his only Son to be suspended on a cruel Cross between Heaven and Earth. God the Father ordained that one day in the future, His only begotten Son, the Lord Jesus Christ, would give His body as a sacrifice and would shed His sinless blood for the sins of the world which includes you and me.

He also foresaw the time when sin on this Earth would be no more. How will this all take place?

The Lord's Three Predictions

First Prediction: At this moment in time, the Lord predicted that the Devil would one day be set before kings, that they may behold him. We read in Ezekiel 28:17d, NIV *"I made a spectacle of you before kings."* The NKJV says, *"I laid you before kings, that they might gaze at you."* In this verse God is revealing an amazing insight into the future when He would one day create man and woman. The Fallen Lucifer would one day be a spectacle to Kings, leaders and all mankind.

This prophetic judgement is being fulfilled today. God did not create man and woman as a robot. He gave them the freedom of choice. This is the reason why you and I must make the right choice between Almighty God or the Devil. Our choices have eternal consequences for good or evil, for time and eternity. This includes our children and their children. Our future destination is either Heaven or Hell. Both are real geographic locations.

Second Prediction: We read in Ezekiel 28:19 NKJV, *"All who know you (Satan) among the peoples are astonished at you. You have become a horror and shall be no more* *forever."* Today Satan and his fallen angels are a astonishment, a horror and a terror to all Mankind. Satan is a Terrorist among the people throughout the world. His aim is to create pain and sorrow, hatred, heart ache, disappointments, death and destruction. He works in many diverse ways, often working through religion and appearing as an angel of light deceiving Mankind and keeping them under constant fear and bondage. However, there is a day coming when Satan shall be no more within the First, Second and Third Heavens. How can this be?

Third Prediction: *"I will bring forth a fire from the midst of you, it shall devour you, and I will bring you to ashes upon the earth"* (Ezek. 28:18 NKJV). How will Lucifer, who is now the Devil, be devoured by a fire that will bring him to ashes upon the Earth? How will this all take place? What is the Devil's final fate?

Chapter 6

First Space Travel & When did it Occur?

The book of Isaiah gives additional insight into what took place after Lucifer sinned. It tells about the time when he was cast down to the Earth. Today, Satan's aim is to weaken the nations and to destroy God's purpose for Mankind on the Earth. We read in Isaiah 14:12, NKJV "*How you are fallen from heaven, O Lucifer, son of the morning! How you are cut down to the ground, You who weakened the nations*!"

In Luke 10:17-18, (NKJV) Jesus said, "*I saw Satan fall like lightning from Heaven.*") Is it possible that He may have been referring to the above event?

Satan's Exploits

After the Fall, Satan purposed in his heart that he would conquer the Three Heavens, the FIRST, the SECOND, and the THIRD HEAVEN. He was no longer satisfied with what God had given to him. He wanted to extend his territorial boundaries. In a certain sense nations and individuals act in the same way today. They are never satisfied with the territory that they have, but are always striving to enlarge their territorial boundaries regardless of the cost. Thus, we have wars, rumors of wars, killings, envy, hatred, jealousy and great suffering and heartache one toward another.

Satan conceived a plan to conquer the First Heaven, the Second Heaven and the Third Heaven. He said in Isaiah

14:13-14 NKJV, "*I will ascend into the heavens (Shomayim), I will exalt my throne above the stars of God; I will also sit on the mount of the congregation on the farthest sides of the north; I will ascend above the heights of the clouds, I will be like the Most High.*"

This declaration of war was conceived in Lucifer's HEART, and was then translated into action. God allowed Lucifer who is now called Satan to go only so far in his attempt to conquer the Three Heavens. He was then cut back to the Earth.

The First Heaven

After the Fall, Satan's first desire was to conquer the First Heaven which is the firmament or hydrosphere that surrounds the Earth. This is the portion of our Earth that is literally teeming with plant and animal life. Satan said, "*I will ascend above the heights of the clouds,*" (Isaiah 14:14 NKJV). The New English Bible says "*I will rise above THE CLOUD BANK.*"

Here we have a description of Earth's first SPACE TRAVEL. Lucifer after the Fall was no longer satisfied with the Earth that God had allowed him to inhabit. He wanted to extend his territorial boundaries. His desire was to become like the most High God. His objective was to conquer the First Heaven by rising above the cloud bank and to ascend into space beyond the Earth. In other words, He was successful in conquering the First Heaven.

This is exactly what Man is attempting to do today. Man is saying let us ascend above the cloud bank. Let us conquer the First Heaven. Let us conquer space (the Second Heaven) and to be like God Himself.

Today Man has conquered the First Heaven. He has risen above the heights of the clouds, in fact he has even reached the Moon, and has sent satellites out to various planets in our solar system. Man is now attempting to conquer the Second Heaven which is the universe of stars and galaxies. What is motivating Man to conquer space and to search for a new place to live?

The Second Heaven

Satan's second desire was to to conquer the Second Heaven, which included the entire physical universe, the millions of galaxies and spheres in outer space. He said, "*I will ascend into Heaven (Shomayim), I will exalt my throne above the STARS OF GOD.*" (Isaiah 14:13 NKJV)

This attempt was two fold, He would first conquer the physical universe, and then he would exalt himself above the STARS OF GOD. The Stars of God are believed to be the angelic Cherubim, or the MORNING STARS that sang together with him during the early part of the First Day of Creation as described in Job 38:7. This was truly a time of great jubilation. Lucifer is believed to have been one of these morning stars, who was delegated by God to the Earth, whereas the other Morning Stars may have been delegated to other spheres throughout the physical universe. Lucifer's object was to conquer the other Morning Stars and to bring them under his subjection and control.

We do not know how far God may have allowed Satan to go in fulfilling his plan, because there is no mention in the Bible of any other sphere besides the Earth as being a place of evil. The Earth is singled out from the rest of the universe as being a special case, where the tragedy of sin first took place, or in other words where evil originated and where evil is now present.

God intervened and only allowed Satan to go so far into the Second Heaven. There are some who believe that he may have conquered a portion of the Universe before he was cast down to the Earth. He may very well have conquered the planets in our solar system, this may be the reason why the planets are today such desolate lifeless places.

The Third Heaven

Thirdly, Satan purposed in his heart to conquer the Third Heaven. His objective was to sit once again not only in the assembly place, but upon the Holy Mount of God. This is where God's throne is located. This time, he wanted to be like the MOST HIGH GOD. *"I will sit also upon the mount of the congregation on the farthest sides of the north." (Isaiah 14:13b NKJV)* *"I will become like the Most High."* (Isaiah 14:14b, NKJV) We now find the Mission Control Centre of the entire universe under attack. Satan's plan was to sit upon the Mount of the Congregation on the sides of the north.

The Bible tells us, *"Beautiful for situation is Mount Zion on the sides of the north, the city of the Great King. God is known in her palaces for a refuge"* (Psalm 48:1-3, NKJV). This is the place that Satan wanted to conquer. Therefore he conceived a plan to force his way back into the Mount of the Congregation which is located in the Third Heaven. He also reasoned that if he could conquer the Second Heaven, he would then be able to get all the Stars of God or heavenly angelic beings to come under his control. He would then be able to operate from a stronger position of power. But God Almighty allowed him to go only so far and then Satan was cast down to the Earth.

This is where Satan has been ever since. The Bible says Satan is *"the prince of the power of the air, the spirit who now works in the sons of disobedience,"* (Ephesians 2:2b, NKJV). Satan is present within the invisible realm of spiritual darkness that surrounds the earth. This is another dimension of space and time. It is like another world within the world where Man is now present on this Earth. See Figure 3-4.

The Bible gives a clue as to where this realm is located. We read in Ephesians 6:10-13, NKJV *"My brethren, be strong in the Lord and in the power of His might. Put on the whole armor of God that you may be able to stand against the wiles of the devil. For we do not wrestle against flesh and blood, but against powers, against the rulers of the darkness of this age, against spiritual hosts in the heavenly places. Therefore take up the whole armor of God that you may be able to withstand in the evil day, and having done all to stand."*

When Did Satan's Exploits Begin, Geologically?

The question arises, when during the geological history of the Earth did Satan determine in his heart that he would Conquer the First, Second & Third Heavens. The Bible gives a clue that Satan first determined to conquer the First Heaven when the Earth was blanketed by a cloud bank. We read in Isaiah 14:14, NKJV "*I will ascend above the heights of the clouds, I will be like the Most High.*" The English Bible says, "*I will rise above the cloud bank.*" This implies that the Earth was covered with a blanket of clouds giving it a greenhouse effect at the time Lucifer purposed in his heart to conquer the Three Heavens.

The geological history of the Earth records three separate occasions when a definite greenhouse effect with a well defined cloud bank was present. The first occasion was during the Birth of the Oceans at the beginning of the Proterozoic Age. The second occasion was during the Second Day of Creation. This was the time when God separated the waters above from the waters below. The third occasion was during Noah's Flood about 4,500 years ago. See Figure 3-5.

First: **The Birth of the Oceans** is described in my book,[1] "*Bridging the Gap: The First 6 Days.*" The Fall of Lucifer brought the Archean Age to a dramatic close. It was at this point in time that God cleansed the Earth with water. The dramatic Birth of the Oceans is the first event that took place after the Fall of Lucifer. It is recorded in Job 38:8-11, NKJV as follows, "*Who shut in the sea with doors, when it burst forth and issued from the womb; when I made the clouds its garment, and thick darkness its swaddling band; when I fixed My limit for it, and set bars and doors; when I said, "This far you may come, but no farther and here your proud waves must stop.*" The science of geology confirms the sudden appearance of ocean water on the Earth at the beginning of the Proterozoic Age.

This is the event that brought the Archean Age to a dramatic close and initiated the Proterozoic Age. The **thick darkness** resulting from Lucifer's sin was now present within the swaddling band of waters that was now surrounding the Earth. This is further confirmed by Genesis 1:2-3, NKJV which says, *"Darkness was over the surface of the (roaring) deep."* Deep is the Hebrew word Abyss which means the deepest part of anything. Now the deepest part of the Earth's crust is below its crust. The roaring fountains of extremely hot waters were being released upon the Earth's surface at this time. See Figure 3-5.

The question arises, was this the time Lucifer determined that he would rise above the cloud bank of the Earth? It could have been, but I personally do not believe this was the time.

Second: During the Second Day of Creation God established a new greenhouse effect upon the Earth by dividing the waters above the firmament (hydrosphere) from the waters below. We read in Genesis 1:7, NKJV *"God made the firmament and divided the waters which were under the firmament from the waters that were above the firmament; and it was so."* This event is confirmed by the science of geology and is described in my book, *"Bridging the Gap: the First 6 Days."* [2]

I personally believe that Satan purposed in his heart to conquer the Three Heavens during the Second Day of Creation for the following reason. The clue is found in the absence of the phrase, "It was good." For some reason God could not say this was a good day.

Years ago the Honorable Ernest C. Manning was Premier of Alberta, Canada. He wondered why the phrase, **"It was good,"** was omitted from the Second Day. He conjectured that it was possible that the Fall of Lucifer may have taken place during the Second Day therefore God could not truly say that this was a Good Day.

I have pondered this thought based upon the Biblical and the geological record. As a result, I have come to the conclusion that the Second Creation Day was the most logical

time when Satan purposed in his heart that he would conquer the Three Heavens. This would have been the most
likely time that Lucifer decided to rise above the cloud bank
of the Earth. In a certain sense the Fallen Lucifer would have
conquered the First Heaven. Thus, God could not say the
Second Day was good because of the exploits of Lucifer to
conquer the Three Heavens on this day.

Third: Noah's Flood: The Mechanics of the Flood of Noah
were very similar to the Mechanics of the Birth of the
Oceans that brought the Archean Age to a dramatic termination. The science of geology now confirms that Noah's
Flood was a global event and that it actually took place
about 4,500 plus or minus years ago. However, it can be
clearly demonstrated that this event was too recent and
was definitely not the time when Lucifer planned to conquer
the Three Heavens. Details of this event are described in a
later chapter.

References for Chapter 6

1. Daae H.D. "Bridging The Gap: The First 6 Days," Genesis International Research Publishers 1989, pp.37-41.
2. Ibib. pp. 56-65.

Chapter 7

The Mystery Surrounding the Second Garden of Eden

There is a mystery surrounding the Second Garden of Eden. The Bible record confirms that this second Garden of Eden was a real place on Earth. The Bible does not give the exact geographical location of this garden, but theologians have always maintained that it was located somewhere in the Middle East region. They also maintain that Adam and Eve were the first human inhabitants of this garden. There has always been confusion as to where the four major river systems flowing out of Eden were specifically located.

The secular world declares the Biblical Garden of Eden to be a mere myth. They reject the idea that Man and Woman were ever created by God. They postulate that mankind first originated by a process called evolution. It has been taught for decades within our schools, colleges and universities that Man has evolved through the primate line. Evolutionary atheists maintain that it is possible to trace the ancestry of Mankind through various species of now extinct hominids, apes, monkeys and prosimians over a period of about 60+ millions of years into the past. In other words, Man is the end result of a long line of progressive, evolutionary developments that have taken place within the primate lineage. The secular world is also saying that Man originated in West Africa, not the Middle East.

How do we resolve this major difference that exists between these two worldviews? Which one is the more scientifically accurate and logical? Does the geological record shed any light upon the authenticity of this Garden of Eden? When did God prepare this garden and where was its most likely location? See Figure 7-1.

A Huge Time Gap Separates the Two Biblical Gardens

According to the science of geology, there is a gap of about 3 billion Earth years separating the first Primordial Garden of Eden from the Second Garden of Eden (See Figure 3-5). Is this realistic? Can the science of geology be trusted? Can Geology give a clue as to where and when this Second Garden was located?

I have had the privilege of studying and exploring many of the geological rock/time units from the base of the Proterozoic Age to the present. They are all real and authentic. They all contain different species of life as shown on Figures 3-5.

God has left two records for modern Man to analyze. One is the record of geology. The other is the record of the Bible. My first book, *Bridging the Gap: The First 6 Days,*[1] reveals the remarkable compatibility that exists between the record of geology and the record of the Bible. Both records were authored, planned, created and formed by the same Amazing Architect and Creator of all creation. Both of these records can now be trusted.

The science of geology has confirmed that the Earth has experienced five Major Ice Ages or Glaciations as follows:
1. The Lower Proterozoic Gowganda Ice Age.
2. The Upper Proterozoic Ice Age.
3. The Upper Ordovician Ice Age.
4. The Lower Permian Ice Age.
5. The Pleistocene Ice Age.

The above Ice Ages are all identified on Figure 3-5'. These Ice Ages are described in my book, "Bridging the Gap: the First 6 Days."[1] They are all major, authentic events.

The Pleistocene Ice Age

The Pleistocene Ice Age is very important because Man made his first appearance on Earth during this period of glaciations. On the basis of geology and radiometric dating, this Ice Age is believed to have extended into the past for about 2.5 million years (Figure 14-1). How can this be true?"

Conflicting Views

There are many conflicting views as to how Modern Man relates to the Pleistocene Ice Age. I trust that as we proceed step by step that this mystery will resolve itself.

Darwinists attempt to relate the evolutionary development of Modern Man to the various stages of the Pleistocene Ice Age. They attempt to trace the primate lineage of Modern Man to the Cro-Magnon and the Neanderthal Men who in turn have supposedly evolved from certain extinct hominid apes such as Homo erectus, Homo habilis, Australopithecus africanus and afarensis etc. They claim to be able to trace Early Man back in time to about 3.0+ million years before the present in Eastern Africa. Darwinists claim Man originated in East Africa and not the Middle East as the Bible claims.

Creation Science persons who believe in **"Flood Geology"** contend that God created the Earth and all plant and animal life and Man in 6 literal 24 hour Creation Days between 6000 to 10,000 years before the present. They believe the Earth was the only object created during the First Creation Day. The sun, moon and Stars which includes all the billions of galaxies were created during the Fourth Creation Day. They believe the entire Pleistocene Ice Age is Post Flood. They believe Adam & Eve were created about 6,000+ to possibly 10,000 years before the present. They also believe all the enormous thicknesses of sediments that belong to the prior geological ages are products of Noah's Flood. See Appendices B & C.

Day Age Geology: We in Genesis International Research Association believe in "Day Age Geology." This means that each Creation Day represents a period of time that could be multi millions of years in duration. We believe Noah's Flood took place about 4,500 plus or minus years ago; that God created Adam and Eve about 6,000+ years ago; that God prepared the Garden of Eden between 6,000+ to 10,000 years ago. We also believe that the Earth could very well be 4.6 + billion years old. We do not compromise evolution and creation. See Figures 7-1 and 3-5.

Other Old Earth Views: Other persons who believe in an Old Earth & Universe concept often have various other concepts as to how the geological record relates with the Biblical record. They often base their views primarily on the other sciences of astronomy, physics, biology and so forth. Many of these concepts are very trustworthy and good. There is often a tendency by some persons to compromise science with evolution.

When Did God prepare the Second Garden of Eden?

It is here believed that the Second Garden of Eden was pre-pared by God sometime between 6,000+ to 10,000 years ago. Pleistocene geologists Ernst Antevs, an American and Gerard DeGreer, a European from Denmark noted a marked temperature rise that took place about 10,000 years ago.[2-4] This change in temperature had a pronounced effect on climate throughout the entire Earth during the Anathermal Age. See Figure 7-1.

Antevs and DeGreer were able to date glacial lake sedi-ments in Northern Europe and in North America for 20,000 and 30,000+ years into the past on the basis of counting the varved annually bedded glacial lake clays and silts.

HISTORY OF MAN

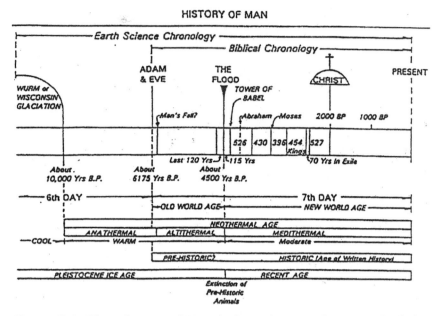

Figure 7-1: The History of Man is based upon the record of the Bible & the record of Geology, Archaeology & Anthropology. The term B.P. means before the present. It is here believed that the Garden of Eden was prepared by God between 6,000+ to 10,000 years ago during the Anathermal Age. God created Adam and Eve about 6,000+ years ago. The Flood of Noah took place about 4,500 years ago. Time units are based upon works by Antevs & DeGreer. Appendix A reveals why Adam & Eve may have been created closer to 6,000+ Years ago rather than about 6,175 years ago. Generated by Don Daae.

Varved clays are formed in fresh water glacial lakes from mud brought by glacial melt water streams. During the summer season one light colored silty laminae is deposited in glacial lakes, whereas during the winter season one dark, greasy laminae is deposited. The couplet is called a varve and is frequently about an inch thick. Sequences of varves are measured in clay exposures and the measurements are graphed correlated and combined in continuous series after a method devised and described by Gerard deGreer and Ernst Antevs. In this manner, chronological records have been obtained from glacial lake sediments in Sweden, Finland, Canada and in parts of Northern USA.

As a result of their excellent field work, they were able to divide the last 10,000 year period into the Anathermal, the Altithermal and the Medithermal ages.

The Anathermal Age

The geological "Anathermal Age" began about 10,000 years ago. It marks the end of the cold Wisconsin (Wurm) Glaciation and the commencement of a pronounced world-wide warming of the climate. This progressive warming was associated with great moisture and luxuriant growth of grass, trees and other vegetation. All the inland lakes in northern Europe and in the USA and parts of Canada were filled with water resulting from glacial melt water. It was a time when a very moist form of precipitation was present throughout the entire Earth. The areas that were previously desert became areas of lush vegetation that were able to provide abundant food for animal life. It is possible that this was the time when the Bible says in Genesis 2:6 NIV, "*but a mist went up from the earth and watered the whole face of the ground.*"

James Howard Wellard[6] confirms that the Sahara Desert region was grown over with lush vegetation that accommodated abundant animal and bird life. This would have been during the Anathermal Age.

The Anathermal Age was indeed an ideal, logical and optimum time for the Lord God to plant and prepare the beautiful Garden of Eden for we read, "*Now the Lord God planted a garden in the east of Eden and there He put the man that He had formed.*" (Genesis 2:8, NIV)

This beautiful garden was prepared for man and woman. Adam and Eve were the first and only human inhabitants of this garden. The question arises what made this garden so different from any other place throughout the Earth? What kind of plant life and what kind of animal life did God create in this garden that made it unique and different from any other part of the Earth?

What Does the Bible say about the Second Garden of Eden?

We read in Genesis 2:8-22 NIV, "*Now the LORD God had planted a garden in the east, in Eden; and there he put the man he had formed. And the LORD God made all kinds of trees grow out of the ground—trees that were pleasing to the eye and good for food. In the middle of the garden were the tree of life and the tree of the knowledge of good and evil. A river watering the garden flowed from Eden; from there it was separated into four headwaters. The name of the first is the Pishon; it winds through the entire land of Havilah, where there is gold. (The gold of that land is good; aromatic resin and onyx are also there.) The name of the second river is the Gihon; it winds through the entire land of Cush. The name of the third river is the Tigris; it runs along the east side of Asshur. And the fourth river is the Euphrates.*"

Then we read in Genesis 2:15-22 NIV, "*The LORD God took the man and put him in the Garden of Eden to work it and take care of it. And the LORD God commanded the man, "You are free to eat from any tree in the garden; but you must not eat from the tree of the knowledge of good and evil, for when you eat of it you will surely die." The LORD God said, "It is not good for the man to be alone. I will make a helper suitable for him." Now the LORD God had formed out of the ground all the beasts of the field and all the birds of the air. He brought them to the man to see what he would name them; and whatever the man called each living creature, that was its name. So the man gave names to all the livestock, the birds of the air and all the beasts of the field. But for Adam no suitable helper was found. So the LORD God caused the man to fall into a deep sleep; and while he was sleeping, he took one of the man's ribs and closed up the place with flesh. Then the LORD God made a woman from the rib he had taken out of the man, and he brought her to the man.*"

The Inhabitants of this Second Garden of Eden

According to the Bible record, God prepared a beautiful garden for Adam and Eve. It was located within a place called Eden. The big question mark is: where was this mysterious garden located? We read in Genesis 2:8 NIV, "*Now the Lord God had planted a garden in the east of Eden; and there He put the man he had formed.*"

According to the Bible, Adam and Eve were the first human beings on planet Earth. They were the first and only human inhabitants of the Second Garden of Eden. There is a mystery that surrounds this Garden of Eden. When geologically did God prepare and plant this beautiful garden? What was it like? What happened to Adam and Eve in this garden? Where was it located? There are many questions we could ask about this mysterious garden that was located at a specific place on this Earth called Eden.

The question arises as to what new species of plant life did God create in this garden in preparation for Man?

What kind of Plant Life did God create in this Garden?

God created and formed species of plants that were food for Man. We read, "*The Lord God made every tree grow that was good for food*" (Genesis 2:9 NIV). The geological fossil record gives us an insight into the type of plants that were present in this garden. **According to geology and the associated science of palynology, the modern fruits and vegetables that we find in abundance on the shelves of our large supermarket stores are recent creations.** Many of the wild berries, plum trees, banana trees and bushes etc. can be traced back much further. However, many of the modern fruits and vegetables as well as crops such as wheat, barley, lentils, and peas were formed and created within the Second Garden of Eden. They are basically food for Man. Since then, they have been transported by Man to all parts of the Earth.

This is confirmed by a famous pre-Historian and archaeologist Dr. Philip Stern[7] who says, *"It was the Middle East that gave Man some of his most important crops such as wheat, barley, lentils, and peas."* Outside of the garden there were many thousands of species of plant life that had been growing wild for millions of years. Some of these were wild fruit trees and shrubs.

What Kind of Animal & Bird Life did God create in the Garden?

Just prior to the creation of Adam and Eve, the Lord God created new species of animal life. We read in Genesis 2:19-20 NIV, *"Now the Lord God had formed out of the ground all the beasts of the field and all the birds of the air. He brought them to the man (Adam) to see what he would name them; and whatever the man called each living creature, that was its name. So the man gave names **to all the livestock**, the birds of the air and all the beasts of the field"*.

This was the final series of animal and bird creations before the end of the Sixth Day. It is important to realize that outside of the Garden of Eden, the Earth was already inhabited by many thousands of species of animal and bird life that had been there for many hundreds and thousands and even millions of years. However, within the garden, entirely new species of domestic animal life were created. It is likely that cattle, sheep, goats, dogs, cats, chickens, turkeys and other animals and birds used by man for domestic purposes were created in the garden at this time. God gave Adam the responsibility of naming each of these domestic animal and bird species in the garden.

Cattle belong to the split hoofed animals. Geology confirms that the wild varieties of split hoofed animals such as deer, moose, buffalo, elk can be traced back in the fossil record for many thousands and even millions of years. Cattle are not found in the fossil record. They are a more recent creation. Wild sheep and goats can be traced back for millions of years, however, domestic sheep and goats are not found in the fossil record. Domestic dogs, cats, chickens etc are recent creations, whereas coyotes, wolves, tigers, and all wild cats, and all wild pheasants, ducks, geese etc. can be traced back for many thousands of years. Domestic animals and chickens cannot survive without the help and assistance of Man. It is hereby maintained that all the animals and birds that God created in the Second Garden of Eden are the domestic varieties that are for Man's benefit.

This is confirmed by a famous pre-Historian and archae-ologist Dr. Philip Stern[7] says, "*It was the Middle East that gave Man some of his most important crops such as wheat, barley, lentils, and peas. **There too, sheep, goats, and cattle were first domesticated.** The use of metal also first began there.*"

Outside of the Garden there were wild animals that had been on Earth for multi thousands and millions of years. Truly, the environment was more hostile outside of this garden. This becomes evident after Adam and Eve sinned. **God had to literally force Adam and Eve to leave the Garden of Eden.** They knew that the outside world would be harsh and cruel. It was cruel because the "Edenic Curse" was present upon all nature except within the confines of the Garden of Eden. This was because of the protective presence of the Tree of Life.

When a person begins to analyze the fossil record of past animal and plant life, one begins to see that God has been carefully preparing the Earth in a most detailed and meticu-lous way for Man. If it had not been for the past creations of plant and animal life, we would not have the advantage of fossil fuels such as coal, natural gas and oil, etc. to provide us with the comforts of life.

What was this Garden of Eden Like?

This was a most magnificent and beautiful garden. It was decked with abundant varieties of fruit trees, shrubs and vegetables that supplied food for Man. All the different types of cereal crops like wheat, oats, flax and so forth that would have supplied food for Man were also in this garden. There were many species of domestic animals such as sheep, goats, camel, cattle, horses, dogs, cats, etc. that are so essential for Man. It also had new species of domestic bird life such as chickens, turkeys, etc. All these new species and varieties of animal and bird creations and cereal grains were unique and different from what existed outside of the garden.

What made this garden unique and special were the two trees in the midst of the garden: the Tree of Life and the Tree of the Knowledge of Good and Evil.

It was indeed a magnificent oasis in the midst of the surrounding sin cursed Earth with its millions of varieties of plant, animal and bird life. It was the closest place to Paradise on Earth, except for one major factor. This was the presence of the Tree of Good and Evil. In other words, **evil was lurking in this garden ready to happen**. The fallen Lucifer was there as an accident ready to happen. **Thus, God gave Adam and Eve a choice either to follow Him or to reject Him and to follow Satan**. This is the same choice you and I must make today.

References for Chapter 7

1. Daae H. D., P.Geol., "Bridging the Gap: The First 6 Days." Genesis International Research Publishers, Calgary, Alberta Canada, 1989.
2. Antevs, Ernest. *Retreat of the Last Ice Sheet in Eastern Canada.* Geol. Survey Canada, Mem. 146, 1925.
3. Antevs, Ernst. *The Recession of the Last Ice Sheet in New England.* Amer. Geog. Soc., Research Ser. 11, 1922.
4. Antevs, Ernest. *Geochronology of the Deglacial and Neothermal Ages.* The Journal of Geology, Vol.61, Number 3, May 1953.
5. DeGreer, Gerard. *GeochronologiaSuecica Principles*, Svenska, Vetenskapsakad, Handl., Vol. 18, No. 6, 1940. Note: The above papers will give the reader an insight into how Antevs & DeGreer were able to date the past 20,000 years of Earth history by means of geology.
6. Wellard, James Howard, "The Great Sahara E.P. Dutton & Co., Inc. new York, 1964. pp. 605 – 606.
7. Stern, Philip Van Doren, "Prehistoric Europe from Stone Age Man to the Early Greeks," NY: Norton, 1971, p.80.

Chapter 8

The Origin of Adam & Eve

The final and crowning act of all God's creation took place about 6000 + years ago, when God created Man, or more specifically, Adam and Eve. This great event is described as follows: "*And God said, Let us make man in our image, after our likeness; and let them have dominion over the fish of the sea, and over the fowl of the air, and over the cattle, and over all the Earth, and over every creeping thing that creeps upon the Earth. So God created man in his own image, in the image of God created he him, male and female created he them.*" (Genesis 1:26-27, NIV)

God formed, created and made man and woman according to a plan full of meaning and purpose. Genesis 1:26 (KJV) says, "*Let us make man in our image, after our likeness.*" This is a plan. It reveals the plurality of the Godhead. It describes the plan that was conceived in the mind of God the Father who is saying to God the Son and God the Holy Spirit, let us make man & woman in our image and after our likeness. This plan was two fold.

The first part of this plan was to create Man in His own image and His likeness. No previous animal was ever created in God's image or likeness. This includes the ape family. Man was unique because he was created in the image and likeness of God. The work involved in creating man & woman was accomplished by God the Son, the Lord Jesus Christ, the Creator of all life. He carried out the perfect will and plan of His Father by creating Man. We read in Genesis 1-27 (KJV): "*So God created (bara) man in His own image, in the image of God created He him; male and female created He them.*" The word create is the Hebrew word (bara), which always implies original creation. Man and woman were not present in any other form or state prior to this act of special creation by the Creator.

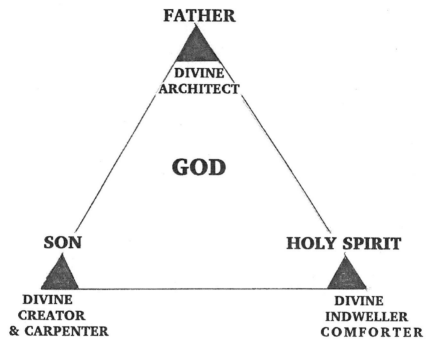

Figure 8-1: The God of Creation, One God with Three Persons. In the beginning God (Elohim) created the Heavens & the Earth (Genesis 1:1). The Hebrew word Elohim is a masculine noun that is always in the plural. It signifies a three in one relationship.

The second part of this plan was to make man & woman after "Our likeness." This little phrase is full of meaning and purpose. It implies a process that begins at birth and continues throughout our life. To be formed after the likeness of God means receiving Him into our lives, to follow, obey, serve, honor, worship, glorify Him in all that we do and say. God said of King David, "*He is a man after my own heart*" (Acts 13:22, NIV). This implies that God could see that David had a tender heart for Him. God was pleased with David because he fulfilled all His plans and purposes during his brief lifetime. David was not a perfect man, but whenever he realized his sin, he was willing to sincerely repent and to confess his sin and to ask for forgiveness. John tells us why God could say this about an imperfect David. We read, "*David served God's purpose in his own generation*" (Acts 13:36 NIV). In other words David fulfilled all of God's purposes and plans for his life during his brief time on Earth. If it were not for David, we would not have the Psalms and many other portions of scripture in the Old Testament. Truly David had a heart for God and lived a meaningful and purposeful life. God also wants you and I to have a heart for Him and to live a meaningful and purposeful life.

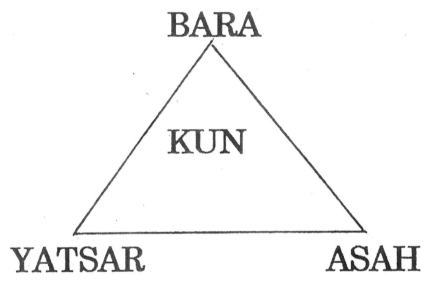

Figure 8-2: The above Four Hebrew Words describe how God planned (kun), created (bara), formed (yatsar) and made (asah) all things. The Hebrew word kun means to plan. Kun is synonymous with God the Father who is the Great Divine Architect and Planner of all Creation. Jesus is the Great Divine Bara which means the Creator. Bara is synonymous with God the Son. He is the One who has created, formed and made all things according to the Plan set forth by His Father.

God has a plan and purpose for every man and woman on this Earth. He is trying to get our attention. God's plan and purpose can only be accomplished if we are willing to humble ourselves and to receive His Son, the Lord Jesus Christ into our heart and lives. Jesus said in John 14:6, KJV, *"I am the way, the truth and the life. No one comes to the Father except through Me."*

How did God Form & Create Adam?

According to the Hebrew Scriptures, Jesus Christ, the Creator of the universe, came down from Heaven's glory to the Earth. He knelt down and formed (yatsar) Adam's body out of the dust of the ground. We read, *"And the Lord God formed (yatsar) man of the dust of the ground, and breathed into his nostrils the breath of life; and man became a living soul"* (Genesis 2:7, KJV). This Hebrew word yatsar means to form something new out of previous existing matter. It implies the work of a Potter who is molding a beautiful vase out of clay.

In like manner Jesus Christ, the Master Potter, was molding (yatsar) a human body out of clay. He then breathed into Adams nostrils the breath of life. The Hebrew word for breath is [ruach], which means life or spirit. When He breathed into man's nostrils the breath of life, He created (bara) life in Man. In this miraculous transaction Man became a living soul (nephesh). In other words, God created (bara) the true life within Adams body which was his spirit and soul. Adam was never in existence prior to this point in time. The relationship between these words is illustrated in Figure 8-2.

In this miraculous, supernatural transaction, the dead dust particles instantly became living flesh and blood. This is what we mean by special creation. Adam was created by God in adult form with a spirit, soul and body. Adam's body was formed out of previous existing clay or dust, whereas his soul and spirit were created out of no previous created matter. When man dies, his body returns to dust. His spirit and soul will go either to Heaven or to Hell. This depends upon the choice that he or she makes.

God realized that Man was lonely by himself and needed a mate, for we read: *"And the Lord God said, it is not good* that the man should be alone; I will make (asah) a helpmate for him" (Genesis 2:18, KJV). God could have matched Adam with some type of animal or ape in the Garden of Eden, but he did not, for we read: "But for Adam there was not found an help mate for him" (Genesis 2:20, KJV).

How did God Form & Create Eve?

When God created and formed Eve, he used a different technique. He did not create her in the same way that he formed and created Adam. But God in his wisdom put Adam into a deep sleep and performed surgery. In this unusual transaction He removed one of Adam's ribs and from this rib God made a woman, for we read: "So the LORD God caused the man to fall into a deep sleep; and while he was sleeping, he took one of the man's ribs and closed up the place with flesh. Then the LORD God made a woman from the rib he had taken out of the man, and he brought her to the man." (Genesis 2:21-22, KJV)

God related Adam and Eve genetically, so that they would be of the same species. Now both of them had a common genetic code (DNA) within their living cells that was capable of reproducing their genetic characteristics in fertile young. Adam realized this genetic relationship, for he says: "This is now bone of my bones and flesh of my flesh: she shall be called Woman, for she was taken out of Man" (Genesis 2:23, KJV).

The Bible says that every human being on the Earth can trace their ancestry back to Adam and Eve, for we read: "And Adam called his wife's name Eve; because she was the mother of all living" (Genesis 3:20, KJV). In other words, Eve is the mother of the entire human race. There is not a person regardless of the color of their skin who is not able to trace his or her ancestry back to mother Eve and to father Adam

What was God's Plan & Purpose for the Garden of Eden?

There was something within this beautiful garden that satisfied the entire body, soul and spirit of Adam and Eve. We read, "*The Lord God made every tree grow that is pleasant to the sight and good for food. The tree of Life was also in the midst of the garden, and the tree of the knowledge of good and evil.*" (Genesis 2:9, KJV).

First, the Lord God made every tree grow that was pleasant to the sight. This satisfied their soul. It is said that the eyes are the windows of the soul. It is through the eye gate that a person perceives the pleasant beauty of the outside world. This gave delightful pleasure and inner satisfaction to their soul.

Second, the Lord God made every tree grow that was good for food. This satisfied their physical body. The many varieties of fruit on the trees and vegetables in the garden were for the nourishment and health of their body.

Third, the Lord God made the "Tree of Life" which was in the midst of the garden as well as the tree of knowledge of good and evil. The tree of Life was to satisfy their spirit and to enhance their spiritual life of understanding with Him.

The Tree of Life   **The Tree of Knowledge of Good & Evil**

Figure 8-3: An illustration of the two trees in the midst of the Garden of Eden. Artwork by Elaine Daae.

God gave Adam definite instructions with respect to these two trees, for we read: *"And the Lord God commanded the Man, saying, "Of every tree of the garden you may freely eat; but of the tree of the knowledge of good and evil you shall not eat, for in the day that you eat of it you shall surely die."* (Genesis 2:16-17, NKJV) God created within Adam and Eve the freedom to make their own choices. As Creator, God did not create them as robots, but gave them the choice to accept Him or to reject Him or to follow Him or to follow the Devil. It is the same choice you and I have to continually make today.

This beautiful Garden of Eden was the closest place on the Earth to Paradise because the Tree of Life was present. Adam and Eve experienced the close and intimate presence, relationship and fellowship of their Almighty Creator God.

However, this garden was not a perfect place because the Tree of the Knowledge of Good & Evil was also present. In other wards there was evil lurking in the Garden, because the Evil One was also present. To make matters worse, death was also present among the animal and plant life outside of the Garden. Is it possible that there was death of insect life, for instance, in the garden? Were the domestic animals that God created in the garden protected from death? If Adam would have stepped on an insect would it have died?

God told Adam that if he would eat of the Tree of the knowledge of good and evil that he would surely die. Was God speaking a language to which Adam and Eve could relate? What we do know is that evil and death were lurking in the garden as an event ready to happen because of the prior Fall of Lucifer and the Edenic Curse.

A Test of Obedience

The first thing God did after He had created Adam was to take him to the two trees in the middle of the Garden. He then commanded Adam in Genesis 2:9 (NKJV), *"Of every tree of the garden you may freely eat; but of the tree of the knowledge of good and evil you shall not eat, for in the day that you eat of it you shall surely die.*" This was a test of Adam's obedience to the Lord. God was speaking a language that Adam could understand. Is it possible that Adam had witnessed death in the garden? Therefore, he understood clearly what would happen to him if he ate of this tree. This is the first mention of evil and death in the Bible.

Theologians abide by the Law of First Mention or First Reference. It states that the first mention of a certain word or phrase in the Bible will give a clue as to its proper inter-pretation later in scripture where its meaning may not be too clear.

If we are willing to "literally interpret" this portion of scrip-ture, then we must conclude that the Fall of Lucifer had already taken place prior to the creation of Adam & Eve and prior to the end of the Sixth Day of Creation. Death is mentioned even before Adam and Eve sinned.

The question arises how long before the creation of Adam and Eve did Lucifer Fall? We can find the answer to this question from the Bible and from the record of geology. See Figures 3-1 & 3-5.

The first mention of darkness, which is symbolic of evil and the Fall of Lucifer is found in Genesis 1:1-2 (NKJV), "*And darkness was on the face of the deep.*" The NIV translation says, "*Now the earth was formless and empty, darkness was over the surface of the deep, and the Spirit of God was hovering over the waters.*" We here discover that the dark-ness of sin resulting from the Fall of Lucifer was already present during the First Biblical Day of Creation. According to the Law of First mention, darkness is synonymous with the workings of evil. Evil is synonymous with death and with the Serpent, who is the Devil. See Chapters 3 and 4 for greater clarification. Also see Appendix C.

How did God Create New Animal Species?

The method God used to create man & woman, which bi-ologists refer to as the species Homo sapiens, is the same method He would have used to create every species of animal life on Earth.

Each of the millions of species of macro and micro animal life that have ever lived from the Proterozoic Age to the present would have been formed and created in the same manner by the Creator. The male species would have been formed and created first in adult form, then the female. The female would have been genetically related to the male just as Eve was genetically related to Adam, so that they would be of the same species. They, then, were able to reproduce fertile offspring from generation to generation.

We read, "*God made (asah) the wild animals each according to their kinds, the livestock according to their kinds and all the creatures that move along the ground according to their kinds*" (Genesis 1:24, NIV).

The word made in this passage is the Hebrew word asah. Asah is always translated made or make. It never implies original creation. However, it means that the specific animal that God has made was formed (yatsar) and created (bara) male and female by the Creator as a unique new species. According to biologists only the species category on the taxonomic table is capable of reproducing fertile offspring.

Plant life was probably formed and created in a slightly different way. It is possible that the Creator would have formed each seed or spore out of the dust of the ground. He would have first created the true life within that seed or spore with all the genetic information necessary for that seed to reproduce itself from generation to generation. For instance when God created plant life in Eden we read, "*And the Lord God made all kinds of trees **to grow out of the ground**"* (Genesis 2:8, NIV).

If the trees grew out of the ground, they must have sprouted from a seed or a spore that had been planted in the soil by God. We also read, "*The land produced vegetation: seed bearing plants and trees on the land that bear fruit with seed in it, according to their various kinds*" (Genesis 1:12, NIV). Here the word "kinds" refer to the biological term species. By definition a species is the only category on the taxonomic chart that is capable of reproducing offspring. See Figure 8-4.

What is Taxonomy?

Taxonomy is an artificial system created by Man to place all species into groupings such as genus, family, group, order, class, phyla for purposes of filing, storing and categorizing all life. All life can be found categorized into one of three known Kingdoms.

There is the Animal Kingdom, the Plant Kingdom and the Third Kingdom in which are found bacteria and viruses. Now no species of animal or plant life could survive apart from the life given to them from the Third Kingdom, which we will call, for the sake of clarification, the Bacteria Kingdom. The life within each Kingdom is known by multi individual species that relate to that Kingdom.

The following Taxonomy Chart shows the species category to be located at the bottom of a certain Kingdom, whereas the phyla is at the top. By definition, only a species is capable of propagating fertile offspring. Thus, all animals belong to a certain species.

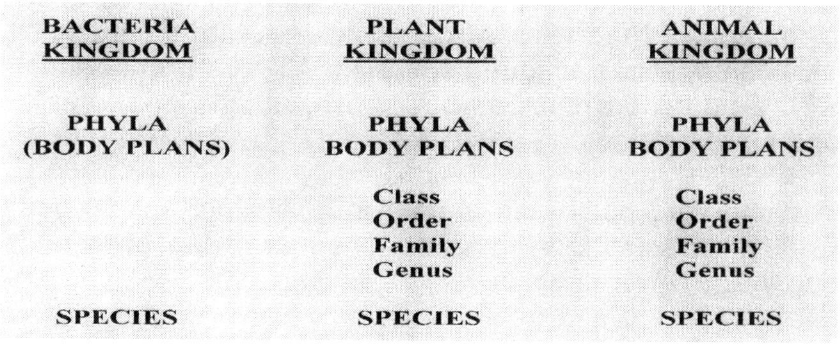

BACTERIA KINGDOM	PLANT KINGDOM	ANIMAL KINGDOM
PHYLA (BODY PLANS)	PHYLA BODY PLANS	PHYLA BODY PLANS
	Class	Class
	Order	Order
	Family	Family
	Genus	Genus
SPECIES	SPECIES	SPECIES

Figure 8-4: A simplified Taxonomy Chart by Don Daae

What is a Species?

When analyzing the life within the three Kingdoms, only a species has the ability to reproduce fertile offspring from generation to generation. In other words, all animal life on Earth today belongs to a specific species. Every species has a unique body plan called a phylum. Each of the 12+ million known species come under the umbrella of one of the 35 plus phyla (body plans) that scientists have identified as being present in the world today.

The groupings such as genus, family, order, class between a species and a phyla were already in place at the time when the first animal life was created. Taxonomy did not evolve as evolutionists would make us believe. Throughout geological time God only created new species. Each new species was created to fit into one of the four body plans (phyla) that were created towards the end of the Proterozoic Age when animal life first began. Then the remaining body plans (phyla) were created during the Cambrian Explosion of Animal life. See Figures 3-1, 3-5 & 8-4.

What is a Phyla?

Phyla constitute the highest biological category or taxa in the animal, plant or bacteria kingdoms. Each individual phylum exhibits a unique architectural blue print or novel structural design. For instance, Man belongs to the Chordate Phylum. The Chordate Phylum is characterized by an animal that has a vertebral column with a notochord. This constitutes a unique body plan. All vertebrate animals with a notochord such as birds, fish, amphibians, reptiles and mammals belong to the Chordate Phylum.

The chordate body plan is one of 35 distinct animal body plans that scientists have identified as being present in our modern world. However, there were 40+, some scientists say 47+ phyla or distinct body plans present during the Cambrian Period. The species that belonged to these extra phyla mysteriously became extinct at the end of the Cambrian Age. Geology records this event as being the first major extinction of animal life on Earth. See Figure 3-5.

Geology & Man

The scientific data of geology and human paleontology verifies a more recent appearance of Man on the Earth at about 6,000+ years before the present. It is believed that God created Adam & Eve toward the latter part of the Anathermal Age. See Figure 7-1.

The Seventh Day

The Creation of Eve did not result in the sudden termination of the Sixth Day of Creation and the commencement of the Seventh Day. It was the Fall of Adam and Eve that terminated the 6th Day of Creation. All of Adam and Eve's children and children's children were born during the Biblical Seventh Day which in turn relates geologically to the Medithermal Age. This is verified by the fact that both Cain and Able had sinful natures. See Figure 7-1.

The Seventh Day is, in reality, the History of man & woman. It is also a time when the God of the universe entered into His rest of creating anything new. We read in Genesis 2:2, NKJV *"And on the Seventh Day God ended His work which He had done, and He rested on the Seventh Day from all the work that He had done."* During the Seventh Day no new stars, planets, comets, solar systems, galaxies or any new species of animal or plant life have been created.

It is important to realize that whatever God has created prior to the end of the Sixth Day continues to experience change. In fact science verifies that all of Creation is experiencing continual ageing and change. The only one who remains without change is Almighty God. We read in Hebrews 1:10-12, NKJV *"You, LORD, in the beginning laid the foundation of the earth, And the heavens are the work of Your hands. They will perish, but You remain; and they will all grow old like a garment. Like a cloak You will fold them up, and they will be changed. But You are the same, And Your years will not fail."* Then in Hebrews 13:8 (NKJV), we read, *"Jesus Christ is the same yesterday, today and forever."*

The ageing process that we witness in nature around us today is the direct result of the Edenic Curse. The Edenic Curse is the result of the Fall of Lucifer that took place during the First Day of Creation. This has sadly affected the First and Second Heavens.

Chapter 9

What Happened to Adam & Eve?

The Bible is silent as to the length of time Adam and Eve were in the Garden of Eden before they disobeyed God and sinned. We are told that Adam was 130 years old when Seth was born (Genesis 5:3). Cain and Able were born after the Fall of Adam and Eve. Knowing that Cain and Abel were born before Seth, Adam and Eve may have been in the Garden for 50 to 100 years before they sinned. Their first two sons were born after they had fallen.

It was in the beautiful setting of the Garden of Eden that the Serpent, who is the Devil, came to the woman and said, "*Has God indeed said, "you shall not eat of every tree of the garden*"? (Genesis 3:1, NIV) This rhetorical question planted a seed of doubt in Eve's mind and she responded, "*We may eat the fruit of the trees of the garden; but of the fruit of the tree which is in the midst of the garden, God has said, "you shall not eat, nor shall you touch it, lest you die.*" (Genesis 3:2,NIV)

God had said "*you shall surely die*" if you eat the fruit of the tree, but Eve misquoted and lessened the impact of the statement by saying, "*Lest we die.*" The Serpent was quick to take advantage of the situation and quoted God in the negative, and responded by saying: "*You will not surely die. For God knows that in the day you eat of it your eyes will be opened, and you will be like God, knowing good and evil*"

(Genesis 3:4 & 5, NIV). Satan was implying that God was holding back something from them.

This prompted Eve to take a second look at the Tree of Knowledge of Good and Evil. We read, *"So when the woman saw that the tree was good for food, that it was pleasant to the eyes, and a tree desirable to make one wise, she took of its fruit and ate. She also gave to her husband and he ate."* (Genesis 3:6, NIV)

The Serpent tempted Eve in a three-fold manner. First, he tempted her body, for she saw that it was good to eat. Second, he tempted her soul, for the fruit was pleasant to the eyes. Third, he tempted her spirit, for the fruit was desirable for gaining wisdom and knowledge. Satan tempts you and I today in the same three fold manner.

After eating the fruit, Eve was a totally fallen, sinful person in body, soul and spirit, whereas Adam was without sin. Now there was a big black barrier of sin that was like **light and darkness** that separated Adam and Eve. This was analogous to the First Primordial Garden of Eden when Lucifer sinned. At that point in time a huge black barrier of sin separated fallen Lucifer from a Holy God.

The Bible makes it clear that Eve was deceived, but Adam was not deceived. His action was deliberate. We read, *"For Adam was formed first, then Eve. And Adam was not deceived, but the woman being deceived fell into transgression. Nevertheless she will be saved in child bearing if they continue in faith, love, and holiness, with self-control."* (1 Timothy 2:13-15, NIV)

Adam realized that the beautiful fellowship between he and his wife was now broken. He sensed the dark valley of light and darkness that now separated them. He deliberately ate of the forbidden fruit because of his great love for his lovely bride. He was not deceived by the Serpent. He ate of the forbidden fruit for the sake of saving his wife Eve for child bearing. This was done because of his great love for his bride which resulted in the furtherance of the human race.

84

Now both Adam and Eve had partaken of the forbidden fruit in direct disobedience to God's Word. They were both at this point in time totally fallen in body, soul and spirit. In Genesis 3:7 (NIV) we read, "*The eyes of both of them were opened, and they knew they were naked, and they sewed fig leaves together and made themselves coverings.*" They were both ashamed for what they had done. Neither of them sought the Lord's direction before they partook of the forbidden fruit. As a result they hid themselves from God. They were embarrassed, guilty and ashamed for what they had done.

Today, when you and I sin, it always brings embarrassment, guilt and shame into our lives. Our first tendency is to hide or to cover our sin and guilt with some kind of cover up.

The First Man-Made Religion

To cover up their guilt and shame they sewed together fig leaves to cover their sin. In other words, they invented the world's first false "Man-Made Religion." We can call this the "Fig Leaf Religion." They attempted to cover their sin by their own religious good works. This is exactly what the world has done ever since. Man has literally created hundreds of false, worldly, "Man Made Religions" in an attempt to gain freedom and to cover their acts of sin. All these acts are futile in the sight of the Lord.

God called to Adam, and asked, "*Where are you?*" (Genesis 3:9, NIV). Adam replied, "*I heard your voice in the garden, and I was afraid because I was naked, and I hid myself.f*" (Genesis 3:10, NIV) Then God asked him, "*Who told you that you were naked? Have you eaten from the Tree of the Knowledge of Good and Evil, which I commanded that you should not eat?*" (Genesis 3:11, NIV). God is asking for a confession, but all he received back were faint excuses.

Adam placed the blame for his sinful disobedience on Eve, for he said, "*The woman whom you gave to be with me, she gave me of the tree, and I ate*" (Genesis 3:12, NIV). Then the Lord turned to Eve and asked her what she had done.

Eve placed the blame on the Serpent and said, "*The serpent deceived me, and I ate*" (Genesis 3:13b, NIV). They were so human.

This act of disobedience had far reaching consequences. It brought Adam and Eve and all their future descendants under the bondage and curse of sin. The close intimate fellowship they had with God prior to the Fall was now broken by a barrier of sin. From this point onward, Adam and Eve were sinners and their fallen nature was transmitted to all their offspring. This is verified in Romans 5:12-14, NIV where we read, "*Therefore, just as sin entered the world through one man, and death through sin, and in this way death came to all men, because all sinned— 13 for before the law was given, sin was in the world. But sin is not taken into account when there is no law. 14 Nevertheless, death reigned from the time of Adam to the time of Moses, even over those who did not sin by breaking a command, as did Adam, who was a pattern of the one to come.*"

It is interesting to note that Adam was a pattern of the one to come. That one was Jesus. Unknown to Adam at this time, he did not realize that the reason why he was willing to die to sin was for the sake of saving his bride for child bearing. Later, at the Cross, Jesus was willing to die for the sins of the world for the sake of saving His bride which is the Church of Christ today.

It is God's will that all men and women come to know Him personally. We read in 1Timothy 2:3-4 NIV, "*I urge, then, first of all, that requests, prayers, intercession and thanksgiving be made for everyone— 2for kings and all those in authority, that we may live peaceful and quiet lives in all godliness and holiness. 3This is good, and pleases God our Savior, 4who wants all men to be saved and to come to a knowledge of the truth.*"

As a result of Adam and Eve's sin, God pronounced specific judgments upon Eve, Adam and the Serpent.

God's Judgement upon Eve

God said, "*I will greatly increase your pains in childbearing; with pain you will give birth to children. Your desire will be for your husband, and he will rule over you.*" (Genesis 3:16, NKJV) There are two parts here; the first refers primarily to the bearing of children, the second to woman's relationship to her husband. In the first part, God is saying that He will multiply two things: sorrow and conception. The number of children born would be multiplied, and the sorrows of life will be multiplied.

God also said to Eve that her desire will be to serve her husband. In other words, her husband would become the head of the home and to be her protector. Later portions of scripture elaborate upon the meaning of this verse. The husband is to love his wife, to cherish her, to support her, to work with her and to help her in the raising of their children.

God's Judgement upon Adam

God said to Adam, "*Because you have heeded the voice of your wife, and have eaten from the tree of which I commanded you saying, you shall not eat of it;*" "*Cursed is the ground for your sake; in toil you shall eat of it all the days of your life. Both thorns and thistles it shall bring forth to you, and you shall eat the herb of the field. In the sweat of your face you shall eat bread till you return to the ground, for out of it were you taken; for dust you are, and to dust you shall return.*" (Genesis 3:17-19, NKJV)

The results of God's pronouncements upon Man were two fold. First, Man had to obtain a living by the sweat of his brow. Second, Man now had an appointment with physical death. Man moved from an ideal life in the Garden of Eden of fellowship with God to a life of broken fellowship involving toil, pain and a struggle for existence outside the Garden.

God pronounced that Man would now have to work by the sweat of his brow. Life from this time and onward would not be easy. God also placed a curse upon the ground at this time, whereby thorns and thistles would begin to grow replacing the previous luxuriant growth of plant life. Thorns and thistles would indicate a change in climate to a progressively warm, dry and arid climate. This implies that the climate worldwide would be slowly changing to accommodate this new type of growth.

God's Judgment upon the Serpent

God also pronounced a prophetic judgment upon the Serpent, the Fallen Lucifer in the Garden of Eden. God said to the Serpent who is now called Satan, "*Because you have done this, you are cursed more than all the cattle, and more than every beast of the field, on your belly shall you go, and you shall eat dust all the days of your life. And I will put enmity between you and the woman, and between your seed and her seed; He shall crush your head and you shall bruise his heel.*" (Genesis 3:14-15, NKJV)

It is believed by Biblical scholars that Satan spoke to Eve through a certain animal in the garden called, "**The Serpent**." Some believe that this serpent was a reptile type of animal that was, hereby, destined to crawl as a snake on the Earth.

The science of archaeology has revealed evidences of Early Man, as well as Modern Man, worshipping snakes, flying serpents, and dragons which are symbolic of the Devil. However one may interpret this portion of scripture, it appears that Satan spoke audibly through a serpent like animal to Eve.

God's Plan of Redemption for Adam & Eve

God in His great mercy and love for Fallen Man provided a plan of redemption for Adam & Eve. This plan is described in Genesis 3:21, NKJV for we read, "*Also for Adam and his wife the LORD God made tunics of skin, and clothed them.*" This verse is literally packed with meaning. It provided a way for Fallen Man & Woman to be united with their Lord in a close intimate and loving relationship once again.

The Lord God clothed Adam & Eve with tunics of skin. What does this mean? It means that a certain clean type of domestic animal within the Garden of Eden such as a Lamb had to die. This lamb's body was sacrificed for Adam and Eve's sin. Its blood was shed as a covering for their sin.

Adam & Eve had a big decision to make. They could have said to the Lord God, we do not want your Blood Religion. We want to keep our Man Made Fig Leaf Religion. But, they made the right decision. They said yes to the Lord God and invited Him to cover them with the coats of skin. They were willing to come under the blood. **They were willing to appropriate God's plan of Redemption for their lives and to come under the covering of the blood.** They now experienced a renewed close fellowship with their Creator once again. Their destination from this point onward was Heaven. If they would have refused God's plan of redemption, their destiny would have been to a lost eternity called Hell.

God's plan of redemption required the death of a clean animal that chewed the cud and had a split hoof such as a lamb, a goat or a bull. This animal had to die; its blood had to be shed as a covering for their sins. This was a practice that "True Believers" practiced from the time of Adam and Eve to Noah's Flood and it continued to the Cross.

Foot Note: We now know that this Lamb pointed forward to the Cross where the future prophesied Seed of the Woman, the True Lamb of God, would one day be suspended on a cruel cross between Heaven and Earth. He would come to sacrifice His body and to shed His sinless blood for the sins of all Mankind.

Adam & Eve: Our Ancestors

According to the Bible, Adam and Eve are the ancestors to the entire human race for we read in Genesis 3:20,(NKJV) *"And Adam called his wife's name Eve, because she was the mother of all living."* The name Eve means life, living, or the first woman. Eve was the first woman, and is the mother of the human race. Every person on Earth can trace their ancestry back to mother Eve, whereas their seed is traced back to Adam (see Matthew 1:1-17 and Luke 3:23-38,).

It is also interesting to note that Luke 3:38 NKJV says, "*The son of Enos, the son of Seth, the son of Adam, the son of God.*" Luke here is tracing the lineage or ancestry of Joseph who was the husband of Mary, who in turn gave birth to Jesus Christ, back in time to Adam. What is important in Luke 3:38 is that Adam could trace his ancestry back to the son of God who is no other than Jesus Christ. He is the One who created Adam in the Garden of Eden.

In other words, the central figure in the genealogy of Adam and to every person who has ever lived on this Earth, including you and I, is our Creator, the Son of God who is no other than the Lord Jesus Christ. See Figures 8-1 and 8-2.

Jesus Christ is truly the central figure in all human history. He is also the central figure in the creation and history of all Creation. This includes the entire Universe of stars, galaxies and the Earth as well as all species of plant and animal life on the Earth. See Figure 3-5.

In Conclusion

As a result of the Fall of Adam and Eve, God's **"Prophetic Clock"** with respect to the future history of all Mankind began to tick. The above three judgments that God pronounced upon Adam, Eve and the Serpent provided the first insight into what the future would begin to reveal.

Chapter 10

What is the Adamic Curse?

The moment Adam sinned, the Adamic Curse began. We read in Romans 5:12, NIV "*Therefore, just as sin entered the world through one man (Adam), and death through sin, and in this way death came to all people, because all sinned.*" **Adam's sinful fallen nature was passed on to all of his descendants.** This is why Romans 5:17-19 NIV says, "*For if by the trespass of the one man, death reigned **through that one man (Adam),** how much more will those who receive God's abundant provision of grace and of the gift of righteousness reign in life **through the one man, Jesus Christ**! Consequently, just as one trespass resulted in con- demnation for all people, so also one righteous act resulted in justification and life for all. For just as through the disobe- dience of the one man (Adam) the many were made sinners, so also through the obedience of the one man (Jesus) the many will be made righteous.*"

The Adamic Curse is the result of Adams sin. This Adamic curse has been passed on to all of Adam's descendents. We are all born with a sinful nature inherited from Adam. Each one of us is destined to one day die. Each one is guilty before Almighty God because of our inherited sinful nature and we are all in need of a Saviour who can cleanse each one of us from all past and present sins.

The second Man, Jesus Christ, willingly went to the Cross. He shed His sinless blood and gave His body as a sacrifice for the sins of all Mankind. This includes you and I. It now remains a choice for every person. The choice is whether we are willing to acknowledge and to receive Jesus Christ as our personal Saviour and Lord or whether we choose to reject Him. Our choice determines our future destination which is Heaven or Hell.

Results of the Adamic Curse

As a result of Eve's sin, God said, "*I will greatly multiply your sorrow and your conception; In pain you shall bring forth children*" (Genesis 3:16, NIV). In other words, women's sorrow will be multiplied because all women will now have a fallen, sinful nature. Sin brings forth sorrow and heart-ache. Secondly, conception will be multiplied. Women will have children and pain will be associated with childbirth. It may even imply that multiple births, such as twins will take place. A change took place in Eve's body at the moment she sinned that has been passed on to all women.

As a result of Adam's sin: God said. "*Cursed is the ground for your sake; in toil you shall eat of it all the days of your life. Both thorns and thistles it shall bring forth to you, and you shall eat the herb of the field. In the sweat of your face you shall eat bread till you return to the ground, for out of it were you taken; for dust you are, and to dust you shall return.*" (Genesis 3:17-19, NIV) As a result of this curse, life became more difficult for Adam. He now had to toil and sweat in a more difficult environment. He would have to labor for his food and for the necessities of life. This more difficult life would eventually result in his return to the ground in death. Every man since Adam has experienced similar hardships, frustrations, toil and eventual death.

Is it possible that God placed this curse upon the ground for Man's sake? As a result of this curse, man would have to work by the sweat of his brow in order to supply his family with food and accommodation. Could this possibly help to remind man and woman of their need for regaining fellow-ship with their Maker?

What was this Curse?

The big question arises, what was the curse that God placed upon the ground when Adam and Eve sinned? Through the science of geology and other Earth sciences, it is now possible to determine certain aspects of this curse.

Two prominent Pleistocene (Ice Age) geologists Ernst Antevs an American and Gerard DeGreer a European from Denmark noted a marked temperature rise that took place about 10,000 years ago.[1-4]This change in temperature had a pronounced warming effect on the climate throughout the entire Earth during the Anathermal Age. See Figure 7-1.

The Anathermal Age was characterized by a progressive global warming of the climate together with abundant moisture. During this age there were no evidences of desert conditions. It would appear that the Earth was a place of luxuriant growth of plant life and animal life. The commencement of the Anathermal Age marks the termination of the Wisconsin Glaciation advance. See Figures 19-1 and 19-2.

The Earth had just experienced the cold Wisconsin Glaciation where massive sheets of glacial Ice of great thickness continued to cover large portions of northern Europe, portions of northern Asia as well as the northern portions of North America, portions of South America and most of Antarctica. See the map in Figure 19-2. Great inland lakes developed along the southern edges of the Pleistocene ice in northern Europe and in northern portions of the United States during the Anathermal Age. These lakes continued to receive melt water from the Pleistocene Ice well into the Altithermal Age.

The Altithermal Age is characterized by the incipient and progressive growth of desert regions with progressive rising temperatures throughout the world as a result of climate change. These desert regions continued to grow and expand during this age. **Is it possible that this abrupt climate change at the beginning of the Altithermal Age was the result of the Adamic Curse?**

Figure 19-1, shows the beginning of the Altithermal Age to coincide with the Fall of Adam and Eve. It is herein believed that the Adamic curse explains the climate change that took place at the beginning of the Altithermal Age.

The Bible says in Genesis 3:17, NIV, "*Both thorns and thistles it (the earth) shall bring forth to you.*" **Thorns and thistles imply a change in climate to a drier and less productive condition throughout the Earth.** Scientists and geologists have observed this progressive climate change throughout the world during the Altithermal Age.

Man was to Populate & Subdue the Earth

God gave Adam and Eve an instruction in Genesis 1:28, NIV "*Be fruitful and increase in number; fill (populate) the earth and subdue it.*" They were to have children and their children were to have children. As a result they were to populate the entire Earth.

According to the sciences of geology, archaeology and anthropology, we can now verify that every continent on the Earth was populated with the possible exception of Antarctica prior to the disaster phenomenon known as Noah's Flood.

The people during the early part of the Altithermal Age were mainly explorers, food gatherers, hunters and nomadic travelers throughout the Earth. People were able to live off the land in rural and small communities because there was a plenteous supply of food.

James Howard Wellard[5] describes the time when the vast Sahara Desert was a moist region of forests and grasslands. Welland says, "*On rock faces in many parts of the Sahara Desert unknown artists have depicted life as they see it, from prehistoric times up to the present, representing 10,000 years of continuous history. The oldest of these engravings are ascribed to the "Hunters" who lived in the Sahara when the desert was forested and inhabited by elephants, giraffes, and aquatic animals.*" Wellard goes on to say, "*The same aura of mystery surrounds the descendants of the Hunters those people who built the "cyclopean" walls which still guard the western approaches to the summit of Zenkekra, and the tens of thousands of rock tombs, or burial mounds, which litter the side of the valley. Their presence indicates a sizeable empire; and if we ascribe to them the immense network of underground tunnels called foggares, it indicates, too, a people of a settled agricultural way of life in contrast to the Hunters who lived by the bow and arrow."*

Welland is describing the Sahara Desert region of northern Africa during the past 10.000 years. Once we begin to subdivide the past 10,000 years into the Anathermal, Altithermal and the Medithermal ages, we begin to see how lush the vegetation in the Sahara region was with abundant animal life during the Anathermal Age. This lush condition of plant and animal life would have extended into the early portions of the Altithermal Age.

It was during the early part of the Altithermal Age that the descendents of Adam and Eve, who were explorers, hunters and food gatherers, would have begun to occupy the Sahara region. These were the people who were eventually forced to move to areas of plentiful water when the desert conditions progressed.

These same people during the latter part of the Altithermal Age began to congregate into areas where the water was more plentiful. It was here where they established farming communities to feed the growing populations of people who lived and worked in towns and emerging cities. As the population increased these were the people who constructed the cyclopean stone structures in northern portions of Africa. It is important to realize that the great industrial developments that took place in Northern Africa and in Egypt were also taking place throughout the world. This is the story that we will be unveiling in the chapters to come.

During the latter half of the Altithermal Age throughout the world great advances were made in animal husbandry, agriculture, and ranching. City growth encouraged animal husbandry, ranching, dairy farms and more sophisticated forms of industrial and mining development. This led into the manufacture of highly polished stone tools, copper tools, and the art of stone casting that resulted in the construction of cyclopean and megalithic stone complex structures worldwide.

This is the story of pre-Flood Early Man who inhabited the world, including north and South America prior to Noah's Flood.

In Conclusion

The reason this dramatic climate change took place worldwide prior to the Flood was because of the curse that God placed upon the ground as a result of Adam's sin. We read in Genesis 3:17 NIV, *"Cursed is the ground because of you."* This was the curse that affected the climate, causing desert areas to expand. This resulted in a scarcity of available food. The people were forced to re-locate to areas where there was a greater supply of water.

Jesus said in Mathew 24:37 (NIV), *"As it was in the days of Noah, so shall it be at the coming of the Son of Man."* In other words, conditions that existed prior to the Flood of Noah will be similar to conditions that will take place prior to Christ's return.

The worldwide Flood brought the Altithermal Age to a dramatic termination about 4,500 years ago. This can now be confirmed by the sciences of geology, archaeology and anthropology. Noah's Flood also commenced a new age called the Medithermal Age.

References for Chapter 10

1. Antevs, Ernest. *Retreat of the Last Ice Sheet in Eastern Canada.* Geol. Survey Canada, Mem. 146, 1925.
2. Antevs, Ernst. *The Recession of the Last Ice Sheet in New England.* Amer. Geog. Soc., Research Ser. 11, 1922.
3. Antevs, Ernest. *Geochronology of the Deglacial and Neothermal Ages.* The Journal of Geology, Vol.61, Number 3, May 1953.
4. DeGreer, Gerard. *GeochronologiaSuecica Principles,* Svenska, Vetenskapsakad, Handl., Vol. 18, No. 6, 1940. Note: The above papers will give the reader an insight into how Antevs & DeGreer were able to date the past 20,000 years of Earth history by means of geology.
5. Wellard, James Howard, "*The Great Sahara*" E.P. Dutton & Co., Inc. New York, 1964. Page 605.

Chapter 11

The Conflict of the Ages Begins

God also pronounced a prophetic judgment upon the Serpent, the Fallen Lucifer in the Garden of Eden. God said to the Serpent who is the Devil, "*Because you have done this, you are cursed more than all the cattle, and more than every beast of the field, on your belly shall you go, and you shall eat dust all the days of your life. And I will put enmity between you and the woman, and between your seed and her seed; He shall bruise your head and you shall bruise his heel.*" (Genesis 3:14-15, NIV)

It is believed by Biblical scholars that Satan spoke to Eve through a certain animal in the garden called The Serpent. Some believe that this serpent was a type of animal that was, hereby, destined to crawl as a snake on the Earth. The science of archaeology often depicts early Man worshipping images of snakes, flying serpents, and dragons which are symbolic of the Devil, who is referred to in the Bible as The Serpent. However, one may interpret this portion of scripture; it appears that Satan spoke audibly through a serpent like animal to Eve. It is also possible that the Serpent spoke directly to Eve in a similar way that he speaks to people like you and I today.

The Conflict of the Ages is predicted in the second part of this prophetic pronouncement. A spiritual conflict and enmity is forecasted to take place between the Seed of the Woman and the Seed of the Serpent. It predicts that there will be a coming Messiah who would one day be born of a woman and who is referred to as the "**Seed of the Woman**." This reference to "her seed'" is peculiar because the male is always considered the one who transmits the seed. This reference is to the virgin birth of the coming Messiah.

Other portions of the Old Testament give additional information as to who the Seed of the Woman may be. We read in Isaiah 7:14 NIV, *"Therefore the Lord Himself shall give you a sign: Behold, the virgin shall conceive and bear a Son and shall call His name Immanuel."* The name Immanuel literally means: **God with Us**. Isaiah the prophet is saying that sometime in the future a certain woman who is a virgin shall miraculously conceive and will give birth to a Son. This Son will be Deity or God incarnate. In other words, **this Son will be the promised Seed of the Woman to the Jews and to all people.**

From the time of Adam and Eve and throughout the Pre-Flood Age, the people of God were made aware of a future time when one day a woman would give birth to the promised Messiah. This promised Messiah would bring eternal hope to all Mankind. He would also replace the plan of redemption that was given to Adam & Eve. This plan involved the death of a clean animal such as a lamb. This lamb had to die its blood had to be shed as a covering of man's sins. The promised Seed of the Woman would also one day die and would shed His blood for the sins of the world once and for all.

This promised Messiah is identified in Matthew 1:18-25 (NIV) as Jesus Christ. We read, *"This is how the birth of Jesus Christ came about: His mother Mary was pledged to be married to Joseph, but before they came together, she was found to be with child through the Holy Spirit. Because Joseph her husband was a righteous man and did not want to expose her to public disgrace, he had in mind to divorce her quietly. But after he had considered this, an angel of the Lord appeared to him in a dream and said, "Joseph son of David, do not be afraid to take Mary home as your wife, because what is conceived in her is from the Holy Spirit. She*

*will give birth to a son, and you are to give him the name
Jesus, because he will save his people from their sins." All
this took place to fulfill what the Lord had said through the
prophet: "The virgin will be with child and will give birth
to a son, and they will call him Immanuel"—which means,
"God with us."*

Satan's Fate was Determined

Satan realized his time was shortened and that his future
was determined. The pronouncement by Almighty God was
this, *"And I will put enmity between you and the woman,
and between your seed and her seed; He shall bruise your
head and you shall bruise his heel."* (Genesis 3:14-15, NKJV).
This statement is packed full of meaning.

As we progress step by step into the future of human history, we will begin to see the strategy that the Fallen Lucifer,
who is known to all mankind as the Devil, Satan and the
Serpent, will take to prevent his own destruction. There
is a coming day when the Seed of the Woman (Jesus) will
crush the head of the Seed of the Serpent. Future Bible
verses clarify that there is a day when this Earth is going to
be delivered completely from Satan's power, influence and
presence. How will this take place?

From this point in time, we will see that the Devil is fighting desperately for his life. During each of the succeeding
periods of human history, Satan will be using different
strategies. However, we will see that Satan is no match for
Almighty God.

Satan is just one of God's created angelic beings who foolishly allowed pride to dominate his actions into a life of sin
and open rebellion against the God of Heaven and Earth. He
has foolishly risen up against Almighty God. His intensions
have never changed since His Fall in the First Primordial
Garden of Eden. His aim at that early time was to deceive
and to lure the angels under his jurisdiction to become like
himself and to rise up in open rebellion against the God who
created them.

Satan's objective is to likewise lure all humans into following him and to encourage them to enter into open rebellion against Almighty God. This commenced **the Great Conflict of the Ages**. It so happens that each one of us is an integral part of this conflict. It is up to you and I to choose who we will follow. Our destination is either Heaven or Hell.

Dissolution of the Second Garden of Eden

Just as God drove Lucifer out of the First Primordial Garden of Eden after his Fall, now God is driving Adam & Eve out of the Second Garden of Eden as a result of their Fall. God was now dealing with fallen, sinful Man. He could not allow sinful Man to continue to inhabit the Garden of Eden. We read, "*Behold, the man has become like one of us, to know good and evil. And now, lest he put out his hand and take of the tree of life, and eat, and live forever. Therefore the Lord God sent him out of the Garden of Eden to till the ground from which he was taken*" (Genesis 3:22-23, NIV).

Adam and Eve were reluctant to leave this beautiful garden. They knew that the world outside of the garden would be more hostile. Therefore God had to force them to leave the garden for we read, "*So God drove out the man; and He placed cherubim at the east entrance of the Garden of Eden, and a flaming sword which turned every way, to guard the way to the tree of life.*" (Genesis 3:24, NIV) God drove Adam and Eve out of the garden and brought "cherubim" down from the Heaven of Heavens (The Third Heaven) to guard its east entrance. Lucifer was one of the cherubim of Heaven before his fall. God sent angelic beings of the same strength and power as Satan himself to prevent Adam and Eve from entering the garden and partaking of the Tree of Life. God also placed a flaming sword which turned every way, to guard the way to the Tree of Life.

The Tree of Life was removed by God from the Garden of Eden and is presently in the Heaven of Heavens, the place where God dwells. "*He who has an ear, let him hear what the Spirit says to the churches. To him who overcomes I will give to eat from the Tree of Life, which is in the midst of the Paradise of God."* (Genesis 2:7) *"In the middle of the street, and on either side of the river, was the Tree of Life, which bore twelve fruits, each tree yielding its fruit every month. And the leaves of the tree were for the healing of the nations."* (Genesis 22:2, NIV)

It would appear as though the Tree of Life was removed from the Garden of Eden shortly after Adam and Eve were forced to leave. The beautiful setting of the garden would have disappeared. It was no longer a place of Paradise, because the Tree of Life was now gone. After a time, this region was probably little different from any other part of the world. Today, the Second Garden of Eden is a barren, desolate, desert type of region. In a later chapter, we will reveal where this garden was most likely located.

It is quite likely that Adam and Eve and their descendents would have entered the garden region soon after the Tree of Life had been removed. They and their descendents would have nurtured the many domestic animals, fruit trees, vegetables and shrubs. Later the domestic animals, fruit trees and vegetables would have been taken to various parts of the Earth including North and South America.

Chapter 12

Earth's First Family: What Went Wrong?

Adam and Eve were the Earth's First Family. It would appear that they settled to the east of the Garden of Eden. This is where they established their first home. It was here that they began to raise a family. They were now in a more hostile environment, without all the benefits of the garden because the Tree of Life was now gone.

Survival would have become the prime requirement as they began to till the soil, to plant vegetables, grain crops, fruit trees, and the like. They would have raised sheep, cattle, horses, dogs, cats, chickens. They would have had dogs and cats as pets. It was here that they began raising their family.

We read in Genesis 3:20 (NIV), *"Adam named his wife Eve, because she would become the mother of all living."* In other words, every human being born on this Earth can trace their ancestry back to mother Eve and to father Adam.

We read again in Genesis 4:1-2 NIV, "Now Adam knew Eve his wife, and she conceived and bore Cain, and said, "I have acquired a man from the LORD." Then she bore again, this time his brother Abel." It is believed that the first two babies born on this Earth were twins. There was one conception and two births.

We read in Genesis 4:2b, *"Now Abel was a keeper of sheep, but Cain was a tiller of the ground."* Abel looked after the sheep. He became the first Shepherd. Cain was a tiller of the ground. He became the first farmer.

Cain & Able Were Put to the Test

Cain and Able were put to the test. They both had inherited an evil, fallen nature from their parents and were under the Adamic Curse. They were also under the Edenic curse, resulting from the Fall of Lucifer. They both had the freedom to make their own choices in life, just like you and I do today.

The first test that was presented to them is recorded in Genesis 4:3-5 (NIV), *"In the course of time Cain brought some of the fruits of the soil as an offering to the LORD. But Abel also brought an offering—fat portions from some of the firstborn of his flock. The LORD looked with favor on Abel and his offering, but on Cain and his offering he did not look with favor. So Cain was very angry, and his face was downcast."* Now what is this all about? Why did God accept Able's offering, but not Cains. They both had a desire to bring an offering to the Lord. On the surface it does not seem fair.

This test had to do with their inherited sinful nature. They both had a fallen nature just like you and I. They both were in need of God's plan of Redemption where they could receive forgiveness for their sins. It is obvious that Adam & Eve had instructed their sons about the need to bring a sin offering to the Lord. Their parents would have told them about God's plan of Redemption which required the death of a clean animal and that the shed blood of this animal would cover their sins. They would also have been told that one day in the future the Seed of the Woman would be born who would cleanse them of all their sins. Now Cain & Able had to make a choice.

Able made the right choice. He brought a blood offering and God accepted his offering. Cain made a wrong choice.

He brought a beautiful offering of fruit & vegetables, etc. This was the work of his hands. God refused this offering because it was not a blood offering.

As a result Cain became very angry. So the Lord pleads with Cain and says, *"Why are you angry? Why is your face downcast?* **If you do what is right, will you not be accepted?** *But if you do not do what is right, sin is crouching at your door; it (sin) desires to have you, but you must rule over it (sin)"* (Genesis 4:6-7 NIV). The Lord is pleading with Cain to bring a blood sacrifice. Otherwise there would be no covering for his sins. But the Lord in his mercy is saying to Cain, if you are not willing to bring a blood sacrifice then you must rule over sin in your life. In other words you must not allow sin to rule over you. This is the same advice that the Lord is giving to every person who has not yet come under the blood.

The Lord is saying to Cain that his ability to reason should be strong enough to keep Satan at arms length. This is brought out in Isaiah 1:18 NIV, *"Come now, and let us reason together," says the LORD, "though your sins are like scarlet, they shall be as white as snow; though they are red like crimson, they shall be as wool."*

In his anger to the Lord, Cain refused to listen to Gods advice. Instead, he listened to the voice of the enemy Satan, the Serpent who was a murderer, a liar and a terrorist from the beginning, for we read in Genesis 4:8 NIV, *"Now Cain said to his brother Abel, "Let's go out to the field. While they were in the field, Cain attacked his brother Abel and killed him."* This is the first recorded murder in the Bible. Then we read in 1 John 3:15, *"Whosoever hates his brother is a murderer; you know that no murderer has eternal life abiding in him."* Cain not only rose up against Almighty God, but he also rose up against his only twin brother because of feelings of envy, jealousy and hatred which resulted in murder.

The Lord came to Cain. He was seeking a confession, *"Where is your brother Abel?* (Genesis 4:9, NIV) Cain's reply was as follows, *"I don't know, am I my brother's keeper?"* Cain was in a state of denial. Then the Lord said, *"What have you done? Listen! Your brother's blood cries out to me from the ground. Now you are under a curse and driven from the ground, which opened its mouth to receive your brother's blood from your hand. When you work the ground, it will no longer yield its crops for you. You will be a restless wanderer on the earth."* (Genesis 4:10-12, NIV)

Cain then said to the Lord in Genesis 4:13-14 NIV, *"My punishment is more than I can bear. Today you are driving me from the land, and I will be hidden from your presence; I will be a restless wanderer on the earth, and whoever finds me will kill me."* Then the Lord in His mercy said to Cain in Genesis 4:15 NIV, *"Not so; anyone who kills Cain will suffer vengeance seven times over." Then the LORD put a mark on Cain so that no one who found him would kill him."* In spite of this mercy from the Lord, there is no record of Cain ever confessing and repenting of his sins. He went his own way and did his own thing in a similar way that Lucifer went his own way and did his own thing.

One can understand the deep sorrow and heartache that Adam and Eve must have experienced at this time to see their first born son perform such an evil and murderous act. They surely grieved deeply over the death of their second son Able. I am sure from this time onward; they became aware that their real enemy was the Serpent, the Devil who was lurking behind the scenes. They sensed the deep hatred and murderous intent of the Devil toward them.

How does Satan Attack Mankind?

The question arises, How does Satan attack Mankind? He is the Evil One lurking behind the scenes. Jesus said, *"He was a murderer from the beginning, not holding to the truth, for there is no truth in him. When he lies, he speaks his native language, for he is a liar and the father of lies"* (John 8:44 NIV). He is full of hate towards God and to all those who follow the Lord and come under the blood. He has mobilized his armies of Fallen Angels, called demons to deceive, destroy, terrorize, and kill and to prevent God's work on this Earth. Satan's aim is to blind the minds of all people and to prevent them from trusting in the Lord God of Heaven and Earth.

In the days of Adam and Eve and their descendents, the people did not know about Jesus Christ as their Savior and Lord. However, during the entire Old Testament period, the people knew that one day in the future, that the promised Messiah, the Seed of the Woman would one day be born. He would be their hope and salvation. This message was preached to the entire world including North and South America through the Messianic genealogy prior to the Flood of Noah. We read, *"And Adam knew his wife again, and she bore a son and named him Seth, "For God has appointed another seed for me instead of Abel, whom Cain killed." And as for Seth, to him also a son was born; and he named him Enosh.* **Then men began to call on the name of the LORD** *(Genesis 4:25-26 NIV). This is the message that would have gone out to all the world.* Every person from the time of Adam and Eve to the Flood had to make a choice between good and evil, that is between God or the Devil.

Jesus confirms this when He said, *"But as the days of Noah were, so also will the coming of the Son of Man be. For as in the days before the flood, they were eating and drinking, marrying and giving in marriage, until the day that Noah entered the ark, and did not know until the flood came and took them all away, so also will the coming of the Son of Man be."* (Mathew 24:37-39, NIV). Jesus is saying that events that preceded the Flood will be similar to events that will precede His second coming. Today, the Gospel of Redemption which is now called Salvation is going out to the entire world. Do you not believe that God's message of Redemption that was proclaimed to Adam and Eve was going out to the entire world prior to the Flood?

This Messianic message of Redemption continued to be preached throughout the interval of time from the Flood to the birth of the Messiah Jesus Christ. Every person from the Flood to the Cross had to also make a choice between good and evil, that is between God and the Devil.

The Descendants of Adam & Eve prior to the Flood?

The question arises who were the descendents of Adam and Eve prior to the Flood? In order to discover the answer to this question we must ask a second question, How many sons did Adam and Eve have? Did every son have a family lineage. All persons who lived prior to the Flood could trace their ancestry back to one of Adam's sons.

Adam and Eve Had Other Children

Adam and Eve had other sons and daughters for we read in Genesis 5:3-4 NIV, "*And Adam lived one hundred and thirty years, and begot a son in his own likeness, after his image, and named him Seth. After he begot Seth, the days of Adam were eight hundred years; and **he had sons and daughters**. So all the days that Adam lived were nine hundred and thirty years; and he died.*" The average life span of Man before the Flood was about 930 years. The only way the human population could grow, was for brothers to marry sisters in the beginning. Many glibly ask the question: Who did Cain marry? He obviously married one of his sisters. The Bible record does not number the other sons of Adam. We can only speculate on the number.

We can conservatively estimate the number of other sons at six and daughters at six. There could have been more. Then the genealogy from Adam & Eve onward would be as follows:

-Cain:
-Able: Murdered by Cain.
-Seth: Replaced Able in the Messianic Lineage
-Four other sons.

This in total would equate to six sons and six daughters. In the course of time each son would have married a sister. Thus, under this scenario there would have been six family groups who were directly descended from Adam and Eve. The reason why I chose six sons is because the Biblical number of Man is six. There could have been a fairly rapid increase in population from this time forth.

There are possibilities that Adam and Eve may have had twelve sons and twelve daughters. The number twelve is a most significant numerical number in the Bible when related to genealogies. For instance, Jacob had 12 sons and Ishmael had 12 sons. If Adam and Eve had twelve sons and twelve daughters then the pre-flood world population would have grown much faster.

The Genealogy of Adam

It is interesting to note that the Bible records only two genealogies before the Flood. The first genealogy is through the line of Seth who replaced Able. The second genealogy is through the line of Cain. The genealogy of Adam & Eve's other sons are not revealed or recorded in the Bible.

The Messianic Genealogy of Adam through Seth

The genealogy of Adam through Seth is referred to as the Messianic Genealogy. It was through this genealogy that God revealed His plan of salvation to all mankind before the Flood and from the Flood to the time of Abraham leading to the eventual coming of the Promised Messiah Jesus Christ.

Almighty God gave the responsibility of transmitting God's Word and His plan of Redemption to all the world through the Messianic Genealogy. We read, "***Then men began to call upon the name of the Lord***" (Genesis 4:26b, NIV). It was through this lineage of Seth that the promised Messiah, the Seed of the Woman, would one day be born. This promise was revealed in the Garden of Eden at the time when God pronounced judgment upon the Serpent.

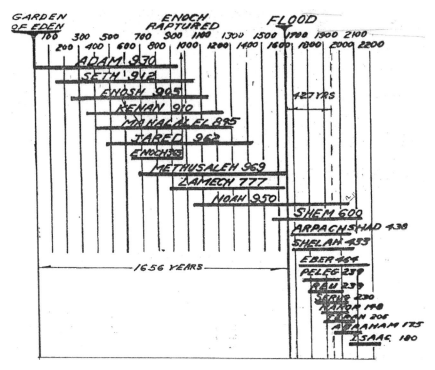

Figure 12-1: The Genealogy of Seth: illustrates the Messianic Genealogy from Adam through Seth to Noah, Shem and Abraham. From the Creation of Adam and Eve to the Flood of Noah is about a 1656 year period of time. There were ten generations from Adam to the Flood. By Don Daae.

The Prophetic Clock

God's Prophetic clock began to tick when God pronounced His future judgement upon Satan. God said to Satan, the Serpent, in Genesis 3:14-15 NIV, *"Because you have done this, I (God) will put enmity between you (the Serpent) and the woman (the promised Messiah), and between your (the Serpents) offspring and hers (the woman's off-spring); he (the promised Messiah) will crush your head (the Serpent), and you (the Serpent) will strike his heel (the promised Messiah)."* This is a paraphrased version of the NIV translation.

From this moment in time, Satan knew that his days were numbered. His aim from that moment onward has been to plan strategies whereby he could prevent his own destruction.

The Messianic genealogy of Adam through Seth to the time of Noah and to Abraham is shown in Figure 12-1. The average lifespan of man prior to the Flood was 930 years. After the Flood the life span was progressively shortened, so that by the time of King David the life span of man was reduced to three score years and ten or to 70 years. We read, "*The length of our days is seventy years or eighty, if we have the strength; yet their span is but trouble and sorrow, for they quickly pass, and we fly away. Teach us to number our days aright, that we may gain a heart of wisdom*" Psalm 90:10 &12, NIV). Many people wrestle with the long lifespan of mankind from Adam to the Flood. It is interesting to note that in the future when the Promised Messiah sets up His Earthly Kingdom for 1000 years, the lifespan of mankind will be lengthened once again to about 1,000 years. Almighty God is the one who controls and determines the average lifespan of mankind.

According to the Messianic Genealogy the time span from Adam to the Flood was about 1656 years. This is based upon the Massoretic Text. This is the genealogical text that most Christian theologians follow. Under this scenario, it is assumed by some that Abraham was born in the year 2166 BC. Others claim Abraham's birth was somewhat closer to 2000 BC. Thus, the about 4500 year date before the Flood could be moved back to accommodate an earlier Flood date. It could also be moved forward to accommodate a later Flood date based upon the Septuagint text. See Appendix A.

Chapter 13

Pre-Flood Cultural & Industrial Developments

The Bible mentions eight specific pre-Flood cultural and industrial developments that characterize the religious, social and economic conditions from Adam and Eve to the Flood of Noah. This Pre-Flood Age was an age of true religion, false religion, world travel, city building and break down of the family unit, great agricultural advances, music, and industrial advances in stone masonry and copper. This age ended with great violence and wickedness.

All of these Pre-Flood cultural and industrial developments are often referred to as Biblical signs that will be repeated once again prior to Christ's Second return. Jesus said in Mathew 24:37 NIV, *"As it was in the days of Noah, so it will be at the coming of the Son of Man."* In other words, worldwide events that preceded the Flood will be similar to worldwide events that will precede His second coming.

The Bible gives information pertaining to the life-style of these early people. The first nine chapters of Genesis were in all likelihood written on clay tablets during the pre-Flood period by the early pre-Flood patriarchs. These records were protected in the Ark by Noah and were later transmitted through the Messianic line from Shem to Abraham and later to Moses.

These pre-Flood developments are recorded in Genesis 4:16-24. Each of Cain's sons lived an average of 930 years.

The last four sons, Lamech, Jabel, Jubal and Tubal-Cain would have been alive when the Flood struck. There were 10 pre-Flood generations recorded in the Biblical genealogy that relate to Cain as well as to Seth.

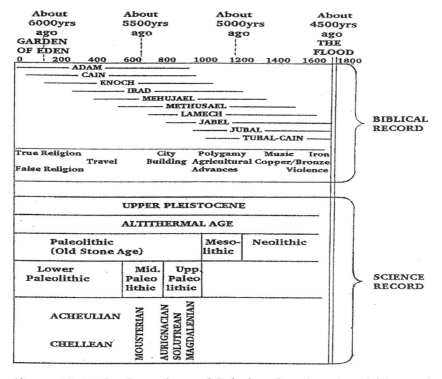

Figure 13-1: The Genealogy of Cain is related to the Altithermal Age. The religious, cultural and science developments are related to the genealogy of Cain where each son is believed to have lived an average of 930 years. There were ten generations from Adam to the Flood. Prepared by Don Daae.

It is also believed that the cultural and industrial developments that took place through the genealogy of Cain were similar and parallel to what took place through the other sons of Adam. They were all involved in the social and economic developments that took place. The new techniques and inventions that developed throughout the 1,656 years culminated in one of the most highly developed civilizations the world has ever known. It was second only to what we are experiencing throughout the world today.

Age of True Religion

It was an age characterized by true religion that began with Adam and Eve. This true religion proclaimed God's plan of Redemption. It was propagated through the Messianic line from Adam to Noah. Blessings went out to all the world through this ancestral Messianic line in a similar manner that the Gospel of the Living God through His Son the Lord Jesus Christ is going out to all parts of the world today. Every person prior to the Flood had an opportunity to either reject or to accept God's plan of Redemption. The same is true today.

God presented his plan of redemption to Adam and Eve, who in turn passed it on to their children from generation to generation. Abel appropriated God's plan of redemption for his life, but was murdered by his brother Cain who rejected God's plan. Seth and Enoch received and proclaimed the true religion of God. The Bible says, *"Then men began to call on the name of the Lord"* (Genesis 4:26b). Seth replaced Abel on the Messianic chain. We read, *"God has appointed another seed for me instead of Abel, whom Cain killed"* (Genesis 4:25, KJV).

The early pre-Flood descendents of Seth were instrumental in carrying out God's purposes for this age and promoting God's plan of redemption to a lost world. However, there are two persons who stand out in particular during this Pre-Flood Age, Enoch and Methuselah.

Enoch was 65 years old when he had a son by the name of Methuselah. Something dramatic happened when this son was born which caused a radical change in Enoch's life whereby he began to walk closely with God thereafter. We read, *"Enoch lived sixty-five years and begat Methuselah. After he begat Methuselah, Enoch walked with God three hundred years, and begat sons and daughters. So, all the days of Enoch were three hundred and sixty-five years"* (Genesis 5:21-23, KJV).

The name Methuselah comes from a combination of words meaning "*When this one is gone, then it shall come.*" Arthur I. Pink,[1] in his book, "Gleanings in Genesis" points out that the name Methuselah is the key to God's revelation concerning the coming of the Flood. The name Methuselah strongly implies that Enoch had received a revelation from God when Methuselah was born. The name Methuselah signifies, "*When he is dead it shall be sent*" This means that when he dies, then the World would be destroyed. There was a divine revelation memorialized in this name. It was as though God said to Enoch, "*Do you see that baby? The world will last as long as he lives and no longer! When that child is taken out, I shall deal with the world in judgment and humanity will perish.*"

We can see what effect this revelation had upon Enoch, which caused him to walk with God. He did not know whether his baby boy would live one day or a hundred years. From this time onward he knew that the moment his son would die the Earth would be destroyed by a judgment from God and the world would come to a sudden end. It is interesting to note that God did not reveal to Enoch how He would destroy the world.

We now know that it was the worldwide Flood of Noah that God used to bring judgment and sudden destruction upon the Old Pre-Flood World. The evidences of Noah's Flood worldwide can now be confirmed and documented by the science of geology. Enoch never dreamed that Methuselah would live for 969 years (Genesis 5:27). It turned out that He became the oldest man that ever lived. The moment that Methuselah died marks the end of the Pre-Flood Age and the beginning of the Flood Age.

It is also interesting to note that Enoch never died. He only lived 365 years. He was taken directly into Heaven. We read, "*Enoch walked with God; and he was not for God took him*" (Genesis 5:24). Enoch and Elijah are the only two persons throughout human history who have never tasted death. They were both taken by God directly into the Third Heaven.

Age of False Religion

This was also an age of false religion. It began with Cain. It was a form of religious apostasy. It was a renunciation or abandonment of the former true religious faith that was practiced by Adam and Eve. Cain was religious in that he offered a fruit offering to the Lord. God rejected Cain's offering because it was not an animal blood sacrifice. God then reasoned with Cain and said to him that if he would go back and bring the proper offering it would be accepted as an atonement for his sins; but if he refused, then his sin would remain and sin would soon control his life. Cain became angry with God, and refused to do what God wanted him to do. The Bible says that, *"Cain went out from the presence of the Lord"* (Genesis 4:16, KJV). It is often said that this event is seen here as the germinal archetype of self-serving, false religion and corruption. This was a deliberate decision by Cain to go his own way, to do his own thing and to follow the way of the Serpent.

From Adam to Noah there was a steady growth and development of false religions, with a corresponding increase of crime, violence and impure living. Just prior to the Flood the situation had become so bad that God looked on the Earth and saw that it was corrupt (Genesis 6:11). Then God said to Noah, *"The end of all flesh has come before me, for the earth is filled with violence through them, and behold, I will destroy them with the earth."* (Genesis 6:13, KJV)

The growth of false religion today is a sign of the pre-Flood days. Jesus said, *"As the days of Noah were, so shall, also the coming of the son of man be"* (Mathew 24:37 KJV). This implies that all the signs that were present prior to the Flood of Noah will also be present prior to Christ's future return to the Earth. Today, the growth of false man made religions is greater than ever before.

Age of Travel

This was an age of travel. After Cain left his homeland, he became a world wanderer. We read, *"Cain went out from the presence of the Lord and dwelt in the land of nod, on the east of Eden"* (Genesis 4:16, KJV). By a deliberate act of his will, Cain chose to go out from the presence of the Lord and to allow evil and the Evil One to dominate his life.

The land of Nod means the land of wandering, which implies a traveling from place to place. He became a restless vagabond and a fugitive on the Earth (Genesis 4:14). Tradition relates that Cain went eastward from Eden to China and to other remote lands. It is here believed that Cain and his descendants went eastward from the Garden of Eden to China, Mongolia, and then to North and South America. Others went westward into Europe, Western Asia and Northern Africa. The reasons for believing this are presented in later chapters.

Age of City Building

The fourth sign of the pre-Flood days was that of "City Building." We read, *"Cain knew his wife, and she conceived and bore Enoch. And he built a city, and called the name of the city after the name of his son Enoch"* (Genesis 4:17 KJV).

This is the first mention of a city in the entire Word of God. When God created man, He did not place him in a city, but in a garden; cities were invented by man, and have ever since been the symbol of wickedness and corruption. Dr. M. R. DeHaan [2] says, *"In the concentrations of populations in our cities, sin develops at a ratio utterly unknown elsewhere. Less than a hundred years ago, we are told, almost 85% of the population of the world lived on farms and in small rural communities. Then came the industrial revolution of the 19th century, with its machinery and labor-saving farm implements and devices, so that millions employed on the farms were no more needed there because of this development of labor saving machinery. As the door of labor closed in agriculture, the newly built factories springing up everywhere to build this same labor-saving machinery called for the services of the same rural young people who were not needed on the farm, and the great shift from the country to the city began. New and better machinery was built, throwing more and more men out of work on the farm, while demanding more and more of them in factories of the cities . . . until today the ratio has been completely reversed, and more than 85% of the entire population now lives in the city, with a corresponding increase of wickedness and crime which characterizes city life."*

Just where to the east of Eden the city was located is a matter of conjecture. City building was a development that culminated during the pre-Flood age. City development reached its climax in the last 120 years prior to the Flood when many great cities were established in various parts of the world. Remnants of these cities and settlements have been found on almost every continent of the world.

Is it possible to believe that the pyramids of Egypt, the great monolithic and cyclopean stone structures that are present in northern Africa, parts of Europe, British Isles, the South Pacific, North and South America and other parts of the world are all pre-Flood in origin? Greater details that describe this majestic Pre-Flood Age are found in succeeding chapters.

Much of the Wooden and copper tools and many of the wooden structures that were associated with these sites would have been destroyed by natural processes of decay, decomposition and by the destructive waters of the Flood.

Age of Polygamy

The fifth sign of the pre-Flood age was that of polygamy resulting from a concentration of the population in the cities. Polygamy, and the breakdown of the home, had their beginning with Lamech. He was the first man in human history to break God's rule of creation. We read, *"And Lamech took unto him two wives; the name of one was Adah, and the name of the second was Zillah"* (Genesis 4:19). DeHaan comments on this sign as follows: *"In the wake of city building came the evil of divorce and polygamy and the breakdown of the home. Because of the concentration of population, and the closer association of the sexes in industry women leaving their homes and children to enter factories and shops and offices this evil broke beyond all restraints."*[3]

Divorce, polygamy and the breakdown of the family unit probably began with local incidents here and there, until, at the time of the Flood, it had become rampant in society.

Age of Great Agricultural Advances

The sixth sign of the pre-Flood age was advancement in agriculture. We read, *"And Adah bore Jabal. He was the father of those who dwell in tents and have livestock"* (Genesis 4:20, NKJV). Jabal was the father of those who have livestock (cattle). This speaks of cattle being used by Man for the first time. This was the beginning of the cattle industry, and it is the first mention of cattle in the Bible being used for Man's profit.

During the Altithermal Age, the climate worldwide became more arid, the desert areas continued to enlarge. The nomadic hunters and food gatherers throughout the world had no difficulty living off the land during the first part of this age because food was plentiful. They were now forced to move to regions of greater water supply where the climate was more conducive for the production of food to feed the people that were gathering in new towns and settlements. Thus, there was a need for the development of the cattle industry to provide milk, butter and food for an ever growing population.

Age of Music

The seventh sign of the pre-Flood period was an age characterized by music for we read, *"His brother's name was Jubal. He was the father of all those who play the harp and flute"* (Genesis 4:21, NKJV). Instruments can be classified into three main divisions: wind, percussion and string. The harp typifies the stringed and the flute the wind. The percussion types are missing for an obvious reason, as they always precede wind and stringed type instruments.

It has been said that music is our fourth great material want; first food, then raiment, then shelter, then music. There is an element within each one of us which calls for something that only music can supply.

Primitive tribal people develop percussion type instruments, such as various types of drums, castanets, cymbals, etc., whereas the development of stringed and wind instruments are of a more advanced type. The Bible is saying that as Man developed in his music, he had now reached the place where the harp and the flute had been invented. This marks the beginning of a new advancement in music before the Flood, which continued to progress and reached its maximum development in the last 120 years, during the time when Noah was building the Ark.

Age of Copper and Iron?

The eighth sign of the pre-Flood age is found in the following passage, "*and Zillah, she also bore Tubal-Cain, an instructor of every craftsman in bronze and iron*" (Genesis 4:22 NKJV). This early period of human history moved into the metallurgical age prior to the Flood. This is the first mention in the Bible of the development of the art of metallurgy. Tubal Cain was an instructor of every craftsman in bronze and iron. This Hebrew word that is translated as bronze and iron can also be translated as copper and metal.[4] Is it possible that Neolithic man may have entered into the bronze and iron age at the very end of the Neolithic Age?

According to the science of archaeology, Man entered the metallic stage of industrial development during the Neolithic Age. It is characterized by the use of copper and stone implements and weapons such as knives, saws, sickles, awls, gouges, hammers, anvils, axes, swords, daggers, spears, arrows and shields.

Important discoveries have been made by archaeologists and others to verify the use of copper during the Neolithic Age. Filby[5] says, "*Investigations of the origin of metallurgy have shown, as was long suspected, that in certain areas metal working goes back almost to the beginning of the Neolithic Period."*

It has been suggested that much of the metal work attributed to Assyria was actually made in Van. There are remains of very old copper mines in Armenia and the earliest copper of Egypt and Mesopotamia may have come from this region.

It is believed that suitable copper ores and wood for smelting furnaces occur in the Caucasus and around Lake Van and in the Elburn Mountains. One of the most likely places for the origin of copper smelting is Armenia.[4] From this centre the knowledge of metallurgy spread to the Middle East, Egypt, Asia and Europe.

Archaeologists would place the beginning of the Bronze and Iron Age to a time that would equate to the Middle Intermediate and 2nd Intermediate Age Age in Egypt which would be Post Neolithic or Post Flood. See Figure 20-2. There are no definite dates for the beginning of the Iron Age. It began at different times in different parts of the world and progressed slowly because of a lack of ready communication. Iron has the tendency of deteriorating and returning to rusty iron oxide over a relatively short period of time.

Age of Violence

The eighth and last sign was violence, which is recorded in the following passage, "Then Lamech said to his wives, Adah and Zillah, hear my voice O wives of Lamech, listen to my speech! For I have killed a man for wounding me, even a young man for hurting me. If Cain shall be avenged sevenfold, then Lamech seventy-seven fold. (Genesis 4:23, 24, KJV)

Violence characterized the pre-Flood age. The evolution of sin is displayed through the life of Lamech. In disobedience to God he departed from God's instruction which stated, *"Therefore a man shall leave his father and mother and be joined to his wife, and they shall become one flesh* (Genesis 2:24, KJV). He is the first person in the Bible to practice polygamy. He allowed sin to dominate and control his life, which led to a progressive rationalization in his mind as to what was right or wrong. Over a period of 930 years his mindset became fixed, and there was no longer any place for God in his life. Lamech's fixed mindset against God was symptomatic of a growing deterioration of human society throughout the world prior to the Flood.

The Bible refers to the last 120 years before the Flood as being a time of great wickedness for we read in Genesis 6:5 (NKJV} *"Then the Lord God saw that the wickedness of man was great on the earth, and that every intent of the thoughts of his heart was only evil continually."* We then read in Genesis 6:11-12 NKJV, *"The Earth also was corrupt before God, and the Earth was filled with violence . . . **for all flesh had corrupted their way upon the earth**."*

Conclusion

The time span from Adam and Eve to the Flood began with a simple and peaceful setting in the Garden of Eden, and ended with a highly industrialized world-wide civilization in many respects similar to our modern age. This age was characterized by true and false religions, world-wide travel, city building, agricultural advances, an abundance of music, and the development of the metallurgical (copper) industry. It was also marked by increasing lawlessness, a breakdown of the family unit and a progressive increase in violence, which culminated with the judgment of the Flood.

These preceding chapters have been presenting the record of pre-Flood Man from a Biblical perspective. However, this record of Early Man is in great contrast to the secular record of Early Man. What is the difference? Is it possible to reconcile the two perspectives of Early Man?

Who was Early Man?

Who was this mysterious Early Man that secular archaeologists and anthropologists are always talking about? Does the science of geology, archaeology and anthropology shed any light upon who this Early Man was? What was he like and what were his accomplishments? How long ago did he live?

Let us now move on to the next chapter and to learn more about Early Man from a secular perspective.

References for Chapter 13

1. Pink Arthur I, "Gleanings in Genesis", Wikipedia, the free encyclopedia, first Published, April 1, 1886. He was a Christian evangelist and Biblical scholar. Also see Google for more information.
2. Dr. M.R. De Haan, "The Days of Noah," Zondervan Publishing House, Grand rapids Michigan USA. 1963, p. 42
3. Ibid. pp. 41-44.
4. See end portions of Chapter 23 for a more detailed description of this metal age at the Medzamor Site in Soviet Armenia.
5. Filby F. A. "The Flood Reconsidered," Pickering & Inglis Ltd., London, 1970, p. 123.

Chapter 14

The Origin of Early Man?

A mystery surrounds the origin of Early Man. He was the one who occupied the so called Old World: Europe, Asia, Africa and Australia and also the New World: North and South America. Where did he come from? What did he look like? What kind of tools did he have? Was he a Stone Age Man? Was he intelligent? What were his accomplishments? Is it possible that this Early Man was in reality Pre-Flood Man? Let us now examine the evidences.

Was Early Man in reality Pre-Flood Man?

This Early Man lived coincident with pre-historic animals such as the extinct giant elephants, such as the mastodon and the woolly mammoth, and the extinct saber tooth tiger, bison, rhinoceros, apes called Hominids and the list could go on and on. Many of these extinct animals were here for many thousands of years. Some were present for 2.5 million years into the past. What happened to all of these now extinct animals? What happened to Early Man?

Darwinian archaeologists and anthropologists always relate Early Man to a certain interglacial period of the Pleistocene Ice Age. In Europe they date him back to about 225,000+ years into the past. In East Africa he has been dated to about 2.0+ million years. In Southeast Asia, he has been dated to 1.0 + million years. In America, he has been dated to 20,000 + years. East Africa is believed to be the birth place of Early Man. What is the logic behind this belief?

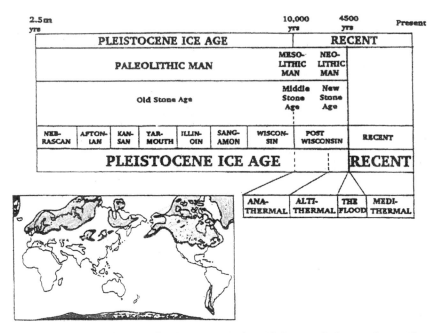

2.5 cm yrs							10,000 yrs	4500 yrs	Present
PLEISTOCENE ICE AGE								RECENT	
PALEOLITHIC MAN							MESO-LITHIC MAN	NEO-LITHIC MAN	
Old Stone Age							Middle Stone Age	New Stone Age	
NEB-RASCAN	AFTON-IAN	KAN-SAN	TAR-MOUTH	ILLIN-OIN	SANG-AMON	WISCON-SIN	POST WISCONSIN		RECENT
PLEISTOCENE ICE AGE									RECENT
							ANA-THERMAL	ALTI-THERMAL	THE FLOOD	MEDI-THERMAL

Figure 14-1: Early Man in Europe, Asia, Africa and throughout the world are always related to the Pleistocene Ice Age. The above map shows the areas of the Earth that were covered with ice during maximum glacial advance. About 10,000+ years ago, the ice cap would have been at its maximum. Prepared by Don Daae.

There is a great misconception among certain Christian people as to the length of the Ice Age. Young Earth Creation Science people believe that the Flood of Noah took place prior to the Pleistocene Ice Age. In other words, they believe that the Ice Age took place after Noah's Flood about 4,350+ years ago. They do not want to admit or accept the evidences of modern day geology and the drilling of wells that have verified that the Pleistocene Ice Age sediments in the Gulf of Mexico are locally up to 9,000+ feet (2,740+ m) in thickness.. In the Beaufort Sea region geophysics and geology estimate these sediments to be about 7,500 feet (2286 m) in thickness. In the Gulf of Alaska drilling and seismic has verified that these sediments are 4,000+ feet (1219+ m) in thickness and that they continue to increase in thickness in a seaward direction from a certain COST well location. The average thickness of glacial sediments throughout the prairie provinces of Western Canada is between 100 - 200 feet (30-60 m) thick. A detailed geological analysis of this age indicates that this Ice Age could very well be about 2.5 million years in length (Figure 3-5).

The Great Stone Age

The modern science of archaeology and anthropology always refer to Early Man as having lived during the Great Stone Age which also equates to the entire Pleistocene Age. The Great Stone Age extends anywhere from about 4500 years ago to some vague beginning hundreds of thousands of years into the past. The Pleistocene Ice Age is divided into three basic divisions: the Old Stone Age (Paleolithic); the Middle Stone Age (Mesolithic), and the New Stone Age (Neolithic). See Figure 14-1. Secular archaeologists and anthropologists have phenomenal problems trying to relate Early Man to the entire Pleistocene Ice Age. Why should this be? What is the reasoning for their belief?

The Old Stone (Paleolithic) Age is believed to extend from about 10,000 to about 2.5 million years into the past. Archaeologists and Anthropologists arbitrarily subdivide the Old Stone Age into the Lower, Middle and Upper Paleolithic.

The Lower Paleolithic extends from the base of the Pleistocene to the base of the Yarmouth.

The Middle Paleolithic extends from the base of the Yarmouth to the base of the Wisconsin.

The Upper Paleolithic extends from the base of the Wisconsin to about 10,000 years before the present. See Figure 14-1.

How authentic are these divisions?

The Middle Stone (Mesolithic) Age extends from about 10,000 to 9,000 years ago. It represents a transitional period from the Old to the New Stone Age.

The New Stone (Neolithic) Age extends from about 9000 to about 4,500 years ago.

The Recent Age extends from about 4500 years ago to the Present. Some say this age may extend to about 5,000 years ago.

The mysterious question arises: Why do secular archaeologists and Anthropologists always want to extend the history of Man to about 2.0+ million years into the past?

The fallacy of these greatly exaggerated Stone Age dates is the premise that Early Man can be related to a certain Pleistocene Ice Age advance or to a warmer interglacial Age. **It is interesting to note that there is not one site of Early Man throughout the world that can be scientifically and truly related to a certain glacial or interglacial Age except to the Post Wisconsin Age!**

Geology is now able to subdivide the Post Wisconsin Age into the Anathermal and the Altithermal Ages. Geology is now able to add the Flood Age and the Post Flood Age which is called the Medithermal Age to Figures 14-1 & 10-1. How can this be?

The Origin of the term "Early Man"

What does the term "**Early Man**" mean and what is its beginning? It is a term that began in England with Charles Darwin and his followers. It refers to the Man that was supposedly in the process of slowly evolving from an ape to a human being. He lived coincident with now extinct animals that characterize the Pleistocene Age.

In 1859, Charles Darwin[1] published his book, "**On the Origin of the Species by Means of Natural Selection.**" Darwin maintained that there was a slow, gradual, random, progressive and naturalistic evolutionary descent of all forms of plant, animal and bacteria life from a common ancestor without the help of any supernatural Being.

After Darwin published his second thesis called, "**The Descent of Man**" in 1871, the sciences of human anthropology and archaeology gained momentum. In it, he advanced the hypothesis that Man had evolved through the primate line from certain extinct forms of apes called hominids and that the ancestors of Man were to be found in Africa or S.E. Asia where modern day apes are present. The gorilla and the chimpanzee are present in Africa whereas, the Gibbon and the Orangutan are present in S.E. Asia. Darwin maintained that these were the areas to research, in order to find the secret as to how Early Man gradually evolved over time. What led Darwin to believe in the evolution of Man?

Darwin's two publications form the cornerstone of the Darwinian Theory of Evolution. The major premise of Darwinian Evolution is that the answer to the evolutionary proof of all life including Man would be found within the fossil record and through the biological and geological sciences.

This thought inspired many young, energetic university professors, graduates and students to go to various parts of the Earth to find the evidences to support the proposed evolutionary development of Man from an Ape ancestry.

Two Basic Types of Early Man

Anthropologists have determined that throughout the world there were only two basic types of true human beings called Homo sapiens that relate to the Great Stone Age Period. They are the Cro-Magnon and the Neanderthal man.

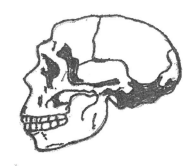
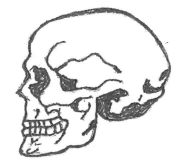

The Neanderthal Man   **The Cro-Magnon Man**

Figure 14-2: Illustrates the facial features of the two types of Early Man. They are the Neanderthal and the Cro-Magnon Men. Drawn and prepared by Don Daae after MacGowan & Hester, P.89.[2]

The Cro-Magnon Man:

The Cro-Magnon man had a pronounced chin, a well domed, narrow Nordic head. He often had a brain capacity greater than 1600 cc. The average brain capacity of Man today is about 1350cc to 1500cc. He is often referred to as a mentally superior kind of man. He was considered a remarkable person in that he painted on the walls of his cave and carved on pieces of bone and elephant ivory pictures of bison, mammoths and boars. His tools are equated with the more superior European Aurignacian and Magdalenian and Solutrean cultures. See Figure 15-1.

The Neanderthal Man:

The Neanderthal man had a receding chin, a low forehead, heavy brow ridges and a long narrow skull from plan view. It is quite surprising that the famous Classical Neanderthal man at one time posed as the first missing link for about 47+ years. He had a brain capacity greater than 1620 cu. cm. This was an amazing endowment for a missing link!

The Neanderthal type man was present in Mongolia, China and Australia. He also co-mingled as a minority to the Cro-Magnon man in south western Asia and Europe (Germany, France, Israel), also in parts of Northern Africa. His stone tools are equated with the Mousterian culture. See Figure 15-1. He was at one time regarded as being inferior and to have preceded the Cro-Magnon man. This view is no longer valid.

The Cro-Magnon and the Neanderthal man were contemporary with the now extinct pre-historic animals at different places throughout the world. Their physical differences appear to be racial.

The Neanderthal man mysteriously disappeared at the end of the Great Stone Age or more specifically at the end of the age of polished stone which is the Neolithic Age. See Figure 14-1. This, in turn, marks the end of the Altithermal Age and the Pleistocene Age, whereas the Cro-Magnon man has survived to the present. What happened to the Neanderthal man?

The Neanderthal Mystery!

The best known name of all extinct species of man is the Neanderthal man. He also inhabited portions of Western Europe during the latter portions of the Pleistocene Ice Age. The original discovery was made in the Neander Valley near Dusseldorf, Germany in 1858. This was one year before Charles Darwin published his book, "The Origin of the Species." Dunbar and Waage [3] say, *"Its striking characteristics and the timeliness of the discovery, led to an immediate appreciation of the significance of the neandertals as a species far more apelike than any living men."* Note: Neandertal is the American spelling.

It was the discovery of the Neanderthal man that convinced Darwin and other Darwinian scientists to believe that Modern Man had evolved from an ape ancestry. He had pronounced eye brow ridges and a receding chin. Modern apes also have pronounced brow ridges and receding chins. Secondly, the Neanderthal man was now extinct. This gave them reason to believe he was an older, more archaic ancestor to the Cro-Magnon man. It was postulated that the Cro-Magnon man had evolved from the Neanderthal man and that the Neanderthal man had evolved from some type of evolving ape hominid.

Dunbar and Waage [4] go on to say, *"Since 1858, several entire skeletons have been recovered and incomplete remains of many men, women and children of the Neandertal race have been found in the caves and rock shelters of Belgium, France, Italy, Spain, Croatia, Crimea, and Palestine. Their stone implements (Mousterian culture), moreover, are found scattered throughout Western Europe, and farther eastward in Asia Minor, North Africa, Syria, northern Arabia, Iraq."* They then go on to say, *"The Neandertals were stocky, short of stature, rarely exceeding 5 feet 4 inches tall. Although they stood upright, the carriage was more like that of a great ape than that of living man."*

As time progressed scientists were able to describe two definite types of Neanderthal men, the Classical (or extreme) and the Progressive types.

The Classical Neanderthal

The classical Neanderthal man is represented by an almost complete skeleton that was found at La Chapelle-aux-Saints in southwest France in 1908. Marcelin Boule,[5] a leading French paleontologist and head of the Natural History Museum in Paris, described the find as a new evolutionary ancestor to Man and as a separate species Homo Neanderthalensis. He made Neanderthal man a monstrous ape-like creature that stood with bent knees and walked on the outside rim of his feet with a rambling gait. He had a pronounced brow ridge, almost chinless, a receding forehead, a big face on which a large, broad nose and protruding jaws were present. He was short in stature, about 5 feet 1 inches tall, so his thick, stocky, heavily muscled body made his face seem larger than it actually was. **Thus was born the world's first acceptable primitive, missing link.**

This description of Boule was to stereotype the descriptions of all future Neanderthal discoveries for over 49 years. The journalists of the day fixed the brutish picture of the Neanderthal man upon the public's mind. It was believed that he was about 120,000 years old, and that he lived during the third (Sangamon) interglacial period of the Ice Age. See Figure 14-1.

Sir Elliott Smith described the Neanderthal man as uncouth and repellent, as follows: *"His short, thick set, and coarsely built body was carried in a half-stooped slouch upon short, powerful, and half-flexed legs of peculiarly ungraceful form. His thick neck sloped forward from the broad shoulders to support the massive flattened head, which protruded forward, so as to form an unbroken curve of neck and back. His heavy eyebrow ridges, retreating forehead, chinlessness, all combined to complete the picture of unattractiveness, which it is more probable than not was still further emphasized by a shaggy covering of hair over most of the body."*[6]

The Neanderthal Hoax revealed

In 1955 two professors of anatomy, William Strauss of John Hopkins University and A.J.E. Cave of St. Bartholomew's Hospital Medical College, London, re-examined the skeleton resting in the Musée de l'Homme, Paris and they dispelled the false notion that he was a primitive missing link. Their report was later published in the Quarterly Review of Biology (IFX (xxxiii, 1957). They say, *"The skeleton, which had belonged to a male 40-50 years old, was rotten with arthritis. This disease had affected the hinges of La Chapelle's lower jaw, his neck and much of his body. The forward thrust of his head noted by Boule was due, in part at least, to a wry neck, and the stunted stature and stooping posture were due to arthritic lesions in his vertebral column. In his youth, La Chapelle had been as tall as the average Frenchman living in the Dordogne today."*[7]

The La Chapelle-aux-Saints man was reconstructed and was found to be five feet four and one half inches tall (164 cm). This was similar to the height of the average Frenchman living in that part of France today. Another factor that was ignored was the exceptionally large brain size of 1620 cc for the La Chapelle-aux-Saints man. This was an amazing endowment for a missing link. The average brain capacity of modern man is 1350 to 1450 cc, whereas the average Neanderthal brain capacity was often over 1600 cc.

Strauss and Cave reported that there is no valid reason for the assumption that the posture of Neanderthal man differed significantly from that of present day men. Other anatomists, after inspecting the bones, arrived at the same conclusion. This disqualified Boules findings, and raised Homo neanderthalensis from a primitive evolving missing link to the status of a true human being **Homo sapiens**.

The Classical Neanderthal man posed as a true primitive missing link between Man and ape for 49 years from 1908 to 1957.

Just as we have different races of people today, it is believed that the Neanderthal man had physical characteristics that set him apart as a race. This distinguished him from the Cro-Magnon man. As we progress in our study, we will begin to see how the description of the Classical Neanderthal man has directly influenced an ape like interpretation of Early Man in Europe, Asia, Africa and all other parts of the world. First we must analyze the Piltdown man.

The Piltown Hoax Revealed

The Piltdown Man posed as a true missing link in textbooks and museums around the world for forty one years, before it was disclosed to be a complete hoax. He was known as Eoanthropus dawsoni, or the "Dawn Man," and was supposedly discovered in 1912 by Charles Dawson and Sir Arthur Smith-Woodward in a Pleistocene age gravel pit in southern England. He was estimated to be between 200,000 to 1,000,000 years old, with a brain case capacity of about 1358 cc.

The Piltdown Man had simian features. A simian feature is generally defined as relating to, characteristic of, or resembling an ape or a monkey. My Webster's College dictionary defines simian as pertaining to, or characteristic of an ape or monkey. To the scientific community throughout the world, the Piltdown Man was proof that modern Man had indeed evolved from an ape ancestry.

In 1953 a newly discovered fluorine technique of dating organic remains was applied to Eoanthropus. It was found that the jawbone contained practically no fluorine and was no older than about the year it was found. The skull had a significant amount of fluorine, but was estimated to be only a few thousand years old. It was revealed that the lower jaw was that of an ape, possibly an orangutan. The cranium (skull) was that of a human. It had the teeth of a chimpanzee that were altered by a combination of artificial abrasion and proper staining so as to appear similar to the molars and canine teeth ascribed to Eoanthropus. The wear of the teeth was produced by artificial filing down. The jaw and teeth were artificially stained to match the cranium. It was believed that one of the bones of the nasal cavity was a small limb bone of some animal. The molar tooth was that of a hippopotamus. From the total evidence it appears that the Piltdown bones and teeth were assembled from a wide variety of sources, some of them outside of Britain itself.

This is an example of where the world was the victim of a most elaborate and carefully prepared hoax. It was concocted with extraordinary skill. It influenced a generation of people into thinking that there were missing links that related modern Man to the Ape family. It started out with an idea from Charles Darwin which became a major premise in the thinking of man, that modern man and apes have descended from a common anthropoid ancestor.

In commentary on this tendency of allowing such ideas to govern one's scientific conclusions, anthropologist Jacquetta Hawkes says *"Accepting this as inevitable and not necessarily damaging, it still comes as a shock to discover how often pre-conceived ideas have affected the investigation of human origins. There is, of course, nothing like a fake for exposing such weaknesses among the experts. For example, to look back over the bold claims and subtle anatomical distinctions made by some of our greatest authorities concerning the recent human skull and modern apes' jaw which together composed "Piltdown Man," rouses either joy or pain according to one's feeling for scientists.*[9]

Paleo-anthropologists driven by their zeal to prove the evolutionary development of man run the risk of creating further "Hominid Hoaxes," and in doing so, fail to see the creative hand of God at work.

Petroleum geologist John Weister had this to say, *"Both science and the public have been duped in the past with the Piltdown hoax. It now appears we have been duped, albeit unintentionally, with a kind of hominid hoax. Since the Piltdown discovery in 1912, we have graduated four generations of students with the impression that science had the fossil evidence to prove we are descended from apes. It is time that students be taught with honesty and candor. We must not be guilty of a cover up of the vast holes in our records and end up with an anthropological Watergate."*[10]

Google reports the following, *"Approximately 1915, French paleontologist Marcellin Boule concluded the jaw was from an ape. Similarly, American zoologist Gerrit Smith Miller concluded Piltdown's jaw came from a fossil ape. In 1923, Franz Weidenreich examined the remains and correctly reported that they consisted of a modern human cranium and an orangutan jaw with filed-down teeth. Weidenreich, being an anatomist, had easily exposed the hoax for what it was. However, it took thirty years for the scientific community to concede that Weidenreich was correct.*

In 1915, Dawson claimed to have found fragments of a second skull (Piltdown II) at a site about two miles away from the original finds.[1] *So far as is known the site has never been identified and the finds appear to be entirely undocumented. Woodward does not appear ever to have visited the site."*

This again reveals the failure of the scientific community to believe the evidences of the famous French anthropologist and paleontologist Marcellin Boule, the American zoologist Grant Smith Miller and the great anthropologist Franz Weidenreich. Instead they chose to believe "The Lie" instead of "The Truth" that was revealed by these imminent scientists.

References for Chapter 14

1. Charles Darwin, "On the Origin of the Species by Means of Natural Selection." 1859.
2. Kenneth MacGowan & Joseph A. Hester, Jr. "Early Man in the New World" published in Co-operation with the American Museum of Natural History. The Natural history Library Anchor Books, Doubleday & Company, Inc. Garden City, N.Y. 1962. p.89.
3. Carl O. Dunbar & Karl M. Waage, "Historical Geology," 1969, Third edition, John Wiley & Sons, Inc. New York / London / Sydney / Toronto. p.501.
4. Ibid. p.501.
5. Marcellin Boule & H. V. Vallois, Fossil Men, Dryden press, New York, 1957, p.123.
6. Dunbar & Waage, p.502, Restoration of the Classical Neanderthal Man.
7. Sir Elliott G. Smith, "The Evolution of Man," London, Oxford University Press, 1924, (pp. 69-70).
8. Quarterly Review of Biology (IFX (xxxiii, 1957). This review has a paper by two professors of anatomy, William Strauss of John Hopkins University and A.J.E. Cave of St. Bartholomew's Hospital Medical College, London.
9. John Klotz, Genes, Genesis and Evolution, St. Louis Concordia, 1965, pp. 365-369.
10. John Weister, The Genesis Connection," N.Y., Thomas Nelson, 1983, p.174.
11. For more detailed information see Google, "The Piltdown Man."

Chapter 15

Early Man in Europe, Asia & Africa

Europe was the birthplace of Darwinism. This is where the Darwinian Theory of Evolution was first proclaimed. As a result, European archaeologists and anthropologists became the leaders in searching for the evidences of Early Man throughout Europe, Asia and Africa. They attempted to explain the history of Early Man by a purely secular and evolutionary perspective.

It is important to realize that northern Europe and portions of northern Asia were covered with great thicknesses of continental ice several thousands of feet thick during the time when Early Man was present in this region. Sites of Early Man are always found to the south of the Pleistocene ice cap. See map on Figure 14-1. What happened to all this ice? This will be answered in later chapters.

The Archaeological Record of Early Man

Archaeology is the science of studying the people, customs, and life of the remote past by excavating and classifying the remains of ancient cities, communities, tools, and monuments.

Darwinian archaeologists have developed a system of dating Early Man based upon the type of stone tool industry found in a certain geological strata or at an archaeological site. The simple and crude chipped stone tools are often shown associated with a more primitive, archaic Man who was assumed to be in the process of evolving from an ape status during the Lower Palaeolithic Age. During the Middle and Upper Palaeolithic ages, the chipped stone tools became gradually more refined as archaic Man slowly advanced in his evolutionary journey as shown in Figure 15-1. We will be analyzing the scientific accuracy of this concept which is always portrayed as a scientific fact to our students.

The method that archaeologists use to determine the age of Early Man by means of stone tools and all other artifacts is called Typology Dating.

Typology Dating

In 1859, Charles Darwin implied that the proof of evolution would be found in the fossil record. The fossil record also includes the bones and the artifacts of Early Man.

In 1865, archaeologist Sir John Lubback, who was a good friend of Charles Darwin, proposed two divisions: the Palaeolithic (Old Stone Age), and the Neolithic (New Stone Age). See Figure 15-1. According to this definition, Palaeolithic Man was only capable of making crude stone chipped implements due to the fact that his brain was just slowly evolving from some former primate. The older stone age tools were naturally more primitive and crude. As time progressed, the tools became more refined based upon Man's evolving brain and his increasing intelligence. The Neolithic Man was distinguished by the making of ground or polished stone implements that were made by rubbing instead of chipping. This gradual, development required many thousands of years to accomplish, so they believed.

MacGowan & Hester[2] say, "*After a time, however, archaeologists found some disturbing discrepancies. Before Neolithic Man grew grain and wove textiles, someone of an earlier age seems to have been making axes from antlers, turning out new artifacts called microliths which were tiny chips of flint that were set in a row along a wooden or bone handle to make a kind of saw or sickle and also producing a partially polished ax with a ground edge, and making crude pots. This was all very upsetting to the old scheme of dividing prehistory into the Palaeolithic and the Neolithic. So Science inserted the term Mesolithic, or Middle Stone Age, between the two, in order to account for the appearance of the new tools."*

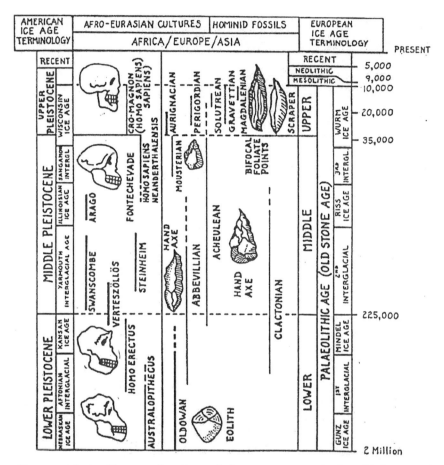

Figure 15-1: Shows the Darwinian system of classifying and dating Early Man by artifacts, hominid bones and geology. What is the basis for believing the above classification and dating? This composite diagram was revised after Dunbar & Waage.[1] Prepared by Don Daae with artwork by Elaine Daae. Palaeolithic is the British spelling.

In 1870, Gustav Oscar Montelius, a Swedish archaeologist, began an elaborate survey of prehistoric implements (artifacts) in which he classified them according to their similarity. Once he had arranged them in their probable chronological order, he had established a system called Typology Dating.

It is often said that typology must remain the basis of any study of industry. It is based on the premise that there has been a slow progressive development throughout the Pleistocene Epoch in the techniques used by Man in manufacturing stone tools and implements. On this basis there is continuity between the different industries. An elaborate chronology of stone tool industries has been established with Earth years attached to the different stone tool assemblages. This typology system is based upon the Darwinian Evolutionary Theory which maintains that Man has evolved by means of a slow, progressive, developmental process. Therefore, the tools must also reflect this slow evolutionary trend.

I agree in principle with the Typology System of classification in that there is always a progressive technological development taking place within a certain civilization or culture of Man. I disagree with the "time principle" attached to the Darwinian Typology Classification System.

The premise of this manuscript is that Early Man was created by God and that he was as intelligent as Man is today. The science of geology has now provided a framework in which a new system of dating Early Man can take place. It is a matter of re-interpreting the data to fit a shorter and a more realistic geological, archaeological and anthropological time span. This system will continue to show a progressive development of the stone tool industries together with advances in agriculture, lumber, city building, music, travel, and many other complimentary industries all taking place relatively speaking at the same time. There is much information to verify that a grand and glorious pre-Flood civilization, second only to ours today, emerged prior to about 4,500 years ago. This equates to the end of the Pleistocene Age.

It is hard to believe that present day evolutionary archaeologists and anthropologists still believe that Modern Man has evolved from an ape ancestry. They are still teaching their students that it is possible to trace the ancestry of modern Man back in time over a period of 2+ million years to the time when Early Man began to slowly evolve from certain extinct forms of apes called hominids. What is the logic behind their reasoning? As we progress step by step, we will be examining their reasoning. See Figures 7-1 and 15-1.

The Anthropological Record of Early Man

Anthropology is the science which deals with Man and especially his origin, development and culture. It also deals with races, customs and beliefs of Mankind. A physical anthropologist will study the fossil bones of hominids and Early Man to determine what they looked like, taking note of their brain capacity, and special characteristics such as the ridges above the eyes, the shape of their chin, skull and body parts etc. to determine how they may have differed from the physical characteristics of present day man.

System of Dating Early Man

A system of dating Early Man has been established by physical anthropologists to relate how Homo sapiens (that is modern man) have evolved from earlier ape like creatures called hominids. It is now believed that the hominids have evolved from an earlier now extinct Great Ape called Ramopithecus that lived 8+ million years ago during the Miocene Age. See Figure 15-3.

Darwinian anthropologists maintain that Cro-Magnon Man has evolved from the Neanderthal Man, who in turn has evolved from Homo erectus, Homo habilis and down the chain to Australopithecus afarensis. Now what is the reasoning behind this evolutionary linked chain? All Darwinian evolutionists are committed to believe that all animal species have evolved from a previous species by an unintelligent, undirected, chance evolutionary process. The fact that an all knowing, all powerful, creative God is capable of creating each unique species at the place where they first appear in the fossil record is not on their radar screen.

It is believed that Homo sapiens evolved from Homo erectus who evolved from Homo habilis, who mysteriously evolved from Australopithecus afarensis. A short while ago, it was believed that Homo habilis evolved from Australopithecus africanus. It all becomes somewhat interesting and a bit confusing. For instance, what is a hominid? See Figure 15-2 and notice that each hominid has human feet and are able to walk uprightly. Apes and monkeys cannot do this? Why?

What is a Hominid?

A hominid is defined as an erect walking primate. It is defined by secular anthropologists as a member of the human family. Australopithecus afarensis, Australopithecus robustus and Australopithecus africanus, Homo habilis and Homo erectus (formerly called Pithecanthropus / Sinanthropus), together with Homo sapiens (true man), are all classified in the same super family Hominoidea. In other words, they are all classified as Hominids.

The Hominids are separated from the Great Apes that lived prior to 8 million years ago by a gap of time. This is often referred to as the 3 to 4 million year gap. See Figure 15-3.

Donald Johanson & Maitland Edey[4] define a hominid as an erect walking primate. They say, *"It is safe to say that a hominid is an erect-walking primate. That is, it is either an extinct ancestor to man, a collateral relative to man or a true man. All human beings are hominids, but not all hominids are human beings. We can picture human evolution as starting with a primitive ape-like type that gradually, over a period of time, began to be less and less ape-like and more manlike. There was no abrupt cross over from ape to human, but probably a rather fuzzy time of in-between types that would be difficult to classify either way. We have no fossils yet that tell us what went on during that in-between time. Therefore the handiest way of separating the newer types from their ape ancestors is to lump together all those that stood up on their hind legs. That group of men and near men is called hominids."*

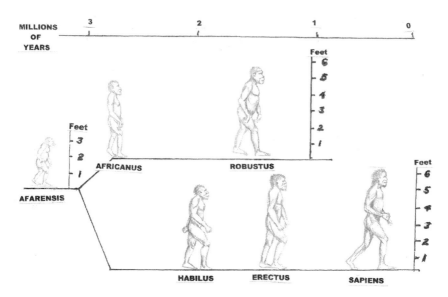

Figure 15-2: This is a Hominid Family Tree. It reveals how Darwinists believe Modern Man (Homo sapiens) have evolved though the Hominids (Homo Erectus and Homo Habilus) from Australopithecus afarenses (Lucy) who lived prior to 3 Million years ago. This figure is based upon Donald Johanson & Maitland Edey's book, "Lucy the Beginnings of Humankind.[3] **Prepared by Don Daae with artwork by Elaine Daae.**

This is the Darwinian explanation of a hominid. It is the basis for believing that modern Man has evolved from an ape ancestry. The fact that Almighty God has created each individual ape species according to a plan is not on their radar screen.

We then come to another question, what is a primate?

What is a Primate?

Primates are warm blooded mammals that have the following dominant characteristics: 1) five fingers on each hand and five toes on each foot. The hand has a opposed thumb, which allows it to grasp objects (apes have 'thumbs' on their feet as well); 2) eyes positioned in the front of a relatively flat face, permitting stereoscopic vision; 3) similar tooth patterns, being roughly U-shaped.

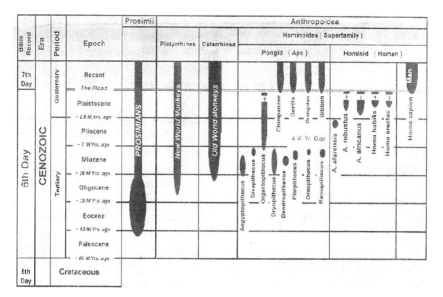

Figure 15-3: Illustrates the Anthropoid Primate record throughout the Cenozoic Era that relate geologically to the Biblical 6th Day of Creation and the 7th Day. Gigantopithecus was the only Great Ape that survived the Miocene Age and continued to the end of the Pleistocene Age. There are those who are still convinced that the Great Apes evolved from the monkeys, who in turn evolved from the prosimians. They all have the characteristics of a primate. This was designed by Don Daae with computer artwork by Mike Gilders.

Man is classified with the primates because he has physical characteristics which are similar to the prosimians, monkeys and the apes. That there are differences between man and the apes is obvious. The point of importance, however, is that these differences indicate that man is, indeed, a wholly discrete species; and that the similarities are only similarities, as similarities exist between many other species created by separate acts of God. Some of these key differences between man and apes are as follows:

1) Man has a heel bone, which enables him to walk in an erect position on two feet. All modern apes are bipedal animals. Lacking heel bones, they are able to walk on their hind feet alone only for short distances.

2) Man has a chin, apes do not.

145

3) The head of a man pivots and is balanced on top of the spinal column. An apes' head is hinged in front rather than on top. When an ape turns its head, its entire body has to turn with it.
4) Only man has a forward convexity of the spine, known as the lumbar curve.
5) The great toe in man is not opposable to the other toes. Apes have thumbs on both their feet and hands.
6) Man has a median furrow in his upper lip, which is lacking in the apes.
7) The lips of man are controlled so that the mucous membrane is visible as a continuous red line.

The Great Apes

The record of geology confirms that all of the eight Great Ape species appeared suddenly out of no where at the beginning of the Miocene Age. See Figure 15-3. They lived throughout the Miocene Age and became extinct at the end of this age, except for Gigantopithecus who continued to survive to the end of the Pleistocene Age. He perished at the time of the great extinctions of animal life about 4500 years ago.

The science of geology confirms the Bible Record that each of these ape species were created during the Miocene Age and they became extinct at the end of the Miocene, except for Gigantopithecus. Geology also confirms that many new species of animal and plant life were also created during this period of time. This is how geologists are able to distinguish the Miocene from older & younger geological ages.

Who Was Lucy?

The skeleton of Australopithecus afarensis was discovered in November of 1974 by an American paleoanthropologist Donald C. Johanson and his graduate student Tom Gray during their second field season in the parched badlands of the Afar Triangle of north central Ethiopia near Hadar. See Figure 15-4. The term Australopithecus represents a new genus of an "Ape like Hominid."

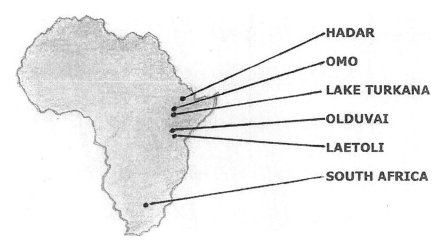

Figure 15-4: A location map in Africa where Hominids have been found. This figure was prepared by Don Daae.

This skeleton is now known as ''Lucy.'' Lucy is unique in that her bones and pieces of her skull were found in the same location. They represent about 40% of a complete skeleton. It was concluded that Lucy was an upright, erect walking hominid that lived about 3.5 million years ago during the geological Pliocene Age. See Figures 15-2 & 15-3. This was based upon the shape of the pelvis and leg bones, which supposedly had similarities to those of modern humans, plus a knee joint that Johanson had found the previous field season. This knee joint, discovered at a different nearby locality resembled that of a modern human. It is doubtful that the knee joint ever belonged to Lucy.

Lucy was a female about three and one half feet tall and had a very small brain measuring from 380 cc to 450 cc. She had a very ape-like head. Thus, she is shown in reconstructions with a human-like body and an ape-like head.

The name Lucy was chosen because the Beatles song "Lucy in the Sky with Diamonds" was playing on the tape recorder in camp while the excited team were analyzing their new discovery. Someone said "**Let's call her Lucy.**" This is how the skeleton, whose catalogue number is AL288, became christened for the world as a new evolutionary ancestor to Modern Man. See Figure 15-2.

In 1975, during the third field season at Hadar, a group of further hominid fossils were found. These included fragmentary parts of thirteen individuals, of which four were juveniles and nine were adults. Johanson referred to them as the "**First Family**," imparting a human-like status to these fossils. The science journals and newspapers of the world proudly proclaimed that another ancestor of Modern Man had been discovered.

Johanson and Tim White went through the painstaking analysis of Lucy's bones together with the "First Family" bones, relating them to similar finds at "Laetoli" where Mary Leakey had discovered a similar set of hominid fossil fragments that were also identified as Australopithecus afarensis of Pliocene Age.

The emphasis was then directed southward to Laetoli in Tanzania. See Figure 15-4.

Regional Geology between Hadar & Laetoli

In order to understand the relationship of the geology at Hadar in Ethiopia with the geology at Laetolia in Tanzania, it is important to get a brief insight into the regional geology between the two locations.

The southern two thirds of Africa is largely Precambrian Shield country. This shield country extends through southern Ethiopia and into Arabia. This is similar to Canada where the Great Canadian Shield covers a large portion of northern Canada. About 75% of the African and Canadian Shield regions consist of granite type crystalline rocks of Archean Age. See Figure 3-5. These granites are intruded with many other darker types of igneous crystalline rocks. They are often referred to as "Basement Rocks". There are certain local areas of the Great African Shield where some younger sediments have been deposited by later invasions of the sea and residual remnants are still present. One such area is at Laetoli.

In northern Ethiopia at Hadar, there are about 1000+ feet (304.8 m) of sediments of Pliocene Age. They increase in thickness in a northeast direction. Geologically, this age spans 2.5 to 7 million years. I do not have any problem with these dates. They fit in with the world wide record of this age. See Figure 15-4.

During Pliocene time a progressively thinner layer of Pliocene sediments extended southward from Ethiopia over the African Shield into the region of Laetoli in Tanzania. Within these Pliocene Age sediments, one will find many species of plant and animal life that are characteristic of this geological age world wide. This is why palaeontologists, anthropologists, palynologists are able to differentiate these different geological time units on a worldwide basis. I have a great respect for all of the above science people. As a geologist, I have had the privilege of spending five summers on geological Field Parties in Canada and Alaska plus two summers doing reconnaissance field work in the NWT of Canada. I understand the work involved.

We do not know how thick these Pliocene sediments were at Laetoli when they were first deposited. However we do know that they increase to over 1000+ feet (304.8 m) in northern Ethiopia. Today, there is only a relatively thin and fairly local outlier of Pliocene sediments in this region of Laetoli. The Pliocene sediments surrounding this Pliocene outlier have been eroded away long ago. These sediments are surrounded and underlain by granite type rocks of Pre-Cambrian Age. See Figure 3-5. The upper portion of this Pliocene outlier has experienced continual erosion since it was deposited.

There is a catch 22 in that several layers of volcanic ash lie directly upon certain portions of these Pliocene sediments at Laetoli. The big question remains: How old are these volcanic ash layers? Are they 3.7 million years old based upon K/Argon dating or could this ash layer be much younger? Today, there is a lush layer of vegetation covering the volcanic ash layer and the Pliocene sediments. This makes it a little more difficult to investigate the geology.

On the basis of fossil assemblages within these sediments, geology confirms that these water laid sediments are of Pliocene age.

In 1935, Louis Leakey found a tooth in these Laetoli sediments that he sent to the British Museum. He had labelled it as a Baboon's tooth. Jonathon & Edey[6] say, "*He did not know that a tooth he had sent to the British Museum .... was a hominid canine. It lay unnoticed until 1979 when it was identified by Peter Andrews of the Museum and White.*" They go on to say, "*He was followed at Laetoli in 1938-1939 by a German named Kohl Larse who recovered a bit of an upper jawbone with a couple of premolars in it, and a well-preserved alveolus---or socket--- for a canine tooth.*" This confirmed and verified the presence of an ape species in these sediments.

Human Footprints at Laetoli

In 1974, Mary Leakey took a field Party to Laetoli. One of her men cut a road through the thicket and found the remains of an ape like hominid. This turned out to be another clue that Australopithecus afarensis (Lucy's Cousin) was present within these Pliocene sediments.

During 1975 and 1976, Mary Leakey continued her field studies at Laetoli. During this time, they were able to increase their knowledge of the Pliocene sediments. Johanson & Edey[7] say, "*Mary and her workers found 42 teeth, some of them were associated with bits of jawbone. One in particular was a fine specimen, LH-4 (Laetoli Hominid 4) with nine teeth in place.*"

What reinforced the idea that A. afarensis (Lucy) walked upright was the sensational discovery of human-like footprints at Laetoli, Tanzania by Mary Leakey and her team in 1976. Johanson & Edey[8] describe it this way, "*Some of the more boisterous members of Mary Leakey's field team were amusing themselves by throwing hunks of dried elephant dung at each other. This may seem a peculiar pastime, but recreational resources are limited on paleontological digs. One who felt this urge was Andrew Hill, a paleontologist from the National Museum of Kenya, who was ducking flying dung and looking for ammunition to fire back, found himself standing in a dry stream bed on some exposed ash layers. One of these had unusual dents in it. When Hill paused to examine them, he concluded they were animal footprints. That diagnosis was confirmed when a larger area was surveyed and other prints found. But no serious effort was made to follow up this extraordinary discovery until the following year, 1977, when a number of large tracks were found by Mary Leakey's son Philip and a co-worker, Peter Jones, and some tracks that looked suspiciously like human foot prints."*

During the Fall of 1977, Mary Leaky came to the USA and told the world about her great discoveries. She held a series of press conferences and interviews. She reported about the human-like footprints and also about Knuckle-walking footprints. Johanson & Edey[9] say that she also reported "*the existence of a water hole around which the animals and birds appeared to have clustered. She even saw some evidence of panic in the tracks, suggesting that the animals had been fleeing the eruption.*" It is believed that the ash deposits came from the nearby Sadiman volcano.

The next season of 1978, Mary Leakey had invited a footprint specialist, Louise Robbins to join her at Laetoli. She also had Peter Jones, Paul Abell and Richard Hay. Tim White also joined the team. Tim White strongly disputed the possibility of the presence of knuckle walking footprints. The discussions became so intense that Mary Leakey even threatened to terminate the Field season. In spite of these disagreements, the search continued. At this location, they discovered more than fifty human like footprints covering a distance of 77 feet. These footprints showed both heel and big toe marks of a human adult and a child. They are described as two erect walking hominids. A photo of these human like footprints are shown in Donald Johanson & Maitland Edey book on page 286 of "LUCY The Beginnings of Humankind." It was published by Simon & Schuster, N.Y., 1981. The human like footprints are also shown on the Google website.

Within this volcanic ash layer they also found numerous footprints of birds, rabbits, fowl, rhinos, giraffes, elephants and several other kinds of animals.

The Age of these Footprints

On the basis of potassium argon (KArg) dating, the volcanic ash was calculated to be 3.7 million years old. Johanson & Edey[11] say, "*Laetoli has attracted paleontologists for more than forty years because its deposits were believed to be very old, extending back into the Pliocene. Recent potassium-argon tests have confirmed that belief. Two tuffs have been dated one at 3.5 million years, another at 3.7 million. The hominid fossils that White was engaged to study fell neatly between them at about 3.7 million years.*"

This all sounds very academic, but one must exercise caution. I have no argument with the Pliocene age being between 2.5 and 7.0 million years. See Figure 15-3. I do have great reservations about the accuracy of the potassium-argon dating method for younger geological ages. Potassium-Argon has a half life of about 1.3 billion years. The decay rate of a radioactive mineral is usually stated in terms of its half life. This is the time it takes for half of the atoms of the parent to decay. After the first half life, there are one-half of the radioactive elements that remains. After the second half-life, then one-quarter is left, then one-eighth is left and it goes on to one-sixteenth, one-thirty-second and so on. Once the rate of decay is known, it is possible to estimate geological age from an uncontaminated sample.

Potassium dates are more accurate for older geological ages, than for younger geologic ages. The error can be substantial for younger geological ages. Even Recent volcanic extrusions can give anomalous and much older readings. Care must be exercised. The above mentioned 3.7 million years before the present could be any where between the present and 3.7 million years ago. In fact it could be as recent as 4500 years before the present. This would equate to the end of the Pleistocene Age. See Figures 19-1, 19-2 & 3-5.

Did Lucy Have Human Feet?

In 1983 scientists Jack T. Stern and Randall Susman, anatomists from the State University of New York at Stony Brook, published a paper entitled, "Detailed Study of Postcranial Skeleton of Johanson's Hadar Specimen." It was published in the American Journal of Physical Anthropology. In summary, this report reveals that the body parts of Lucy were more ape-like than man-like. They say,[12] *"Their long curved heavily muscled hands and feet were to meet the demands of full or part time arboreal life. They were adept tree climbers. Their bipedal gait was that of a chimpanzee or spider monkeys. Their pelvis structure had a marked resemblance to the Chimpanzee. The knee joint fell outside the range of human variation."* This description by two qualified scientists does not relate to an upright walking hominid. They make no mention that Lucy had a heel bone, that would enable her to walk upright.

Stern and Susman are saying that Lucy had ape like feet. In other words, Lucy should now be re-constructed with an ape-like head, ape-like body and ape-like feet. No ape-like creature such as Lucy is able to walk upright like a human because apes do not have a heel bone. Only human beings have a heel bone. This enables all humans to walk erect, that means up right. See Figure 15-2. We can now remove Lucy, Homo afarenses, from the Hominid Family tree.

How old are the Laetoli Footprints?

The question arises how do we explain the human like feet at Laetoli? The only reason, Darwinists believe that Lucy had human feet is based upon the Laetoli footprints. This volcanic ash deposit could be as young as 4,500 years. This roughly equates to the termination of the Pleistocene Age. This also equates to the time when the Great Extinction of Pre-Historic Animal Life took place. See Figures 19-1 and 19-2.

I am not implying that Lucy became extinct about 4500 years ago because geologically speaking Lucy became extinct about 3.0+ million years ago.

The true age of the volcanic ash is being conveniently ignored and hidden by the scientific community. As a result a scientific error is being perpetuated.

Every geologist realizes that new and unique species of animal and plant life suddenly occur during each specific geological age. This enables man to map the same age of sediments from place to place on a worldwide basis.

I had the privilege of being closely involved with three offshore COST wells along the east USA offshore, as well as a COST well in the offshore Gulf of Alaska and a COST well in the Bering Sea region. Three of these wells along the USA east coast drilled through Tertiary, Cretaceous and Jurassic sediments. The other two wells were drilled primarily in Tertiary sediments. See Figure 3-5. I marvelled at how palaeontologists and palynologists were able to determine the specific ages of the Pleistocene, Paleocene, Miocene, Oligocene, Eocene, Paleocene, and the details of the Cretaceous and Jurassic ages by means of the many unique species of plant and animal life. They were also able to determine the many magnetic reversals of the north and south poles that have taken place during the different geological ages.

It is obvious that evolution was not responsible for the systematic order of the fossil record, because it is based upon a non intelligent, undirected process. Evolution is unable to explain the sudden appearance of new species of plant and animal life. Only an all intelligent, all knowing, Creator God is able to create new species of plant and animal life and is able to establish such unique order on a world wide basis. Unfortunately, a highly intelligent, all powerful Creator God is not on their radar screen.

How to Re-Interpret the Hominid Family

Figure 15-2, reveals the Darwinian interpretation as to how the Hominids from Afarensis (Lucy) to Homo Sapiens (Modern Man) have evolved over a period of 3.6 million years. Each Hominid is shown with human feet. Why? The only reason for believing these hominids had human feet is based upon the human footprints in the volcanic ash at Laetoli. The so called Hominids should now be re-constructed with Ape-like heads, body and feet. Let us now look more closely at each of the so called Hominids.

Australopithecus Afarensis

Australopithecus Afarensis (Lucy) should now be re-constructed with an apes head, body and feet. Under our scenario, Afarensis was created as a unique ape-like species by an all-powerful, all Knowing Creator God during the Pliocene Age about 3.6 million years ago.

It must be remembered that a big time gap separates Afarensis from the over lying volcanic ash deposits. These human footprints are within the over lying volcanic ash layers and are not within the Pliocene sediments. These volcanic sediments are now believed to relate to Stage One of Noah's Flood. Stage One deposits can now be identified at select places throughout the entire Earth. See Appendix F.

Australopithecus Africanus & Robustus

Fossil bones of Australopithecus africanus & robustus have been found in South African limestone caves and in East Africa at Olduvai Gorge in Tanzania and in the Lake Turkana region to the north in Kenya. See map of Africa on Figure 15-4.

Richard Leakey[13] describes A. africanus as follows, "*They must have been about 120 cm (4 feet) tall, and to judge from their leg and hip bones, they were capable of standing upright and walking and running on two legs. Their brains were not much larger than those of gorillas, but their bodies were smaller. This means that the gracile australopithecines were probably a little more intelligent than gorillas or chimpanzees.*" Richard E. Leakey, Human Origins, New York, 1982, p. 27.

Richard Leakey describes A. robustus as follows, "*A large male would have weighed about half as much again as a gracile australopithecus. It would have been about 150 cen-timetres (5 feet) tall, but very heavily built, like a gorilla. Its broad, flat face, strong jaws and large teeth were better suited for chewing large quantities of tough food."*[14]

East African robust australopithecines are somewhat big-ger than those in South Africa. Both animals are very simi-lar. The general consensus among paleo-anthropologists is that they are within the range of variation of the same species. Their average brain capacity of is about 550 cc. The average brain capacity of humans are between 700 to 1700 cc. Small baby's and children would be in the 700+ category.

C. E. Oxnard[15] says, "*Finally, the quite independent informa-tion from the fossil record of more recent years seems to indicate absolutely that these australopithecines of half to 3 million years from sites such as Olduvai and Sterkfontein are not on a human pathway.*" This confirms the reason why Figure 15-3 shows that Australopithecus africanus and ro-bustus are definitely not ancestral to Homo sapiens. There is no reason based upon the fossil record to maintain that they had human-like feet and walked upright as shown on Figure 15-2.

Homo Habilis

There is a mystery surrounding the Homo habilis skeletal remains in Units 1 & 11 at the Olduvai Gorge Type Section. The big question arises, do these fragmentary skull and body bones relate to human beings as Louis Leakey main-tained or are they transitional hominids that are ancestral to modern Homo sapiens? A plausible interpretation is pre-sented in chapter 16 which greatly alters the Darwinian in-terpretation. Once we realize the true story of the regional geology in East Africa and the Olduvai Gorge Type Section, we can now confidently remove Homo habilus from Figure 15-2. Homo habilus is not a transitional link in the supposed evolution of Man.

Homo Erectus

The mystery surrounding Homo erectus is described and resolved in Chapter 17. Read the concluding paragraph in Chapter 17. This insight greatly alters the Darwinian interpretation. In fact, once we see the true story behind Homo erectus, we can now confidently remove Homo erectus as being a transitional link in the supposed evolution of Man from Figure 15-2. This means that there are now no hominid ancestors to be found in Africa or Asia during the Pleistocene Age that will link modern Homo sapiens (modern man) to any Pleistocene Australopithecus hominid.

On the basis of geology, archaeology and anthropology we are now witnessing the demise of the Darwinian view of hominid evolution in East Africa and Asia. The classic story of hominid evolution has been a false fabricated interpretation of the fossil record in East Africa and Asia since the time of Charles Darwin and his associates.

Who is Hominid Ardi?

The Google[16] website now relays the following information, *"Nearly 17 years after plucking the fossilized tooth of a new human ancestor from a pebbly desert in Ethiopia, an international team of scientists today (Thursday, Oct. 1, 2009) announced their reconstruction of a partial skeleton of the hominid, Ardipithecus ramidus, which they say revolutionizes our understanding of the earliest phase of human evolution. The female skeleton, nicknamed Ardi, is 4.4 million years old, 1.2 million years older than the skeleton of Lucy, or Australopithecus afarensis, the most famous and, until now, the earliest hominid skeleton ever found. Hominids are all fossil species closer to modern humans than to chimps and bonobos, which are our closest living relatives."*

Google[17] goes on to say, *"This is the oldest hominid skeleton on Earth," said Tim White, University of California, Berkeley, professor of integrative biology and one of the co-directors of the Middle Awash Project, a team of 70 scientists that reconstructed the skeleton and other fossils found with it.*

"This is the most detailed snapshot we have of one of the earliest hominids and of what Africa was like 4.4 million years ago."

Google[18] continues, *"The team's reconstruction of the 4-foot-tall skeleton and of Ardi's environment – a woodland replete with parrots, monkeys, bears, rhinos, elephants and antelope – alters the picture scientists have had of the first hominid to arise after the hominid line that would eventually lead to humans split about 6 million years ago from the line that led to living chimpanzees."*

I would advise the reader to go to Google to retrieve a picture of Ardi @ www. probable appearance in anterior view of Ardipithecusramisdus ("Ardi"). Each person will have to arrive at their own interpretation.

Google[19] says, *"Based on a thorough analysis of the creature's foot, leg and pelvis bones, for example, the scientists concluded that Ardi was bipedal – she walked on two legs – despite being flat-footed and likely unable to walk or run for long distances. In part, this primitive ability to walk upright is because Ardi was still a tree-dweller, they said. She had an opposable big toe, like chimpanzees, but was probably not as agile in the trees as a chimp. Unlike chimps, however, she could have carried things while walking upright on the ground, and would have been able to manipulate objects better than a chimp. And, contrary to what many scientists have thought, Ardi did not walk on her knuckles, White said. ""Ardi was not a chimpanzee, but she wasn't human,"* stressed White, who directs UC Berkeley's Human Evolution Research Center. *"When climbing on all fours, she did not walk on her knuckles, like a chimp or gorilla, but on her palms. No ape today walks on its palms."* Ardi's successor, Lucy, was much better adapted for walking on the ground, suggesting that *"hominids became fundamentally terrestrial only at the Australopithecus stage of evolution."*

In 1983 scientists Jack T. Stern and Randall Susman,[20] anatomists from the State University of New York at Stony Brook, published a paper entitled, "Detailed Study of Postcranial

Skeleton of Johanson's Hadar Specimen." It was published in the American Journal of Physical Anthropology. In summary, this report reveals that the body parts of Lucy were more ape-like than man-like. Their long curved heavily muscled hands and feet were to meet the demands of full or part time arboreal life. They were adept tree climbers.

Why do Darwinists refuse to even mention this report by qualified scientists Stern and Susman on Lucy? Are they guilty of concealing scientific evidence?

It is important to realize that Ardi is in reality an older cousin of Lucy. Ardi was found in the same Pliocene sediments in Ethiopia, but a little lower in the section. She would naturally be older than Lucy. Ardi was a tree-dweller. She had an opposable big toe, like chimpanzees. Humans do not have an opposable big toe. Only humans have a heel bone enabling them to walk uprightly. There is no mention that Ardi had a heel bone.

Until now, the oldest fossil skeleton of a human ancestor was Lucy, the 3.2-million-year-old partial skeleton, discovered in the Afar depression of Ethiopia near Hadar, in 1974 and named Australopithecus Afarensis.

In 1992, however, while surveying a site elsewhere in the Afar region, near the village of Aramis, Gen Suwa, a Middle Awash Project scientist discovered a tooth from a more primitive creature more than 1 million years older than Lucy. After more fossils of the creature were found in the area from some 17 individuals, Suwa, White and project co-leader Berhane Asfaw published the discovery in the journal Nature in 1994.

Although that first paper initially placed Ardi in the Australopithecus genus with Lucy, the team subsequently created a new genus – Ardipithecus – for the hominid because of the fossils significantly more primitive features. In other words, Ardi is now named Ardipithecus Ardi which implies Ardi belongs to a different species. This all becomes very interesting.

Until the discovery of Ardi, only Australopithecines were considered in the Hominid category. This places Ardi in the pre-hominid category. See Figure 15-2. Who is fooling who?

Google relates how Tim White said, *"Ardi, who probably weighed about 110 pounds, had a brain close to the size of today's chimpanzees – one-fifth that of Homo sapiens – and a small face. Males and females were about the same size. The hominid's lack of resemblance to either chimp or modern humans indicates that the last common ancestor of apes and humans looked like neither, he said, and that both lines have evolved significantly since they split 6 million years ago."*

Concluding Remarks regarding the Hominids

For a true scientist to postulate that Modern Man has evolved from Homo erectus, Homo habilis, Australopithicus afarensis (Lucy) & now Ardipithecus Ardi is not based upon scientific fact, but upon pure human speculation and imagination. This reveals the tenuous nature upon which the Darwinian hypothesis of human evolution is based.

We now conclude that H. afarensis, H. africanus, H. robustus and H. erectus were all ape like creatures. They should all be re-constructed with an apes head, body and feet. They should now be removed from the Hominid Family as shown on Figure 15-2. This reveals that the species categorized as Homo sapiens are unique and different from any other ape or monkey species. All Homo sapiens are true human beings. They are our true ancestors. They are no different from you and I today. See Chapters 16 & 17 for greater confirmation.

Modern Apes

Where did the modern apes come from? Did they also evolve from the Hominids? Anthropologist Donald Johanson[21] who wrote "Lucy, The Beginnings of Human kind" states, *"modern gorillas, orangutans and chimpanzees spring out of nowhere, as it were. They are here today; they have no yesterday, unless one is able to find faint fore shadowing's of it in the dryopithecids."* Now what or who are the dryo-pithecids? Dryopithecus was one of the eight great apes that have been identified in sediments of the Miocene Age. See Figure 15-3.

The big question remains, how can one explain the sudden appearance of the modern apes towards the end of the Pleistocene epoch? Where did they come from? Is it possible that these modern apes may have been created by Almighty God in the Garden of Eden about 6,000 to 10,000 years ago? Is it possible that they were the only apes that were preserved in Noah's Ark? Did the other apes or so called Hominids perish at the time of Noah's Flood? See Figure 7-1.

Early Man Identified

It can now be determined that only two types of Early Man were present in Europe, Asia and Africa prior to Noah's Flood. They were the Cro-Magnon and the Neanderthal men. All the other men such as the Heidelberg, the Verteszollos, the Swanscome, the Steinheim, the Fontéchevade and the list could go on and on are all related to either the Cro-Magnon Man or to the Neanderthal Man. See Figure 14-2.

The Heidelberg Man

The Heidelberg man consists of a lower jaw complete with teeth that were dug out of the 78 foot level of a commercial sand pit a few miles southwest of Heidelberg, Germany. It is often called the "Mauer" mandible, because it was found in the Mauer sands. It was also found associated with the bones of extinct elephants, rhinoceros, and other animals. On the basis of the animal assemblage, the Heidelberg lower jaw was dated at about 500,000 years old. See figure 15-1.

Some anthropologists believe the Heidelberg jaw should be assigned to Pithecanthropus (Homo erectus). Other anthropologists believed it may belong to the same ancestral lineage such as Montmaurin man and the first Neanderthals.

The Heidelberg (Mauer) mandible has remained somewhat of a mystery and an enigma. Anthropologist Coon[22] says, *"Because there is no Mauer cranium we do not know to which species, Homo erectus or Homo sapiens, Heidelberg man belonged. Both the teeth and the narrow intercondylar width fit a higher grade than the other features of the bone itself, and both the jaw and its teeth fail to fit into the pattern of any of the other four lines of human evolution seen elsewhere in the world. Mauer therefore stands at the base of a line of its own."* Coon is implying that due to the absence of the skull cap, the other evidences would support him to be more similar to the Homo sapiens.

This 500,000 year age is very suspect. If this mandible is acknowledged to be within the range of variation of the human species which it appears to be, then, geologically, he lived sometime during the Altithermal Age between 6000+ to 4500 years ago. The Heidelberg Man is associated with prehistoric animals that became extinct at the time of Noah's Flood at about 4500 years ago. He was found 78 feet below the surface of the ground. This could be explained due to the severe reworking of sands and gravel during Stages 1 and 3 of Noah's Flood. If the mandible does not belong to the human species, then the Heidelberg jaw may belong to a certain ape species and be somewhat older. This now seems unlikely. The mystery remains unresolved due to its incomplete fossil remains.

Vérteszöllös Man

On August 21, 1965 Lazlo Vértes found part of a skull (the occiput) in a travertine quarry near Vérteszöllös, 30 miles west of Budapest, Hungary. Three human teeth had been recovered from the site earlier, as well as charred animal bones which had been split open for the marrow. The men who lived there were familiar with the use of fire. Numerous stone implements were found, and are noteworthy because they are so crude. There are no hand-axes, only simple choppers made from big pebbles like those used in Olduvai Gorge about 1.5 million years ago. The accompanying bones of extinct animal would indicate he was about 400,000 years old according to the Darwinian interpretation.

Anthropologist Howells[24] dates the occipital to the middle or later part of the Mindel glaciation and thus clearly within the Homo erectus time zone. See Figure 15-1. He maintains that the bone is moderately thick, and shows a well defined ridge for the attachment of neck muscles, such as seen in all erectus skulls. Howells also reported that Andor Thoms of Kossuth University in Hungary examined the occiput and estimated it had a brain capacity of 1400 cc, which is well within the Homo sapiens range. On the basis of this evidence, it was concluded that the Vérteszöllös man was a subspecies of Homo sapiens.

In other words, the evidence indicates that the Verteszollis man was another Homo sapien who was in reality a Neanderthal man. It is here concluded that the Vérteszöllös Man was a true human being. No ape hominid has ever been found with a brain capacity of 1400 cc. In fact, his brain was larger than the average human brain capacity of today. The crude Oldowan type of implements would indicate that he was not advanced in his stone industry. This would place him near the beginning of the Altithermal Age. He may also have been one of the earliest explorers to migrate north-westward into Europe from the region of the Garden of Eden.

Swanscombe Man

The third oldest European fossil of Man is the Swanscombe skull. In 1955, an occiput and two parietals were found separately in a gravel pit 24 feet below the surface, near Swanscombe, England on the south shore of the Thames River a few miles east of London. The skull was dated at 250,000 years old on the basis of extinct species of animal bones and stone implements of Middle Acheulean age. Many hand axes and flake tools were found. See Figure 15-1.

The skull is a female who possibly died in her early twenties, with a cranial capacity of 1325 cc. Some anthropologists have hesitated to classify the Swanscombe skull as Homo sapien. However Hooton[25] says *"There is no denying the conclusion that Swanscombe is either a mid Pleistocene Homo sapien or something so close to it that the differences are zoologically inconsiderable"* The Swanscombe is often classified as a so-called Archaic Homo sapien, when in reality his or her brain capacity is well within the range of variation of the Cro-Magnon species and of present day man.

It becomes common sense that the Swanscombe people were direct descendants of Adam and Eve who had developed the acheulian techniques of manufacturing stone implements. They may have been among the original inhabitants of England. The lady discovered may have been previously buried, however during the Flood 4500 years ago her bones may have been reworked and re-deposited in the gravel pit where she was found. This may explain why the one parietal was found about 25 feet away from the occipital within the same depth. The associated animal bones were of extinct species that became extinct at the time of Noah's Flood about 4,500 years ago.

This part of southern England was never glaciated, although glacial outwash gravels and sands are found. There is no real reason to believe that these gravel sands are of Middle Pleistocene (second interglacial) age. This is only guess-work, and no absolute dates have been established. These sands were very likely redistributed and reworked at the time of Noah's Flood about 4500 years ago.

Steinheim Man

The Steinheim skull was discovered in 1933 near Steinheim, Germany, not far from Heidelberg. Associated animal bones, some now extinct, established that this skull was about 200,000 years old according to Darwinists. It is fairly complete, except that the lower jaw, most of the upper teeth, and some of the more delicate facial bones are missing. It is believed to be a female who was killed by a crushing blow to the left eye.

In 1962, G.H. Von Koenigswald[26] said of the Steinheim man: "*By underplaying its Neanderthal characteristics we can easily change it into Homo sapiens, by exaggerating these characteristics we can turn it into extreme Neanderthal man. However, the sapiens characteristics seem to be the more pronounced of the two.*" This would mean she is a true human being more akin to the Neanderthal Man.

No tools or implements were found in association with the skull, and the date of 200,000 years is highly suspect. She is definitely Homo sapien.

This discovery convinced many persons that this Early Neanderthal lady predated the Cro-Magnon man. She was considered to be a person of great antiquity. It was reasoned that she had been in Europe for over 200,000 years. This again illustrates the narrow reasoning of a secular anthropologist who is committed to propagating the Darwinian theory.

However, the discovery of the Fontechevade Man revealed the opposite.

The Fontéchevade Man

In 1947 the Fontéchevade Man was discovered in a cave at Fontéchevade France. Upper strata of the cave floor disclosed a cultural record ranging from the remains of Recent Man in the upper layers to the remains of Stone Age Man in the lower layers. Tools and debris of the Neanderthal Mousterian culture were found at the bottom resting upon the cave floor. The term Mousterian always relate to stone tools made by the Neanderthal Man.

However, archaeologist Henri-Martin realized that the floor consisted of a thick layer of stalagmite deposit. She decided to dig through this calcareous layer to see what was below. As she broke through this layer, she discovered 20 feet of additional sedimentary deposits. A new tool industry and culture was found in the lower levels, called the Tayacian Industry. Crude flake tools were found, rather than worked cores. On the basis of associated fragments of extinct fossil mammals, the deposit was dated as third interglacial (between 75,000 to 125,000 years old). However, a human skullcap and a fragment of a second skull was found. It did not resemble the Neanderthal man, but was more akin to the Cro-Magnon man.

For the first time, clear evidence was found that a more modern form of Man preceded the Neanderthal. This helped to confirm that the Neanderthal was not our direct ancestor, but was preceded by the Cro-Magnon man in Europe. It helps to confirm that the so-called archaic Homo sapiens, such as the Vérteszöllös and the Swanscombe were in reality Cro-Magnon as well.

The date of 75,000 to 125,000 years for the Fontéchevade man is suspect and is based upon an unscientific, greatly exaggerated evolutionary model. It is realistic to believe that he was a direct descendant of Adam and Eve, and that he lived during the early part of the Altithermal Age.

The Sites of Early Man in Europe & the Middle East

The question arises, is there a direct relationship between the sites of Early Man in Europe and with sites of Early Man in the Middle East? They are all amazingly similar. Figure 15-4 is a schematic cross section that relates the geological and archaeological cultural ages from Europe to the Middle East Persian Gulf region.

Mas d'Azil Cave Site in France

We will begin by relating a certain site in France with three separate sites in the Persian Gulf region. This site was discovered in 1887 by a French Archaeologist E. Piette. A simplified description of the Mas d'Azil Cave Site is given by Boule. He describes two Palaeolithic (Old Stone Age) levels, overlain by a Mesolithic (Middle Stone Age) level that is in turn overlain by a Neolithic (New Stone Age) level. This site is related to similar age levels at Ninevah, Ur and Fara.

The left side of Figure 15-8 illustrates the different cultural layers of Man found in the Mas d'Azil Cave in France. The Flood Age is shown to abruptly terminate the Neolithic Age in both regions. The bedrock is of an older geological age that is devoid of human remains.

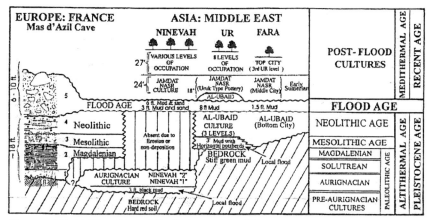

Figure 15-5: The Mas d'Azil Cave Site[27] **is compared with Ninevah, Ur & Fara Sites. Interpretation by Don Daae.**

Layers 1 & 2 of the Mas d'Azil Cave Site[27] relate to the Palaeolithic Magdalenian Age. **Layer 1** is about 4 feet 7 inches thick. It consists of clay, silt and sand mixed with larger pebbles. It is almost barren of artifacts and rests on limestone bedrock. **Layer 2** is about 11 ft. 6 inches thick and consists of silt and clay with hundreds of laminae. It is cut by several ashy layers of incinerated earth. In these layers of occupation are abundant bones of the extinct red deer and rare bones of reindeer. Artifacts include harpoons of red deer and reindeer antlers, needles and artistic engravings.

Layer 3 is of **Mesolithic Age**. It varies in thickness from 4 inches to 2 feet 6 inches. It is a bed of cinders, reddish incinerated earth and charcoal with wild fauna. There are abundant remains of the red deer and beaver, but not a trace of the reindeer. Artifacts include flat perforated harpoons of deer-horn, painted pebbles with some pebbles polished at ends. The upper part consists of a surface marked by a line of stones. In the lower part are beds of ashes.

Layer 4 is of **Neolithic Age**. It consists of banded masses of ashes with beds of charcoal and innumerable snail shells. Artifacts include polished stone implements, pebbles worn with usage at the points, together with fragments of pottery. Thickness is variable up to a maximum of 7 feet (2.1m). Polished stone implements are characteristic of the Neolithic Age.

Layer 5 is, herein, related to the Flood Age. It is a rubble layer, 6 to 10 feet in thickness, consisting of blocks of rock that have been detached from the roof of the cave. They are in-filled with finer sediment. In the upper portion were found Gaulish and Bronze Age objects that are definitely of a Post Flood Age. These objects were obviously introduced later.

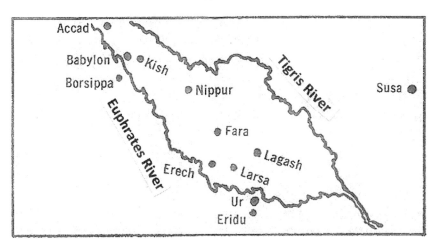

Figure 15-6: A revised Map of the Middle East as it was during the Early Sumerian period. This land is also called Ancient Sumer. The Euphrates River to the left & the Tigris River to the right flowed southeast ward into the Persian Gulf. Map from Halley [28]

Within the rubble layer were polished stone axes and pottery of Neolithic Age. These artifacts are definitely Pre-Flood. The thickness of this rubble layer varies from 6 to 10 feet (1.8 to 3.1m) It would have required high energy, powerful tsunami type of flooding to have deposited this type of rubble.

Archaeologists date this above sequence into the past at about 4,000 to 15,000 years more or less based upon typology and carbon 14 dating. What is very important to note is that this rubble Flood layer is of post Neolithic Age. This equates to the time when Noah's Flood took place throughout the world. Keep this in mind as we examine many other sites of Early Man throughout the world.

Three Middle East Sites

Figure 15-4 illustrates the archaeological findings of three ancient Archaeological sites in the Mesopotamian triangle region north of the Persian Gulf, namely, Ur, Fara and Ninevah. These three sites are, in turn, related to the findings at the Mas d'Azil Cave Site in France.

As we discuss the ancient history of Ur, Fara and Kish there will be differences of opinion as to its interpretation. First let us look at the archaeological evidences, then to see how they relate to geology.

Dr. Fredk. A. Filby[29] says, *"The story really commences with the excavations by Dr. H. R. Hall in 1919 of the little mound of al'Ubaid, four miles north of Ur. These deposits yielded interesting remains of pottery and various flint and obsidian tools of the Neolithic Age."*

The view I have been presenting is that Noah's Flood terminated the Neolithic Age throughout the world. Now let us see whether there is evidence that the Neolithic Age was terminated by a massive flood in this region surrounding ancient Babylon. See Figure 15-8.

After Noah's Flood life began, in what the Bible describes as, the land of Shinar. This is in reality Ancient Sumer and this period of human history equates to the **Early Sumerian Age**.

The Bible clearly states that after the Flood, Noah and his family had first settled to the east of Shinar, where they probably began to raise their families. They then moved from the east into the fertile land of Shinar, which is described in Genesis 11:1 & 2, (NKJV) as follows, *"Now the whole Earth had one language and one speech. And it came to pass, as they journeyed from the east, that they found a plain in the land of Shinar, and they dwelt there".*

Deposits at Ur

In 1930, Dr. Leonard Woolley led a joint expedition of the Museum of Pennsylvania and the British Museum at Ur. He sank a shaft 75 feet by 60 feet and went down 64 feet. This shaft penetrated 8 levels of occupation. See Figure 15-8.

The Jamdat Nasr Culture: Woolley encountered 18 feet of pottery rubbish of the Jamdat Nasr Culture which is of Early Sumerian Age. This is definitely Post Flood. He found evidence of a pottery factory where wastes had been thrown out. In this "kiln" stratum he encountered pottery of the Erech or Warka type where a heavy potter's wheel was found. These layers are described by Filby. [29]

Below this level Woolley encountered a thin layer with the painted **al'Ubaid type of pottery which is typically of Neolithic Age**. Now this layer appears to be out of place and should be classified as Pre-Flood. Should it not be positioned below the Flood layer?

Interpretation: The al'Ubaid culture at Ur above the Flood Layer is believed to be a carry over by Noah & his family members after the Flood. It is believed that Noah and his family returned to this fertile Middle East region after leaving the Ark. They would have brought with them all the Neolithic tools and pottery that were preserved in the

Ark. This al'Ubaid culture, soon phased into the overlying Jamdat Nasr Culture that characterizes the Early Sumerian Age. It is very possible that Ur was the home of Noah after the Flood?

Flood Deposit: A few graves from above penetrated down into this Flood layer. A copper spear-blade which typifies Neolithic age and a number of terra-cotta figurines were found in these grave sites.

Halley[30] says this, "*Dr. C.L. Woolley, found (1929), near the bottom of the Ur mounds, underneath several strata of human occupation, a great bed of solid water laid clay 8 feet thick without admixture of human relic, with yet the ruins of another city buried beneath it. Dr.Woolley said that the 8 feet of sediment implied a very great depth and a long period of water, that it could not have been put there by any ordinary overflow of the rivers, but only by some vast inundation as the Biblical Flood. The civilization underneath the flood layer was so different from that above it that it indicated to Dr. Woolley a sudden and terrific break in the continuity of history*." This 8 foot clay unit at Ur is typical of a "Stage Two Deposit" of Noah's Flood, where the Earth experienced a period of worldwide quiescence. See Appendix F for greater clarification. See Appendix F.

Al'Ubaid Culture: Below the Flood layer were at least three levels of occupation and the pottery of the decorated al'Ubaid type. The al'Ubaid culture is classified as being of **Neolithic Age.**

Underlying the al'Ubaid level was a 3 foot (0.9m) layer of mud with horizontal potsherds. This is considered to be a local flood deposit that was lying upon bedrock of an older age. This is where the evidence of human activity ceased at Ur.

Dr. Fredk A. Filby has done a commendable and exhaustive study of geological and archaeological evidences that relate directly to Noah's Flood throughout Europe and the Middle East. It is an important book to read. However, he maintains that Noah's Flood took place at the end of the Paleolithic Age. He rather believed the Flood evidence that Dr. Woolley brings forth in the Persian Gulf region was a later and a more local flood deposit. As a geologist, I believe Dr. Filby has failed to realize that the end of the Pleistocene Age equates to the end of the Neolithic Age and not the Paleolithic Age. He also failed to identify the different stages of Noah's Flood. See Figure 15-8 and Appendix F.

Filby[31] gives additional data that relates to the site at UR beyond that of Halley as follows, *"In 1929 (Sir) Leonard Woolley, -- drove a shaft down to virgin soil and in so doing discovered an 8 foot layer of clean, water laid silt, with pottery of the al'Ubaid type both above and below it. This he and his wife both concluded was laid down by the Genesis Flood. During the following season Woolley sank a very much larger shaft 75 feet by 60 feet and went down finally to 64 feet. This shaft penetrated eight levels of houses and then went through no less than eighteen feet of pottery rubbish – evidence of a pottery factory where 'wastes' had been thrown out. Some red and black painted fragments were the same as those discovered at a site called Jamdat Nasr, 150 miles north of UR. Still lower in this kiln stratum the pottery became much plainer and belonged to the Uruk (Erech or Warka) type, and a heavy potter's wheel was found. Below this level came the hand-turned, painted al'Ubaid type of pottery – just a thin layer—and then the so called Flood silt. A few graves from above penetrated down into this and in one there was a copper spear blade. A number of little terra-cotta figurines were found. The flood silt here was 11 feet thick, absolutely uniform and clearly water-laid, subject to the action of gentle currents and composed of material brought down from the middle reaches of the Euphrates. Below it were at least three levels of occupation and the pottery was again of the richly decorated al'Ubaid type."* It is interesting to note, that Dr. Leonard Woolley referred to the Flood layer as clean mud, not silt. This mud layer relates directly to Stage Two of Noah's Flood. See Appendix F.

Deposits at Fara

Fara is located midway between Babylon and Ur. See Map 15-9. At one time Fara was situated along the Euphrates River. Now it is 40 miles to the east. There are a group of low lying mounds beaten by the desert sands. Dr. Eric Schmidt, of the University Museum of Pennsylvania, excavated them in 1931. **He found the remains of three cities:** The top city was contemporaneous with the 3rd Ur Dynasty. The middle city was of Early Sumerian Age which included Jamdat Nasr type pottery; and the bottom city was pre-Flood. This was based upon Dr. Eric Schmidt's interpretation who had found a Flood layer between the Middle city and the bottom city. It consisted of yellow dirt, a mixture of sand and clay. It was definitely alluvial, water laid without relics of human occupation. This flood layer is correlated with the Flood layer at Ur.

Fredk A. Filby[32] says, "*A similar layer of mixed clay and sand eighteen inches thick was found at Fara (ancient Shuruppak, legendary home of Ut-Napish-tim or Noah), but this too comes between the Jamdat Nasr type of pottery and the remains of the earliest dynasties.*"

Halley[33] describes the city below the Flood Layer at Fara as follows, "*Underneath the flood deposit was a layer of charcoal and ashes, a dark colored culture refuse which may have been wall remains, painted pottery, skeletons, cylinder seals, pots, and pans, and vessels.*" Dr. Eric Schmidt classified this lower layer as the Al-Ubaid culture which is of Neolithic age.

Deposits at Ninevah

Ninevah is located about 300 miles north of Ur. Dr. Mallowan, Director of the British Museum, conducted excavations at Ninevah in 1932-33. He sunk a 90 foot shaft into the Great Mound. The different layers are described by Filby.[16]

Post Flood Age: At a depth of 27 feet from the surface, excavators found Jamdat Nasr type pottery of Early Sumerian

Age. The Jamdat Nasr type pottery was found between 27 to 51 feet.

Flood Age Deposit: Below this 51 foot interval they found a 6 foot layer of black mud with pebbles, underlain by 3 feet that consisted of thirteen layers of inter-bedded mud and sand. Filby[34] says, "*The excavators consider that this represents a well-defined pluvial period and that it coincided with an important climate change.*" In other words, it represented a Flood Layer that was deposited at the end of the Altithemal Age.

At the base of the Flood layer, they found a copper pin. This copper pin relates to the Neolithic Age. Then Filby[35] says, "*A copper pin was found at this level, being the earliest found. It would seem then that this deposit might be much nearer in time to the 8-11 feet silt at Ur. And in that case the evidence for Noah's Flood would be still deeper.*" Filby disagrees with my interpretation, because he firmly believed Noah's Flood took place at the end of the Paleolithic Age. See Figure 15-8 & 19-2.

It is to be noted that there is an absence of human relics of Mesolithic or Neolithic Age below the Flood Deposit. The reason for this is the absence of people living at this particular site during this particular interval of time or it was a time of no deposition. It is also possible that Stage One of Noah's Flood may have eroded the Neolithic and the Mesolithic age sediments away. See Appendix F.

Pre-Flood Age: Below the above Flood Deposit is an earlier civilization called "**Ninevah 2**" with charred wood, red and black painted pots and a thin layer of mud. Still lower is **Ninevah 1** where the pottery was plain with no ornamentation. The artistic remains of Ninevah 1 and 2 are said to be somewhat like those of the Aurignacian culture, which would place this interval in the latter part of the Paleolithic Age. See Figure 15-8.

Below Ninevah 1 at the 81 foot depth, is a 3 foot layer of black mud. This can also be interpreted to be a local flood layer. Below this was very hard soil where all evidence of human activity ceased. Filby.[35]

Deposits at Kish

The ancient city of Kish is contemporary with Ur and Fara. It is located on the east edge of Babylon, on the banks of where the Euphrates River used to flow. See Map 15-9.

In 1928-29, Dr. Stephen Langdon, of the Field Museum-Oxford University Expedition, found a 5 foot bed of clean water-laid clay sediments in the lower ruins of Kish, indicating a flood of vast proportions. It contained no objects of any kind. Dr. Langdon suggested that it may have been deposited by Noah's Flood mentioned in the Bible.

Halley describes the layers beneath the Flood layer as follows, *"Underneath it (the Flood layer), the relics represented an entirely different type of culture. Among the relics found was a four wheeled Chariot, the wheels made of wood and copper nails, with the skeletons of the animals that drew it."*[36] In other words the animals that drew this chariot were still present beneath the shafts. This confirms the suddenness and the magnitude of this Flood event. The presence of copper nails is indicative that these people had entered into the copper age which is characteristic of the **Neolithic Age**.

In Conclusion

By comparing the site at Kish with the sites at Ur, Fara, Ninevah and with the Mas d' Azil Cave in France, we begin to see the immense magnitude and the widespread enormity of the Flood event that swept through this region about 4500 years ago. As we progress we will see that this Flood event relates directly to Noah's Flood.

Geological evidences now reveal that the Biblical Flood of Noah terminated the Neolithic Age on a worldwide basis. It terminated the Pleistocene Age, the Altithermal Age and ushered in a new age called the Recent or the Medithermal Age. See Figure 19-1.

References for Chapter 15

1. Carl O. Dunbar & Karl M. Waage, "Historical Geology," 1969, Third edition, John Wiley & Sons, Inc. New York / London / Sydney / Toronto. p.490.
2. Kenneth MacGowan & Joseph A. Hester, Jr. "Early Man in the New World" published in Co-operation with the American Museum of Natural History. The Natural history Library Anchor Books, Doubleday & Company, Inc. Garden City, N.Y. 1962. p. 36.
3. Donald Johanson & Maitland Edey, "LUCY The Beginnings of Humankind." Simon 7 Schuster, N.Y., 1981, p. 286.
4. Johanson & Edey, pp. 18-20.
5. Johanson & Edey, p.283.
6. Johanson & Edey, p.244.
7. Johanson & Edey, p.244. ok
8. Johanson & Edey, p.245. ok
9. Johanson & Edey, p.246. ok
10. Johanson & Edey, p.249. ok
11. Johanson & Edey, p.244. ok
12. Jack T. Stern and Randall Susman, "Detailed Study of Postcranial Skeleton of Johanson's Hadar Specimen," published in the American Journal of Physical Anthropology, 1983. ok
13. Richard E. Leakey, Human Origins, New York, 1982, p. 27. Ok P Johanson & Edey, p.246.
14. Ibid. p.27. ok?
15. C.E. Oxnard, "Convention and Controversy in Human Evolution," Homo 30, 1981, p,242. ok
16. Google website.
17. Google website.
18. Google Website.
19. Google Website. Also Figures 15-6 & 15-7.
20. Kenneth MacGowan & Joseph A. Hester, Jr. "Early Man in the New World" published in Co-operation with the American Museum of Natural History. The Natural history Library Anchor Books, Doubleday & Company, Inc. Garden City, N.Y. 1962. p. 36.
21. Donald Johanson & Maitland Edey, "LUCY The Beginnings of Humankind." Simon 7 Schuster, N.Y., 1981, p. 318.

22. Coon, Carleton S., "The Origin of the Races," N.Y.: Publisher, p. 492. Ok
23. Hooton, Ernest Albert, "Up from the Ape." N.Y.: Macmillan, p. 363
24. Howells, W.W."The Origins of the American Indian Race Types." 1940, pp.46-53. Also see Howells, W.W. "Homo erectus-Who, When and Where." A Survey Yearbook: Physical Anthropology. Pp. 1-23.
25. Hooton, Ernest Albert, "Up from the Ape." N.Y.: Macmillan, p. 363
26. Von Koenigswald G.H.R., "The Evolution of Man." Ann Harbor, Michigan. p. 57. 1962. It was translated from German by Arnold J. Pomerans in the University of Michigan Press. Ok
27. Boule M & H. Valois, "Fossil Men a Textbook of Human Palaeontology, Thomas & Hudson, 1957.
    Note: For further information see Google www. Mas d'Azil site. It says, "The paleolithic cave site known as Mas d'Azil is located in the Pyrénées of France, and was excavated by Edouard Piette in the 19th century. Mas d'Azil is the type site of the Azilian culture of the Late Paleolithic, and contains bone carvings interpreted by Piette as indicating the domestication of reindeer and horses. Occupations at the site range in date from 17,800 to 6500 years BC."
28. Halley H. H., Halley's Bible Handbook, Zondervan, May 1976, References to Ur are at pp.77-79 & 87-89 & p. 95, 46, 51.
29. Filby Fredk. A. M.Sc., PhD., "The Flood Reconsidered." Pickering & Inglis Ltd., 1970. pp. 27-28.
30. Halley, p. 77.
31. Filby, p.30
32. Filby, p.30
33. Halley, p.77. ok
34. Filby, p.30. or
35. Filby, p.30. o
36. Halley, p.78-79.

Chapter 16

Early Man in East Africa & Olduvai Gorge

Louis S. M. Leakey (1903-1972) is known for his discovery of fossils and artifacts that were related to human evolution. He was a true paleontologist and anthropologist. His parents were English missionaries to the Kikuyu tribe at a mission station in East Africa at Kabete, ten miles from Nairobi Kenya. It is said that Louis grew up more African than English.

At the age of 13, he discovered mysterious stone tools. This ignited his passion for prehistory and led him to learn more about the people who made them and who at one ancient time lived in this region. In 1922 he started studies at Cambridge University, but a rugby accident the following year left him unable to continue his study. He left to help manage a paleontological expedition to Africa. He returned in 1925 to resume his studies, and graduated in anthropology and archaeology in 1926.

While at Cambridge University, he was inspired by the Darwinian Hypothesis that Modern Man had evolved from an ape ancestry and that the proof of human evolution could be found within the fossil record. The logical place for him to go to in order to find the proof of evolution was to his home country of Kenya in East Africa where modern day chimpanzees and gorillas were present. It was here that he diligently sought the evidences to support the evolutionary development of Man from an Ape ancestry.

Over the next few years, he conducted a number of excavations in East Africa mainly in the Olduvai Gorge region. In 1930 Cambridge awarded him a Ph.D. for his work.

Google says, "*In 1928 Louis married Frida Avern, an Englishwoman he had met in Africa. While in England in 1933, he met Mary Nicol, a scientific illustrator, and soon started an affair with her despite the fact that he had one young child and a pregnant wife. Mary joined him for his next expedition to Africa, and returned home to live with him in 1935. In 1936, his wife Frida filed for divorce, and Louis and Mary married late that year.*"

He and his wife Mary began a long series of anthropological and archaeological observations which has made East Africa a classic in relation to the evolution of Early Man. He began his work along the East African (Gregory) Rift Valley in south west Kenya and northern Tanzania. He made the Olduvai Gorge one of his main areas of interest. He and his wife Mary also extended their activities within the East Rift Valley and to adjacent areas such as Lake Victoria to the west and Laeotoli to the south (Figure 16-1).

Louis S. M. Leakey (1903-1972) is best known for his discoveries of fossils and projectile point artifacts which he and his associates related to Human evolution. By the time he died, he had pushed back the cradle of humanity from a few thousand years to two plus million years. It is sometimes said that he helped refute the Biblical creation record of Adam & Eve and replaced it with a Naturalistic Darwinian Theory of Evolution. This was to the chagrin of his Christian parents.

The Olduvai Gorge Type Section

The Olduvai Gorge is the classical Darwinian Type Section to which all other sites in East Africa and the world are related. A second comparable location is the Koobi Fora site along the east side of Lake Turkana about 1000 miles north of Olduvai where the geology and palaeontology are similar. However, this site is also related to Olduvai for its confirmation.

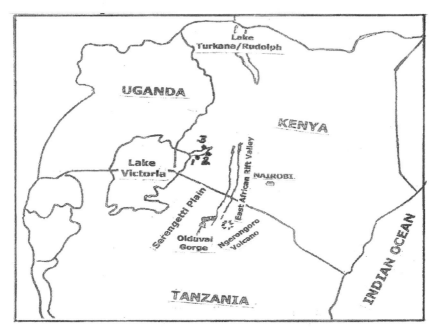

Figure 16-1: Map of Kenya, Tanzania & Uganda showing the various sites where Louis and Mary Leakey did most of their Field Work. Prepared by Don Daae. See Louis Leakey's Memoirs. [12]

The Olduvai Gorge Type Section is used by secular archaeologists and anthropologists as a basis for dating Early Man in Europe, Asia and all other parts of the world. Thus, it is very important to examine the geology of the Olduvai Gorge Type Section to see whether this is appropriate to do. See Figure 16-2.

Where is the Olduvai Gorge located?

The famous Olduvai Gorge is located in the northern part of Tanzania and is about 70 miles (112.6 km) south of Kenya. It is also located along the southeast border of the Serengeti Plains in northern Tanzania. These plains are famous for their wildlife Safari Tours. It is also situated along the western edge of the main north/south trending East African (Gregory) Rift

Valley. See Figure 16-1. The Olduvai Gorge is also located about 120 miles (193 km) west of Lake Victoria.

The Geology of the Olduvai Gorge

The geology of the Olduvai Gorge is relatively simple. The great African Precambrian Shield extends into the Olduvai Gorge region. It consists primarily of granite type rocks. Geologists have found that the Olduvai area was a previous lake bottom with a relatively thin layer of lake sediments overlying the Pre-Cambrian granite. Above the thin fresh water lake sediments are mysterious pluvial sediments that have been mapped as beds 1, 11, 111, & 1V. Each of these units contain a great mixture of Pleistocene animal and plant life. Thus, it has been interpreted as being primarily of Lower & Middle Pleistocene Age.

Above unit 1V the Leakey's found a thin overlying Bed V that they believed to be of Upper Pleistocene Age with an estimated age of about 17,000 years before the present. Surface layers reveal artifacts of Recent Age that relate to the modern Masai tribal African people who inhabit this region today.

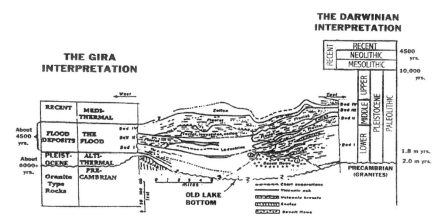

Figure 16-2: This is a revised version of a geological east west cross-section through the famous East African Olduvai Gorge Type Section. It shows the Darwinian interpretation on the right side and the GIRA Interpretation on the left side. The middle portion of diagram is from the textbook "Historical Geology" by Dunbar & Waage, [1] Prepared by Don Daae.

After the deposition of these four Pleistocene units, a mysterious east-west strong flowing river cut a deep east/west trending steep sided gorge that empties into the major north-south trending East African Rift Valley a short distance to the east. This deep gorge is called the Olduvai Gorge. It has exposed all of these four units from top to bottom. The entire strata are only about 90 meters (300 feet) in thickness. It contains the remains of extinct Pleistocene animals, birds together with the Palaeolithic artifacts (stone tools) of Early Man. The mystery is where did all the water come from to cut this deep gorge? Also where did the pluvial (flood) waters come from to deposit units 1, 11, 111, & 1V?

Louise Leakey[2] upon examining the Olduvai sediments concluded theses four units were deposited by pluvial waters. These Pleistocene sediments cover a vast area of central Africa. At the Pan African Congress of January 1947, Louis and others argued that glacial episodes in Europe & North America relate to pluvial periods in Africa. Prof. F.E. Zeuner insisted that periods in the Northern hemisphere coincided with drier conditions in the equatorial zone. This theory of pluvial waters was replaced by the theory that inland lakes were being filled with water to their limits resulting in the deposition of these sediments.

Where did all the water come from to deposit this vast amount of sediment over such a large regional area of Central and East Africa and also throughout the Lake Victoria region to the west and the Lake Turkana region to the north? Up to this time, Louis Leakey maintained that East Africa was a highland region that was undergoing drier conditions during the previous Pliocene Age with continual erosion taking place up to the time when these water laid sediments were deposited.

The Darwinian Interpretation

The Darwinian interpretation of the Olduvai Gorge Section is shown on the right side of Figure 16-2. The underlying granite rocks are of Pre-Cambrian (Archean) Age. Directly above the granite and below Bed 1 is a relatively thin layer of fresh water lake sediments that has been dated as being of Early Pleistocene Age. The igneous basalt intrusive along the lower right side is from an earlier extrusion.

The overlying sedimentary units 1, 11, 111, 1V & V are believed to range in age from about 1.8 million years at the base to Recent times at the top. This sequence of sediments has a combined maximum thickness of about 300 feet (90 meters). Bed 1 is believed to be of Lower Pleistocene Age. Beds 11, 111, & 1V are believed to be of Middle Pleistocene Age. Bed V above Bed 1V is believed to be of late Upper Pleistocene Age. Compare Figures 14-1 to 16-2 to get a mental image of the Pleistocene Age and the extremely long time span involved in depositing Beds 1 to 1V.

Bed 1 is a pluvial or water deposit. Abundant fossil remains have been found within Bed 1, such as fish, alligators, hippos, together with broken and dismembered fossil fragments of birds, many extinct types of mammalian life such as the giant pre-historic deinothere elephants. Extinct species of ape like animals such as Homo robustus, Homo africanus, and Homo habilis are present. **According to the Darwinian Theory, these ape or hominid remains are believed to be the ancestors to modern Man!**

Washed-in Paleolithic (Old Stone Age) type projectile points are also present in Bed 1. See Figure 15-1. **No actual sites of Man have been found within Bed 1.** Pluvial means the sediments, debris, bones and stone projectile points were brought in by fast flowing water. The question arises, where did the great volumes of pluvial waters come from?

The Darwinian scenario at Olduvai Gorge envisages the base of Bed I to be about 1.8 million years old. This is based upon the potassium argon dating of a thin volcanic ash layer near the base of Bed 1. It is thus reasoned that Early Man was present in this area for at least 200,000 prior years. This extends the age of Early Man to about 2 million years into the past. Geology has since extended the age of the Pleistocene Age from 2.0 million to 2.5 million years which has added further complications to this interpretation.

Another perplexing mystery to this interpretation is this: if these washed in tools were made by Early Man, then they would have been made by Early Man who would have lived prior to 1.8 million years ago or prior to the deposition of Bed 1? What was this Early Man like? One could logically rationalize that the above ape like Hominids within Bed 1 must have evolved from Early Man who lived in Africa prior to the deposition of Bed 1.

Beds 11, 111 and 1V are believed to be of Middle Pleistocene age because they lack the larger types of mammals such as the giant pre-historic deinothere elephants. Washed-in acheulian and other Paleolithic stone tools and projectile points are found at various levels. **No actual sites of Man have been found within these beds.** However, disarticulated fossil fragments of Australopithecus robustus and africanus, Homo habilus and Homo erectus have been found, together with many other extinct mammal fossil fragments. See Figure 15-2. According to the Darwinian Theory, these ape-like hominid remains are believed to be the ancestors to modern Man.

This Type Section at Olduvai Gorge reveals a big dilemma. Archaeologists and anthropologists have determined that Early Man lived prior to the deposition of Bed 1. If that is the case, then the ape-like hominids must have evolved from Early Man? What was this Early Man like?

What was this Early Man Like?

Richard Leakey [3] in his book Human Origins says, "*Geologists can tell us what the landscape was like. They can locate lakes, rivers, streams and valleys and put together a detailed picture of the ancient countryside.*" Now he is describing the older surface that is underlying beds 1, 11, 111 & 1V at Olduvai and in the surrounding region. Leakey goes on to say, "*Using these reconstructions the archaeologists can plot where the sites were located. In this way we can find out whether our ancestors preferred to camp by the lakeshore on the shady banks of a river or out on the open plains.*"

It was upon this landscape at the base of bed 1 that Mary Leakey discovered 16 archaeological sites on the eastern side of the lake and 2 sites on the western side. This is where Early Man lived. Mary Leakey was able to describe two different types of sites.

There were permanent sites where Early Man actually made a permanent camp and other sites where they stopped temporarily to cut up animal carcasses. These sites were along rivers that flowed into a previously existing relatively fresh water lake. This lake was rich in water life, such as fish, hippos and alligators. Extinct and modern mammals and birds were present among the surrounding trees and grassland areas. All indications reveal that the climate was moist with luxuriant land and water life during the time that Early Man lived in this region. In other words, all these archaeological sites relate to an age prior to the deposition of Bed 1.

Anthropologist Glynn Isaac worked closely with Richard Leakey. Glynn Isaac described this two million year Man at Olduvai as follows, "*The evidence of the hominid fossils and the evidence of the artifacts together suggest that these early artisans were nonhuman hominids.*" [4] This means they were extremely primitive, ape like and were in the very early stages of evolving from an ape-like creature called a hominid. Why would Glynn Isaac describe these early people in this way? The reason is clear. His reasoning was determined by the dating of the volcanic ash layer near the base of Bed 1 at about 1.8+ million years old. This fit into the Darwinian interpretation that Bed 1 was of Lower Pleistocene Age. See Figure 16-2 and 19-1. We now know that potassium argon dating can be very unreliable in younger Tertiary sediments. This date could very well be much younger. It could even be within the past 5,000 year period.

The question remains, how scientifically correct and reasonable was Glynn Isaac's interpretation?

Richard Leakey[5] who is the son of Louis and Mary Leakey says, "*My mother has made very detailed plans of all the ancient camps sites, and at two of these she thinks that the people may have built some kind of shelter. At one site, the signs are that there was a sort of wind-break; at another, she thinks they may have even managed to build a proper hut. Here she found a series of quite large stones arranged in a circle. As the inside of the hut would have been used for sleeping, most of the tools and broken bones were scattered over the ground outside the circle. A circle of stones does not seem much evidence of a hut, but even to this day people living in the arid, windy areas of northern Kenya support the struts of their grass huts with stones. When the hut burns down, or the wood is eaten by termites, all that remains is a circle of stones just like at Olduvai."* Assessing this remarkable evidence one can conclude that these early people were just as intelligent and advanced as the tribal people of Africa today. They were equally as intelligent, as you or I. In other words, this is not a description of a two million year old type of a nonhuman type of hominid that was in the early stages of evolving. This was a true Homo sapien (human being) that was just as skillful at making projectile points as are the African people living in that area of Tanzania today.

Richard Leakey is the son of the famous Louis Leakey and his wife Mary. They were the original ones to discover and to interpret the sediments at Olduvai. Mary Leakey was a world class archaeologist. Richard Leakey was quoting his mother's description of the various tools and sites of this Early Man. It is quite different to that of Glynn Isaac. To Richard Leakey, this Early Man was just as intelligent as the native Africans living in that part of Africa today. Does this description of Early Man at Olduvai appear to represent a non human type of hominid? Does this Man appear to be a 1.8 to 2.0+ million year old Man?

It is upon this type of reasoning of Glynn Isaac that secular Darwinian scientists want to extend the time when Early Man lived to many hundreds and thousands of years into the past. In this case, they are trying to extend the time to about 1.8+ million years into the past.

There are three archaeological sites at or near the base of Bed 1 where Mary Leakey[6] found the remains of an elephant, a deinothere (an extinct type of giant elephant) and another giant extinct elephant. They had become bogged down in wet, muddy, swampy ground. It was speculated that Early Man then came and butchered them for their meat as revealed by the presence of Acheulian (Oldowan) Stone Age tools. To the Darwinists, this is proof that Early Man lived contemporary with these extinct elephants. The evidence would indicate that these giant now extinct animals were all bogged down, destroyed and in some cases re-deposited by powerful flood waters. The artifacts were washed in at the same time. The question is this, where did the powerful pluvial or flood waters come from?

We would totally agree with the Darwinists that this Early Man lived contemporary with these extinct elephants and the entire above mentioned ape hominids. We believe that the powerful tsunami tidal waves relate to Stage 1 of Noah's Flood. This would explain why these giant, extinct forms of elephants became bogged down in a wet, muddy swampy ground. In fact Louis Leakey confirms that all the units 1, 11, 111, & 1V are all pluvial (Flood) deposits and they all contain Achuelian type of artifacts. Further work will determine whether beds 1, 11, 111, and 1V would relate to Stage 1 of Noah's Flood. The fact that only Paleolithic (Old Stone Age) tools are present would give credence to relating them to Stage 1 of Noah's Flood. See Appendix F.

The Leakey's also found a thin overlying **Bed V** that they believe is of Upper Pleistocene Age with an estimated age of about 17,000 years before the present. Above this are occasional evidences and artifacts of Recent Age that relate to the modern Masai tribal African people who inhabit this region today.

Olduvai is similar to other Early Man Sites?

The above description of the Olduvai section is very similar to the sections of Early Man throughout North and South America, Mongolia, China, Europe and Asia. This site can therefore be classified as a Type Section for identifying similar sites of Early Man throughout the Earth.

The artifacts in units 1 to 1V are all of Paleolithic Age at Olduvai Gorge. See Figures 19-1, 19-2 & 15-1. The artifacts of Mesolithic and Neolithic Man are absent at Olduvai. However, they are present nearby. It is interesting to note that Louis and Mary Leakey discovered several Mesolithic and Neolithic sites nearby. For instance, in 1935, Mary Leakey found a Mesolithic site a short distance to the north of Olduvai at the granite outcrop of Naibadab Hill. She found a scatter of artifacts and potsherds. Mary also described the famous Neolithic site in the Ngorongoro volcanic crater that is located a short distance to the east of Olduvai. See Figure 16-1. It is obvious that this Neolithic site was preserved because the Ngorongoro volcano was inactive during Noah's Flood. Mary located several burial mounds of Neolithic Age in East Africa. These burial mounds are similar to the Neolithic burial mounds found at the Stonehenge Site in England. I have had the privilege of exploring and analyzing one of the British Stonehenge Neolithic mounds which are amazingly similar to the mounds in Africa.

Dr. J.de Haeizeler of Belgium excavated Mesolithic / Neolithic sites at the SW corner of Albert Lake that is just NW of Lake Victoria. Other scientists have found Mesolithic/ Neolithic sites on the west shore of Lake Turkana. Mary Leakey found Neolithic sites at Hyrax Hill near Lake Nakurau in the Rift Valley. She found stone artifacts of pottery, stone tools made of obsidian, also remains of seventy different individuals, and much more. Mary Leakey also found the prehistoric drawings on the sides of cliffs at Kisese /Cheke that were similar to Late Paleolithic paintings that were found in caves in France.

These sites and many more have uncovered a wealth of information including the polished and refined stone tools, the many bones of Man and burial mounds that are similar to Mesolithic / Neolithic sites found in England at the famous Stonehenge sites. The distribution of similar Paleolithic, Mesolithic and Neolithic sites reveal the widespread presence of Early Man throughout all Europe, Asia and Africa.

The GIRA Interpretation of the Olduvai Gorge

An alternative Interpretation of the Olduvai Gorge Section is shown on the left side of Figure 16-2. Beds 1, 11, 111 and 1V are shown as pluvial or flood Deposits. They have all the characteristics of being deposited as pluvial deposits as Louis Leakey has verified time and time again. It is, herein, believed that they were deposited by Noah's Flood about 4500 years ago. Instead of these deposits being 1.8 to 2.5 Million years of age, they are in reality only about 4500 years old. They have all the earmarks of re-worked Pleistocene sediments, because they contain washed in Pleistocene animal and plant remains. These four units are post-Pleistocene and pre-Recent in Age. See Figure 19-1.

Under this post-Pleistocene scenario, all of Africa and all continents throughout the world have experienced a relatively thin covering of sediments that relate directly to Stages One, Two and Three of Noah's Flood. See Figure 26-2.

During Stage Three of Noah's Flood, the Earth experienced several additional, powerful tsunami waves that produced great erosion and carved large and small river channels throughout the Earth. These powerful tsunami waves would in most places have completely eroded and redeposited all or a partial amount of the first and second deposits into newly formed alluvial deposits generally within the newly formed river channels. Today, these large and small river channels have only a small little river or creek meandering through them. For greater details see APPENDIX F.

Under this scenario, the underlying granites at Olduvai Gorge are of Precambrian Age. The lower basalt flow may very well be related to the north/south trending deep seated East African Rift Valley that is located a very short distance to the east of the Olduvai Gorge. This great Rift Valley involved the separation of the Earth's crust allowing exteremely hot liquid basaltic extrusions to rise and to intrude adjacent country rock. According to the regional geological history of Africa, the north/south trending East African Rift Valley began to form during the Pleistocene Age. Thus, the question arises, what is the East African Rift Valley?

Richard Leakey[7] describes the East African Rift Valley as follows, *"Flying over the valley in an airplane one sees the sides rising, sometimes as much as 2000 meters (6000 feet) above its floor. In places the valley is 60 km (50 miles) wide. It is lined with huge cliffs and escarpments and dotted with volcanoes surrounded by vast lava flows."* then he goes on to say, *"Twenty million years ago this huge rift was only a shallow depression. As the depression deepened cracks began to form in the earth's surface creating the cliffs and escarpments we see today."* Thus we see that it is a pronounced north south trending failed arm of a triple junction structure that is further described in Chapter 29. See Figure 29-3.

The lacustrian (lake) sediments that underlie Units 1,11,111,1V relate to a previously existing lake bottom that geologists have mapped. These lake sediments would be of Anathermal and Altithermal ages which is of Late Upper Pleistocene Age. See Figures 19-1 & 19-2.

In other words, these so called Pleistocene Units 1, 11, 111 and 1V are not 1.8 to 2.5 million years of age as Darwinists claim. They are water lain Flood Deposits that relate directly to Noah's Flood and are about 4500+ years old. They are Post Pleistocene and Pre-Recent pluvial sediments as shown on Figure 16-2.

The only true late Pleistocene insitu sediments at Olduvai Gorge are the underlying lake sediments. These lake sediments lie upon PreCambrian granites of Archean Age. However, they are believed to be of Anathermal and Altithermal Age Figure 19-1.

It is upon these shoreline lake sediments and upon river channel sediments that flowed into this previous existing lake that Mary Leakey identified 18 archaeological sites of Early Man. They all pre-date beds 1,11,111, and 1V on Figure 16-2. All the artifacts that Mary found relate directly to Early

Man called the Paleolithic (Old Stone Age) Man who lived during the Altithermal Age. These were the Old Stone Age hunters and food gatherers who were forced to move into areas where there was a more plentiful supply of water and food. This resulted from the encroaching desert conditions which in turn, resulted from global climate changes during this age.

It was common for these early people to settle along the shoreline areas of lakes and rivers where food and water were more plentiful. It was along the west and east shore-lines of this ancient Olduvai Lake that Mary Leakey found 18 archaeological sites of Early Man.

Richard Leakey said that some camps appeared to be per-manent, others were temporary places. These Early Men and women were food gatherers and hunters. They lived off the land. According to geological evidences the climate in this portion of Africa was moist with abundant vegetation and animal and bird life at this particular time. These Early Men and women would have been Pre-Flood hunters and food gatherers. Once we look into the over all history of East Africa, we soon realize that there were neighboring people who had already entered into what is called the Mesolithic and the Neolithic stages of development.

Richard Leakey8 says, *"Most of the camp-sites were located by the water's edge, and at one of the biggest there are fossil remains of papyrus reed which shows it was swampy. The animal bones found at the camp-sites look as if they were broken deliberately; on some of them you can even see cut marks made by stone tools cutting away the meat. Antelope meat seems to have been their favorite food, with three toed horses and zebras a close second. The bones of fish and turtles also suggest they were making good use of the lake itself. When other sorts of food were scarce it looks as as though our ancestors were not above eating small birds and even chamelions."* This also verifies that the three toed horse lived during the Altithermal Age and became extinct at the time of Noah's Flood. The three toed horse is often falsely referred to as an evolutionary ancestor to our modern (one toed) horse. Now we know they were contemporary and were just different species.

Evidences of Noah's Flood at Olduvai

We can now conclude that the above beds 1, 11, 111 1V are all Flood Deposits. The Gira Interpretation would relate these four sedimentary units to four separate powerful tsunami tidal waves that swept across this portion of Africa during the time of Noah's Flood. They would relate directly to Stage One of Noah's Flood. See APPENDIX F.

Stage One: During Stage One of Noah's Flood, unit 1, would have been deposited by the first powerful tsunami tidal wave. Mary Leakey found the remains of a giant buffalo, a giant extinct elephant and a gigantic deinothere which is another large extinct type of elephant. The sediment is chacterized by clay, sand, gravel and boulders that are mixed with a definite layer of volcanic ash. This volcanic ash is near the base of bed 1. Volcanic ash is very diagnostic of Stage One of Noah's Flood in other areas of the Earth.

Potassium argon dating gave this ash a date of 1.8 million years. This date is highly suspect. Even recent volcanic eruptions can give anomalous readings. Regional geology is the best and most accurate method of dating volcanic activity that relates to Early or Modern Man. Geology has the distinct advantage of relating similar events of Early Man throughout the world to confirm its approximate age.

Beds 11, 111 and 1V would be the product of three additional, successive powerful tsunami tidal waves to sweep across this region of Africa. These beds would all relate to Stage One of Noah's Flood. The animal remains in Beds 11, 111 and 1V appear to be more reworked and and are more disarticulated. See Chapter 25 for a greater insight into Noah's Flood Disaster Scenario.

Stage 2: It would appear that Stage 2 deposits of Noah's Flood are absent at Olduvai. If present, Stage 2 deposits would consist of clay with minor mixtures of fine silt that may or may not be interspersed with varying quantities of volcanic ash.

Stage 3: The several powerful tsunami tidal waves that characterize Stage 3 of the Noah's Flood Disaster Scenario would be responsible for the erosion of the deep Olduvai Gorge that now exposes the entire 300 feet (91.4m) of sediments. Today only a small little river is present trickling through this gorge.

The large deposits of loess that are found in many parts of the Earth are believed to relate to Stage 3 of the Flood scenario. Whether the upper portions of Units 1V or V are rich in loess, I am not sure. See Appendix F.

Post Flood Deposits: The surface artifacts of the Masai tribal African people are of Medithermal (Recent) Age. These artifacts are associated with a thin layer of younger possibly wind blown sediments.

Louis Leakey's Memoirs

In later years Louis Leakey 9 published his Memoirs between the years 1932-1951. It is entitled, "L.S.B. LEAKEY BY THE EVIDENCE with a caption at the base, MEMOIRS 1932-1951. It gives an insight into the great work that he and his wife Mary accomplished during this interval of time together with their assistants. It must also be realized that Louis and Mary had arrived in this region during the 1930's. Their work in the Olduvai region and other nearby places continued into the 1960's and 70's.

The Google website relates that during the 2nd World War Louis performed intelligence work, but in between his war-time responsibilities he and Mary continued to do geological and archaeological work. In 1941, he was made an honorary curator of the Corydon Museum (later the Kenya National Museum), and in 1945 he accepted a poorly paid position as curator of the museum so that he could continue his paleontological and archaeological work in Kenya. In 1947, Louis organized the first Pan-African Congress of Prehistory, a successful event which helped restore his reputation and introduced many scientists to the large amount of important work that the Leakey's had accomplished since the Kanam / Kanjera debacle.

He and Mary continued to excavate and explore at many sites during the 1950s, especially at Olduvai Gorge in Tanganyika (now Tanzania). Although the discovery of an important Miocene ape fossil in 1948 had given them some attention and led to more funding, money constraints always limited the amount of work they could do. Nevertheless, they continued to make significant discoveries.

The Google website also describes some of their achievements as follows, "*In 1959, Mary found their first significant hominid fossil, a robust skull with huge teeth. It was found in deposits that also contained stone tools and Louis, typically, inflated its importance by claiming it was a human ancestor and calling it <u>Zinjanthropus boisei</u>. To everyone else, it seemed markedly unhuman, and most similar to robust australopithecines. Even so, it was a major find that gave them tremendous publicity. The National Geographic magazine printed the first of many articles about the Leakeys and their finds, and gave a large amount of funding which allowed the Leakeys to greatly increase the scope of their excavations at Olduvai. Within a few years they had found many more hominid fossils, including some that were far more plausible human ancestors and toolmakers than Zinj. In 1964, Louis, along with Phillip Tobias and John Napier, named the new species <u>Homo habilis</u>. Although originally controversial, habilis would eventually be widely accepted as a species.*"

In 1983, Mary retired from active fieldwork, moving to Nairobi from Olduvai Gorge, where she had lived for nearly 20 years. She died in 1996 at the age of eighty-three.

The Kanam/Kanjera Sites: Victoria Lake

In March of 1932, Louis Leakey together with his assistants went to the Kavirondo Gulf area of Lake Victoria in West Kenya. See map 16-1.

At the **Kanjera Site,**[10] he found fragments of four human (Homo Sapien) skulls which dated to Middle Pleistocene Age. On the basis of the fossils within this unit, Leakey realized that this unit related to the Middle Pleistocene beds at the Olduvai Gorge. These human fossils were older than any other human bone fragments found in East Africa to that point in time according to Leakey.

On Figure 16-1 is a map of Lake Victoria. The Kanjera Site is close by the Kanam Site. They are both located at a smaller adjoining lake to the west and are labelled as Number 1.

At the nearby **Kanam Site**[11] one of his African workers made an exciting discovery. He found a fossilized human jaw fragment which Louis Leakey dated to beds of Lower Pleistocene Age. This was based upon the fossil assemblage of extinct animals within this unit as they related to the so called Lower Pleistocene beds that were present at the Olduvai Gorge Section. This was indeed exciting because this Homo Sapien jaw was older than any other human bone fragment known to that point in time.

Shortly after Louis Leakey brought these remarkable findings to Britian. Leakey says, *"Back in Britain these sapien specimens were bitterly disputed."*[12] The big question arises, why were they disputed? The answer is clear because under the Darwinian Theory modern human beings (Homo sapiens) had not as yet evolved during the Lower and Middle Pleistocene Ages. See Figures 15-1 & 19-1 & 2. Thus, it was impossible for these human skull fragments to have been found in their original place according to the British scientists. They must have been buried later. Louis Leakey was convinced that these human specimens were found insitu.

Under our Flood scenario, the sediments at lake Victoria were an extension of the Post Pleistocene Flood Deposits at Olduvai Gorge. Of course, the British Darwininian Establishment could not conceive of Modern Man being preseent in 1.8+ million year old deposits. This precipitated a continuing dilemna for Louis Leakey.

In 1935, Louis Leakey published the above finds with careful drawings. They showed the Old Stone Aged Kanjera hominids unquestionably of the Homo sapiens type with long parallel sided skulls and with brain capacities greater than the average humans today. Louis Leakey[13] says, "*Since a larger brain capacity was considered an ultra modern characteristic, many of my colleagues who had previously supported my interpretation decided to join ranks with those who preferred to place the specimens into a suspense account.* **So began the long controversy that was to rage for the next 34 years.**" The large brain capacities were more analogous in size to the Cro-Magnon and the Neanderthal skulls that were found in Europe.

Louis Leakey[14] said, "*The Kanam jaw fragment proved to be controversal because it included the chin, together with a small part of each side. Most of the teeth were missing, few remained on the right side. Unfortunately, both the lower margin and the hind part of the jaw were missing. The jaw was heavily mineralized and had been dug out from the face of a small cliff in one of the Kanam West Gullies by a member of my African team whose name was Juma Gitau. The discovery was accidental, since he was engaged in digging out a molar tooth of an extinct type of elephant known as deinotherium. This had not been seen by any scientist while insitu, that is in its original position.*"

Leakey[15] says, "*As soon as he noticed that it was still embedded in the hard adhering rock, he summoned my student Donald Macinnes, who in turn called me to the spot. Juma had recognized that the specimen was human because one of the fragments of a hominid tooth was visible. I only partially cleaned away the rock in preparation for the Cambridge Conference, so geologists could see the nature of the matrix that it had been found.*"

Leakey[16] continues, "*At England, he proceded to clean the specimen with great care. He noticed a lump wih a strange bony growth, so he took it to Sir Frank Collier Royal College of Surgeons, then to the Dental Department who was a leading specialist in mandibular abnormalities. It was* concluded that it was an ossified sarcoma. This was pub-lished in the index of his book. **Because of the bony growth it was difficult to determine whether the Kanam jaw ever possessed a feature known as the simian shelf – a ledge of bone that unites the two halves of the lower jaw on the inside.** The general view of anthropologists at that time was bound to be present in all true primitive hominids. It was decided to cut a sec-tion with technicians at the Imperial College of Science in London. **This revealed two things: 1. Natures extent of the bony growth. 2. The fact that the specimen never possessed a simian shelf.**"

Then Louis Leakey[17] says, "*Oponents then claimed, firstly, that the Kanam Jaw did not belong to the Lower Pleistocene deposits and that I must have been mistaken in believing that the specimen had been found in situ. Secondly, they suggested as an explanation that the specimen of modern man had somehow found its way down a crack into the earlier deposit of Lower Pleistocene Age.*" [17]

Louis Leakey could not accept this view and continued to maintain that the specimen was a genuine insitu Lower Pleistocene fossil. Leakey says,[18] "**The Piltdown skull and jaw** at that time had such a strange acceptance by all but a few scientists." In other words the Kanam skull did not have a simian feature that was characterized by the Piltdown Man, thus to them, it had to be a modern man that had fallen through a crack. If it had a simian feature, then they could have related it to the Piltdown Man of England. The Piltdown Man was a big hoax. He is described at the end of Chapter 14.

In his memoirs Leakey writes, "**The rejection was a great disappointment and was certain that one day he would be vindicated in the eyes of the scientific world. The part played by prejudice was strong in the 30's and remains to this day.**" [19]

Was Homo Habilis at Olduvai a true Human?

Homo habilis is shown on contemporary evolutionary charts as being an ancestor to the Homo sapiens. The first discovery at Olduvai was made in 1960, when Jonathan Leakey found a jaw with two cranial fragments of a child within the upper half of Bed I at Olduvai Gorge. This was clearly not a gracile or a robust australopithecine. It was named "Johnny's Child" after its founder. A second discovery, "Cindy," was found in the middle portion of Bed II. She had a lower jaw and teeth, some bits of an upper jaw, and a patch of skull. A third discovery, "George," was made near the base of Bed II, comprised of teeth and very small skull fragments. A fourth discovery, "Twiggy," was represented by a crushed and flattened cranium and seven teeth. See Figure 16-3. Louis Leakey gave them all human names. Why would he do this?

Louis Leakey insisted that they belonged to a new genus, Homo. His assistant, Tobias, calculated their mean brain capacity at 642 cc. To Leakey, this placed these fossils into a higher category of a more advanced species, so he called them Homo Habilis.

Jonanson & Edey[20] say, "The question was, "How small a brain can we accept in a human?" Then he says, "Le Gros Clark later shrank the human brain minimum to 700 cc. Again this was an arbitrary figure: it measured the capacity of the smallest fossil human skull then in possession. But LeGros Clark, even as he set this standard, realized that a newer find might force him to lower it again."

Johanson & Edey[21] describes a conversation between Louis Leakey and other scientists, "So was Homo habilis human or an australopithecine? Definitely human, said Leakey, Napier and Tobias. His brain was a whole size larger than the australopithecine brain. His teeth were different, more human-like. His skull was a different shape, more humanlike. His skull was a different shape, again more humanlike. The rest of his skeleton was very much that of a modern man." Wow, is it possible that these were fragments of true human beings? They may have belonged to babies or smaller children.

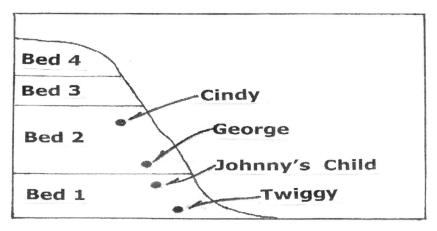

Figure16-3: The Olduvai Gorge showing how Twiggy, Johnny's Child, George and Cindy relate to beds 1 and 2. Darwinists refer to these unique finds as relating to Homo habilis. Could they be true human beings or Homo sapiens as Louis Leakey maintained? Prepared by Don Daae.

Johanson & Edey[22] report as to how the conversations evolved, "*Definitely not, said a great many critics. They charged that Tobias calculation of a brain of 642 cc was questionable, because of the poor quality of the samples. They criticized the conclusions about the teeth. They pointed out that not enough was known about the rest of habilis' skeleton to warrant any positive ideas about it at all.*"

Johanson & Edey[23] say, "*On the matter of teeth the Leakey team was in a stronger position. It had found human like traits in habilus' molars and premolars. They were narrower than those of Australopithecus when measured crossways from cheek to tongue, and longer from front to rear.*" Again the Darwinian critics said that those differences in shape were not significant. Thus, a big disagreement arose against the Leakey interpretation that homo habilis was more human than ape like. The case was argued back and forth, but could not be resolved without more evidence.

Another find was made in the region to the north, just east of Lake Turkana in 1972. One of the Kamoya's team, Bernard Ngener, found a skull believed to be two million years old. It was found in a lower unit that would relate to Unit 1 or 11 at Olduvai. Johanson & Edey[24] report, "*It was assembled from many fragments found up and down the slope, and assembled over a period of weeks. While almost complete, the face was lacking pieces. Its brain cavity was estimated at about 800 cc (with a 200 cc margin of error), much larger than the 450 to 550 cc of australopithecus.*" On this basis, it was classified as Homo habilis. In other words, it fit into the human category. Now Lake Turkana is in northern Kenya bordering the north south trending East African Rift Valley. The sediments at Olduvai are the same age to those at Lake Turkana. Lake Turkana area is designated by many anthropologists as the cradle of humankind. Lake Turkana is shown on Figure 16-1.

Lake Turkana was named Lake Rudolf in honor of Crown Prince Rudolf of Austria by Count Sámuel Teleki de Szék and his second-in-command Lieutenant Ludwig Ritter Von Höhnel, a Hungarian and an Austrian, 6 March 1888.

The Darwinian establishment has done every thing possible to prove that Homo habilis is not a human as Louis Leakey maintained. If they would dare to admit that Louis Leakey was right, then Homo habilis would have to be removed from Figure 15-2. This would indeed cause their Darwinian Theory to collapse. They are not willing to see their Theory collapse. Instead, they are willing to promote a false theory rather than admitting the truth?

Concluding remarks about Homo habilis.

On the basis of the Gira Interpretation, beds 1, 11, 111 & 1V at Olduvai Gorge are all a product of Stage One of Noah's Flood. These sediments are only about 4500 years old. This throws an entire new light upon how we interpret the Hominid fossils.

Leakey believed Homo habilis was a true human because his brain was a whole size larger than the australopithecine brain. His teeth were different, more human-like. His skull was a different shape, again more human-like. The rest of his skeleton was very much that of a modern man. This was hotly disputed by the Darwinian Establishment who could not conceive that a true human could be found in Middle and Lower Pleistocene sediments. To them this would mean modern Man was living between 1.0 ti 2.0+ million years ago. To believe that Homo habilis was human would indeed throw the entire Darwinian Theory of man into a nightmare. Thus, the Leakey's were forced to believe, by the Darwinian establishment, that these human like bones were only an evolving Hominid.

Louis Leakey was confronted at Olduvai Gorge by the same problem that he was confronted with at the Kanjera and the Kanam Sites. It was the 1.8 million year K-Arg date of the volcanic ash in Bed 1 at Olduvai that was the sole reason for believing that these were true Pleistocene sediments. We now know that Potassium/Argon dates can be very unreliable for younger geological ages.

The Darwinian Establishment could not conceive that a great portion of east, central and west Africa could have been covered with a thin covering of Flood Deposits that contained Pleistocene plant and dismembered animal life that was in reality Post Pleistocene and Pre-Recent in age. In other words, these sediments are a Flood Deposit originating from Stage One of Noah's Flood. See Figures 16-1, 16-2 & 19-1.

To the Darwinists, the Flood of Noah is not on their radar screen. To them, the concept of Noah's Flood is mere foolishness. After looking at all the evidences based upon the record of geology, archaeology and anthropology, we can now see who the foolish ones actually are.

Deep down Mary and Louis Leakey knew that the 18 archaeological sites of Man found by Mary Leakey below Beds 1, 11 111 & 1V were made by true Human Beings. The projectile points that are found within the above units are all of Paleolithic Age. They appear to have been washed in by pluvial (flood) waters. This explains why no actual sites of Early Man have been found within the Olduvai sedimentary units.

Thus, it was no surprise to them to see bone fragments of child and adult true human beings scattered throughout these fluvial sediments.

Truly, it is time for the scientific Community to vindicate Louis Leakey as he has requested.

The fact that the animal fossil remains at the Kanjera and the Kanam and Olduvai Sites are largely disarticulated gives strong credence to the possibility that they had been washed in by powerful tsunumi tidal waves that relate directly to Noah's Flood. In actual truth, these so called Pleistocene sediments were Flood Deposits that were only about 4,500 years old and not 1.8 million years.

How Widespread were these Flood Deposits?

In 1947 Louis and Mary Leakey[25] were invited to the Angold Diamond Mine site in Northern Angola by the Chief geologist Dr. J. Janmart. The purpose was to determine the age of the sediments containing diamonds on the basis of archaeology.

The whole region was blanketed by variable thicknesses of red wind blown sands. The sands made it difficult to locate buried gravel deposits. After looking at the geology, Louis and Mary examined the Paleolithic (Old Stone Age) artifacts that were distributed within the gravel deposits. They were similar to the finds at the Olduvai Type Section in Tanzania and in Kenya. It was concluded that the majority of gravels were of Middle Pleistocene Age and a few younger deposits dated as Upper Pleistocene. No sites of Man were found. All artifacts were deposited by swiftly flowing waters.

They also found that Pleistocene gravels and sands were overlying an older bed of gravels of Miocene Age. This was based upon the fossil remains. In other places there were evidences of eroded weathered, rusty gravels intermingled with Miocene gravels. These contained some acheulian artifacts and were labled as Lower Pleistocene.

It was found that in all the diamond mine sites that were of high economic worth, the diamonds were found in gravels that contained acheulian artifacts. These were labled as Middle Pleistocene gravels based upon the geology at Olduvai.

In Conclusion: The geological evidences confirms that the so-called Lower and Middle and Upper Pleistocene sediments with acheulian type artifacts should now be classified as flood deposits that relate directly to Noah's Flood. They were deposited by powerful tsunami type tidal waves that swept across eastern, central and western Africa. These sediments were in reality all related to Noah's Flood disaster scenario. All of these sediments acknowledges the enormity of the tsunami waves that were associated with Noah's Flood.

It is also concluded that Homo habilus should be removed from Figure 15-2. It has now been verified by the Leakey's and others that all the so called Homo habilus skull and body bones throughout Eastern and Central Africa relate directly to true human beings that are true Homo Sapiens.

Why Louis Leakey should be Vindicated

On the basis of our GIRA Interpretation, we can now demonstrate why Dr. Louis Leakey should be vindicated by the science community. If any person was a true anthropologist and scientist, it was Dr. Louis Leakey. He also had the strong support of his wife Mary who was an extra ordinary archaeologist. They both were true pioneers in East Africa for many years.

Louis and Mary Leakey did much to unravel the mysteries surrounding Early Man in East Africa. They were the pioneers who unravelled the mysteries of the Olduvai Gorge Type Section. They were very involved in identifying the so-called Lower, Middle and Upper Pleistocene units 1,11, 111 & 1V. See Figure 16-2.

Louis Leakey was able to identify and to relate the sedimentary units at the Kanam & Kanjera Sites in the Lake Victoria region with the Olduvai Gorge section. They were also able to relate the same units at the Angold Diamond Mine Site in Angola with the Olduvai Gorge Secton.

On the basis of the now extinct animal life and the Paleolithic artifacts of Early Man Louis Leakey was able to discern the relationship of these geological units from place to place. Only a qualified field person with great geological skills would be able to do this. The Leakey's were also able to demonstrate that these same so-called Pleistocene units were present throughout all of central Africa from Kenya through Tanzania to Angolia.

The big question arises why was there a conflict of interpretation between the armchair, British Scientists and himself. Louis Leakey[26] says, *"**So began the long controversy that was to rage for the next 34 years.**"*

Louis Leakey realized that these ultra secular Darwinists were willing to conceal the true scientific evidences inorder to propagate their false interpretation. If they would have admitted that these (Homo habilus) skull fragments were true human skull fragments, then their admittance would have blown away their Darwinian Theory of the slow gradual evolution of Early Man from an ape ancestry. These secular Darwinists could not allow this to happen in spite of true scientific evidence to the contrary. They rather chose to conceal the evidence and to believe "The Lie," rather than "The Truth."

It is now time for the science community to vindicate a truly great Anthropologist and a self learned geologist Dr. Louis Seymour Bazet Leakey (1903-1972). If they do not have the courage to do so, we certainly will.

References for Chapter 16

1. Carl O. Dunbar & Karl M. Waage, "Historical Geology," 1969, Third edition, John Wiley & Sons, Inc. New York / London / Sydney / Toronto. p.496.
2. Leakey Louis S.B., "By the Evidence Memoirs, 1932-1951, Harcourt Brace Jovanovich Inc., NY & London, 1974. P. 201.
3. Leakey Richard E. Human Origins, Dutton Publ., NY, 1982, p.34.
4. Ibid, p.35.
5. Ibid. p.36.
6. Ibid. p.36.
7. Ibid. p.15.
8. Ibid. p.36.
9. Leakey Louis S.B., "By the Evidence Memoirs, 1932-1951, Harcourt Brace Jovanovich Inc., NY & London, 1974. p. 15.
10. Ibid. p. 16-18. The Kanjera Site.
11. Ibid. The Kanam Site p. 19.
12. Ibid. P. 20,
13. Ibid. p. 20-21. The Kanjera Skulls.
14. Ibid. p.21. The Kanam Skull.
15. Ibid. p.21. The Kanam Skull.
16. Ibid. p.21 The Kanam Skull.
17. Ibid. p.21-22.
18. Ibid. p.21-22
19. Ibid. p. 22.
20. Donald Johanson & Maitland Edey, "LUCY The Beginnings of Humankind." Simon & Schuster, N.Y., 1981, p. 100.
21. Ibid. p.102
22. Ibid. p.102.
23. Ibid. p.102.
24. Ibid. p.102.
25. Leakey Louis, Ibid. P. 211-220
26. Leakey Louis, Ibid, p.21.

Chapter 17

Early Man In SE Asia, Australia & China

The Darwinian vision inspired Dubois, a young Dutch army physician, to go to the Island of Java in S.E. Asia. In 1891, Dubois discovered a hominid skull cap that was thick walled with enormous eye-brow ridges. Later he found two molar teeth and a premolar. A thigh bone was found 50 feet away from the head parts in the same strata. It was the thigh bone that looked like a modern human thigh bone that convinced Dubois that its owner must have walked upright. He thus related the thigh bone with the head parts and constructed the second missing link called "**The Trinil Man**." The skull portions were named Pithecanthropus 1. The brain capacity was estimated at 914 cc, intermediate between the anthropoid ape and man. The teeth were ape-like. Dubois later pointed out that the ratio of brain mass to the length of the femur in Pithecanthropus 1 is exactly what it would be if a gibbon's cranium would be enlarged to that of Pithecanthropus 1.

Gish[1] says, "*Dubois failed to reveal that he had also discovered at nearby Wadjak and at approximately the same level two human skulls (known as the Wadjak skulls) with a cranial capacity of about 1550-1650 cc, somewhat above the present human average. To have revealed this fact at that time would have rendered it difficult, if not impossible, for his Java Man to have been accepted as a "missing link." It was not until 1922, when a similar discovery was about to be announced, that Dubois announced the fact that he had possessed the Wadjak skulls for over thirty years. His failure to reveal this find to the scientific world at the same time he exhibited the Pithecanthropus specimens was deplorable since this constituted concealment of important evidence."*[1] See Figure 17-1.

What is truly amazing is the fact that the three modern human skulls, called the Wadjak skulls, were never described in the literature by Dubois or by the other famous European anthropologists. Were these skulls Neanderthal or Cro-Magnon? Was this concealment of evidence done with ulterior motives?

Two famous anthropologists from France, Frances Marcelin Boule and Vallois made the following conclusions after having analyzed Pithecanthropus I and the associated femur, *"If we possessed only the skull and the teeth, we should say that we are dealing with beings, if not identical with, at least closely allied to, the Anthropoids. If we had only the femora, we should declare we are dealing with Man."*[2]

Dubois became famous throughout the world as the discoverer of the ape man that was just in the process of evolving from an ape ancestry.

Anthropologist Mueller, Jr. believed that the teeth of Pithecanthropus I were those of a fossil orangutan, and anthropologist Hooton was inclined to agree. This view was supported by the evidence of other specimens. In Pithecanthropus II, most of the skull vault is present except for the right side of the frontal bone. It had a cranial capacity of only 750 cc, and is believed to be the skull of a female. The skull of Pithecanthropus B consists of the greater part of the right half of the mandible. The second premolar and all three molars are preserved in their sockets. The molars increase in size from the first to the third. This is not the case in modern man. In other words, these famous anthropologists realized that the three specimens of Pithecanthropus 1, 11 & B, were all from an arthropod ape species that became extinct. The question arises, when did they become extinct?

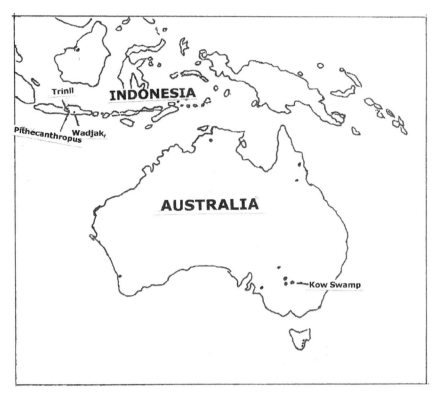

Figure 17-1: Map of S.E. Asia and Australia. It shows some of the locations for Early Man throughout the region that are mentioned in the text. There are several other locations mentioned at www. Kow Swamp Man Australia that are shown, but are not named on this map. Prepared by Don Daae.

Fifteen years before his death, Dubois came to the conclusion that Pithecanthropus 1 may have been a giant gibbon, and not an ancestor to man. In embarrassment, Dubois hid the bones of the Trinil Man below his bedroom floor. This decision may have been influenced by his final acknowledgement of the Wadjak skulls. **The Trinil Man was in reality Pithecanthropus who became known as the Java Man and later as Homo erectus.**

During the 1900's, this Pithecanthropus Ape Man has often been illustrated in school, college and university textbooks as proof of Darwinian evolution. We are told that **Pithecanthropus marks the beginning of the very**

earliest form of "Early Man" that was in the process of evolving from an ape ancestry. He had a receding chin and pronounced ridges above his eyes. This model revealed that his brain was just beginning to evolve to the place where he was able to make primitive stone tools. He was always pictured with simple tools in his hands.

Descriptions of the three Waljak Skulls are amazingly absent. It is now concluded that these Homo sapien skulls belonged to the Neanderthal Man. The famous French anthropologist Marcelin Boule who discovered the classical Neanderthal Man in France makes this observation. Marcelin Boule and Valois say, *"In its principal characters, the Trinil skull cap is really intermediate between that of an ape-like chimpanzee and that of a Man of really low status, such as the Neanderthal Man."*[3] At that time Boule considered the classical Neanderthal Man to be of very low status because of the incorrect way he had described the classical Neanderthal Man in France. For 47 years the classical Neanderthal Man of Europe was considered a true missing link between modern Homo sapiens and evolving hominids. See Figure 14-2.

The Java Site: A Typical Flood Deposit

In Conclusion, this surface layer of sands and gravels on the island of Java have been thoroughly examined since the time of Dubois. It contains the remains of extinct apes like Pitehcanthropus 1, 11, and B. It also contains the remains of several skull and bone fragments of Early Man. Scientists have never found any supporting evidence to verify that Pithecanthropus was a pre-Human. Neither have they found any sites of Early Man within these pluvial sediments.

This is another typical example of a regional pluvial or Flood Deposit. It contains the remains of now extinct animal life and also of Early Man. It was deposited by powerful tsunami tidal waves that swept through this region during Stage One and Three of Noah's worldwide Flood. Instead of being about two million years of age, this deposit is now believed on the basis of regional geology to be about 4,500 years old. See Figure 19-1.

I have had the privilege of viewing aerial photographs throughout S.E. Asia. They reveal that prior to modern times this entire region was above sea level. It is possible to see the submerged branching, dendritic drainage pattern of ancient rivers that flowed throughout this vast region of Indonesia prior to being submerged by the present level of the ocean. These submerged river channels are Post Flood. After Noah's Flood the level of the ocean remained about 180 feet (55m) below our present sea level for at least 500+ years. During this time Australia and Southeast Asia were connected by a land bridge.

Early Man in Australia

The Australian Man from the Kow Swamp area of Australia had pronounced brow ridges that are characteristic of the Neanderthal Man. This confirms that the Neanderthal Man was present in Java and in Australia. This does not negate the fact that the Cro-Magnon Man may also have been present in this region as well.

The Kow Swamp website says, "*Initial descriptions of the Kow Swamp crania focused on the morphology of the fronto-facial region and overall size and robusticity (Thorne and Macumber 1972). It was argued that they displayed a complex of archaic characteristics not seen in recent aboriginal crania. Archaic features were primarily concentrated on the mandibular body and on the cranium forward of the coronal suture. In particular a combination of receding frontal squama, massive supraorbital regions and a supraglabella fossae "preserving an almost unmodified eastern erectus form" (1972:319). These features indicated to the authors "the survival of Homo erectus features in Australia until as recently as 10,000 years ago" (1972: 316).*"[4] See www. Kow Swamp Man Australia.

It is interesting to note that anthropologists and archaeologists in Australia are still referring the Australian Early Man who has Neanderthal features as a form of Homo erectus.

Thorne and Macumber's original article was published by Nature 238:316 in 1972. They found the remains of over thirty individuals from the Kow Swamp site. They refer to these individuals as the Kow Swamp Man. The fact that they lived within the past 10,000 years on the basis of science, makes one realize that these individuals are true Neanderthal Homo sapiens.

According to Darwinian anthropologists, Homo erectus lived between 40,000 to 100,000+ years ago. Whereas, this Kow Swamp Man is only about 10,000 years old. See Figure 15-2. The Kow Swamp Man is just as modern as all the Neanderthal men that were present throughout Europe, Asia, North Africa as well as in North and South America prior to Noah's Flood.

Early Man in China: the Peking Man

In 1921, two molar teeth were recovered from a pocket of bone remains at a cave site near the village of Choukoutien, China. This site was located about 25 miles southeast of Peking, now Beijing. On the basis of a third tooth in 1927, together with so called primitive stone tools, they were named Sinanthropus pekinensis by an American anthropologist Davidson Black, establishing evidence for the existence of an ancient hominid known as "The Peking Man."

This discovery of the Peking Man was heralded throughout the world by the news media as verification of the Darwinian evolution of Man. This was the third proof from the fossil record that Early Man was in the process of evolving from an ape ancestry.

In 1928, Dr. W. C. Pei, palaeontologist in charge of excavations, found fragments of crania, two pieces of lower jaw, and numerous teeth. In 1929 he found a well-preserved skull cap resembling the Pithecanthropus skulls in Java. Eventually 30 skull caps, 11 lower jaws, and about 147 teeth were found. These fossil finds were derived from the so called "Lower Cave Level" after fragments of ten other specimens all identified as the remains of modern Man were found in the "Upper Cave Level".[5]

Among the remnants in the Lower Cave level, the Sinanthropus Skull III was ascribed by Black to an adolescent and by Weidenrich to a child 8 or 9 years of age. Boule and Vallois[6] p.192 *say that viewed from the top and side, it bears a striking resemblance to Pithecanthropus, and that Skull II in its general contour was more like that of Pithecanthropus. They concluded that the structure of Sinanthropus skull is still very ape-like in its totality. The brain capacity for the first skulls discovered was about 900 cc, and up to 1200 cc for two skulls found in 1936. The features of the lower jaws were ape-like, including the teeth: except for the shape of the dental arcade which was parabolic, as in man, rather than U-shaped, as in apes".* This led Boule and Vallois to conclude that the jaw bones and teeth of Sinanthropus denote a large primate more closely allied to man than any other known great ape, although the differences are less than those within a single species (namely, Neanderthal Man). They insisted that the fossils be included in a single genus, and since Pithecanthropus enjoys priority, they re-named the Choukoutien creature Pithecanthropus pekinensis. **As a result, anthropologists have reclassified Pithecanthropus and Sinanthropus in a single genus and species called Homo erectus.** The purpose was to give these hominids a more human connotation. Now after viewing Figure 15-2, can a person honestly believe that Homo erectus is the closest ancestor to Modern Man? The answer is a definite no.

Gish points out a word of caution and says, "*Today we have no skulls or fragments of Sinanthropus (except two teeth and a few fragments that have been recovered during the past two decades), no reconstructions which include actual fossil material. All we have available are the models fashioned by Weidenreich. How reliable are these models? Are they accurate casts of the originals, or do they reflect what Weidenreich thought they should look like? Why do his models differ so greatly from the earlier descriptions? I consider these models of Weidenreich to be totally inadmissible as evidence related to the taxonomic affinities of Sinanthropus. If such a case were ever brought to court, there would not be the slightest doubt that such hearsay evidence would be ruled inadmissible."*[7]

Weidenreich believed the hunter to be Sinanthropus himself, whereas French anthropologists Boule and Vallois disagree and say, *"To this hypothesis, other writers preferred the following, which seemed to them more in conformity with our whole body of knowledge: the hunter was true Man, whose stone industry has been found and who preyed upon Sinanthropus. Later on they say: We may therefore ask ourselves whether it is not overbold to consider Sinanthropus the monarch of Choukoutien, when he appears in the deposit only in the guise of a mere hunter's prey on a par with the animals by which he is accompanied."*[8]

It becomes obvious that Sinanthropus was the victim of hunters and the hunters were the true Men that occupied the Upper Cave level. Black and Weidenreich used to always maintain Sinanthropus was the hunter and that the stone tools were made by Sinanthropus. According to Boule the tools were not primitive. The gravers and scrapers and other tools were of fine workmanship and had many features not found in France until the Upper Palaeolithic. These were Mousterian tools that would relate to the Neanderthal Man of Europe who we now know was contemporary with the Cro-Magnon Man.

In both the Upper and Lower Cave levels, one finds evidences of man lighting fires. The stones have a layer of soot on one side and enormous heaps of ashes were found at both levels. The fact that the fossil remains of ten human individuals of modern type were found at the upper level gives credence to the belief that true Man was the hunter and the ape-like creature Sinanthropus was the hunted. Due to the quarrying of rocks for building purposes, these upper and lower levels no longer exist.

Concluding Remarks

We can thus, conclude that the sediments in Java are Flood Deposits of about 4,500 years before the present. These sediments contain the bone remains of Early Man and animal life that lived prior to Noah's Flood. This verifies that the Neanderthal Man and the Cro-Magnon Man were both living to the end of the Neolithic Age. The only difference is this: The Neanderthal Man became extinct at the time of Noah's Flood, whereas the Cro-Magnon Man has survived to the present day via Noah and his family. See Figures 15-1 and 19-1.

We can also conclude that Homo erectus is a name derived by French and Chinese anthropologists during the 1930s when they realized that the Java Pithecanthropus and the Chinese Sinanthropus were of the same ape species. The big question is this: during 2009, how comfortable would you be with modern day anthropologists who are trying to tell the world that Homo erectus is modern man's closest relative as shown on Figure 15-2. The human like feet and body of Homo erectus can now be permanently replaced by ape like feet and body. **We can now confidently remove Homo erectus from Figure 15-2**

References for Chapter 17

1. Duane T. Gish Ph.D., "Evolution: The Challenge of the Fossil record." P. 181, Creation-Life #Publishers, Master Books Division, El Cajon, CA.
2. Marcellin Boule & H. V. Vallois, Fossil Men, Dryden press, New York, 1957, p.123. (was #8)
3. Ibid, p. 167.
4. See www. Kow Swamp Man Australia. Their original paper was published in Nature 238:316, 1972.
5. Daae H. Donald, "Bridging the Gap: The First 5 Days." Genesis International Research Publishers, pp. 165-168, 1989.
6. Boule & Vallois Ibid, p. 192.
7. Gish, p.195. was#12.
8. Boule & Valois, p. 196.

Chapter 18

Early Man in Mongolia

A reconnaissance geological report by geologists Charles Berkey from Columbia University and Frederick Morris of the American Museum of Natural History relate interesting surface observations in their 1927 report, "Geology of Mongolia."[1] A map of this region is shown on Figure 18-1.

Berkey and Morris[1] allude to the discoveries of Early Man in Java, China and Mongolia as follows, "*They are represented by a Palaeolithic culture discovered in the Ordos by the distinguished explorers Pere Emil Licent (1925) and Pere Teilhard de Chardin (1924) and one Palaeolithic and two Neolithic stages (sites) found in the Gobi by our own Expedition. Licent and Teilhard de Chardin found primitive stone implements, not unlike those of* **the Neanderthal man of Europe, and bones of extinct animals in gravels which were laid down before vast deposits of "loess"** *were formed in northern China.*" They go on to say,[2] "*Of the three stages found by the Third Asiatic Expedition, the palaeoliths are apparently much like those of the Mousterian culture in Europe. ---- all we dare say is that several stone-age civilizations lived in Mongolia long ago, and it is reasonable to think that they represent many successive invasions of the land by tribes which brought much of their culture with them.*"[2]

It is interesting to note that the Palaeolithic tools of the Neanderthal Man of Europe are characterized as Mousterian stone tools. These same Mousterian tools have also been found in Mongolia, China, northern Africa, the Middle East, and throughout North and South America. This verifies the fact that Early Man occupied almost all regions on this Earth prior to Noah's Flood.

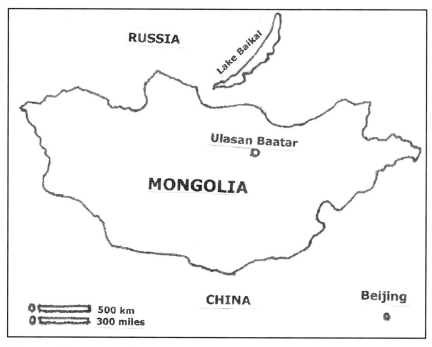

Figure 18-1: Map of Mongolia with Russia to the north and China to the south. The capital city is Ulasan Baatar.

Berkey and Morris[2] confirm that these primitive stone implements were similar to those used by the **Neanderthal Man** of Europe and that they were found with the bones of **extinct Pleistocene animals** in gravels that were laid down before the vast deposits of "loess." In other words, the Neanderthal Man lived in this area of Mongolia. Their tools were mixed with the bones of the pre-historic animals in gravels that would relate to Stage One of the Noah's Flood.

Loess deposits are often found associated with Stage 3 of Noah's Flood. This is another clue that these Neolithic sites are Pre-Flood. These loess deposits are associated with the latter stages of Noah's Flood deposits world wide.

According to my Webster's College Dictionary,[3] loess is a loamy, usually yellowish and calcareous deposit formed by wind. It is common in the Mississippi Valley and in certain northern parts of USA and in Europe and Asia.

Berkey and Morris[4] relate interesting surface observations in their 1927 report, Geology of Mongolia. As they journeyed through Mongolia they noted recent changes in climate. They write, *"We find many evidences of climatic changes: in the building and partial destruction of several alluvial fans along the Altai front; in the ancient beaches at Tsagan Nor; in the re-dissection of the gently sloping walls of hollows; in* ***the renewed dissection of smooth surfaces which formerly supported a richer carpet of vegetation than at present;*** *in renewed dissection of the Gobi erosion plane; in the carving of broad valleys by streams which have vanished and whose channels are now filled with wind blown sand; in the failure of rivers to reach their terminal lakes; in the shrinking of the meander-curves of rivers, as shown by the large abandoned meandering scarps; in the drying of salt lakes to form salt pans; in old drawings cut upon rocks by a vanished race, picturing animals that lived in woodlands, though the region is now bare of trees."* The artwork portrays the work of Pre-Flood Man who lived during the time when the land was covered with luxuriant vegetation during earlier Pre-Flood days. This quotation by Berkey and Morris is another description of erosional dissection of the landscape caused by powerful tsunami tidal waves resulting from Stages One, and Three of Noah's Flood. See Figures 25-1 & 25-2.

The surface features that are described by Berkey & Morris in Mongolia are similar to features of this particular age throughout Europe, Asia, Africa, America and in all parts of the world.

According to the science of geology, the Pleistocene Age came to an abrupt termination about 4,500 years ago by a Flood of worldwide dimensions.

References for Chapter 18

1. Charles P. Berkey & Frederick K. Morris, "Geology of Mongolia;" A Reconnaissance Report based on the Investigations of the Years 1922-23 in Natural History of Central Asia Vol.11, 1927; The American Museum of Natural History, New York,1927. p.386.
2. Burkey & Morris. p.13.
3. Webster's College Dictionary, 1995, publ. in New York, Toronto, London, Sydney, Aukland.
4. Burkey & Morris. p.386.

Chapter 19

Early Man in America

A mystery surrounds the Early Man who occupied North & South America long ago. Where did he come from? What did he look like? What kind of tools did he have? Was he a Stone Age man? Was he intelligent? What happened to him?

This Early Man lived in America coincident with the now extinct prehistoric animals such as the mastodon, the woolly mammoth, the horse, the lion, the saber tooth tiger, the camel, a pig six feet tall, and giant sloths the size of an elephant. The list could go on and on. Many of these extinct animals were here for many thousands of years. Some were here for more than two million years into the past. What happened to all of these now extinct animals? When Christopher Columbus discovered America in the year 1492, there weren't any horses or any of these pre-historic animals nor was Early Man present. Why?

Archaeologists have classified this Early Man on the basis of their tools, stone hammers and projectile points as having lived in America between 6,000 to about 12,000 years before the present. Some extend this date to over 40,000 years. What happened to this Early Man, who archaeologists often refer to as Paleo-Indian? Did he also become extinct? This is the big mystery!

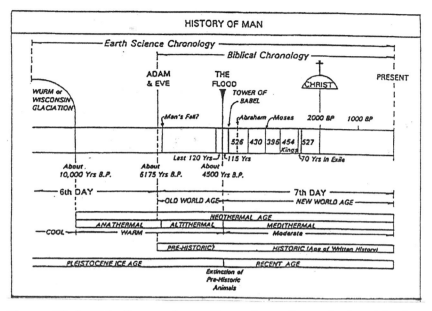

Figure 19-1: This figure shows the astounding relationship that exists between the record of geology and the record of the Bible over the past 10,000 years. Prepared by Don Daae.

The North & South American Man

Archaeologists are agreed that Early Man did not originate in America. He arrived here from Asia. The most likely time that Early Man arrived was during a warmer interglacial ice age.

The Pleistocene Ice Age can be divided into five glacial advances and four warmer interglacial ages going back in time to about 2.5 million years (Figure 19-2). I agree with the geological sciences that the Pleistocene Age began about 2.5 million years ago. However, I disagree with anthropologists and archaeologists who vainly attempt to relate Early Man to the various stages of the Ice Age beyond 10,000 years into the past.

The Secular Interpretation classifies Early Man into three categories: the Palaeolithic (Old Stone Age), the Mesolithic (Middle Stone Age) and the Neolithic (New Stone Age). The secular view believes Early Man first appeared in Africa about 2+ million years ago. Our GIRA Interpretation relates Early Man to the Post Wisconsin Age which in turn relates to the Anathermal and the Altithermal Ages. Modern Man is related to the Recent Age which also equates to the Medithermal Age. The Flood Age separates the Altithermal and Medithermal Ages. See Figure 19-2.

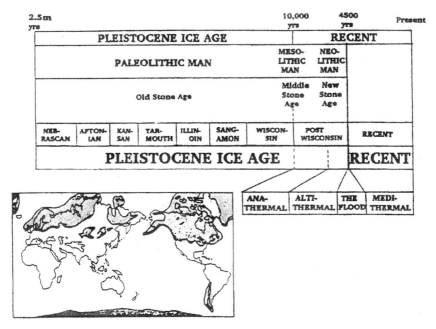

Figure 19-2: Illustrates the Pleistocene Ice Age and how Early Man in America and throughout the world relate to the Ice Age. A map shows the areas of the Earth covered by ice during maximum glacial advance. Prepared by Don Daae.

Archaeologists and anthropologists in America have been constantly attempting to relate Early Man to different earlier interglacial and glacial periods. They have failed to find real evidence to relate Early Man to an earlier interglacial ice age, other than the Post Wisconsin Age. See Figure 19-2.

The most likely time that Early Man migrated from Asia through Mongolia to Alaska was somewhere between 4,500 and 10,000 years before the present. This manuscript maintains that Early Man arrived in America during the upper to mid part of the Altithermal Age. See Figure 19-1.

According to Pleistocene glaciologist Antevs[1] the climate throughout the world began to get progressively warmer about 10,000 years ago. An ice corridor began to form in a northwest direction through west central Alberta extending northward into the Yukon Territories and westward through the central part of Alaska. This ice corridor provided a pathway for Asian Man from Mongolia to enter North America. See map on Figure 19-3.

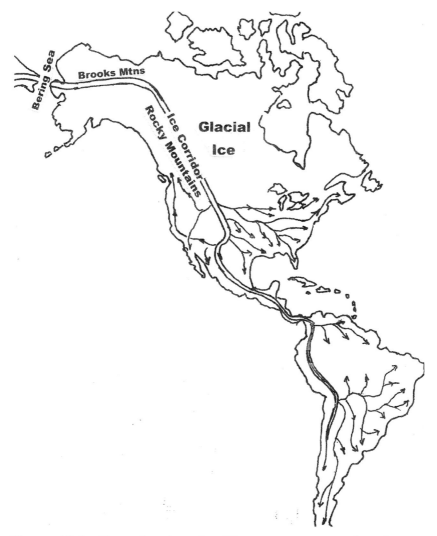

Figure 19-3: Map showing the Migratory routes of Early Man from Asia to America. This Figure was prepared and revised by Don Daae after Sauer[2] 1944 & MacGowan & Hester[3] 1962.

It was along this ice corridor that archaeologists have identified the artifacts of Early Man. They are generally always inter mixed with the bones of the woolly mammoth, mastodon, horse, camel, saber toothed tiger and other extinct mammals within rubble zones along this ice corridor. The early Klondike miners who were digging for gold along this corridor encountered many of these artifacts and animal remains in the rubble muck. In Alberta, Archaeologists have found the artifacts of Early Man in certain areas along this Ice Corridor, especially in the more southerly portions of the province.

During the time when Early Man was in North & South America great thicknesses of continental ice several thousands of feet thick still covered all of Canada to the east of the ice corridor & throughout the Mountain areas of the Rocky Mountains and the interior mountains to the west.

Due to the increasing temperatures during the Anathermal and the Altithermal ages the ice kept continually melting allowing Early Man to penetrate certain local areas that were formerly covered by ice. MacGowan & Hester [4] have this to say, "*There can be no question that some parts of this route were used by early man – and extinct mammals, too. His ancient spear points have been found in the muck beds of Fairbanks mingled with the fossilized bones of elephant, bison, camel, horse, and an extinct jaguar once called the Alaskan lion.*"

The above map of North and South America reveals that Early Man only inhabited the areas to the south of the major Pleistocene Ice sheet. It becomes obvious that during the lower half of the Altithermal Age the population of Early Man increased dramatically. Figure 19-3 reveals that by the latter part of the Altithermal Age there were advanced settlements throughout Southern USA, Mexico, Central America and South America. We will analyze some of these civilizations in greater detail in Chapter 22.

Projectile Point Classification of Early Man in the America's

The archaeological classification of Early Man in Alberta and North & South America is shown in Figure 19-4. According to a booklet, "The Record In Stone" by J. T. Humphreys [5] (1967), the dates of Early Man are shown to begin about 11,000 years BC and to terminate about 6,000 years BC. Then, there is a 3000 year break separating Early Man from the North American Indian. What is the reason for this break?

In 1987, a revision of this booklet by J.T Humphreys and Michael C. Wilson [6] show a 1400 year separation between the Early-Man and the North & South American Indian. However, this later edition has also extended the Clovis Point back to 12,000 years BC which is 14,000 years before the present.

Figure 19-4 displays the names of the various projectile points of Early Man in Alberta and North America to be between 6000 to 11,000 years BC. This equates to 8,000 to 13,000 years BP (before the present). The names of the North American Indian projectile points are found ranging in age from the present to about 3000 years BC which equates to 5,000 years BP.

Figure 19-4 reveals the sharp break that exists between the Indian cultures and the cultures of Early Man who occupied North and South America beyond 6000 BC. Who was this Early Man? We all know what the American Indian looked like, but what did this Early Man look like?

Some archaeologists and anthropologists do not want to acknowledge the pronounced break that separates these two cultures. They would have us believe that due to climate change the prehistoric animals died out and the few remaining humans continued the Indian Culture.

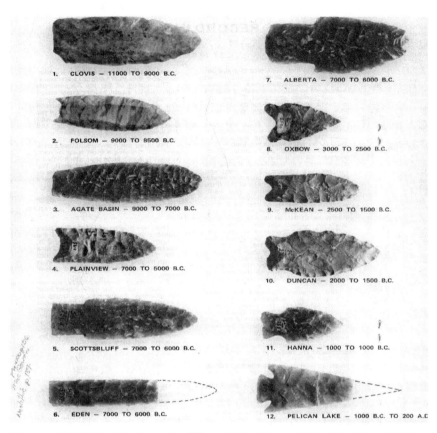

1. CLOVIS — 11000 TO 9000 B.C.
2. FOLSOM — 9000 TO 8500 B.C.
3. AGATE BASIN — 9000 TO 7000 B.C.
4. PLAINVIEW — 7000 TO 5000 B.C.
5. SCOTTSBLUFF — 7000 TO 6000 B.C.
6. EDEN — 7000 TO 6000 B.C.
7. ALBERTA — 7000 TO 6000 B.C.
8. OXBOW — 3000 TO 2500 B.C.
9. McKEAN — 2500 TO 1500 B.C.
10. DUNCAN — 2000 TO 1500 B.C.
11. HANNA — 1000 TO 1000 B.C.
12. PELICAN LAKE — 1000 B.C. TO 200 A.D

Figure 19-4: Typical projectile points from Alberta. Permission by J.T. Humphries."[7]. See Footnote at end of Chapter.

What did this Early Man in America look like?

Secular Darwinian anthropologists and archaeologists maintain that Early Man originated in Africa. He evolved from certain African apes called hominids, such as Homo habilus and Homo erectus, who in turn evolved from Australopithecus afarensis. As evolution progressed, this evolving hominid became known as a true human being referred to as Homo sapiens. They also maintain that there were two types of Homo sapiens that they refer to as the Neanderthal and the Cro-Magnon men.

They maintain that Early Man's intelligence slowly evolved over many hundreds of thousands of years reaching its optimum today. This is the reason why Early Man could only manufacture very primitive tools and projectile points in the beginning. This is also the reason why archaeologists and anthropologists want to extend the age of Early Man to earlier stages of the Pleistocene Ice Age. See Figure 15-1.

Two Basic Types of Early Man

Anthropologists have determined that throughout the world there were two basic types of true human beings called Homo sapiens that relate to the Great Stone Age Period. They are the Cro-Magnon and the Neanderthal Man.

The Cro-Magnon Man

The Cro-Magnon Man had a pronounced chin, a well domed, narrow Nordic head. He often had a brain capacity greater than 1600 cc. The average brain capacity of Man today is about 1350cc to 1500cc. He is often referred to as a superior kind of man. He was considered a remarkable person in that he painted on the walls of his cave and carved on pieces of bone and elephant ivory pictures of bison, mammoths and boars. His tools are equated with the more superior European Aurignacian and Magdalenian and Solutrean cultures. See figure 14-2.

It is interesting to note that the Cro-Magnon man was not present in North and South America.

The Neanderthal Man

The Neanderthal Man had a receding chin, a low forehead, heavy brow ridges and a long narrow skull from plan view. It is quite surprising that the famous Classical Neanderthal Man, that at one time posed as a missing link for 47 years, had a brain capacity greater than 1600 cu. cm.

The Neanderthal type Man was present in Mongolia, China and Australia. He also co-mingled as a minority to the Cro-Magnon Man in western Asia, Europe (Germany, France,

Israel), also in parts of Northern Africa. His stone tools are equated with the Mousterian culture. He was at one time regarded as being inferior and to have preceded the Cro-Magnon Man. This view is no longer valid.

Both the Cro-Magnon and the Neanderthal man were con-temporary. They are both always associated with the now extinct pre-historic animals. Their physical differences ap-pear to be racial. However only the Neanderthal Man was present in North and South America.

The Neanderthal man mysteriously disappeared throughout the world at the end of the Great Stone Age or more spe-cifically at the end of the age of polished stone which is the Neolithic Age. This, in turn, marks the end of the Altithermal Age and the Pleistocene Age, whereas the Cro-Magnon man has survived to the present. What happened to the Neanderthal man? See Figures 19-1 and 19-2.

The Early Man in North & South America

Anthropologists have found numerous skeletons of these Early Men in North and South America. It is interesting to note that all of these finds have physical characteristics that relate to the Neanderthal Man of Europe, Asia and Africa. They have a receding chin, pronounced ridges above their eyes. From plan view, their skulls were long and narrow. They are invariably found in association with the extinct pre-historic animals. Many of these sites are related to or underlie severe pluvial sedimentary flood deposits.

The Type Section for Early Man in America

The Santa Lagoa Man is considered the Type Section for describing Early Man in America. All later discoveries of Early Man in North and South America are related to this important discovery. He had Neanderthal characteristics.

In 1835, Danish naturalist Lund (130) left Europe for America. For some unknown reason, he began to explore caves in Brazil. MacCowan & Hester[9] say, *"He examined over*

200 caves, and in six of them he found human remains. For eight or nine years, he was dubious about his finds, but he was convinced in 1844 when he found human bones and the skulls of men mingled with the bones of extinct mammals all equally fossilized." The extinct animal remains made him aware of the antiquity of his findings. The fact that they were equally fossilized made him realize that they were of the same age. However, it was the peculiar characteristics of the human skulls that made Lund realize that this was indeed a different type of man.

MacGowan & Hester[10] say, *"These skulls were long and narrow, while those of most Indians and other Mongoloid peoples are relatively short and broad."* They go on to say, *"**The Lagoa Santa** (Man) had very heavy brow ridges; their skulls were straight sided and had keeled vaults. The total effect was archaic. This was to prove a basic type to which all the later finds of the bones of early man could be related."* In other words, the **Santa Lagoa Man** became the model or **Type Section** for relating all future findings of Early Man throughout North and South America. **He had the characteristics of the Neanderthal Man.**

The Confins Man:

In 1933, a neighboring cave in Brazil was excavated by the Brazilian Academy of Science of Minas Gerais. It was here that they discovered the **Confins Man**. He had all the basic characteristics of the Lagoa Santa Man.

MacGowan & Hester [11] describes the Confins Man as follows, *"They found the molars of a young mastodon under a few feet of dirt inside the entrance. Deeper down and further back, they discovered fossils of the horse, giant sloth, mastodon, and other extinct mammals. Finally they came on a nearly complete human skeleton. They had cut through a layer of stalagmitic material and more than six feet of alluvial soil to reach the bones of the Confins man, and so they knew that he had died during or just before a period of great moisture. They write of this as the post Pleistocene, or Pluvial. Post-Pleistocene means, of course, Postglacial, and Pluvial means a time of much rain."* Is it possible that this time of pluvials or great flooding could relate to Noah's Flood? Were these extinct animals washed into this cave?

It is interesting to note that the termination of the Confins Man and all the pre-historic animals by pluvial or flood waters was Post Pleistocene. This confirms Figures 19-1 and 19-2 that it was Noah's Flood that terminated the post Wisconsin, the Neolihic and the Atithermal ages. This momentous event gives an insight into the Flood Age. At this time in history, all the so called pre-historic animals such as the mastodon, woolly mammoth, horse, camel, giant sloths, etc. and pre-Flood Man mysteriously perished throughout all the world.

The Punin Man

Since 1923, additional skulls were found in Equador and Chile in association with the extinct horse, camel, ground sloth and mastodon. The man found in Ecuador is called the **Punin Man**. [12] He was found with the fossils of the extinct horse, camel and mastodon. He also all had the same basic Neanderthal facial characteristics of the Lagoa Santa Man.

North American Skulls and Bones

The Sandia Man

A significant discovery was made in 1936 by Frank C. Hibben in New Mexico at the Sandia Cave. In his dig he found the remains of the Pueblo Indian near the surface. In the underlying sediments he found a layer of stalagmite travertine one half to six inches thick that was deposited during a period of great moisture. Sealed below, he found classic folsom points, scrapers and the evidence of extinct animals. As he dug deeper, he found another sterile seal. It was two inches to two feet in thickness. It was of yellow ochre which is a substance induced by fir and spruce under moist conditions. MacGowan and Hester [13] quote Kirk Brown as saying, *"Fir and spruce require more cold and more moisture than the neighborhood of Sandia provides at present—which argues that the ochre was manufactured during the last pulsation of the fourth and final glaciations more than 11,000 years ago*. MacGowan & Hester [13] say, *"The two periods of moisture indicate that the cave was inhabited by Folsom man toward the end of the last glaciations, or 9,000 to 11,000 years ago, and by the Sandia man still earlier. Unless, of course, you wish to believe, as some do, that both pluvial periods were Postglacial."* It is interesting to note that the end of the Postglacial equates to the end of the Altithermal Age. Noah's Flood would then be responsible for bringing this age to a dramatic close. See Figures 19-1 & 19-2.

MacGowan & Hester [14] report, *"Since the discovery of the human bones in glacial gravels near Trenton, New Jersey, three skeletons of some importance and a number of skulls that resemble those of the Lagoa Santa and Punin have been found in the United states."* In other words the Neanderthal man was also in the United States.

Between 1931 and 1935, three different finds of skulls and skeletons were found in the Minnesota region during the digging of gravels or road building. They are the Minnesota Man which was in reality a girl, the Brown's Valley Man with a solutrian type of spear point, and the Saulk Valley Skull. [15]

The Melbourne Man:

In Florida during 1925, the famous Melbourne Skull was found. The evidence revealed that a mammoth or mastodon stepped on the skull of this man and left it flat like a pancake. Experts reconstructed this skull. MacGowan & Hester [16] say, *"The Melbourne man had a long, narrow, flat-sided head, the low forehead, and the strong brow ridges typical of most craniums found under conditions that suggest antiquity."* He also was a Neanderthal Man.

Other Early Men

MacGowan & Hester [17] refer to findings of Early Man at Lansing, Kansas where the skull was buried under 20 feet of Loess; a number of skulls found below hardpan in California;

a number of skulls discovered in Texas, Lower California, California coastal area; and the Sacremento Valley. They all bear evidence of being Early Man. The significance of loess is that it is characteristic of deposits that relate to the 3rd Stage of Noah's Flood. See Appendix E.

MacGowan & Hester[18] also refer to various finding of Early Man in Mexico associated with extinct mammals.

The Neanderthal Man in America Confirmed

Archaeology has now confirmed that the Early Man in North & South America was directly related to the Neanderthal Man of the Old World. How did the Neanderthal Man get to America? The question arises: Who was the Neanderthal Man? Why did he become extinct and when? Did The Neanderthal Man become extinct at the same time as the great mammals? Is it possible to date the time when Man & the Great Mammals became extinct? The answer is yes.

Both the Cro-Magnon and the Neanderthal Man were present in the Old World of Europe, Africa, and Asia. However, the Neanderthal Man mysteriously became extinct in the Old World at the end of the Neolithic Age, but the Cro-Magnon man has continued to the present. How can this mystery be explained?

Who Were the Neanderthal & the Cro-Magnon Men?

Anthropologists and Archaeologists are able to determine the physical features of the Neanderthal and the Cro-Magnon men. The big question remains who were they? Where did they come from? What are their roots?

The Great Mystery

A great mystery surrounds the extinction of the Great Mammals & the Neanderthal Man throughout the world. Various attempts have been made by scientists to solve the mystery surrounding the extinction of the great mammals and of the Neanderthal Man. All of these attempted theories fail to adequately explain how and when they vanished. It was not only the large, clumsy and gregarious mammals that became extinct; also varieties of toads, mollusks, rabbits, the dire wolf, three types of antelope, the short faced bear, the saber-toothed tiger, the giant beaver, a small horse, and a number of birds and the list could go on and on.

The big question arises, where did the modern, now living new species come from, such as the modern antelope, bison, musk ox and the list could go on and on? These are the mammals that suddenly replaced the extinct mammals. Where did the modern North & South American Indian come from? They had distinctly different racial characteristics from the Neanderthal man. The unanswered questions are astounding.

MacGowan & Hester[19] describe the puzzling great numbers of extinct mammals present in the deep Alaska muck beds along the Ice Corridor. They quote Frank Hibbens who says, *"Their numbers are appalling. They lie frozen in tangled masses, interspersed with uprooted trees. They seem to have been torn apart and dismembered and then consolidated under catastrophic conditions. Eden and Plainview spear points and perhaps one Clovis have been found in these chill beds. Skin, ligament, hair, flesh, can still be seen."* See figure 19-4 in order to identify the Pre-Flood spear points.

A Challenge Presented

MacGowan & Hester[20] present a challenge with respect to the Alaska finds as well as to Early Man throughout America. The challenge is stated as follows, *"If scientists can solve this mystery before the high-pressure water stream of the miner disperses the evidence, perhaps we shall be nearer solving one of the greatest and most tantalizing problems involved in the story of early man --- **the date of the extinction of the great mammals.**"* We have the answer to this mystery. It is called the GIRA Interpretation.

The Challenge Explained

The preceding portion of this Chapter 19 has already described the above mystery challenge presented by MacGowan and Hester. The extinctions of the great mammals mark the termination of the Neolithic and the Altithermal age. The termination of the Altithermal Age also corresponds to the termination of the Pleistocene Age. This termination was characterized by a period of pluvial or great moisture. Pluvial also means a time of much rain. This in turn relates to the time of Noah's Flood. This manuscript gives strong evidence in the previous chapters that Noah's Flood was world wide. It was a real event as future chapters will reveal. Figures 19-1, 19-2 give strong evidence that Noah's flood took place about 4500+ years before the present.

The date of the extinctions of the great mammals and the time of Noah's Flood is further verified in Chapter 20 at about 4,500 years before the present on the basis of the Egyptian Type Section. See Figure 20-2. This date marks the termination of the Neolithic Old Kingdom Age.

There are only two authentic quality records that can give a clue to the mysterious extinctions of the great mammals and of the Early Neanderthal Man in America. One is the record of Science. The other is the record of the Bible. No other so called holy book gives authentic information with respect to Noah's Flood.

The GIRA Interpretation

In the GIRA Interpretation, we have been able to demonstrate that these two records are astoundingly accurate and compatible. It is based upon the record of geology, anthropology, and archaeology combined with the authentic record of the Bible. We are able to show this remarkable compatibility going back over the past 10,000 years.

By uniting these two records, it is possible to solve the mystery as to who the Neanderthal man was and where he originated. We can also solve the great mystery as to the precise geological age when of the extinction of the Neanderthal Man and the Great Extinction of animal life took place.

The GIRA Interpretation also explains how a new grouping of modern mammals and the American Indian and the Inuit suddenly appeared in North & South America during the early stages of the Medithermal Age. See Figure 19-1.

The Record of Science

The record of science can be trusted. However, the interpretation of this record cannot always be trusted. It is always necessary to compare the findings of Early Man with the findings of Early Man elsewhere, in order to get a more comprehensive picture of what the evidence is saying and meaning.

To correctly interpret the record of science depends upon the basis of our interpretation. If you apply a total secular based interpretation, then the results become very confrontational and variable even among their own peers. It then results in a lot of guesswork and futile striving.

The Record of the Bible

The record of the Bible can be trusted. However, the interpretation of this record cannot always be trusted. It is always necessary to compare scripture with scripture in order to get a more comprehensive picture of what the Bible is saying and meaning.

The prerequisite of interpreting the Bible record correctly is found in 2 Peter 1:20-21 which says, *"Knowing this first, that no prophecy of Scripture is of any private interpretation, for prophecy never came by the will of man, but holy men of God spoke as they were moved by the Holy Spirit."* In other words, anyone who tries to privately interpret the Bible without earnestly seeking God's interpretation through His Holy Spirit is liable to bring out a wrong interpretation which becomes confrontational and variable. It then results in a lot of guesswork and futile striving.

To interpret the Biblical scripture accurately, one must always consider the context and compare it with other scripture. This respects the clear meaning without trying to find hidden meanings in it.

What Does the Bible record have to say about Early Man.

God's Purpose for Early Man

The Bible record gives an insight into the origin and purpose of the Human Race. It describes how & why Almighty God created, formed and made the first Man and Woman on the Earth whom He named, Adam & Eve. God did not create them as robots, but He gave them a free will to follow Him or to reject Him. He created Man for a purpose. His main purpose in creating man and woman on this Earth was that they would recognize Him as their Creator and would give Him honor and glory. We read, *"I have created him for my glory, I have formed him, yes I have made him."* (Isaiah 44:15)

God's Instructions for Early Man

God instructed Adam & Eve to have children. They were to populate the entire Earth. They were to be good stewards of looking after the Earth. God promised to provide them with food to eat. We read in Genesis 1:28-30 NIV, *"God blessed them and said to them, "Be fruitful and increase in number; fill the earth and subdue it. Rule over the fish of the sea and the birds of the air and over every living creature that moves on the ground."* Then God said, *"I give you every seed-bearing plant on the face of the whole earth and every tree that has fruit with seed in it. They will be yours for food. And to all the beasts of the earth and all the birds of the air and all the creatures that move on the ground—everything that has the breath of life in it—I give every green plant for food."* And it was so.

The Earth sciences of geology, anthropology, archaeology reveals that Early Man, who equates to Pre-Flood Man, has carried out this instruction by inhabiting every continent throughout the Earth with the possible exception of Antarctica.

Two Lineages Only

The Bible Record reveals only two lineages of Early Man prior to Noah's Flood. They are the lineage of Cain & Seth. See Chapters 12, 13, and 14.

It is interesting to note that the lineage of Cain was terminated or became extinct at the end of the Pre-Flood Age by Noah's Flood. However, the lineage of Seth to Noah has continued to the present day. Every human being on Earth today can trace their ancestry back through Noah to Seth and of course to Adam and Eve. But, not one person today can trace their lineage back to Cain.

The Science Record of anthropology and archaeology has revealed only two lineages of Early Man. They are the Cro-Magnon Man and the Neanderthal Man. They maintain that the Neanderthal man became extinct at the end of the Neolithic Age, whereas the Cro-Magnon Man has continued to the present time. This record compliments the Biblical record.

Cain the Father of the Neanderthal Man

Is it possible that Cain and all his descendants would have had Neanderthal facial characteristics? Is it possible that Seth and all his descendents would have had Cro-Magnon facial characteristics? In other words, Cain was the Father of the Neanderthal Race and Seth was the Father of the Cro-Magnon Race.

The life of Cain fits the life of the Neanderthal Man. We read, "*Then Cain went out from the presence of the Lord and **dwelt in the land of Nod on the east of Eden**"* (Genesis 4:16). The literal meaning of Nod means wandering. Cain became a world wanderer and explorer. He and his wife dwelt to **the east of Eden**. It was there that they dwelt and raised a family.

The average lifespan of Man prior to the Flood was 930 years. Thus, it is possible that Cain and his wife in later years wandered with members of their family eastward into southeast Asia, Australia, China, Mongolia, eastern Siberia and then into Alaska. This entrance into Alaska could have taken place when Cain was possibly 300+ years old. The question arises, how could they have crossed the Bering Sea between Russia and Alaska?

This was the time when large portions of northern Europe and Asia as well as the northern portions of North America were covered with vast thicknesses of continental glacial ice. See Figure 19-3. A large portion of the Earth's water was locked in the ice; therefore the level of the ocean is believed to have been possibly 325+ feet (99 meters) lower than at present. Today, the present depth of water in the Bering Sea region is less than 180 feet. These early Neanderthal persons would have been able to walk across the Bering Sea region into Alaska on dry land.

Early Man would have travelled through Alaska along the ice corridor that now extended through the Yukon Territories, northeast British Columbia, and western Alberta and into the United States. See Figure 19-3.

They would have seen tremendous thicknesses of glacial ice to the east and west that were many thousands of feet thick. They would have encountered the many species of now extinct animals such as the woolly mammoth, the camel; the saber tooth tiger and the list could go on and on.

What happened to these now extinct animals? What happened to the many thousands of feet of glacial ice that covered most of Canada & the northern part of the USA? When did the Neanderthal man enter North and South America on the basis of geology?

Early Man entered America during the Altithermal Age

Adam & Eve were created at the end of the Anathermal Age. Their children were all born during the Altithermal Age. See Figures 19-1 & 19-2. According to Antevs, the Earth experienced pronounced warming about 10,000 years ago. The Anathermal Age is characterized by progressive global warming with much moisture and luxuriant plant and animal life. The portions of the Earth that are desert regions today were areas of lush vegetation that provided abundant food for all animal life and for Early Man. It was not until about 6,000+ years before the present during the Altithermal Age that the Earth began to experience progressively drier conditions.

The progressive global warming that began about 10.000 years ago resulted in the melting of portions of the glacial ice. This allowed an ice corridor to develop through Alberta in a northwestward direction through the Yukon into Alaska. This ice corridor provided an open door for the Neanderthal man to enter North America and eventually South America. This was the beginning of a new civilization of people that would eventually inhabit all of North and South America. See Figure 19-3. Is it possible that they may have built the large megalithic and cyclopean, Neolithic Stone structures in central North America and South America?

The big question arises: On what basis can we honestly relate the Neanderthal Man to the geological Altithermal Age? Is it possible to date the approximate time when man arrived in America and when the Great Extinctions of Animal life and Early Man took place? The answer is yes. The Key to unlocking this mystery is found in the Egyptian Type Section? The answer again is yes.

The Key to unlocking the mystery surrounding Early Man is found in the Egyptian Type Section. What is the Egyptian type Section? See the next chapter.

References for Chapter 19

1. Antevs & DeGreer p.69.
2. Carl Sauer, 1944, Geographical sketch of Early Man in America." Vol.34 (p.70)
3. Kenneth MacGowan & Joseph A. Hester, Jr. "Early Man in the New World" published in Co-operation with The American Museum of natural History. The Natural history Library Anchor Books, Doubleday & Company, Inc. Garden City, N.Y. 1962. P.22.
4. Ibid, p.21.
5. Jim T. Humphries, "Record in Stone," 1967 p.3.
6. Jim T. Humphries, & Michael C. Wilson, 1987, "Record In Stone." This is an update.
7. Ibid, of Jim T, Humphries, Record in Stone 1967.
8. MacGowan & Hester p.89.
9. Ibid. p.130 Santa Lagoa Cave described.
10. Ibid. p. 130: The Santa Lagoa Man Described.
11. Ibid. p.131, The Confins Man.
12. Ibid. p.132. Punin Man described.
13. Ibid. p.164. The Sandi Man.
14. Ibid. p.164. The Sandi Man.
15. Ibid. p.132. Early Man in the USA.
16. Ibid. p.132. The Minnesota, Brown's Valley & the Saulk Valley Skulls are described.
17. Ibid. p. 132,The Mebourne Man.
18. Ibid. p. 134, Discovery of the Kansas & California men.
19. Ibid. p.137 to 138. Early Man in Mexico discussed. All had features of the Neanderthal Man.
20. Ibid. p.203. This quotation was taken from Frank Hibben's book.
21. Ibid. p.203.
22. Ibid. p.203.
23. Charles Berkey & Fedrick Morris. p.
24. Pere Emil Licent (1925) & Pere Tellhardde Chardin (1924).
25. Daae H. Donald, "Bridging the Gap: The First 6 Days." p.

Note: Jim T. Humphries wrote the little booklet entitled, "Record in Stone," 1967. He also co-authored a second updated booklet with Michael C. Wilson in 1987. I first met

Jim at the B.A. Geological Lab in Calgary, Alberta in the spring of 1956, when I was privileged to be on a Structural Geological Field Party in the Rocky Mountains between Jasper & Banff.

In the Spring of 1957, I began as a permanent employee with British American Oil Co. Ltd. that was later taken over by Gulf Oil Canada. Jim Humphries was in charge of our geological induction classes. I always admired his teaching abilities.

In 1969 & 1970, I had the opportunity of spending considerable time at the Geological Lab under Dr. Andrew Baillie. Jim Humphries became one of my mentors. He also introduced me to the science of Archaeology and to the Archaeological Society of Alberta. He gave me a copy of his booklet, "Record In Stone" that was published by the Archaeological Society of Alberta in 1967. This is what initiated my interest and study of Archaeology and also an interest in Early Man, artifacts and projectile points.

I was transferred to Edmonton for six years. Then I was transferred back to Calgary. Since then, I would occasionally call Jim about certain archaeological or geological matters. He always had a logical answer. It was Jim who introduced me to the Mazama Volcanic Ash deposits in Calgary. I have had the privilege of sharing this booklet with other geologists. Whenever, I had a question I would call him. He was always willing to discuss and to share his knowledge about archaeology and geology. I will always have a warm place in my heart for a great geologist and archaeologist, Jim Humphries. He has now gone to be with His Maker.

I will always cherish a statement that Dr. Andrew Baillie, who was in charge of the Gulf Oil Geologic Lab, said to me when I left the Lab in 1970. He said, "Don you are able to see geology in three dimensions. This is a valuable trait for a geologist to have."

Chapter 20

The Egyptian Type Section Unlocks the Mystery of Early Man

On the basis of the GIRA Interpretation, the Egyptian Type Section unlocks the mystery of Early Man throughout the Earth. It also unlocks the mystery to the geological age when Early Man first began to migrate to all regions of the Earth. This includes Europe, Asia, Africa, and Australia, North and South America and the islands of the sea. How is this possible?

No place has been under such intensive investigation and study from a geological, archaeological, anthropological and pre-historical perspective than Egypt. The key to unveil many of the perplexing mysteries and misconceptions of Early Man in other parts of the Earth is found in the Egyptian Type Section. Thus, a knowledge of Early Man in Egypt is of vital importance.

Introduction to Egyptian History

A group of three great, mysterious, pyramids in Egypt near Giza, about four miles southwest of Cairo, are numbered among the Seven Wonders of the ancient world. These three pyramids together with about 75 other lesser pyramids extend for a distance of about 25 miles from north to south along the west side of the Nile River. They are, primarily, associated with the 3rd, 4th, 5th and 6th Dynasties of the Old Kingdom Age.

Figure 20-1: The Three Great Pyramids of Egypt. Photo by Evelyn Daae

These three pyramids are the remnants of a great and glorious pre-Flood civilization that came to an abrupt end about 4,500 years ago. See Figure 20-2. The scientific evidence suggests that this age came to an end by erratic changes in climate and by a mysterious inundation of marine water. Egyptologists maintain the evidence does not indicate military invasion. What brought this mysterious age to a dramatic close? Why are the pyramids of Egypt referred to as one of the Seven Wonders of the Ancient World?

The Geological and Biblical history is shown on the left side of Figure 20-2. It documents a Flood Age break at about 4,500 years ago. This break separates the Pre-Flood Age from the Post Flood Age. This coincides with the break that separates the Old Kingdom Age from the First Intermediate Age. According to Egyptologists, the break between the Old Kingdom Age and the First Intermediate Age took place about 4,500 years ago. In 1995, I had the privilege of showing the above Figure 20-2 to an Egyptologist while in Cairo, Egypt. She took it with her to analyze. The next day, she said to me that the dates and what is shown on it are correct.

This pronounced Flood Break can now be traced worldwide. It always occurs at the end of the geological Altithermal Age. It can be documented throughout Africa, Europe, Asia as well as throughout North & South America.

This break is found at the end of the Old Kingdom Age in Egypt. It represents both a geological and an historical hiatus.

GEOLOGICAL TIME	BIBLICAL CHRONOLOGY	EGYPTIAN CHRONOLOGY	EARLY EGYPTIAN HISTORY	ARCHAEOLOGY
	0			
	CHRIST'S BIRTH		PTOLEMAIC PERIOD	
		332 BC	GREEK CONQUEST BY ALEXANDER THE GREAT	
	500 BC EXILE 597 BC IN BABYLON	(753 YRS)	21–31 DYNASTIES	
RECENT — MEDITHERMAL AGE	1000 BC 1051 BC KING SAUL	1085 BC		
	EXODUS 1446 BC	(482 YRS)	NEW KINGDOM 18–20 DYNASTIES	
	1500 BC	1567 BC (219 YRS)	2ND INTERMEDIATE 13–17 DYNASTIES HYSKOS INVASION	IRON TOOLS
		1786 BC (254 YRS)	MIDDLE KINGDOM 11–12 DYNASTIES / PYRAMID AGE	BRONZE TOOLS
	2000 BC	2040 BC		
	ABRAHAM 2166 BC	2196 BC ?	1ST INTERMEDIATE 7–10 DYNASTIES	
FLOOD	APPROX. 2500 BC 120 YRS	APPROX. 120 YEAR GAP		
		(480 YRS) 2676 BC	OLD KINGDOM 3–6 DYNASTIES / PYRAMID AGE	COPPER TOOLS
		(304 YRS)	EARLY DYNASTIC (THINITE) PERIOD 1–2 DYNASTIES	NEOLITHIC (NEW STONE AGE)
PLEISTOCENE — ALTITHERMAL AGE	3000 BC	2980 BC	PRE-DYNASTIC, ARCHAIC OR PRE-HISTORIC AGE	PALEOLITHIC (OLD STONE AGE)
	3500 BC		CLIMATE DRIER (ENCROACHING DESSERTS) HUNTERS CLIMATE MOIST	FLINT TOOLS WOODEN TOOLS
	APPROX. 4000 BC			

Figure 20-2: Illustrates Egyptian History from about 4,000+ B.C. to the time of Christ. On the left side, the Geological and Biblical Records are related to Egyptian History. The Pleistocene and the Altithermal Ages terminate at the end of the Old Kingdom Age. Why? Interpretation by Don Daae.

Some Pertinent Details in Egypt

1. **The Old Kingdom Pyramid Age** relates to the 3rd, 4th, 5th and 6th Dynasties. Egyptologists relate the Old Kingdom Age to the **Neolithic** Age.
2. **The Early Dynastic Thinite Age** precedes the Old Kingdom Age. It is represented by the 1st and 2nd Dynasties. This was a transitional period that could be classified as **Mesolithic** in age.
3. **The pre-Dynastic Age** precedes the Thinite Age. It relates to the archaeological **Paleolithic** Age. All of these Egyptian Ages relate directly to the geological Altithermal Age. See Figure 20-2 and 19-1.

The Discovery of Plywood

The Egyptians were carpenters. It becomes evident that Egyptians had stone tools throughout the Pre-Dynastic Age. Copper tools have been found within the latter part of the Pre-Dynastic Age. Egyptologist Davidovitz says, *"Carpentry appeared in Egypt at the end of the pre-Dynastic period, around 3500 BC, when copper tools were sufficiently developed to enable them to do woodworking."*[1] Then he goes on to say, *"Throughout all epochs, the Egyptian carpenter was a remarkable craftsman. He invented all manner of preparing wood joints and made them with skill: dowelling, mortices and tendons, dovetails, glueing, veneering, and marquetry. Wood being scarce in his country, he was the inventor of plywood."*[2]

Truly, the early Egyptian carpenter of this age was a remarkable craftsman. Egyptologist Davidovitz says, *"In a sarcophagus made during the Third Dynasty [around 2650 BC] there was actually a fragment of plywood found which was made from six layers of wood, each about 4 mm (0.15 inches) thick, held together by small flat rectangular tendons and tiny round dowels. Where 2 pieces had to be joined side by side, their edges were chamfered so as to unite exactly. The grain direction in successive layers is alternated, as in modern plywood, to provide greater strength and to avoid warping."*[3] He also explains how this plywood was used for casting the enormous stone blocks that compose the pyramids. What do we mean by casting stone?

In order to understand the significance of stone casting, it is necessary to discover what happened to change the lives of Early Man, not only in Egypt, but throughout the entire world. What was this big, enormous discovery? In order to understand the importance of this discovery, we must focus our attention upon the Old Kingdom Age in Egypt.

The Discovery of Stone Making

One of the greatest discoveries in human history was the discovery of stone making which led to Stone building. This amazing feat took place during the Third Dynasty. The first Pharaoh of the Third Dynasty was Zanakhit. He was followed by Zoser.

Pharaoh Zoser gave the responsibility of constructing the first pyramid to his architect by the name of Imhotep. Davidovitz says, "*Imhotep left an unforgettable legacy. Historically, the lives of few men are celebrated for 3,000 years, but Imhotep was renowned from the height of his achievements at about 2700 BC, into the Greco-Roman period. Imhotep was so highly honored as a physician and sage that he came to be counted among the gods.*"[4] He was later deified.

Figure 20-3: Zoser's Pyramid on the right and Zoser's Funerary Complex on the left. Purchased from Thinkstock.

King Zoser gave Imhotep great honor. Davidovitz says, "*Imhotep had many titles, Chancellor of the King of Lower Egypt, the First after the King of Upper Egypt, Administrator of the Great Palace, Physician, Hereditary Noble, High Priest of Anu, (On or Heliopolis), Chief Architect for Pharaoh Zoser, and, interestingly, Sculpturer, and Maker of Stone Vessels.*"[5]

What was his big accomplishment? He invented the art of stone making and producing building blocks of polished stone. Davidovitz says, "*The words describe "stone" with a beautiful, smooth surface, a feature characteristic of fine, agglomerated casing stone so smooth that it reflects the Sun.*" [6]

The Saqqara website says, "*Saqqara has the distinction of being the site of the first large stone structure built in the world. The place where humans began to strive for the impossible, where the imagination gained the power to transform reality.*" It then goes on to say, "*The chap responsible for the step pyramid was Imhotep, Djoser's Vizier. He is credited as being the inventor of building in stone and was a man of many talents - Architect, physician, master sculpture, scribe, and astronomer. He must be the first true genius in recorded history and his impression on the Egyptians was profound because later generations revered him as a god of wisdom.*"[7]

The Birth of the Neolithic Age

Archaeologists describe the Neolithic Age as the age of polished stone. Imhotep was the inventer of the polished stone. Egyptologists Davidovitz says, "*During this era, hard stone vessels made of slate, metamorphic schist, diorite, and basalt first appeared. All but indestructible, these items are among the most unusual and enigmatic of the ancient world. In a later era, 30,000 such vessels were placed in an underground chamber of the first pyramid known as the Third Dynasty Step Pyramid of Saqqara*".[8]

There is a mystery how these magnificent, highly polished vessels were made. The laborious carving, grinding, and polishing methods are not a satisfactory explanation because of the great hardness of the basalt and diorite stones. Davidovitz gives solid evidence and support that they were made by the more logical casting method.

The Neolithic Age relates to the Old Kingdom Age in Egypt. However, the knowledge of stone making resulted in the construction of megalithic and cyclopean stone structures that are found in various countries throughout the world such as the Middle East, Northern Africa, Western Europe, the British Isles, as well as in North and South America.

The archaeological Neolithic Age can also be called the Pyramid Age especially in Egypt and in North and South America. The Neolithic projectile points produced by Early Man throughout the world are also characteristically more highly refined and polished.

The abrupt Termination of the Neolithic Age

The last Pharaoh of the Old Kingdom Age in Egypt was Pepi II. He lived about 2500 years BC. He reigned for 94 years, the longest of any Pharaoh in history. His pyramid was built better than most of this period, and it is still relatively well preserved. Davidovitz and Morris, say, "*Within a few years after his death, Egypt was no longer a united nation. The country was in a state of anarchy, for a period lasting more than 200 years. Political and social revolution and "high mortality" rates characterize the epoch. Having no proof, scholars speculate that the fall of the Old Kingdom Age was from long and continuous mismanagement. Some scholars conjecture that "erratic changes in climate" produced food shortages against which the kings were powerless.*"[9]

The Biblical Flood best explains the abrupt termination of the Old Kingdom Age in Egypt. It was characterized by high mortality rates, a state of anarchy, chaos and confusion. There are no evidences of invading forces.

The inundation of Egypt by Noah's Flood waters could very well explain why many of the smaller stone monuments, funerary complexes and valley temples were in some cases completely buried by gravels, sands, silts and clays many feet thick.

The Queen's Chamber in the large pyramid was entered for the first time by recent explorers, they found that the walls were encrusted with salt. Tompkins says, *"The walls of the Queen's Chamber are unblemished limestone blocks, beautifully finished, but early explorers found them mysteriously encrusted with salt as much as 1/2 inch thick."*[10] The mystery intensifies because this pyramid is well above sea level and according to Egyptologists it is only about 4600+ years old. It is, herein, postulated that the sea inundated this pyramid about 4500 years ago at the time of the Great Flood, depositing this layer of salt.

The end of the Neolithic Age equates with the end of the Old Kingdom Age (Figure 20-2). Monuments built during the succeeding First Intermediate Age were sparse and were made of poor quality material. Buildings never stood higher than 30 feet and were most left unfinished or have perished. Ceramic pottery replaced stone, metal and faience in vessels. This verifies an abrupt change in history and culture from the Old Kingdom to the First Intermediate Age.

During the Old Kingdom Age, the Pharaohs worshipped the great god Khnum at the ancient capital city of Memphis located near present day Cairo. The Pharaoh and people of the First Intermediate Period began worshipping a new god, Amun. The capital city was established at Thebes, that is, about 120 miles to the south at Luxor. This reflects a major discontinuity or hiatus in Egyptian history. The Egyptian god Amun is still worshipped and highly recognized in parts of Egypt today.

Another reason for believing the Old Kingdom Age was destroyed by Noah's Flood is to be found in unique erosion damage to the Sphinx as is described below.

The Egyptian Sphinx

Today, Egyptologists generally attribute the construction of the Sphinx to Pharaoh Khafra of the Old Kingdom Age. Geological studies of the mysterious Sphinx have added new light as to its possible age. The severe erosion of body parts of the Sphinx and the hollow in which it is located indicates that water has been a damaging agent in the past. It has been found that slow erosion of the limestone occurs when water is absorbed and reacts with "salt" in the rock.

The controversy surrounds the source of the vast amounts of water responsible for the erosion. Scientists have determined that three distinct and separate repair operations have been completed on the Sphinx between the New Kingdom Age and the Ptolemaic rule (about a 1000 year period). The study indicates that the Sphinx was already in its current state of erosion when these early repairs were made. No appreciable damage was done since the original damage. Nor is there further damage to the bedrock of the surrounding hollow, an area that never underwent repair. Therefore the damage was done sometime prior to the New Kingdom Age.

Figure 20-4: The Egyptian Sphinx. In the foreground are the Temple Mount structures that were buried by sand and gravels revealing the megalithic stone blocks that were carefully laid in place by Early Man. Photo by Evelyn Daae.

Geologists have also found that layers of silt and sand have built up around the Sphinx which has been accompanied by a gradual rise of the water table, so that today the water table is 30 feet higher than it was during Kafra`s reign.

There are two popular theories attempting to explain the erosion damage as follows: The first is that water slowly rose into the body of the Sphinx and caused damage, then lowered again. In response to this theory, Davidovits and Morris say, "*During Khafra`s time the water table was about 30 feet lower than it is today. For the rising groundwater theory to hold, an unbelievable geological scenario would have to have taken place. It would mean that from 30 feet lower then today's water table, water rose to about 2 feet into the body of the Sphinx and the surrounding hollow, where it caused erosion for roughly 600 years, and then stopped its damaging effect.*"[11] It is obvious that this theory has major unsolved problems.

The second theory suggests that the source of water stemmed from the wet stage of the last ice age, about 10,000 to 15,000 years B.C., when Egypt underwent severe flooding. This theory advocates that the Sphinx was constructed prior to 10,000 BC. This does not fit in with current Egyptian historical chronology.

I would like to propose a third theory. This suggests that the worldwide, Biblical Flood was responsible for raising the water table, and causing extensive erosion damage to the Sphinx. Much of the erosion damage to body parts of the Sphinx resulted from chemical reaction of the salt water with the limestone, whereas initial damage would have resulted from the abrasive action of salt water, silt and sand as several powerful Stage 1 and Stage 3 tsunami tidal waves would have swept across Egypt at this time. As soon as the Flood waters subsided, the water table would have eventually lowered, thus preventing any further erosion damage. The Flood waters would also have been responsible for depositing the great thicknesses of in filled silt and sand around the base of the Sphinx and the pyramids.

Early Man in Egypt

The term Early Man always relates to the Paleolithic. Mesolithic and the Neolithic ages. Thus, the Man that lived in Egypt is analogous in age to the Early Man that lived in all other parts of the Earth at this particular time. This is the reason why Egypt becomes a **Primary Type Section** *for dating Early Man throughout the entire Earth.*

Archaeologists and anthropologists would want to extend the Paleolithic Age far beyond 4,000+ B.C to many hundreds of thousands of years into the past. However, they would have little or no disagreement with the dates assigned to the Mesolithic and the Neolithic ages that are shown on the above Figure 20-2. These are the ages that are generally accepted by Egyptologists. However, Egyptologists often do extend the time frame of the Pre-Dynastic age to an older age. I do not believe that it is necessary to extend the age of Man a great distance into the past beyond 6,000+ years.

Why is the Egyptian Type Section so Important?

The Egyptian Type Section is important because it is able to stand alone on the basis of detailed studies of geology, archaeology, anthropology and all the natural sciences as a basis for dating Early Man.

On the basis of our GIRA Interpretation of East Africa, Egypt is the Type Section, not the Olduvai Gorge Section for unlocking the Mystery of Early Man throughout the world.

In other words, the key to unlocking the mystery of Early Man and finding the correct interpretation for the "Olduvai Gorge Type Section" is also found in "The Egyptian Type Section."

What caused Egypt's Sudden Demise?

It was Noah's Flood that caused the Sudden Demise of the great Neolithic, Pre-Flood Egyptian Civilization.

References for Chapter 20

1. *J. Davidovitz & M. Morris, "The pyramids: An Enigma Solved." Hippocrene Book, NY, 1988, 2nd printing, p.72.*
2. *Ibid., p.72.*
3. *Ibid., p.72-73.*
4. *Ibid., p.127.*
5. *Ibid., P.129.*
6. *Ibid., p.129.*
7. *Quote from the Internet website.*
8. *Ibid., p.7.*
9. *Ibid. p.207.*
10. *Peter Tompkins, "Secrets of the Pyramid," Harper & Row, NY, 1978, p.12.*
11. *Davidovitz, p.21 & 22.*

Chapter 21

A Glimpse into this Mysterious Pre-Flood Worldwide Civilization

Is it possible that the mysterious megalithic and cyclopean stone structures present worldwide could possibly be related to a glorious pre-Flood civilization? The Young Earth Creation Science people are forced to disbelieve this possibility, because they believe Noah's Flood occurred prior to the Pleistocene Ice Age. The natural sciences of archaeology & anthropology deny the reality of Noah's Flood. Their denial is based upon their false secular, Darwinian interpretation. But what does the evidence really tell us?

Archaeology has unveiled the remnants of a past, glorious, pre-Flood civilization at various places throughout the Earth. Is there a relationship between the megalithic and cyclopean stone structures in Egypt with those found in the Middle East, Northern Africa, Western Europe, England, Mexico, Easter Island, Central and South America and other parts of the world.

There is an **air of mystery** that surrounds each of these regions as to the precise time in which they were constructed. Could they be contemporary? There is a similarity in the type of stone blocks. For example at Tiahuanaco, Bolivia, there are stone blocks that measure 36 feet by 7 feet and weigh up to 200 tons, yet their quarries are conjectured to be 30 or even 90 miles away. Some of these stone blocks are black volcanic andesite that is extremely heavy and hard. These rocks would blunt our finest steel tools, yet no such tools for fashioning them have been found. The builders were still able to shape these stones to fit together to an accuracy of one fiftieth of an inch. Was this all accomplished by the carving and hoisting method or is it possible that the art of stone casting was known world wide and that these people did have ways of communicating? Is it also possible that the highly polished stone tools that characterize the Neolithic age may have been made synthetically by Man? Future detailed scientific research should give additional answers to many of these perplexing mysteries.

It would appear that there was also a similarity in climate change throughout the Earth. During the Paleolithic (Old Stone Age) Period, the people were essentially nomadic food gatherers and hunters. They lived off the land. In North Africa, Egypt, Europe, and the Middle East as well as in North and South America the climate was moist, warm and favorable for the growth of lush vegetation and abundant animal life. The climate gradually became drier; the desert areas began to expand. People were forced to congregate towards lakes, oases, rivers and shoreline areas where water was more plentiful. This resulted in dramatic advancements in agriculture in order to feed the growing populations. This led to industrial development, city growth, and better communication and eventually to the construction of cyclopean and megalithic structures. Thus, a progressive development appeared worldwide from the Paleolithic (Old Stone Age) to the Mesolithic (Middle Stone Age) to the Neolithic (New Stone Age). There are now strong scientific evidences that it was the worldwide Flood of Noah that abruptly terminated this great Stone Age Period.

We will begin our study with Northern Africa where the above transition is so very evident, then to other parts of the world in an attempt to unravel the ancient mysteries associated with a by-gone glorious worldwide civilization. This chapter will attempt to relate some of the cyclopean and megalithic stone structures to the pre Flood age, stating reasons why this is a reasonable assumption.

Cyclopean Structures in North Africa

There is a remarkable relationship that exists between the Paleolithic, Mesolithic and Neolithic ages of the Egyptian Type Section with that of Northern Africa. Certain cyclopean structures in Lybia are believed to be of Neolithic age. James Howard Wellard[1] describes the time when the vast Sahara Desert was a moist region of forests and grasslands. It was in these areas that the early hunters and food gatherers inhabited vast areas of Northern Africa. As the climate became more arid, these hunters were forced to migrate to areas along the coastal regions of the Mediterranean and into Egypt where there was a more plentiful source of water.

Archaeologists have found immense networks of underground tunnels and foggares. This indicates that these people had developed a more settled agricultural style of life. The people built cyclopean walls and tens of thousands of rock tombs and burial mounds have been found. This age is characteristic of the Neolithic and has a remarkable similarity to that of Egypt. Wellard[2] says, "*Cyclopean stone structures are present in northern Africa that date back to early times.*" He describes some of the archaeological evidences found in Libya and in the Sahara desert region, "*On rock faces in many parts of the Sahara Desert unknown artists have depicted life as they see it, from prehistoric times up to the present, representing 10,000 years of continuous history. The oldest of these engravings are ascribed to the "Hunters" who lived in the Sahara when the desert was forested and inhabited by elephants, giraffes, and aquatic animals.*" Wellard goes on to say, "*The same aura of mystery surrounds the descendants of the Hunters those people who built the "cyclopean" walls which still guard the western approaches to the summit of Zenkekra, and the tens of thousands of rock tombs, or burial mounds, which litter the side of the valley. Their presence indicates a sizeable empire; and if we ascribe to them the immense network of underground tunnels called foggares, it indicates, too, a people of a settled agricultural way of life in contrast to the Hunters who lived by the bow and arrow.*" [2]

In Africa, the Anathermal Age is characterized by moist humid conditions. It was during the Altithermal Age that the desert regions began to grow. The climate slowly became less moist. As the desert regions expanded, the people were forced to leave their more easy hunting and food gathering style of life to a more settled style. They were forced to congregate to places where water was more plentiful. It was in these areas that settlements, towns and cities began to grow.

During the latter half of the Altithermal Age great advances were made in animal husbandry, agriculture, and ranching. City growth encouraged animal husbandry, ranching, dairy farms and more sophisticated forms of industrial and mining development. This led into the manufacture of highly polished stone tools, copper tools, and the art of stone casting that resulted in the construction of cyclopean and megalithic stone complex structures.

The boat / naval industry was also progressing. This resulted in communications on a local, regional and eventually on a worldwide basis similar to our present age. However, they were not quite as sophisticated. What took place in the Middle East and Africa was also taking place in America and other parts of the world.

The Oasis Theory

The climate changes that were advocated by an American geologist, Raphael Pumpelly in 1904 compliment the changes that took place in Northern Africa. He formulated what has become known as the "***Oasis Theory of Agricultural Origins***."

Two prominent geologists from Columbia University Ryan and Pitman say, "*For over seventy years Pumpelly traveled throughout China and Mongolia describing landforms and mapping rock formations. In 1904 near Ashkhad on the fringe of the Kara Kum desert east of the Caspian Sea in what later became Turkestan, Pumpelly uncovered signs of early farming at the edge of an oasis. Throughout his extensive travel he had noted that the climate in central Asia had become significantly drier in the wake of the last Ice Age. He wondered whether during this desiccation Stone Age hunters and gatherers had found themselves clustered together around the edges of the remaining water holes along with wild animals and plants. Perhaps in order to conquer new means of support these people took the crucial cultural leap leading to the genetic manipulation of plants and animals called domestication."* [3]

Ryan and Pitman[3] describe the life of Vere Gordon Childe who some have proclaimed as the greatest pre-historian in Britain and probably the world. In 1946, he was appointed as Director of the Institute of Archaeology at the University of London. In 1926, he began a field study of the archaeological sites along the Danube River valley in Hungary and Yugoslavia toward the Black Sea region. He studied the Vinca culture which is now believed to be of Neolithic age. Childe observed that traders, prospectors, and primitive metallurgists had set up towns, and villages to support the mining of gold, copper and tin for export to the Near East. He was impressed by the pins, earrings and daggers with artistic style that reminded him of Palestinian and Asian handiwork. He noted Mediterranean seashells among the artifacts in Vinca graves. He observed that the Vinca people possessed a wide spectrum of natural resources to attract homesteaders whose farms were always near abundant water supplies.

With respect to Childe's view of the origin of farming, Ryan and Pitman quote a portion of Childe's book The Danube in Prehistory as follows, *"A revolution whereby man ceased to be purely a parasite and ... became a creator emancipated from the whims of his environment."*[4] In other words, Childe supported Pumpelly's conclusions with respect to the "Oasis Theory" that as the climate became more arid, the nomadic hunters and food gatherers began to gather together for survival purposes around oases or lakes where there was a plentiful supply of game, plants and water. This led to an agricultural and industrial revolution that characterizes the Vinca culture and civilization in Europe. In other words, the climate changes in the Danube region were similar to climate changes in northern Africa, Egypt, the Middle East and in other regions of Asia. The Oasis Theory also compliments the climate changes that characterize the Altithermal Age in North and South America and in Europe as advocated by Pleistocene geologists.

The Pyramids of Egypt

The Great Pyramids of Egypt are striking remnants of a great Stone Age Civilization. There are about 75 pyramids in number representing mainly the Old Kingdom Age. They extend for a distance of about 25 miles from north to south. They occur in several groups on the west side of the Nile River. Only the pyramids associated with the 3rd, 4th, 5th, and 6th Dynasties of the Old Kingdom Age are believed to be pre-Flood (see Figure 3).

Figure 21-1: The three Great Pyramids of Giza. They are located just to the southwestern edge of Cairo. Photo's taken by Evelyn Daae.

The Great Pyramid of Khufu (Cheops in Greek) is the largest pyramid and represents the peak in engineering design. Sir Flanders Petrie said, *"It's the greatest and most accurate structure the world has ever seen."*[5] It covers a space of 13 acres. Its base forms a square, each side of which was originally 768 feet, though now, by the removal of the outer casing, it is only 750 feet. The outer surface now forms a series of steps, each with an average height of 3 feet or more. Its height was originally 481 feet, and is now 450 feet. It contains approximately 2.6 million building blocks each weighing from 2 to 70 tons.

The Great Pyramid of Khufu is said to contain about 2,600,000 carefully cut blocks of limestone, ranging in weight from 2 to 70 tons each. They fit together with extreme precision. There are two major methods suggested to explain its construction. The first is the carving and hoisting method, the second is the casting method.

The Carving & Hoisting Method

Egyptologists who subscribe to *"The Carving and Hoisting Method"* each block was quarried, dressed, transported, and fitted very closely believe together. Halley says, *"It is believed that the stone blocks were cut from a quarry 12 miles to the east, floated across the Nile during inundations, and then drawn up long sloping earthen construction ramps by large gangs of men tugging at ropes, raised and brought into place by means of wedges driven alternately on one side and then the other on platforms with cradle like bottoms. It is said to have required 1,100,000 men 10 years to build the causeway, and another 20 years to build the pyramid itself; all in forced labor: working classes and slaves, driven under the pitiless lash of the task master."* [6]

The Casting Method

The Casting method was proposed and elaborated upon by Davidovits.[7] He proposes the revolutionary Casting Theory or Agglomeration Concept that each pyramid stone was cast in place as a type of manmade concrete. Davidovits gives credit to a French chemist, metallurgist and ceramist Henry Le Chatelier (1850 - 1936), who was the first to discover that the ancient Egyptians produced man made stone and made stone vessels, jewelry and tools.

Davidovits, as a biochemist, was the first person to reproduce the synthetic pyramid stone in his laboratory and to apply the technology to the construction theory. As

Davidovits and Morris point out, there are many theories of construction and they are all based on the carving and hoisting theory, but these do not solve the irreconcilable problems. For instance, with flint stone and copper tools, how did they make the pyramid face absolutely flat? How did they make the faces meet at a perfect point at the summit? How did they make the tiers so level? How could the required number of workers maneuver on the building site? How did they make the blocks so uniform, and some of the heavier blocks were placed at great heights? How was this all done in about 20 years? Certainly, there must have been a better way?

Davidovits says "*Only the casting theory instantly dissolves all of the logistical and other problems. The casing blocks each weigh about 10 tons and are clearly the product of stone casting. Joints between the casing blocks are barely detectable, fitting as close as 0.002 inch according to Petries' measurements. They are smooth and of such fine quality that they have been mistaken for light-gray granite.*" [8]

In the Great Pyramid, there are hundreds of stone blocks that make up the core masonry. They weigh 20 tons or more and are found at the level of the Grand Gallery and higher. Each block fits together with remarkable precision, so that one cannot fit a razor blade between them. Davidovits and Morris[9] say "*With chemistry, the task of pyramid construction was easily accomplished with the tools of the Pyramidal Age. No carving or hoisting was required. The implements needed were simply those used to lay sun-dried mud bricks, a hoe to scrape up fossil shell limestone, a basket to transport ingredients, a trough in which to prepare ingredients, a ladder, a square, a plumb line, a builder's trawl, and wooden molds.*"

In other words, the wooden molds were made of plywood. They would shovel fossil limestone sand into the wooden molds together with water. However, in order to produce a solid crystalline rock, certain types of mafkat minerals were added. **These minerals were mined from a special mineral mine site in the Sinai Peninsula. Davidovits**

documents where these minerals were located. Many of the Old Kingdom Age Pharoahs had engraved their names in rocks at this mine site. Once these mafkat minerals were mixed with the limestone sand, the chemical reaction would solidify the mixture, so that the mold could be removed within three to four hours.

They would then set up the wooden molds in an adjacent position and would repeat the procedure. The scientist who discovered how to mix these mafkat minerals together with other rock types was a genius by the name of Imhotep. Normally, the limestone sand within the plywood molds would never have hardened into solid rock. However, with the addition of the Mafkat minerals, they would harden in a few hours.

The complex of stone monuments and temple structures in front of Khafra's Pyramid are the most well preserved of the Giza Group. In the Valley Temple south of the Great Sphinx are two levels that are made of blocks weighing 50 to 80 tons a piece and assembled with tongue-and-groove joints. Some of these blocks weigh up to 500 tons. Mortar joins the different blocks. Inside the Valley Temple are granite blocks in perfect condition exhibiting the fabulous jigsaw joints which go around corners? This supports the use of cast stone which was a method discovered by Imhotep.

I, personally, had the privilege of examining these temple complexes on a tour to Egypt. The gigantic stones of various kinds are mind boggling.

The power of kings to build great pyramids began to dissipate after the 4th Dynasty. Still the times were prosperous, and the period is not characterized by war, but by a revolution in art and literature. Trade flourished and Egypt had a fleet of ships in the Mediterranean. Davidovits believes the building decline may have been also caused by a depletion of mineral resources.[12] It would appear that the Pharaoh's from the 4th, 5th and 6th Dynasties were more interested in trade and commerce than in pyramid building. The fleet of ships and the development of improved vessels would have contributed to the advancement of knowledge, communication and science throughout the world during that latter part of the Neolithic Age.

By the 6th Dynasty, Egypt was less powerful and the power of the kings seemed no longer to have been absolute. The Pharaohs appeared to concentrate their attention more on foreign expeditions, trade and enterprises.

Pepi II was the last great Pharaoh of the 6th Dynasty and of the Old Kingdom Age. He reigned for 94 years, the longest reign of any pharaoh in history. His pyramid was built better than most of this period, and it is relatively well preserved. Davidovits says, *"Within a few years after his death, Egypt was no longer a united nation. The country was in a state of anarchy, lasting more than 200 years. Political and social revolution and High Mortality rates characterize the epoch. Having no proof, scholars speculate that the fall of the Old Kingdom was from long and continuous governmental mismanagement. Some scholars conjecture that erratic changes in climate produced food shortages against which the kings were powerless."* [10]

Evidences of Noah's Flood

It is possible that the world wide Flood of Noah was responsible for the sudden destruction of the Old Kingdom Age (see Figure 20-2). This would explain the high mortality rates, and the state of anarchy, chaos, and confusion. As the powerful tsunami tidal waves of Noah's Flood swept across Egypt it would explain why many of the funerary complexes and Valley Temple Mounts were in many cases completely buried by gravel, sand and silt, and why the Queen's chamber in the Great Pyramid was encrusted with salt on the walls so much as half an inch thick, when it was entered for the first time. Tompkins says, *"The walls of the Queen's chamber are unblemished limestone blocks, beautifully finished, but early explorers found them mysteriously encrusted with salt as much as one-half inch thick."* [11]

During the First Intermediate Age Social disruption and upheaval persisted from the 7th to the 10th Dynasties. Monuments built during this era were sparse and were made of poor quality material. Buildings never stood higher that 30 feet and most were left unfinished or have perished. Pottery replaced stone, metal and faience in vessels. See Figure 20-2.

The Neolithic Age in Egypt

It is evident that the Neolithic Age was well on its way prior to the commencement of the First Dynasty. Davidovits & Morris say, "*During this (prehistoric) era, hard stone vessels made of slate, metamorphic schist, diorite and basalt first appeared. All but indestructible, these items are among the most unusual and enigmatic of the ancient world. In a latter era, 30,000 such vessels were placed in an underground chamber of the First Pyramid of the Third Dynasty Step Pyramid of Saqqara.*"[12] All these vessels have a smooth, glossy, polished appearance and bear no trace of tool marks. They are considered the most beautiful of all fine stone objects. These high quality polished vessels were only made in Egypt during the Neolithic Age.

The Flood could very well explain the dramatic shift in religious deities at the end of the Old Kingdom Age. During the Old Kingdom Age, the people worshipped the great god Khnum at the ancient capital of Memphis near present day Cairo. A new god Amun was introduced after the Old Kingdom Age. The Pharaohs and people began worshipping the god Amun and their capital city was established at Thebes or present day Luxor and Karnak about 190 kilometers to the south. These factors show a distinct cultural discontinuity of history from the Old Kingdom Age to the First Intermediate and later Egyptian Ages.

The cyclopean and megalithic structures that characterize the (Neolithic) Old Kingdom Age in Egypt are described in our GIRA Newsletter vol.10, no.2, and in greater detail in an article entitled, "Early Egyptian History" at www.gira.ca.[13] These cyclopean pyramids and associated temple structures in Egypt relate to the Old Kingdom Age. They bear remark-able similarities to other cyclopean and megalithic struc-tures throughout the world.

The GIRA Newsletter Vol. 12, No. 2 at www.gira.ca relates the geology, archaeology and anthropology of East Africa to the Egyptian Type Section. There is also a remarkable relationship that exists between the Paleolithic, Mesolithic and Neolithic ages of the Egyptian Type Section with the region of Mesopotamia, the Middle East, Europe, Asia and northern Africa. The scientific evidences give strong support that Noah's Flood was a real event that was responsible for abruptly terminating the Neolithic age in Egypt about 4,500 years ago (See Figure 20-2).

The Middle East

A similar abrupt change took place in the Middle East at the very same time. Halley [14] describes the Flood deposits that are present at the ancient cities of Ur, Fara, Kish and Ninevah that consist of a black layer of clay and silt sepa-rating the pre-Flood and the post-Flood cultures. Above this flood layer is found the Jamdat Nasr or Early Sumerian cultures, whereas below are the highly decorated pottery of the Al-Ubad cultures of Neolithic Age. Halley describes the findings of Dr. Stephen Langdon's Field Museum-Ozford University Joint Expedition in 1928-29 as follows: *"A bed of clean water-laid clay, in the lower strata of the ruins of Kish, 5 feet thick, indicates a flood of vast proportions. It contains no objects of any kind. Dr. Langdon suggested that it may have been the Flood mentioned in the Bible. Underneath it the relics represented an entirely different type of culture. Among the relics found was a four-wheeled chariot, the wheels made of wood and copper nails, with the skeletons of the animals that drew it lying between the shafts."*[15] The Flood scenario would explain why the skeletons of the ani-mals that drew it were still lying beneath the shafts. See Figure 15-8.

Obviously, the Flood came in suddenly bringing about an abrupt termination of this former Neolithic, Mesopotamian civilization. Halley describes some of the relics of the pre-Flood cities in the Middle East as follows: *"painted pottery, flint implements, tools of obsidian, turquoise vases, copper axes, copper mirrors, hoes, sickles, various implements of stone, flint, quartz, fish hooks, models of boats, an underground kiln, specimens of the most beautiful vitrified pottery, cosmetics which pre-historic women used for darkening their eyebrows and eyelids, brick ruins of temples painted red or covered with plaster, pottery artistically painted in intricate geometric patterns and figures of birds, even a chariot and architectural accomplishments that indicate an astonishingly advanced civilization."*[16] Many of these relics and tools are very similar to the ones found in Egypt as part of the Neolithic Old Kingdom and Early Dynastic Ages.

It is obvious that the pre-Flood people in the Middle East and in Egypt were both experiencing an advanced form of civilization when it was abruptly terminated. There are no indications of invading forces in either case, but they were suddenly destroyed by a climate change. A flood of great proportions such as Noah's Flood would explain its sudden termination.

Terrace of Baalbek, Damascus

North of Damascus in eastern Lebanon lies the Terrace of Baalbek. It is a platform which consists of three massive megalithic blocks. Each block weighs about 750 tons and are 65 x 12 x 15 feet in size. The Temple of Jupiter is constructed upon this platform. There is a fourth block in a nearby quarry that is perfectly cut and is believed to weigh nearly 2000 tons. Archaeologists do not know its origin.

Davidovits & Morris describe the ancient outer wall of the acropolis at Baalbek saying, *"Three blocks are so large that they have acquired their own name, "the trilithon." Each of these blocks measured sixty-four feet long and thirteen feet wide. Estimated to weigh 1200 tons apiece, they are situated in the wall at a height of twenty-five feet above the ground. It is estimated that it would require the force of 25,000 men to raise these stones. The placement of the trilithon has puzzled the most expert engineers. In the temple of Jupiter at the site, one of the huge stones weighs 2000 tons."*[17] It is possible that these cyclopean stones were cast in place by the casting method. The Terrace of Baalbek is a remnant of the Great Stone Age Period. It is believed to be of Neolithic Age.

The Acropolis at Athens Greece

There is a mystery as to the origin and history of the Acropolis at Athens Greece. It is another megalithic wonder of the ancient world. Google says, *"While the earliest artifacts date to the Middle Neolithic era, there have been documented habitations in Attica from the Early Neolithic (6th millennium BC). There is little doubt that a Mycenaean megaron stood upon the hill during the late Bronze Age. Nothing of this megaron survives except, probably, a single limestone column-base and pieces of several sandstone steps. Soon after the palace was built a Cyclopean massive circuit wall was built, 760 meters long, up to 10 meters high, and ranging from 3.5 to 6 meters thick. This wall would serve as the main defense for the acropolis until the fifth century."*

It is interesting to note that the Acropolis dates back to the Neolithic Age. This megalithic stone structure is equivalent in age to the Pyramids in Egypt. This equates to the time when the megalithic stone structures in Egypt, North Africa, the Stonehenge's in the British Isles, the Menhirs of France and the megalithic pyramidal structures in the Americas were being constructed.

There are several smaller Acropolis structures in Greece that would also equate to the Neolithic Age.

Monuments in the Americas

Numerous megalithic pyramidal stone structures are present in Mexico, the Yucatan, Central America and parts of South America. Some of these cyclopean and megalithic structures are of similar size and shape to the pyramids of Egypt and are of Neolithic Age. See Chapter 22 for details.

Plateau of Marcahuasi, Peru

High in the Andes Mountains of Peru, not far from Nazca, on the plateau of Marcahuasi, Raymond Drake reports, *"Dr. Daniel Ruzo in 1952 discovered a most remarkable assemblage of giant sculptures representing human beings, animals, and birds, notably a lion and several condors, symbols of the Sun God. Many of the figures are only prominent when viewed from a certain angle, particularly in the sunlight. Two altars twelve feet high suggest that the prehistoric builders must have been Giants, perhaps those Giant Gods who, according to the Hunaca Indian legends, dwelt in the high places. Many carvings depict camels, lions, elephants, penguins, which as far as is known never existed in South America. Daniel Ruzo proved that they had been made by giants 12 feet tall . . . Like the statues on Easter Island, they radiate an aura of transcendent wisdom akin to the Sphinx."* [20] According to geology, these prehistoric animals such as the camel, lion, elephant were present throughout all North and South America prior to about 4,500 years ago. The carvings of prehistoric animals like the camel, lion and elephant would imply a Pre-Flood origin.

Easter Island

About 300 miles westward from the coast of Peru is Easter Island where there are several hundred colossal statues carved out of hard volcanic rock. They are between 10 and 66 feet high, and weigh as much as 50 tons. Originally they wore hats that weighed more than 10 tons each. The eyes of these statues radiate an aura of transcendent wisdom and eeriness akin to the Sphinx in Egypt.

Recent excavations have discovered hidden caves containing decayed remains of tablets, wooden images, and small wooden sculptures. The tablets are covered with finely carved and stylized figures, which seem to be a form of picture writing. To date no one has been able to translate any of the tablets, and no satisfactory method of interpreting the symbols has been found.

Who could have constructed these megalithic, gigantic statues? Is there a connection between the gigantic statues in Peru and these on Easter Island? Could they have been built by the strange nephilim that lived on the Earth during the 120 year period prior to the Flood? However we interpret these stone statues, one conclusion can be made, that is, they belong to the Great Stone Age period known as the Neolithic.

European Stone Monuments

Great stone monuments dating back to prehistoric times are scattered along the coastal areas of western Europe, some on nearby sea islands, and a few inland (in Great Britain in particular). It is estimated that 40,000 to 50,000 of these monuments occur in major prehistoric sites along the west coasts of Malta, Spain, France, the British Isles and Scandinavia. The most popular is the megalithic gray rocks of the Carnac menhirs in France, and Stonehenge's in Britain. Many of these giant rocks weigh many tons and make up the menhirs, dolmens, passage graves, the alignments, and the circles, all of which were carefully put into place by Neolithic Man.

The constructions are variously referred to as cyclopean and megalithic. According to Stern, *"Cyclopean structures are built by placing very large stones on top of one another very much as bricks are laid, whereas the essentials of megalithic construction are either the single large slab or the large slab as walling stone with another slab resting on two or more large walling stones as a capstone, a sort of house of cards architecture."* [21]

Menhirs of Carnac, France

Along the western coast of Brittany, France at and near Carnac are thousands of large megalithic rocks placed in long parallel rows that run for miles. The individual stones often are graduated in size, with the largest ones placed nearest to the culminating point of the alignment. These individual giant rocks are often referred to as "Menhirs" and are usually long, slender stones standing on end. A few have been roughly shaped, some even have been carved, but most of them are natural rocks that were brought to the site where they were given special significance by their location and their spatial relationship to one another.

The largest of all the menhirs is nearly 70 feet high. It was called the Breton giant of Locmariaquer. However, it fell centuries ago and broke into five huge pieces when it hit the ground. Scattered among the thousands of menhirs in Brittany are dolmens, which consist of a large capstone supported by walled rocks together with other megalithic monuments.

Men who have analyzed the megaliths at the various pre-historic sites in Western Europe have found similarities in the rock carvings as well as the types of pottery. This would indicate that the people communicated with each other from place to place. Stern describes the time when these megalithic structures were possibly constructed, *"Since the megalithic monuments were built after men had learned how to make utensils out of baked clay, shards and even some unbroken vessels have helped to date and trace the origins, affiliations, and trade routes of the men who brought foreign-made pottery into Europe. And since the monuments continued to be built well into the period when copper and bronze implements came into use, the megaliths bridge the long span of time between the Stone Age and the Age of Metals."*[22] This description of history would fall into the Neolithic Age and would be contemporary with the Thinite and the Old Kingdom Age in Egypt.

The Stonehenges

Stonehenge in Somerset, England is a circle of huge stones, some of which weigh over 50 tons. According to Gaverluk and Hamm [23] each stone was cut and shaped to the size required to relate to the total structure. The main feature of the monument is a circular trench 400 feet in diam-eter. Inside this circle was a rectangle with the four station stones imbedded in the circle itself. The longer sides of this rectangle faced the northwest, where, through a portico some 200 feet away, could be seen the 18.5 foot heel stone. If Stonehenge were built 30 miles north or south of its present latitude, then the position of the station stones would no longer have formed a perfect rectangle in relation to the observations and the heel stone. It was possible for these ancient people to make predictions of solar and lunar eclipses through the arrangement of the stones in Stonehenge I and III. There is actually more than one circle of huge stones at various locations in England. They are collectively referred to as Stonehenge.

Figure 21-2: The Stonehenge Site. Purchased from Thinkstock.

At one time it was believed the Druids were responsible for their construction, but now their origin is believed to be much older. Archaeologists are now saying that the Stonehenge people are of Mesolithic and Neolithic age. On this basis the Stonehenges are contemporary with the Menhirs of France and the Egyptian "Old Kingdom Age?" They should now be classified as Pre-Flood.

Neolithic Metal Mines in Europe, Asia, and the Middle East

Several copper mines have been found in Europe, Western Asia, and the Middle East that date back to the copper and Neolithic ages or to pre Flood times. Deposits of copper ore were mined at an early date by open pit at Ai Bunar in Bulgaria, also at Chinflon in Spain, at Mount Gabriel in Ireland, and at Mitterburg in Austria.

In the Veshnoveh area of Iran, an ancient copper mining site was found with galleries 40 metres (131 feet) long. In most of these ancient mines the miners worked with the same kind of stone mauls that were found at Rudna Glava, Yugoslavia which are characteristic of the Neolithic Age.

Rudna Glava Copper Mine

One of the oldest known copper mines was found at Rudna Glava, Yugoslavia. This is described by J. Borislav.[24] During the 1900's open pit operations revealed older mine shafts that date back to Neolithic times. It was found that Early Man mined horizontally for flint bearing strata and dug vertical shafts up to 20.1 meters (66 feet) vertically to recover copper ore veins. The basic tool of excavation was a stone maul. It is believed they heated the rock and then threw water on to break it. Many pottery vessels were found. Their culture is named Vinca and it is late Neolithic in age. Archaeological findings throughout the Balkans indicate that these people were active in manufacturing copper tools, weapons, ornaments, copper axes and chisels.[24] In view of the fact that this early mining development was of Neolithic Age would verify that it is pre-Flood in age.

Copper Mountain in Oman, Saudi Arabia

Along the west coast of the Gulf of Oman is an ancient copper mine that dates back to Sumerian times. Sumerian records speak about "Magan," the distant copper mountains from which shiploads of coveted metal were brought home by way of Ditmun. Heyerdahl visited this site in 1977 as he sailed his reed ship from ancient Sumer in the Persian Gulf to Pakistan, then westward through the Gulf of Aden to Djibouti, Africa. He met with Dr. Costa, Oman's archaeological adviser to examine the remains of a structure somewhat similar to a Sumerian Ziggurat. Between the structure and nearby mountains was the site that had been mined for thousands of years. Heyerdahl reports, *"The terrain between us and the mountains was strewn with unmistakable evidence of a copper mine. Slag carpeted the ground everywhere. It seemed a nearby mountain had been razed, and all that remained of a more distant one was a monumental stone arch, testimony to the entrance of some long ago mine shaft. Copper's importance to a Bronze Age society can hardly be overestimated, and it is little wonder that Magan was so highly regarded by Sumerians. Magan and modern Oman would seem to be one and the same."*[25]

Sumer is the first civilization to emerge after the Flood. It is characterized by the building of ziggurats. The Bible says that Noah and his family settled in the land of Shinar, which is in the region of Sumer. The world's population had to increase from a total of eight persons. Thus it would have taken years before the world's population would have been large enough to begin large scale mining operations at Magan (Oman) during the Sumerian Age. The most logical time for this flourishing mining centre was prior to Noah's Flood. In all likelihood, Noah and his family would have known about and would have been familiar with this rich copper site.

Medzamor Site in Soviet Armenia

One of the oldest metallurgical mines in the world was recently discovered at Medzamor in Soviet Armenia. Charroux says, *"Dr. Koriun Meguerchian has discovered the oldest metallurgical factory in the world. Experts have established that it was built 5000 years ago. At Medzamor, vases and objects made of all the common metals have been found such as knives, spearheads, arrowheads, clasps, rings, bracelets, etc. The foundry had a series of vats, hollowed out of rock, in which ore was crushed, pounded, washed, refined, and enriched until pure metal was obtained. Twenty* *five furnaces have been uncovered, but **more than two hundred are thought to be still buried.** Medzamor was an industrial centre of the period derisively **called the Neolithic.** Craftsmen worked with copper, bronze, lead, zinc, iron, gold, tin, arsenic, antimony, manganese, and also steel tweezers, slender and shiny have been found. Fourteen varieties of bronze were smelted in the plant and used for different purposes."* [26]

This discovery has been verified by scientific organizations in the Soviet Union, the United States, France, Britain and Germany. It would appear that this highly advanced metallurgical factory site was in full operation during the latter part of the Neolithic Age just prior to the Noah's Flood. However, bronze is a combination of copper and tin. This would normally place the age of this site according to the science of archaeology into the post Flood Age to about 2040 to 1786 BC. See Figure 20-2.

The problem is further mystified by the presence of iron and steel tools. The Iron Age is believed to have appeared about 1786 to 1567 BC and the steel Age sometime later. See figure 20-2. It would appear that a new beginning of human history began after Noah's Flood. Is it possible that we have evidence of history repeating itself at Medzamor in Soviet Armenia?

The Medzamor Site reveals that Early Man during the latter stages of the Neolithic Age had in fact surpassed the technology of making just Copper tools. They had discovered the art of smelting copper and tin together to get bronze? It also appears as if these Neolithic people had already entered the Iron & Steel Age. We read in Genesis 4: 23 (NIV) which says, *"Zillah also had a son, Tubal-Cain, who forged all kinds of bronze and iron."* **The implication in this passage is that the Pre-Flood people had finally passed beyond the Copper Age and had actually entered into the Bronze and the Iron Age just prior to Noah's Flood.** Future research will further unlock the mystery of this age. Is it possible that we are underestimating the scientific advancements and accomplishments that took place during the final stages of the Neolithic Age just prior to Noah's Flood?

See Google: the Medzamor Site in Soviet Armenia for further information.

Flood Deposits at the Medzamor Site

It is interesting to note that the Neolithic Medzamor Site has been covered with younger sediments. The above description of the site reveals twenty five furnaces were uncovered, but more than 200 furnaces are believed to be still buried. How would geology explain the sedimentary burial coverings? This could have been accomplished by wind or water. In this case, it would have been by water based upon the sudden termination of similar Neolithic sites throughout this region and throughout the world by Noah's Flood.

Figure 15-4 describes the sudden termination of the Mas d'Azil Cave Site in France, together with the Middle East sites of Ninevah, Ur and Fara. Geology reveals that all of these Neolithic sites were abruptly terminated by Flood waters. The Egyptian Type Section reveals the sudden termination of the Neolithic Old Kingdom Age by sea water. Many of the funerary complexes and valley temples in Egypt were in many cases completely buried by gravel, sand and silt. See Figure 20-2.

On the basis of the Calgary Alberta Type Section, it is now possible to identify the Stages 1, 2 & 3 of Noah's Flood throughout the world. This should be done at the Medzamor Site in Armenia. See Appendix F.

Brief Summary of Events

Archaeology has confirmed that Early Man had entered the copper age during the Neolithic Age in Europe, Africa, Asia, the Middle East, China, Mongolia and in North and South America.

Archaeology now confirms that Early Man had entered the copper, bronze, and iron and steel Age during the Neolithic at the Medzamor Site in Armenia.

Archaeology now vindicates the authenticity of the Biblical record that man had entered the bronze and iron age prior to the Flood for we read, "*Zillah also had a son, Tubal Cain, who forged all kinds of tools out of **bronze** and **iron**"* (Genesis 4:22 NIV).

The Bible record confirms that the world experienced a population explosion prior to Noah's Flood. We read in Genesis 6:1-2, "*When men began to increase in numbers on the earth and daughters were born to them, the sons of God saw that they were beautiful and they married any of them they chose."*

Archaeology and anthropology has also revealed that large concentrations of people lived in Central and South America, Europe, Asia, the Middle East, Egypt, etc. at the time these large structures were constructed. It is estimated that millions of people were required to construct the giant pyramids of Egypt and America. The logical time for the pyramids and the other cyclopean stone structures to have been built would have been prior to the Flood. After the Flood the Earth's population remained relatively small for many centuries and there would not have been sufficient people to construct these great colossal and cyclopean structures.

It is concluded that the Egyptian Type Section is the key for unlocking the mystery of all the Stone Age sites throughout the world that are classified as Paleolithic, Mesolithic and Neolithic.

It is concluded that there was a similarity of climate change throughout the Earth. The science of geology is able to realistically divide the last 10,000 years into the Anathermal, the Altithermal, the Flood Age and the Medithermal Age.

It is concluded that Global extinctions of prehistoric animals and Man characterize the termination of the archaeological

Great Stone Age. Prehistoric animals like the sabre tooth tiger, giant elephants such as the woolly mammoth and the mastodons, giant sloths and so forth together with Man all perished at the end of the Great Stone Age period except for Noah and his family.

It is concluded that Geological evidences supporting Noah's Flood are found throughout the Earth. The Calgary, Alberta Type Section has representations of all three stages of Noah's Flood which are stages 1, 2 & 3. See Appendix F. This qualifies the Calgary Site to be a typical Type Section that can be used to interpret all other Flood Sites through-out the world.

Jesus Christ made a most interesting statement. We read, *"As it was in the days of Noah, so shall it be at the coming of the Son of Man"* (Mathew 24:37 NIV). In other words, events that took place prior to the Flood of Noah will be similar prior to His second coming. However, God has promised that He will not destroy the Earth the second time with water.

References for Chapter 21

1. Wellard, James Howard, *"The Great Sahara"* E.P. Dutton & Co., Inc. New York, 1964. The quoted reference is from a scientific magazine article on page 605. Similar info is also found in the above reference.
2. Wellard, p. 606.
3. Ryan William & Pitman Walter, *"Noah's Flood"* with a caption *"The New Scientific Discoveries about the Event that Changed History,"* Simon & Schuster, Rockerfeller Centre, N.Y., 1999, p. 165.
4. Ryan & Pitman, p.167.
5. Halley, p.93. He quotes Sir Flanders Petrie.
6. Halley, p.93. He describes the Carving & Hoisting Method of Pyramid building.
7. Davidovits Joseph and Margie Morris, "The Pyramids: An Enigma Solved," Hippocrene Books, N.Y., 1989, p.184.
8. Davidovits, p.184.
9. Davidovits, p.71.
10. Davidovits, p. 193-207.
11. Tompkins, Peter, "Secrets of the Great Pyramid," Harper & Row, N.Y., 1978, p.12.
12. Davidovitz, p.119.
13. www.gira.ca for article entitled, "Early Egyptian History."
14. Halley, p.71-79.
15. Halley, p.71.
16. Halley, p.71.
17. Davidovitz, p.8-9.
18. Drake, W. Raymond. "Gods and Spacemen in the Ancient West." N.Y.: New American Library, 1974, p.141.
19. Drake, p. 148.
20. Drake, p.6-7.
21. Stern, Philip Van Doren,. "Prehistoric Europe from Stone Age Man to the Early Greeks" N.Y. Norton, 1969, p.250.
22. Stern, p.258.
23. Gaverlock & Ham. p.83.
24. Borislav J. *"The Origins of Copper Mining in Europe,"* Scientific American, May, 1980. He quotes Jovaovic, p.152-167.

25. Heyerdahl Thor, 1990, "*The Tigris Expedition*," published in Great Britain by Gerge Allen & Unwin, 1980. The quote is from a scientific Journal which I am unable to find, but is also found in Chapter 7.
26. Charroux, Robert, "*Forgotten Worlds*," N.Y., Popular Library, 1973, p. 64

Chapter 22

The Inca, Maya, Aztec, Toltec Mystery Revisited

In Chapter 19, we discussed the Early Man who occupied North and South America prior to Noah's Flood. Anthropologists have identified this Early Man on the basis of his facial bone structure as the Neanderthal Man. Archaeologists have identified this Early Man on the basis of his stone tools as being directly related to the Palaeolithic, Mesolithic and the Neolithic ages. They also believe this Neanderthal Man occupied all of regions to the south of Canada. This included all of the United States, Mexico, Central America and all of South America. See Figure 19-3. If this is the case, then he would have been contemporary with the Early Man who occupied the Old World countries. Thus, he would have lived prior to Noah's Flood. See Figure 20-2.

Do we know anything about the great accomplishments of this Early Neanderthal Man in America? Is it possible that his accomplishments only apply to some simple stone age projectile points and simple copper tools that mysteriously also relate to similar tools in Africa, Europe, Asia. Was he capable of constructing megalithic and cyclopean stone structures in North and South America? Is it possible that archaeologists and anthropologists are ignoring his greater accomplishments?

Archaeologists say that Early Man in America had stone and copper tools that were similar to the stone and copper tools that characterize the Palaeolithic, the Mesolithic and the Neolithic ages in the Old World. If this is true, then it means that he should have experienced building and technical developments that would also be characteristic of these three ages.

Archaeologists and anthropologists often talk about Paleoindians in America. Is it possible that the term Paleoindian actually refers to the Neanderthal Man?

Was there a close connection between the Old World of Africa, Europe and Asia with the New World of North and South America? How close was this connection?

Ancient Peoples in North & South America

Ancient peoples in North and South America did not call themselves Inca, Aztec, Toltec or Maya people. Archaeologists assign such names to distinguish the cultural history of the various groups of Indian people who are living and have lived in North and South America for many years. It is not known for sure what these ancient Americans called themselves.

Would it be more plausible to refer to these ancient so called Inca, Aztec, Toltec and Maya people as two separate and distinct groups such as the Neolithic Neanderthal People followed later by the American Indian People? Let us now see whether this is possible to do?

The Inca Sites in Peru / Bolivia

Figure 22-1 is a map of South America where nine specific sites of Early Man have been discovered. Archaeologists classify these mysterious sites with the Inca People. Some brave persons date these sites as far back as 20,000+ years before the present. The traditional majority want to classify these sites with the Inca people who constructed these cyclopean and megalithic structures between 1000 BC to1500 AD at which time the Spaniards came to America.

Figure 22-1: Map of South America showing nine specific sites of Early Man. This map was prepared by Don Daae. This information was based upon the excellent work of Thomas C. Patterson in his book, "Archaeology the Evolution of Ancient Societies."[1]

Many modern day archaeologists, anthropologists and other people are relating the Inca people with the North and South American Indian tribes. However on the basis of the Biblical record, the origin of the Indian people began about 120+ years after Noah's Flood at the Tower of Babel dispersion. This is when the origin of the modern nations took place. How is it possible to resolve this continuing dilemma?

In reality, it would have taken the American Indians tens of years to have migrated to America from Mesopotamia in the Middle East region after Noah's Flood. It would have also taken considerable time for the Indian people to have increased in numbers to populate this vast region of North and South America. Obviously, the American Indians would have eventually encountered these ancient mysterious Neolithic megalithic and cyclopean Stone Age sites. These ancient sites would have been an amazing mystery to the early Indian people. It would be equal to the mystery that you and I experience when we visit and read about these sites and wish to earnestly solve.

Let us now investigate some of these sites. Figure 22-1 is a map of South America that identifies nine sites. They are the Tiahuanaco, Cucso, Huari, Tutishcainyo, Chuquitanta, Ancon, Chavin, Chanchan and the Real Alto Sites. We will only look into the Tiahuanaco and the Cusco Sites.

The Tiahuanaco Site

The Puma Punku ruins at Tiahuanaco, Bolivia startles the imagination. It is located along the shores of an ancient Lake called Titicaca. It reveals a massive, four-part, now collapsed building. One of the construction blocks from which the pier was fashioned weighs an estimated 440 tons and several other blocks lying about are between 100 and 150 tons. The quarry for these giant blocks was on the western shore of Lake Titicaca, some ten miles away. See www. Puma Punku in Tiahuanaco for photos.

The ancient builders left no written records. There is a mystery as to who constructed these megalithic and cyclopean stone structures. Is it possible to correctly identify these ancient people who constructed these magnificent structures?

We read on the Google website that there is no known technology in the entire ancient world that could have transported stones of such massive weight and size. It is said that the Andean people of 500 AD, with their simple reed boats, could certainly not have moved them. Even today, with all the modern advances in engineering and mathematics, we could not fashion such a structure. How were these cyclopean blocks made? Another question arises, what gigantic force could have caused the collapse of some of these massive buildings?

When the Puma Punku ruins at Tiahuanaco were first discovered many were largely covered with sediment. After several decades of excavation some of the walls have been uncovered and treasure hunters opened a depression in the top. This structure was built originally to open towards the east.

Is it possible to explain how this temple became covered or buried with sediments? Could this have been the result of Noah's Flood that terminated the Neolithic Age about 4,500 years ago?

Puma Punka

The internet describes the Puma Punku structures at the Tiahuanaco site. It is the remains of a large number of megalithic blocks of stone on the ground, evidently smashed by a devastating earthquake. However, closer inspection shows that these stone blocks have been fabricated with a very advanced technology. Even more surprising is the technical design of these blocks. All blocks fit together like interlocking building blocks.

The question arises, how were these monstrous, gigantic stone blocks moved into place and what was their purpose? They literally weigh many tons.

Tiahuanaco is a mystery because of its age and peculiar stone technology. Today there is little doubt that Tiahuanaco was a major sacred ceremonial centre and focal point of a culture that spread across much of the region. These ancient people built a stone pyramid known as the Akapana. It is located along the Peru/Bolivia border.

The Cusco Site

Cusco, historical capital of the Inca Empire, was declared (in 1983) a World Heritage Site by UNESCO. It is located in Peru which is just across the border from Bolivia; it serves as a major tourist attraction. It is unique in its location, appearance, its megalithic stone structures and its mysterious origin. It is open to the world that warmly welcomes the visitors, who astonishingly watch its strange look.

Cusco is surrounded by impressive archaeological remains like the Machu Picchu citadel, the Saqsayhuaman fortress, the Ollantaytambo complex and picturesque towns such as Pisaq, Calca and Yucuay.

It is reported that the Incas built the huge fortress and religious site of Sacsayhuaman on a hill above Cuzco at Machu Picchu. This site is 8,000+ feet (2438m) in elevation above sea level. When the Incas built the Machu Picchu fortress of Sacsayhuaman, they shaped massive rocks with great precision. The construction of sites like Sacsayhuaman is a remarkable achievement for a society that did not have the wheel or iron tools. Many of these blocks weigh many, many tons. How were they transported from great distances to this site? How were they shaped to fit together with such precision? Did the Inca Indian people build these monstrous cyclopean and megalithic structures? Or is there another explanation? See Google @ www Inca fortress of Sacsayhuaman for an insight into the entrance door and the massive stone blocks.

Most rocks underlying Cusco, the Urubamba River Valley and Machu Picchu are igneous, comprising parts of several vast Andean plutons (intrusions) similar to those that form the principal core complexes within the Coast Range of North America. Although many guidebooks describe the intrusive rocks of Peru as "granites" most appear to be diorites, quartz diorites and granodiorites.

Figure 22-2: The Inca Machu Picchu fortress of Sacsayhuaman. Purchased from Thinkstock.

By going to the internet, one realizes that all of these pre-historic sites along the west coast of South America have megalithic and cyclopean stone structures that have remained a
puzzlement to archaeologists and to all mankind. It is not
necessary to postulate that these were super human beings.
They were normal human beings like you and I. They had
discovered a secret that made all of this massive construction possible. What was this secret discovery? This secret will
be revealed as we progress with our study of Early Man.

Other Archaeological Sites

There are several other sites of the same age along the
west coast of South America. They are located at Huari,
Tutishcainyo, Chuquitanta, Ancon, Charvin, Chanchan and
Real Alto. See Figure 22-1. I would encourage our readers
to explore these additional sites in South America. This will
enhance your knowledge of the advanced industrial and
social developments that took place during this mysterious
and unique age. This mystery will be revealed later!

In our study, we will now leave South America. We will now
begin to unravel the mystery of Mesoamerica that is located
in the southern portion of North America.

Mesoamerica

Mesoamerica is the area extending approximately from
the central portion of Mexico in the north to Nicaragua
and Costa Rica to the south. Diverse ancient and mysterious civilizations flourished that were also characterized by
megalithic and cyclopean Stone structures and pyramids.
Who were these ancient people?

These civilizations are known today by names like the Toltec,
Aztec, Olmec and Maya Peoples. Who were these people
and when did these mysterious civilizations flourish. The
different Archaeological Sites are plotted on Figure 22-3.

We will begin by viewing the peoples who lived at Teotihuacán.
This ancient City is located about 25 miles northeast of

Mexico City. Today, the elevation of Teotihuacán is about 7,000 feet (2,134m) above sea level. It is located on a high plateau region with mountains to the west and also to the east.

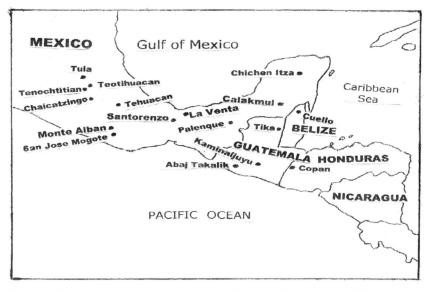

Figure 22-3: Map of Mesoamerica. It was the home of Early Man who lived prior to the Flood of Noah. This map shows 16 sites where mysterious Neolithic Stone structures were constructed. Prepared by Don Daae. There are undoubtedly other smaller sites yet to be discovered. The reader may wish to see the work of Thomas C. Patterson. [2]

The Teotihuacan Site

Teotihuacan is the largest known ancient site of Early Man in Mesoamerica America. Its history is an exciting mystery. It was once a thriving city, than suddenly its population disappeared. The name Teotihuacan means "the place where gods were born." It is also commonly held to mean "the place of reeds." Why did its population suddenly disappear from that site? See www.Teotihaucan Pyramids, Mexico.

The Pyramid of the Sun has a square base. It measures 738 feet (225m) on each side and rises 210 feet (64m) high. By comparison, the Great Pyramid of Khufu (Cheops in Greek) in Egypt has a square base that was originally 768 feet (234m) and originally rose to an height of 481 feet. The Pyramid of the Moon measures 492 feet (150m) on each side and its height is 138 feet (42 m).

The traditional view is that the Pyramids of the Moon and the Sun were built between 2 A.D. and 225 A.D. Is it possible that these Teotihuacan Pyramids could be Neolithic Structures that were built about the same time as Neolithic Age Pyramids in Egypt? If this is true then they should have been built prior to 4500 BC. See Figure 20-2.

Archaeologists speculate that Teotihuacan was abandoned about 700 A.D. for unknown reasons. The great mystery surrounding Teotihuacan is the origin of the city's original inhabitants. Archaeologists who study Teotihuacan history subscribe to one of two ideas; either that the elite sections of the city were burned to the ground or that a neighbouring group such as the Toltec's sacked and burned the city. Then it was later inhabited by the Aztecs.

Figure 22-4 is a view from the top of the Temple of the Moon viewing the Avenue of the Dead. The Pyramid of the Sun is seen in the distance to the left. Photo from Google website and purchased through Thinkstock.

There are no written records or a code to decipher that shed any light on this matter. Even the original name the city was given by its original builders is unknown. The nomenclature of the site, including the name Teotihuacan, was bestowed upon the city primarily by the so called Aztecs after the city's demise. In the Nahuatal language the name Teotihuacan means, "The city of the gods."

Two geologists and I had the privilege of climbing the pyramid of the Moon. We were told that there used to be an altar to their god at the top. We had an excellent view of the Avenue of the Dead and the Pyramid of the Sun as well as all the temple complexes. We could view the Palace of Quetzalpapalotl, another of the more famous structures that celebrates Quetzal-Mariposa, a mythical bird-like butterfly. This is a must place to see on your vacation to Mexico.

As we were walking among the temple complexes; we encountered the Temple of the Feathered Serpent. As I observed this fierce, devilish looking gigantic stone creature with wings, I wondered whether Cain or his descendents had personally been in this vicinity. The Bible record implies that Cain and his family group became world travellers and explorers. Cain was a person who followed and worshiped the Serpent, the Fallen Lucifer. See Chapter 12.

The Serpent obviously became the main object of worship by these Early Teotihuacán People. This does not mean that there were no believers to the True God of Heaven and Earth in Teotihuacán. It probably implies that the majority of people were worshipers of the Serpent who is no other than the Devil himself.

Who were the people of Teotihuacan?

As we learned in Chapter 19, Cain became the Father of the Neanderthal people of Europe and Asia. Archaeologists and anthropologists also confirm that the Palaeolithic, Mesolithic and the Neolithic people who inhabited all of North and South America were Neanderthal people. It is here concluded that the first inhabitants of Teotihuacan were the Neanderthal people. The average life span of all mankind before the Flood was 930 years. Thus, Cain's followers would have been the residents in this region prior to Noah's Flood.

The Traditional Origin of Teotihuacan

The present day view is that the city of Teotihuacán was built in the highlands of central Mexico about 150 BC and became one of the largest cities in Mesoamerica. At its height, the city covered an area of approximately 20 square kilometres and was home to 125,000 people including immigrants from all parts of America.

Our GIRA Interpretation is that Teotihuacán was constructed during the 120+ year period prior to Noah's Flood. This would equate to about 2,620+ to 2,500 years BC. These pyramids were constructed in a similar way that the great pyramids in Egypt were constructed. It is thus assumed that these people would have learned the art of stone making from Egypt.

Modern day archaeologists claim that the construction of the famous Teotihuacán Pyramid of the Sun began in about 100 B.C. This Pyramid is the second largest in Mesoamerica. Of course, the Great Pyramid of Cholula is the largest in the world. It is located about 60 miles south of Teotihuacan.

Monte Alban Site: Mexico

Soaring above the valley and city of Oaxaca are the hilltop ruins of Monte Alban. It is the second largest ceremonial site in Mesoamerica. It is only exceeded in size by Teotihuacan near Mexico City. One ancient name of the site was *Sahandevui*, meaning, "at the foot of heaven." The ruins are extremely old. Elaborate yet currently undeciphered hieroglyphs found here are among the most ancient writings in all of Mesoamerica. Equally mysterious are the strange rock carvings known as *danzantes*, which depict humanoid figures with strange facial features.

Modern day archaeologists maintain that the first known buildings in Monte Alban were constructed between 1000 to 800 BC, but most of these are now destroyed or buried beneath later Zapotec structures. The Zapotec occupation of the site dates from 100 BC and most of the enormous structures standing today date from the classic phase of 300 to 900 AD when Monte Alban had become the principal ceremonial site of the Zapotec empire. The complex contains great plazas, numerous pyramids, a ballcourt, underground passageways, and over 170 tombs.

The Google website describes Monte Alban as having been a highly refined and complex astronomical observatory centre. A curiously shaped arrowhead structure, situated at an angle of 45 degrees to the main axis of Monte Alban, Mound J was aligned with the point in the western sky where Alnilam, the center star of Orion's belt, sets. The traditional view is that Monte Alban was built sometime between 100 BC and 200 AD, Mound J also has astronomical alignments with the setting positions of the Southern Cross and Alpha and Beta Centauri, and the rising position of Capella.

Is it possible that this site is more ancient and was actually constructed during the Neolithic Age prior to 2500 BC? See Figure 20-2.

San Lorenzo Site

The San Lorenzo Site is located along the southern shoreline of The Gulf of Mexico. The colossal Olmec Head at the San Lorenzo Site weighs about 18 tons. This head is believed to be the portrait of a ruler. It does not appear to have the characteristics of the Neanderthal or the Cro-Magnon Man. Nor does he have the definite characteristics of any modern day race of people. How were stone images of this magnitude made by these early people? What is the true origin of these people? Is it possible that the mysterious Biblical Nephilim may have looked like this colossal head? See the Olmec head at <u>www. San Lorenzo Collossal Head</u>.

Genesis describes the strange union that took place between the "sons of God" and the "daughters of men," which brought about unprecedented evil, violence, and crime upon the Earth. We read in Genesis 6:1-8 NIV "¹*When men began* *to increase in number on the earth and daughters were born to them, ²the sons of God saw that the daughters of men were beautiful, and they married any of them they chose. ³Then the LORD said, "My Spirit will not contend with man forever, for he is mortal; his days will be a hundred and twenty years." ⁴The Nephilim were on the earth in those days—and also afterward—when the sons of God went to the daughters of men and had children by them. They were the heroes of old, men of renown. ⁵The LORD saw how great man's wickedness on the earth had become, and that every inclination of the thoughts of his heart was only evil all the time. ⁶The LORD was grieved that he had made man on the earth, and his heart was filled with pain. ⁷So the LORD said, "I will wipe mankind, whom I have created, from the face of the earth—men and animals, and creatures that move along the ground, and birds of the air—for I am grieved that I have made them. ⁸But Noah found favor in the eyes of the LORD."* In other words, God is saying that He will give the Earth an additional 120 years, then judgment will come.

The strange marriage union between the mysterious sons of God and the daughters of men resulted in the birth of a race of Nephilim of great stature with supernatural wisdom and powers, and of exceedingly great wickedness. LaHaye / Jenkens³ say, *"Some prophecy scholars teach that "Nephilim," the Hebrew word for "giants" doesn't merely mean tall men but supernatural creatures, the product of angels ("the sons of God") and the daughters of men. Whatever their case, the most important lesson we can learn from this passage is that their wicked lifestyle caused God to unleash the flood. Their lifestyle included three specific sins:*

1. *Sexual perversion.*
2. *The thoughts of their hearts were turned to evil continually.*
3. *Routine living and disregard to the consequences of impending judgment."*

At the time of the Flood these fallen angelic beings who took on human form were cast into the pit where

they are today awaiting judgement. The writer Jude gives convincing evidence that the sons of God were fallen angels. He compares the sins committed to that of Sodom and Gomorrah as follows, *"And the angels who did not keep their positions of authority but abandoned their own home— these he has kept in darkness, bound with everlasting chains for judgment on the great Day."* (Jude 1:6, NIV).

Jude is here referring to the select group of fallen angels who did not keep their proper domain or first estate before Noah's Flood. These fallen angels committed a grievous sin which precipitated the judgement of the Flood, and resulted in their banishment by God into the 'pit' where they are continually in chains under darkness awaiting the judgement of the Great Day. They are no longer present on the Earth today. Is it possible that the Olmec Head may represent the features of the so called, "sons of God"?

Whatever the Olmec Head represents, it must be remembered that the primary object of worship for these people was "The Serpent" who is another name for the Fallen Lucifer. Even today, it is the Devil's primary aim to get all people to follow and to worship him. These fallen angels were subservient to the Serpent.

Yucatan Peninsula, Mexico

There are several Maya Sites in the region of the Yucatan Peninsula which are located in the south west portion of Mexico. In this chapter we will only select the locations that will give the reader an insight into the megalithic and cyclopean nature of these ancient sites. I would encourage readers to check out the other sites on Google.

The Chichen Itza Site

The Maya name *Chichen Itza* means "At the mouth of the well of the Itza." According to the Google website, this name derives from *chi'*, meaning "mouth" or "edge", and *ch'e'en*, meaning "well." Itzá is the name of an ethnic-lineage group that gained political and economic dominance in the north eastern Yucatan Peninsula. The name is believed to derive from the Maya *itz,* meaning "magic," and *(h)á,* meaning "water." Itza in Spanish is often translated as "Brujas del Agua (Witches of Water)."

If there was an earlier name for this city, then it implies that an earlier people than the Maya Indian people built these cyclopean stone structures. Who could they have been? The original people were worshippers of the Serpent. At Yucatan, there is also a pyramidal structure with the head of the Serpent. It is our belief that these people were direct descendents of Cain who was a Serpent worshipper? In other words Cain was a worshipper of the Fallen Lucifer whose name is referred to as "The Serpent" in the Garden of Eden.

Figure 22-5: The pyramidal shaped pyramid at the Chichen Itza Site in northern Yucatan. See Google@www.chichen itza. The great attraction for the tourists at Yucatan are the ancient mysterious megalithic pyramidal stone structures. Purchase from Thinkstock.

This does not imply that true worshippers of Almighty God were not also present. Jesus said in Mathew 24:36-39 NIV, *"No one knows about that day or hour, not even the angels in heaven, nor the Son, but only the Father. As it was in the days of Noah, so it will be at the coming of the Son of Man. For in the days before the flood, people were eating and drinking, marrying and giving in marriage, up to the day Noah entered the ark; and they knew nothing about what would happen until the flood came and took them all away. That is how it will be at the coming of the Son of Man."* It is important to realize that the Message of Redemption was proclaimed to the entire world prior to Noah's Flood in a analogous way to how the Gospel is being proclaimed throughout the entire world today.

Why the Pyramidal Structures?

Why did Early Man want to build these megalithic and colossal pyramidal structures? Is it possible they were built to appease their god, the Serpent. Is it possible that they believed that if they would build these pyramidal structures that this would bring them into a closer relationship with their god, the Serpent.

At the summit of the Mexican Pyramid of the Sun and Moon was an altar to their god. These early people believed that by constructing these colossal pyramidal structures and by their good, hard and laborious works that this would in some magical way help them to earn brownie points and to gain acceptance and entrance into Heaven. They believed it would bring them into a closer contact and relationship with their god, the Serpent.

Cain became a Serpent worshipper and a world traveler. His aim was to work his way into heaven by good works and to appease the Serpent who became his god.

Cain's mindset was the same as Nimrod's after the Flood who said, *"Come, let us build ourselves a city, and a tower whose top is in the heavens; let us make a name for ourselves, lest we be scattered abroad over the face of the whole earth,"* Genesis 11:4 NKJV. As a result God passed judgment upon the Tower of Babel and upon Nimrod. After the Flood, history was about to repeat itself except for the Divine interception of Almighty God.

Other Sites of Interest

The following are additional Sites in Mesoamerica for the reader to explore in order to gain a greater insight into these mysterious people who constructed these cyclopean stone structures. See Figure 22-3.

Chichen Itza.	Tula
Tenochtitian.	Calakmul.
Fehuacan.	Cuello.
Monte Alban.	Palenque
San-Jose Mogota.	Tikal.
La Venta.	Abaj Takalik.
San Lorenzo.	Copan

Mysterious Pyramids Offshore Cuba!

In May 2001, engineer Paulina Zelitzky, President, ADC Corporation, Victoria, B. C., Canada and Havana, Cuba, announced the discovery of megalithic and cyclopean structures 2,200 feet below sea level at the western tip of Cuba. (The reader can find the following conversations on the Google website: "www.update of deep water Pyramids Offshore Cuba."

We read this quotation in the above website, *"In November 19, 2001 Havana, Cuba the story about a possible mega-lithic site half a mile down off the western tip of Cuba first broke this past May when a Reuters News Service reporter interviewed the deep ocean engineer who first reported un-usual side scan sonar of the discovery. Her name is Paulina Zelitsky."*

Ms. Zelitsky was born in Poland, studied engineering in the Soviet Union, was assigned to work on a secret submarine base in Cuba during the Cold War, and eventually defected to Canada. There she met her current husband, business-man Paul Weinzweig. Now the couple own and operate a company called Advanced Digital Communications, or ADC, with offices in both Victoria, British Columbia, and Havana, Cuba. Their specialty is deep ocean exploration.

We read, "*Now this year, Ms. Zelitsky reports that about 2,200 feet off Cuba's western tip she has found a huge land plateau with clear images of what appears to be man made large-size architectural designs partly covered by sand. From above, the shapes resemble pyramids, roads and buildings. Those dimensions are similar to the estimated sizes of some of the deep under water megalithic structures ADC International, Inc. has on sonar images. On video tape, there are also singular, large, granite-like stones that are curved with an unidentified line detail, or squared off, or one that seems to be a pyramid-shape rising up out of a rectangular stone.*"

The following is a dialogue between a reporter and Ms. Zelitsky regarding an inquiry about hieroglyphic writings on the sides of these stone structures. She responded by saying, "*Yes, thank you. I was overhearing, my husband and I don't want you to make any bad mistakes mixing Greek, because it is not Greek. It has the same tendency, but it is not Greek. We don't know what it is and scientists are try-ing to decipher it.*"

The reporter asks the question, "RIGHT. IT HAS SOME RESEMBLANCE IN LETTERING TO GREEK, BUT IS NOT GREEK. AND THERE ARE SOME LIKE PICTOGRAPHS THAT WOULD FALL INTO THE HIEROGLYPHIC CATEGORY AS WELL?"

Answer by Ms. Zelitsky, "*Yes, and symbols as well. There are different signs, more like American nature, like they have found in Central America Pyramids. And strong delineation of the structures which suggest pyramidal type, American pyramidal type, not Egyptian pyramidal type.*"

Question by reporter, "OK, YOU MEAN BY THE GLYPH SYMBOLS THAT WOULD BE FOUND IN MESOAMERICAN PYRAMIDS?"

Answer, "Yes."

Question by reporter, "AND AN EXAMPLE IS THAT CROSS MADE OF OVALS CROSSING EACH OTHER?"

Answer by Zelitsky, "*Yes. Yes, and other symbology, other cosmic type depictions. And you find this in Cuban caves around the island, not only in the south but in the north. And those caves are underwater caves. One cave I know of is on land and it has this type of symbology as well.*"

Question by reporter, "AND WHEN ARCHAEOLOGISTS HAVE STUDIED THE CARVINGS IN THE CAVES ON CUBA, HAVE THEY BEEN ABLE TO MATCH THOSE SYMBOLS AND GLYPHS TO ANY OTHER PRE-EXISTING KNOWN LANGUAGE? "

Answer by Zelitsky, "*They are trying to match it to Central American, but it is distinctive on its own. It's very difficult to say that ancient American symbology is identical to this. It is not identical. It's similar, but not identical.*"

Answer: "*After hearing about the symbol of crossed ovals and mysterious lettering, I began searching. I called the Archaeology and Anthropology Department at the University of Pennsylvania which has one of the finest collections of Olmec, Mayan and other Mesoamerican artifacts in the world. This weekend I spent several hours searching the library's rare books of Mayan and Mesoamerican glyphs. I could not find a single cross of ovals until I opened up a book called The Language of the Sea Peoples. There in a section comparing hieroglyphs from the Minoan island of Crete with hieroglyphs known as 'Linear C Language" used by an ancient Minoan culture called 'Luwian,' I found it.*"

Is it possible that during this time of Early Man, which would be Pre-Flood Man that there was travel and communication taking place between America and the Old World? Crete is next door to Egypt. It was in the Mediterranean where the Pharoah's of Egypt had their fleet of ships that would have been capable of sailing to America.

This is another conversation between a reporter and a certain qualified person with respect to the offshore Cuban Pyramidal Structures. Question: "WELL, AN INTERESTING POSSIBLE DISCOVERY IN THIS UNDERWATER MEGALITHIC SITE THAT'S UNDER RESEARCH IS THAT IN SOME OF THE SONAR DATA, NOT THE VIDEOTAPE, BUT THE SONAR DATA, THERE ARE SOME RETURNS THAT SUGGEST THAT THERE MIGHT BE METAL, LIKE METAL ON THE TOPS ON SOME OF THE OBJECTS. WOULD THE USE OF METAL AS SHEETING ON STRUCTURES BE SOMETHING THAT WOULD BE ASSOCIATED WITH THE RESEARCH ON ATLANTIS?"

Answer: "*Well, now we are getting really close to the Atlantean realm. Plato tells us that at the height of their prosperity to show off their wealth, they would actually sheet their outer walls of the city with great sheets of **high grade copper** which didn't exist in Europe in large numbers like North America. So, here were people who used a design technique, an architectural technique of including sheets of precious metal in their walls and now we are finding this supposedly at a site underwater off of Cuba. I would say now we are beginning to narrow in on a cultural commonality.*" Where did they get this copper? Could this copper have come from northern Michigan, USA?

The Pyramids Offshore Cuba Explained

The perplexing question is this: How can one explain the fact that the offshore pyramids are 2200 feet below sea level. The only science that can explain the dramatic structural Earth Movements at this time is within the geological sciences.

By conducting detailed geophysical and geological surveys along the western coastline of Cuba, this problem can be resolved. It is obvious that a vertical normal fault is present along the western edge of Cuba. Displacement along this fault has submerged these megalithic pyramids and other stone structures so that today they are 2200+ feet (671+m) below sea level. It must also be remembered that the sea level during this Neolithic age was about 328 feet (100 m) lower than it is today. This also explains why many of the caves in Cuba are presently below sea level.

A well known British Pleistocene geologist, Professor Charlesworth, in his 1957 book, THE QUATERNARY ERA,[4] wrote: "*The Pleistocene indeed witnessed Earth-movements on a considerable, even catastrophic scale. There is evidence that it created mountains and ocean deeps of a size previously unequalled-- the Pleistocene indeed represents one of the crescendi in the earth's tectonic history. The movements affected about forty million square kilometers of the ocean floor, i.e. 70 % of the total surface of the Earth. Asia was subjected to powerful and far- reaching disturbances; the fault troughs of the Dead Sea, Red Sea, Jordan Valley, Gulf of Aden, Persian Gulf, and Arabian Sea received their present form. Earth movements elevated the Caucasus; the amount since Mindel time (i.e. the second stage of the Ice Age) is estimated at 3,900 feet (1,189 m) and raised Lake Baikal region and Central Asia by 6,700 feet (2,042 m). Similar changes took place around the Pacific and in North China the uplift was estimated at 10,000 feet (3,040 m).*"

Dr. Lester King, Professor of geology at Natal University, South Africa, in his 1962 book, THE MORPHOLOGY OF THE EARTH [5] (p.33) stated, "*The greatest uplift has taken place in the Himalaya. The modern **Andes** were created by violent Pleistocene up-arching. There is, of course, much evidence of a late vertical movement of the Himalaya from Tibet into Europe, the Mountain Garland, Hindu Kish, Elbruz, and Caucasus are everywhere the product of uplifting during Pliocene to Recent times.*"

We are now able to pinpoint the exact time when these great structural movements took place throughout the Earth. It was at the end of the Altithermal Age. See Figure 19-1. This was the dramatic Earth shaking event that took place worldwide at the time of Noah's Flood. This event terminated the Pleistocene Ice Age. It also explains the sudden termination of the Pyramid Age throughout North and South America as well as in Egypt and other places throughout the world.

We read a description of what took place prior to the Flood by the only person who knows all things. Jesus said in Mathew 24:38-39 (NIV), "[38]*For in the days before the flood, people were eating and drinking, marrying and giving in marriage, up to the day Noah entered the ark;* [39]*and they knew nothing about what would happen until the flood came and took them all away. That is how it will be at the coming of the Son of Man.*"

Paleoindian Sites offshore Miami

The following article on Google Says[6], "*According to Gagliano and Blackwelder less than 100 Paleoindian sites are recorded in Florida. These known sites are scattered around the state and their recording is primarily a result of accidental discoveries. Many more Paleoindian sites undoubtedly exist, but they are located offshore on the continental shelf, in terrestrial wet areas, or are deeply buried. These inaccessible locations make it difficult to identify Paleoindian sites, and our ignorance of them has biased our interpretation of Paleoindian culture.*"[6]

For greater details see Google @ www. Gagliano and Blackwelder less than 100 Paleoindian sites are recorded in Florida.

We read, "*The Paleoindians lived in a Florida twice the size it is today. At the time they lived, sea level was 60-100 m (197 ft- 328 ft.) lower, exposing vast expanses of the present continental shelf.*" (Gagliano 1977; Blackwelder et al, 1979).[6]

We also read, "*Present-day coasts were inland, even upland, areas. The late Pleistocene shore lines in the Gulf of Mexico were located as much as 120 to 150 km (75-93 miles) seaward of their present locations. It is not difficult to see why Paleoindian period coastal sites have yet to be discovered in Florida-they are submerged beneath scores of fathoms of ocean water, tens of kilometres offshore.*" (Stright 1986; Garrison 1989).[6]

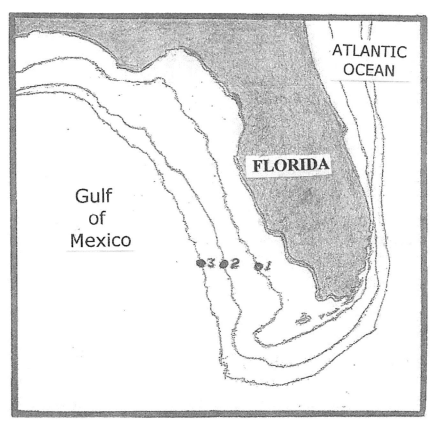

Figure 22-6: A Map of Florida revealing two offshore older shorelines. It was Prepared by Don Daae after the map by Gagliano and Blackwelder. See Google www. Gagliano and Blackwelder[6]

This map illustrates two separate shorelines: one at 60 m (197 feet), the other at 100m (328ft). I have found that the upper 60 m (197 foot) shoreline can be documented worldwide. I personally believe *this Upper Shoreline at 197 feet is Post Flood.* The lower shoreline at 100m (328 feet) would be pre-Flood. In other words, the sea level was about 100m (328 feet) lower than at present during the Pre-Flood Neolithic Age when the cyclopean and megalithic pyramid stone structures were being constructed throughout Mesoamerica.

The Post Flood Shoreline

The level of the ocean remained at about 180 to 197 feet below the present sea level for at least 500+ years after Noah's Flood. Then, for some reason the level of the ocean was raised to our present sea level. The minor varying depth range can be explained by varying local crustal read-justments that continually take place from time to time.

Scientists have found a distinct shoreline about 180 feet (55 m) below the present sea level at various places through-put the world. This is believed to be the level of the ocean after Noah's Flood. For instance, oceanographer Dr. Robert Dill presented research results from the submersible Deep Star submarine off the west California coast at a Canadian Society of Petroleum Geologists (CSPG) Alberta Geological luncheon in Calgary Alberta in the Fall of 1968. He showed the filming of the sea life on the sea bottom offshore near Long Beach California utilizing the Deep Star Submarine. At the 180 foot (55m) depth, one could see an older shore-line with numerous tree trunks standing erect. Specimens of wood were dated by carbon-14 and found to be about 5,000 radiocarbon years of age. Similar observations of this shoreline were made by the Deep Star Submarine in various other parts of the world.

At that time, I personally checked bathymetric maps along the North Slope of Canada and Alaska and in the Bering Sea region where I was working the geology at that time. I dis-covered that there were places where the bathymetric maps showed a distinct steepening of the contours at about the 180 to 200 foot level, indicating the presence of an old shore-line. The depth of water between Alaska and Russia through the Bering Sea region is much less than 180 to 200 feet in depth. Therefore this land area would have been above sea level for a certain period of time after Noah's Flood.

According to Dr. Lester King[7] of Natal University, a large extension of southeast Asia has recently sunk beneath the sea until only islands and peninsulas remain visible where formerly land was continuous. If the sea level was 180 feet lower, then Australia would have been joined to Southeast Asia by a land bridge.

I had the privilege of seeing the Bathymetric and aerial photo maps throughout SE Asia. A certain geology Professor from the University of Honolulu showed me the work he was doing for a certain American Professor of archaeology. He showed me the Bathymetric aerial photo maps throughout SE Asia to Australia. We observed the shallow recently drowned dendritic river systems that were presently sub-merged by sea water. We both surmised that if the shore-line was 180 feet lower when these dendritic river channels were formed, then all of this south eastern region of Asia would have been above sea level. Also Australia would have been joined to SE Asia by a land bridge. This geologist also verified that there is a shoreline about 180 feet in depth surrounding the Hawaiian Islands.

Lowering the level of the sea by 180 feet would have al-lowed the Indian and Eskimo people to migrate into North and South America after Noah's Flood. A large portion of the North Sea in Europe would also have been dry land. In other words, the British Isles would have been attached to France by an extensive land bridge. The lower sea level would have facilitated the migration of animals to many places via land bridges that today are separated from the mainland by sea water.

Pre-Flood Shoreline

I have no definite knowledge of the deeper shoreline that is presently offshore Florida. However, I have always as-sumed that the there had to be another shoreline as one approached closer to the continental shelf edge.

It becomes obvious that during the Neolithic Age the shore line world wide would have been in the vicinity of 328 feet (100 m) below our present sea level. This would have been the shoreline that existed during the Pyramid Age when all these cyclopean and megalithic stone structures were being constructed in America as well as throughout the world.

I believe we can safely say that the eastern coastline of Mesoamerica should now be expanded to include Florida, Cuba and all the islands within the Caribbean Sea Region.

My Personal Thoughts

During the 1960's and 1970's, I had the privilege of being a participant in overseeing an exploration program in the off-shore regions of the USA. The company that I was employed with were interested in determining the oil and gas offshore potential along the east coast of the USA, the Gulf of Alaska and the Bering Sea region in preparation for future offshore land sales. This resulted in the participation with about 23 other major Companies by running group geophysical sur-veys throughout these regions. Every major Company had their geologists and geophysicists interpreting the regional geology and geophysics for potential oil and gas prospects. This resulted in the drilling of five COST WELLS. The first well was drilled in the Georges Banks Basin just south of Nova Scotia, Canada. The second well was drilled in the Baltimore Canyon Basin to the east of New York. The third well was drilled along the Florida Embayment region. The fourth well was drilled in Gulf of Alaska offshore. The Fifth well was drilled in the St. George Basin in the Bering Sea region of Alaska.

When we were exploring the eastern offshore USA, I re-call the conversations regarding the mysterious Bermuda Triangle and how certain ships and planes had mysteriously disappeared. However, we could not detect any abnormal anomaly to be present in this region on the basis of seismic. This wetted my appetite to purchase the different books that pertained to the Bermuda Triangle and the Pyramids of Mesoamerica and South America. At that time, I vowed if I were to write a book about this region that I would be as pragmatic and scientific as possible in my interpretation.

Our geological and geophysical program was to relate the onshore geology with the offshore. The seismic lines invari-ably covered the offshore region extending to and overlap-ping the outer continental shelf edge.

Later, I had the rare privilege of evaluating the coastal and offshore oil and gas potential of Belize in Central Mesoamerica. See Figure 29-9. This again whetted my appetite in wanting to know more about the strange megalithic pyramidal-shaped stone structures that are present in Belize.

Mysterious Northern Michigan Copper Mines

The following is a dialogue between a reporter and a scientist regarding the ancient copper mines in northern Michigan, USA. (Note: The reader can find the following conversations on the Google website at: www.Northern Michigan Copper Mines.

Question: AND THIS WAS THE 5,000 MINES OF THE NORTHERN PENINSULA OF MICHIGAN THAT ARE EACH ABOUT 60 FEET DEEP?

Answer: *"Well, the average depth is probably like 20 feet deep for the pit mines, but there were many pit mines that were excavated through solid rock 60 feet down. So, whoever did that obviously had a technology far beyond anything that was known to the native Americans at that time who were not interested in anything more than float copper they picked up off the ground. But this is one of the great - I hate to use the word conspiracy, but it certainly is suppressed evidence that American scholars have known about for more than 100 years that there was a huge copper mining enterprise in upper Michigan that lasted from 3,000 B. C. to 1,200 B. C. (5,000 – 3,200 years BP) those magic dates again in which a minimum of half a billion pounds of the world's highest grade copper was excavated and disappeared."*

Answer: *"Copper was first mined in this area by an ancient vanished race between 5,000 and 1,200 bc. These miners left no burial grounds, dwellings, pottery, clay tablets or cave drawings. What was left behind was thousands of copper producing pits and more thousands of crude hammering stones with which the pits had been worked. The*

ancients apparently worked the copper bearing rock by al-
ternately using fire and cold water, to break the copper ore
into smaller pieces from which they could extract the metal
with hand held hammering stones or stone hatchets. With
this copper, they made tools."

"Scientists and engineers estimate that it would have re-
quired 10,000 men 1,000 years to develop the extensive
operations carried on throughout the region. It is estimated
that 1.5 billion pounds of copper were mined by these un-
known people. The pure copper of Lake Superior has been
discovered in prehistoric cultures throughout North and
South America."

"The mystery of their origin remains unsolved. The mystery
of their disappearance remains unsolved. Many hammered
copper knives, arrow and spear heads and axes were re-
covered at ancient mining sites. Some fine examples are on
display at Fort Wilkins." (See Google: Update on underwater
Megaliths-Windows Internet Explorer)

In Conclusion: the mystery of the Northern Michigan Copper
Mines is hereby resolved. This massive Copper Mine Site
in Northern Michigan was discovered and developed by
the now extinct Neanderthal people. Archaeologists always
relate the Copper Age to the Neolithic Age. This gives an
added clue as to the great technological advancements that
took place during the Neolithic age in America. It is obvious that this man was capable of transporting this precious
copper ore to all of Mesoamerica and beyond.

It is interesting to note that the Northern Michigan Copper
Mines bear a remarkable similarity to the mysterious,
Neolithic Rudna Glava Copper Mines in Yugoslavia. See
Chapter 21 for details.

Mesoamerica Enlarged

Mesoamerica should now be enlarged to include the entire
region of Central America, Mexico, the Caribbean Islands
and Florida. It should now be extended northward to the

southern limits of the Pleistocene Ice edge and to the Ice corridor that extended northward into the Yukon and Alaska. See map on Figure 19-3. Let us now continue.

Mysterious Poverty Point Site, Louisiana?

Poverty Point is a major archaeological mystery. A website description of this site is as follows, "*The mystery centers on the ruins of a large prehistoric Indian settlement, the Poverty Point site. There on a bluff top overlooking Mississippi River swamp lands in north-eastern Louisiana is a group of artificial mounds and embankments. It is not the earthworks themselves that are so mysterious. Eastern North America is, after all, the land of the "Mound Builders."*

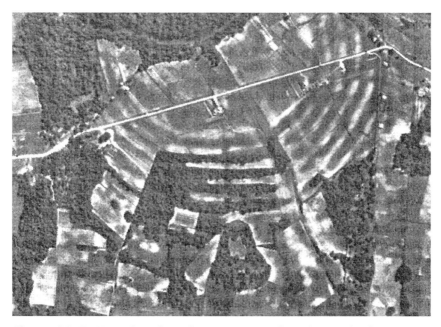

Figure 22-7: Map showing the Poverty Point Site, Loiusiana, USA from Google website. Purchase from Thinkstock.

One interpretation suggests that these people are thought to be a highly advanced, extinct race. However, no one seems to have had the courage to identify who these extinct people were? The origin of this race is still a mystery.

The Google Website Site says, *"They now are known to be ancestors of Native Americans, such as the Creek, Choctaw, Shawnee, and Natchez. The real mystery lies in the size and age of the earthworks. They are among the largest native constructions known in eastern North America, yet they are old, older than any other earthworks of this size in the western hemisphere."* They have only found the human remains of Indian people at this site. Also, radiocarbon dates according to Google, would indicate that the earthworks were built between fourteen and eighteen centuries before the birth of Christ. The dates 1400 and 1800 years B.C. would equate to 3,400 to 3,800 years before the present. This could very well have been the time that the North American Indians would have arrived at this site.

My Interpretation: Is it possible that these now extinct Poverty Point people were the Neanderthal people who lived during the Neolithic (Copper) Age prior to Noah's Flood? There is a remarkable similarity between this site and the Neolithic Stonehenge Site in England. See photo on Figure 21-2. Medical Researcher Dr. Mike Collins from the University of London and his lovely wife Jan guided my wife and I on a tour of the British Stonehenge's. We observed these mysterious megalithic stone structures that are now considered to have been constructed during the Neolithic Age. We walked along the circular ridge that encircles the famous Stonehenge and wondered as to its purpose? There are unsolved mysteries surrounding these structures. We also visited a Burial Mound and observed the inside rooms. I found this most interesting because I used to give lectures on the burial mounds in East Africa which are characteristic of the Neolithic Age. Likewise, these three burial mounds at the Poverty Point Site in Virginia also bear a remarkable resemblance to the burial mounds in Europe and East Africa.

When did the North American Indians arrive?

The question arises, what is the most likely time that the Indian people would have arrived into North America? All modern day races of people originated at the Tower of Babel

Dispersion. This would have been about 120+ years after Noah's Flood which is believed to be about 4,500 years ago minus 120 years equates to about to about 4,380 years B.P. It would have taken considerable time after the Tower of Babel Dispersion for the American Indians to populate America.

At that time, almost all Indians living north of Mexico were small bands of migratory hunters and food gatherers. Such societies do not ordinarily build huge earthworks like those at Poverty Point. Large-scale construction is possible when large numbers of people settle down in villages and after political forces grow strong enough to shift some labour from the hunt and harvest to the civic and ceremonial.

The google website asks these questions, "*How did the conditions necessary for large-scale construction appear at Poverty Point while everyone else in America north of Mexico was still following a simpler way of life? Was Poverty Point one of the first communities to rise above its contemporaries to start the long journey toward becoming a truly complex society? If Poverty Point did represent the awakening of complex society in the United States, how and why did it develop?*"

It goes on to say, "*Was it created by immigrants bearing maize and a new religion from somewhere in Mexico? Was it developed by local peoples who had been stimulated by ideas from Mexico? Did it arise by itself without any foreign influences? Did it come about without agriculture? Could hunting and gathering have sustained the society and its impressive works?*"

The website than says, "*These sorts of questions perplexed archaeologists. Limited data and disagreement over these issues made Poverty Point a real archaeological puzzle. New research has begun to clarify some of these things. We no longer regard Poverty Point as a geographic or developmental irregularity, but it remains one of the most unusual archaeological cultures in eastern North America.*"

The website also brings out that Poverty Point was the ultimate destination for incoming goods as follows, "*Poverty Point stone dealers tapped into a wide range of resources from the North American midcontinent:* **copper from the Great Lakes***, galena—a native lead ore—from the Upper Mississippi River in Iowa, soapstone from the Appalachian piedmont, and tons of flint and other materials from the Ouachita Mountains, Missouri's table rock, southern Illinois's Shawnee Hills, Kentucky's Knobs, Tennessee's Appalachian foothills, and places in-between. There is even a piece of obsidian from Wyoming's Rockies. Practically all stone supply areas could have been reached by express dugout using the Mississippi's net of rivers and creeks. It is evident that there was trade connections from many different regions of the USA during this time.*"

An Alternative Interpretation: The Neanderthal men and women are the most likely peoples to have constructed this enormous site at Poverty Point, Louisiana. They were the ones who constructed the Cyclopean and Megalithic Sites in Mesoamerica and in South America. To get an insight into how densely North and South America was populated by Neanderthal people during the Pre-Flood Neolithic Age see the map on Figure 19-3. This map reveals that the Neanderthal man inhabited all areas south of the Pleistocene Ice. This included the USA, Mexico, Central America and most of South America.

It becomes obvious that the Poverty Point site was constructed by the Neanderthal Man during the Neolithic Age just prior to Noah's Flood. Anthropologists maintain that the Indians constructed this site because the bodies that were found at this site had Indian features. This can easily be explained by the fact that these early Indians came across this site with the same wonderment that peoples from Europe, Asia and Africa had when they first visited this site. It is only natural that they would have made this as a place of residence.

One of the mysteries of all these sites is the lack of anthropological evidences to believe that the Neanderthal type man constructed these amazing structures at Poverty Point and at other sites throughout Mesoamerica because of an amazing scarcity of human skeletal remains.

The reason for this is the longevity of Pre-Flood Man that was on an average of 930 years. The deaths would have been minimal. All the persons who lived at this site were very likely less than 930 years of age. Thus, they were all, for the most part, swept away by the powerful Tsunami tidal waves resulting from Noah's Flood.

The Mystery of North & South American Paleo-History

It is now possible to resolve the mysterious Paleo-History of North & South America. We can now truly find a reasonable answer as to the origin of the ancient people who inhabited North and South America prior to the appearance of the modern day Indian people.

The Neanderthal Man was responsible for constructing these mysterious cyclopean and megalithic structures in various parts of North and South America. But, why is the Neanderthal Man not recognized in America by archaeologists, anthropologists as a builder of these structures?

A Big Problem Exists

Creation Science (Young Earth) Creationists believe that God created the Earth between 6,000+ years ago and that Noah's Flood took place about 4,350 plus or minus years ago. Thus, they maintain that all these megalithic and cyclopean stone structures in North and South America as well as in Egypt, Africa and Europe are all Post Flood and were built by American Indian groups. Thus, they cherish the idea of referring to the Inca, Aztec, Toltec and Maya people as being the ancestors to the modern American Indians who were responsible for constructing these gigantic stone structures. See Appendices A, B & C.

Creation Science people believe the entire Pleistocene Ice Age is Post Flood. Therefore, all the mysterious, ancient Stone-Age sites in North and South America must be Post Flood. They go along with the secular view that these early Maya, Inca, Toltec and Aztec people are ancestors of our modern day Indian Groups.

Creation Science persons ignore the fact that the Pleistocene sediments in the Gulf of Mexico are up to 9,000+ feet (2,743m) in thickness. In the Mackenzie Delta region of the NWT the thickness of the Pleistocene sediments increases from about 50+ feet at Aklavik and Inuvik to over 1500 feet (457m) in the Mackenzie Delta region to about 7,500 feet (2,286m) in the Beaufort Sea. This is based upon seismic and drilling. I had the privilege of working the geology and viewing the geophysics in this area with a Major Oil & Gas Company.

I also had the privilege of participating in the drilling of an offshore COST well in the Gulf of Alaska with 23 other major oil and gas companies. This well was drilled to a depth of about 13,000 feet (3,962). It encountered 4,000+ feet (1,219.2m) of Pleistocene sediments that on the basis of seismic data were increasing in thickness in a seaward direction.

Throughout the Western Prairie Provinces of Canada there is an average of 200 feet (61m) in thickness of Pleistocene gla-cial sediments increasing to 800 feet (243.8m) in places.

If the Pleistocene Ice Age sediments are Post Flood in age, how can Creation Science persons account for this great thickness of sediments being deposited after Noah's Flood at about 4,350 years ago. Where is their evidence of Pre-Flood Man? They must look to the bottom of the geologic column! This would have to be at the base of many tens of thousands of feet of water-laid sediment. So the mystery continues.

The Secular Darwinian Worldview denies Noah's Flood entirely. Therefore they do not see a break separating the

Neolithic Stone Age people from the North American Indians. They would tend to believe that the people who built these cyclopean structures were the ancestors to the present day American Indians.

A few of the more brave secular scientists maintain that many of these cyclopean stone structures could be 6,000 to 20,000+ years in age. However, they never give credit to the Neanderthal Man. They rather give credence to the traditional secular view that the North and South American pyramids and the other great Stone Age structures were constructed about 1000 BC to about 1400 AD by ancestors of the American Indians.

Unfortunately, modern day anthropologists and archaeologists continue to maintain that the Neanderthal man was inferior to the Cro-Magnon Man. They believe that the Cro-Magnon man evolved from the Neanderthal Man about 40,000 years ago. See Figure 15-2. Thus, they erroneously believe that the Neanderthal man in America did not have the mental capabilities of constructing megalithic and cyclopean stone structures. Anthropologists have confirmed that the Neanderthal man had a brain capacity of over 1600 cu cm. It is evident that he was brainier than the average man today who has an average brain capacity of about 1450 cu cm.

The Scientific Affiliation of Christian Scientists in the USA is one of the older and larger Christian Science groups. I was a member of this organization for several years. They generally deny that Noah's Flood was global. They generally contend that Noah's Flood was restricted to the Middle East Region. Thus, they would go along with the secular view that the North American Indians are descendents of the ancient people who built these many megalithic and cyclopean pyramids and other stone structures.

All of the three above groups are living in a state of denial that there is a gap that separates the American Indians from the original (Early Man) people who truly were responsible for constructing these megalithic stone structures.

The Traditional Interpretation of the Inca, Toltec, Aztec, Olmec and Maya People is that these Megalithic and Cyclopean Stone structures were constructed sometime between 1000 BC to about 1500 AD at which time the Spanish people from Europe came to America. The question arises, is there a better interpretation?

The GIRA Interpretation

Our GIRA interpretation is based upon the amazing compatibility that exists between the scientific data of geology, archaeology, anthropology and the Bible record. As a result we are able to confirm that all the worldwide megalithic and cyclopean stone structures were built by Neolithic Pre-Flood Man who lived during the 120+ year prior to Noah's Flood. They were direct descendants of Adam and Eve. See Figure 19-1.

We read in Genesis 1:28 (NIV) that God said to Adam and Eve, *"Be fruitful and increase in number; fill (populate) the earth and subdue it. Rule over the fish of the sea and the birds of the air and over every living creature that moves on the ground."* In other words, the descendents of Adam and Eve were to populate the entire Earth prior to the Flood. This is confirmed by the three sciences geology, anthropology and archaeology that every continent, except possibly Antarctica, was occupied by Early Man prior to Noah's Flood.

We are now able to determine that the Flood of Noah was global and that Early Man actually inhabited North and South America as well as the Old World prior to about 4,500 years ago when Noah's Flood took place.

In Chapters 14-19, we were able to determine that the Cro-Magnon and the Neanderthal Men were present in Europe, Asia, Africa, whereas, only the Neanderthal Man occupied North and South America. See Chapter 19.

We conclude that the Neanderthal Man was "primarily" responsible for building the megalithic and cyclopean stone structures throughout North and South America. However, He was unable to do this without the help of the Cro-Magnon Egyptian people. Thus, we must analyze the amazing discovery of Stone Making and the Egyptian type Section.

The Egyptian Type Section

The Egyptian Type Section in Egypt reveals the true ages of all the megalithic and cyclopean Stone Age pyramids and structures throughout Northern Africa, Europe, Asia and now North and South America.

The Egyptian Type Section also reveals the key to understanding how these cyclopean and megalithic structures were made by mere human beings like you and me.

In Chapter 20, we discussed the two great discoveries that led to stone making in Egypt. The first big discovery was the making of plywood. The second was the discovery of Stone making.

The Discovery of Plywood

The Egyptians were great carpenters. It becomes evident that Egyptians had polished stone and copper tools throughout the Pre-Dynastic Age. Copper tools have been found within the latter part of the Pre-Dynastic Age as well as throughout the Neolithic Age. See Figure 20:2.

Egyptologist Davidovitz [8] says, *"Carpentry appeared in Egypt at the end of the pre-Dynastic period, around 3500 BC, when copper tools were sufficiently developed to enable them to do woodworking."* Then he goes on to say, *"Throughout all epochs, the Egyptian carpenter was a remarkable craftsman. He invented all manner of preparing wood joints and made them with skill: dowelling, mortices and tendons, dovetails, gluing, veneering, and marquetry. Wood being scarce in his country, he was the inventor of plywood."*

Truly, the early Egyptian carpenter of this age was a remarkable craftsman. Egyptologist Davidovitz [9] says, *"In a*

*sarcophagus made during the Third Dynasty there was ac-
tually a fragment of plywood found which was made from
six layers of wood, each about 4 mm (0.15 inches) thick,
held together by small flat rectangular tendons and tiny
round dowels. Where 2 pieces had to be joined side by side,
their edges were chamfered so as to unite exactly. The grain
direction in successive layers is alternated, as in modern
plywood, to provide greater strength and to avoid warping."*
He also explains how this plywood was used for casting the
enormous stone blocks that compose the pyramids. What
do we mean by casting stone?

In order to understand the significance of stone casting, it
is necessary to discover what happened to change the lives
of Early Man, not only in Egypt, but throughout the entire
world. What was this big, enormous discovery? In order to
understand the importance of this discovery, we must focus
our attention upon the Old Kingdom Age in Egypt.

The Discovery of Stone Making

One of the greatest discoveries in human history took place
in Egypt about 400+ years prior to the Flood. It was the
discovery of stone making which led to stone building. This
amazing feat took place during the Third Dynasty. The first
Pharaoh of the Third Dynasty was Zanakhit. He was followed by Zoser. See figure 20-3.

Pharaoh Zoser gave the responsibility of constructing the
first pyramid to his architect by the name of Imhotep.
Davidovitz says, *"Imhotep left an unforgettable legacy.
Historically, the lives of few men are celebrated for 3,000
years, but Imhotep was renowned from the height of his
achievements at about 2700 BC, into the Greco-Roman
period. Imhotep was so highly honored as a physician and
sage that he came to be counted among the gods.*[10] He was
later deified.

King Zoser gave Imhotep great honor. Davidovitz says,
*"Imhotep had many titles, Chancellor of the King of Lower
Egypt, the First after the King of Upper Egypt, Administrator*

of the Great Palace, Physician, Hereditary Noble, High Priest of Anu, (On or Heliopolis), Chief Architect for Pharaoh Zoser, and, interestingly, Sculpturer, and Maker of Stone Vessels."[11]

What was his big accomplishment? He invented the art of stone making and producing building blocks of polished stone. Davidovitz says, "The words describe "stone" with a beautiful, smooth surface, a feature characteristic of fine, agglomerated casing stone so smooth that it reflects the Sun." [12]

The Saqqara website[13] says, "Saqqara has the distinction of being the site of the first large stone structure built in the world. This was the place where humans began to strive for the impossible, where the imagination of Man gained the power to transform reality." See Figure 20-3. It then goes on to say, "The chap responsible for the Step Pyramid was Imhotep, Djoser's Vizier. He is credited as being the inventor of building in stone and was a man of many talents - Architect, physician, master sculpture, scribe, and astronomer. He must be the first true genius in recorded history and his impression on the Egyptians was profound because later generations revered him as a god of wisdom."

The Birth of Stone Making in Egypt began during the Third Dynasty about 150+ years before Noah's Flood. This marks the beginning of the Neolithic Age which is also called the Age of Polished Stone and copper tools.

Pharoah Khufu's Boat Discovered

Another big discovery in Egypt was Pharoah Khufu's boat. Davidovitz[14] says, "In the 1950's, an excavation of one of the pits near the Great Pyramid yielded a sacred funerary boat by Khnumu-Khufu. To the delight of archaeologists, the acclaimed artifact was preserved in perfect condition. The boat was measuring 120 feet, had a displacement capacity of over 40 tons." Davidovitz goes on to say, "Khufu's boat is far more seaworthy than any craft of Christopher Columbus's day. The famous mission of Thor Heyerdahl in

1970, from Morocco to Barbados in a papyrus reed boat, makes it clear that ancient Egyptian ships were capable of intercontinental travel."[15]

The big question arises, is there any evidence that mysterious boats reached America during the Neolithic Age? This is an area that requires greater study.

A Strange Boat Found at Lima Peru

W. Raymond Drake[16] reports, *"Eusebius Newcombergus, The Jesuit, in his fifth book of natural History, says that near the Port of Lima as the people were working a goldmine they found a ship on which were many characters very different from ours. Had this vessel been tossed ashore in some cataclysm and buried thousands of years ago en route to lost Lemuria?"*[15] The First or Third Stages of Noah's Flood Disaster Scenario would explain why this vessel had been tossed ashore and buried by cataclysmic type waves. See Figure 25-2 and APPENDIX F.

It must be remembered that the shore line world wide would have been in the vicinity of 328 feet (100 m) below our present sea level. This would have been the shoreline that existed during the Pyramid Age when all these cyclopean and megalithic stone structures were being constructed in America as well as throughout the world. The place for scientists to search in order to unlock the mystery of the above mentioned boat is in the vicinity of this submerged shoreline. Who knows what interesting mysteries are awaiting be discovered not only in Peru, but throughout the world.

It is very plausible that Early Man had ships that were capable of commuting from the Old World to the New World prior to Noah's Flood. Pharoah Kufu had a fleet of ships in the Mediteranean during his 94 year reign prior to Noah's Flood. It is very likely that many of these ships were capable of intercontinental travel. Only half of the story has now been told. It is also highly plausible that Early Man were able to communicate on a world wide basis. Von Daniken's

Book, "The Chariots of the God's," may have more to tell us than we are able to imagine.

I trust that this manuscript will continue to open up a new window of learning and the discovery of secrets from the past that will be mind boggling.

In Conclusion

Noah's Flood Disaster Scenario best explains the sudden destruction and termination of the Neolithic Age in North and South America as well as throughout the entire world.

References For Chapter 22

1. Patterson Thomas C., "ARCHAELOGY The Evolution of Ancient Societies," Prentice Hall, Inc. Englewood Cliffs, New York, New Jersey 07632, p.256.
2. Patterson, ibid. p.275.
3. Tim LaHaye / Jerry B. Jenkins, "Are We Living in the End Times?" Tyndale House Publishers, Inc. Wheaton, Illinois, p. 344.
4. Johnson George & Tanner Don, "The Bible and the Bermuda Triangle," published by Logos International, Plainfield, New Jersey 07060, 1973.
5. Professor Charlesworth A well known British Pleistocene geologist, In his 1957 book, *The Quaternary Era, Vol.1,* p: 604-605.
6. Dr. Lester King, Professor of Geology at Natal University, South Africa, in his 1962 book, "The Morphology of the Earth." p.33.
7. Dr. Lester King. As above p. 33.
8. Davidovits Joseph and Margie Morris, "The Pyramids: An Enigma Solved," Hippocrene Books, N.Y., 1989, p.72.
9. Davidovitz says, p.72.
10. Davidovitz says p. 72-73.
11. Davidovitz says, p. 129.
12. Davidovitz says, p. 129.
13. The Saqqara website.
14. Davidovitz says, p.16. Khufu's boat.
15. Davidovitz. p. 207.
16. W. Raymond Drake, 1974, "Gods and Spacemen in the Ancient West." 1974, p.203, Published by arrangement with Sphere Books Limited, 30/32 Gray's Inn Road, London WCIX *JL, England. A Signet Book, New American Library, Times Mirror.

Chapter 23

The Last 120 Years: Age of Great Despair

The 120 years prior to the Flood of Noah witnessed one of the most advanced worldwide civilizations. It was second only to our advanced worldwide civilization of today. There are indications that communication, travel, knowledge; industrial development were of a global nature. People and nations throughout the Earth had a means of sharing achievements, and technological skills.

The great pyramids of Egypt, the great pyramids of Central and South America, the colossal statues on Easter Island, the stone monuments of Britain, the Terrace of Baalbek north of Damascus, the Acropolis in Greece, the Megalithic Menhirs of Carnac in France, and many more are all contemporary and belong to a great worldwide civilization that reached its height of grandeur just prior to Noah's Flood.

The human population began with Adam and Eve about 6000+ years ago, when God commanded them to populate the Earth for we read, *"Be fruitful and multiply, fill the earth and subdue it"* (Genesis 1:28, NKJV). After the Fall, the Lord God informed Eve that the birth rate will now commence to multiply for it is recorded, *"I will greatly multiply your conception"* (Genesis 3:16, NKJV). Twins, triplets, and large families were probably the rule prior to the Flood.

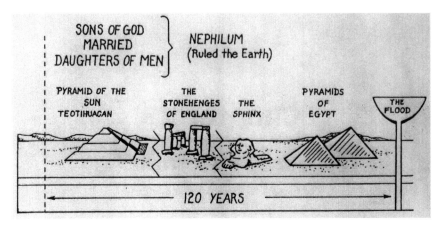

Figure 23-1: Illustrates the final 120 years prior to Noah's Flood. Prepared by Don Daae.

The Earth's population growth increased much faster before the Flood than after because people lived an average of 930 years. Disease would not have been as common. It is interesting to note that Noah was 500 years old when Shem, Ham and Japheth were born. People had children when they were several hundred years old as disease, illness and bodily weaknesses were relatively uncommon. At about 120 years before the Flood the population curve began to rise vertically, similar to what the world is experiencing today.

This 120 year period throughout the world was characterized by a progressive increase in evil and great violence. A strange group of fallen angels in some mysterious way took on human form and had relationships with the daughters of men. Children were born called Nephilum who were half demon and half human. Ordinary human beings would have been co-workers, and in many cases subservient and under their control, especially towards the end of this mysterious 120 year age.

The Nephilim

Who are the strange and mysterious Nephilim who dominated the Earth during the last 120 years prior to the Noah's Flood? According to the Bible record they were the children who were born into this world as a result of a strange and mysterious marriage relationship between the sons of God and the Daughters of Men. As a result of this relationship, God had no other option, but to destroy the ancient world of mankind, except for one family. Why was this event such a serious offense to Almighty God?

Chapter 6 of Genesis describes this strange union that took place between the "sons of God" and the "daughters of men," which brought about unprecedented evil, violence, and crime upon the Earth. We read in Genesis 6:1-8 *"Now it came to pass, when men began to multiply on the face of the earth, and daughters were born to them, that **the sons of God** saw the daughters of men, that they were beautiful; and they took wives for themselves **of all whom they chose**. And the Lord said, "My Spirit shall not strive with man forever, for he is indeed flesh; yet **his days shall be one hundred and twenty years**"* Genesis 6:1-3 (NKJV). In other words, God is saying that He will give the Earth an additional 120 years, then judgement will come. This is confirmed in Genesis 6:4-8 (NKJV),*"There were giants (nephilim) on the earth in those days, and also afterward, when the sons of God came in to the daughters of men and they bore children to them. Those were mighty men who were of old, men of renown. Then the Lord saw that the wickedness of man was great in the earth, and that every intent of the thoughts of his heart was only evil continually. And the Lord was sorry that He made man on the earth, and He was grieved in His heart. So the Lord said, "**I will destroy man who I have created from the face of the earth, both man and beast, creeping thing and birds of the air, for I am sorry that I have made them**. But Noah found grace in the eyes of the Lord."*

The strange marriage union between the mysterious sons of God and the daughters of men resulted in the birth of a race of Nephilim of great stature with supernatural wisdom and powers, and of exceedingly great wickedness. LaHaye /Jenkens [1] say, *"Some prophecy scholars teach that "Nephilim," the Hebrew word for "giants" doesn't merely mean tall men but supernatural creatures, the product of (fallen) angels ("the sons of God") and the daughters of men. Whatever their case, the most important lesson we can learn from this passage is that their wicked lifestyle caused God to unleash the flood. Their lifestyle included three specific sins: Sexual perversion. The thoughts of their hearts were turned to evil continually. Routine living and disregard to the consequences of impending judgment."*

There are two schools of thought in Christian literature as to who these sons of God were. It can mean either one of two things: (1) they were the godly descendents of Seth, who were calling upon the name of the Lord (as in Genesis 4:26), or (2) they were a specific group of fallen (demonic) angels who took on human form (Job 1:6).

The First School of Thought

The first school of thought maintains that the sons of God represent the godly descendants of Seth and the daughters of men who were the descendants of the godless line of Cain. They maintain Genesis 6:2 denotes that these two genealogies intermarried, regardless of the prohibition throughout the Old and New Testaments against the people of God marrying those who are not of the people of God. They often quote the New Testament portion which says in 2 Corinthians 6:14 NKJV, *"Be ye not unequally yoked together with unbelievers. For what fellowship has righteousness with unrighteousness? And what communion has light with darkness?"* Under close scrutiny, this view presents many difficulties. Some of the issues are:

1. The marriage union appears to be only between the daughters of Cain and the sons of Seth. Why are the male descendants of Cain and the female descendants of Seth omitted? Why are the male descendents of Adams other sons omitted? The question to those who hold to this view is: were all the descendants of Seth female and those of Cain male?

2. Were all the descendants of Seth believers, and those of Cain unbelievers? The Bible is clear that Seth and Cain as well as all their descendants had fallen natures. It is

obvious there would have been believers and unbelievers in both lines.

3. Are the children of believers and unbelievers different
   in their physical and mental makeup? The answer is no.
   However in this strange union of Genesis 6:1-7, the children are referred to as giants or "Nephilum" implying
   fallen people of great stature and unusual intelligence.
   Today one's faith has no physical, mental, or emotional
   effect upon one's offspring.

As well, it is difficult to explain how an unequal yoke of
mixed marriages of humans, namely the sons of godly Seth
and the daughters of ungodly Cain could have precipitated
the judgement of the Flood. This view lacks credibility.

The Second School of Thought

The second school of thought, held here, takes the position
that what took place was far more serious. This view maintains that the "sons of God" were a certain group of fallen
angels (demons) who took on human form. They had left
their first estate and took on human form and had sexual
relationships with all whom they chose. The daughters of
Men included women throughout the Earth, regardless of
whether they were of the line of Seth, Cain or whoever. It
is obvious that during this 120 year period **women lost all
their rights**. Evil persons, in this case the sons of God, took
advantage of women and brought them under bondage.

The children of this strange, unholy union are referred to as
Nephilim. The Hebrew word 'Nephilim' is used in the original text and means "fallen ones". Nephilim is translated as
"giants" in the New Revised King James version and comes
from the Hebrew verb 'naphal' which means to fall.

M.R. DeHaan [2] says the following, "*We may therefore translate the verse in Genesis 6, "There were fallen creatures of
fallen ones in the earth in those days; when the sons of God
(fallen angels) came in unto the daughters of men. In other
words, after the sons of God had sexual relationships with
the daughters of men, children were born to them, who are*

called Nephilim. These children were half human and half demon, accounting for their unique physical stature, and supernatural wisdom, power, and wickedness."

DeHaan[3] says, *"These demon beings are called the 'sons of God,' a term repeatedly applied to angels in the Old Testament, both fallen and unfallen. The unfallen angels are called sons of God. Job says that at the creation of the worlds the morning stars sang together, and all the sons of God shouted for joy (Job 38:7). But the same expression is also used for angels after their fall. In Job 1:6 we are told, "Now there was a day when the sons of God (fallen angels) came to present themselves before the Lord, and Satan came also among them."* (Job 1:6).

This is repeated in the next chapter, *"Again there was a day when the sons of God (fallen angels) came to present them-selves before the Lord, and Satan came also among them"* (Job 2:1, NKJV). De Haan [4] says, *"Here the fallen angels are called the sons of God and Satan was one of them."*

The writer Jude gives convincing evidence that the sons of God were fallen angels. He compares the sins committed to that of Sodom and Gomorrah as follows, *"But the angels who did not keep their proper domain, but left their own habitation, He has reserved in everlasting chains under darkness for the judgment of the great day"* (Jude 1:6, NKJV). Jude is here referring to the select group of fallen angels (demons) who did not keep their proper domain or first estate as the King James translation states. These fallen angels committed a grievous sin which precipitated the judgment of the Flood, and resulted in immediate ban-ishment by God into a portion of hell called "The Pit" where they are continually in chains under darkness awaiting the great judgment day. They are no longer present on the Earth today.

A clue as to what their sin was is given in the next verse, *"as Sodom and Gomorrah, and the cities around them in a similar manner to these, having given themselves over to sexual immorality and gone after strange flesh are set an example, suffering the vengeance of eternal fire. Likewise also these dreamers defile the flesh, reject authority, and speak evil of dignitaries."* (Jude 1:7 & 8, NKJV) Their sin was the same as that of Sodom and Gomorrah, which was fornication, and engaging in unnatural sexual relationships.

The Apostle Peter confirms and corroborates the testimony of Jude that the sons of God were fallen angels (demons) who sought to corrupt humanity in the days of Noah before the Flood. In 2 Peter 2:4-7 (NKJV) we read, *"For if God did not spare the angels who sinned, but cast them down to hell (the Pit) and delivered them into chains of darkness, to be reserved for judgment; and did not spare the ancient world, but saved Noah, one of eight people, a preacher of righteousness, bringing in the flood on the world of the ungodly; and turning the cities of Sodom and Gomorrah into ashes, condemned them to destruction, making them an example to those who afterward would live ungodly; and delivered righteous Lot, who was oppressed by the filthy conduct of the wicked (for that righteous man, dwelling among them, tormented his righteous soul from day to day by seeing and hearing their lawless deeds)."*

Satan's Strategy

Satan's strategy was to directly attack motherhood to prevent the Seed of the Woman (Jesus Christ) from ever being born into the world. Satan's aim was to corrupt all flesh on the Earth, so as to prevent the possibility of the Seed of the Woman, the future Messiah from ever being born through woman as Savior of the world. In other words the flesh of all family groups at this point in time was becoming corrupted by being a combination of human and demonic. Satan's plan to corrupt motherhood was being accomplished. The only family at the very end of this age that was exempt appears to have been that of Noah and his family.

As a result God had no other choice, but to destroy this ancient Pre-Flood Age because all flesh had become corrupted. He chose to destroy this age by the Worldwide Flood of Noah.

Just after Adam and Eve sinned, God declared war upon Satan by declaring, *"And I will put enmity between you and the woman, and between your (Satan's) seed and her seed, He shall bruise your head and you (Satan) shall bruise His heel"* (Genesis 3:15 (NKJV). God said that the Seed of the Woman (Christ) would one day ultimately defeat the seed of the Serpent (the Anti-Christ). Therefore Satan knew that his time was short and his main objective from that time forward was to defeat God's purpose and program in providing a Redeemer and Savior for Mankind.

Before the Flood, Satan chose to defeat God's plan by corrupting all human flesh, so that the predicted Seed of the Woman could never be born by woman. Thus, God had no alternative but to destroy all human flesh on this Earth at that time and He chose to do so by sending the Flood.

Why were Noah and His Family Spared?

In other words what happened to all the other believers? Were Noah and his family the only remaining believers on the Earth? The answer is yes. How could that be?

When the Flood struck, Noah and his family were the only humans who survived. Prior to the Flood taking place, all true believers would have been put to death sometime during this 120 year period for their faith in the True God by evil men who were under the control of Satan and his demons.

The last righteous believer to die prior to the Flood was Methuselah. He was now 969 years old. We read in Genesis 5:21-22 (NKJV), *"When Enoch had lived 65 years, he became the father of Methuselah. And after he became the father of Methuselah, Enoch walked with God."* Dr. DeHaan[5] says, *"Somehow the birth of this baby boy, who was to become famous for his longevity, had such a profound effect on father Enoch that it caused him to walk with God ever after. The reason for this was a revelation concerning a divine judgment which was imminent."* In other words, there was memorialized in the name of his son a message that when he dies, then judgment would come. Enoch did not know whether his son would live 10 years or 200 years. It ended up that Methuselah lived 969 years. It was then that the Flood became imminent.

The very day Noah and his family entered the Ark, Methuselah died. Noah and his family were the only righteous persons left on the Earth just prior to the Flood taking place. They were the only eligible persons at this point in time to begin life again after the Flood.

Jesus said in Mathew 24:37 (NKJV), "But *as the days of Noah were, so also will the coming of the Son of Man be.*" Jesus is revealing to us what will happen on Earth before His second visible return which is His Glorious Return to this Earth. There is a remarkable comparison of events that will take place prior to Christ's "Glorious Return" and to the time before the Flood. Remember, the future rapture of the church will take place prior to Christ's Glorious Return.

The Pre-Flood Age came to an abrupt Termination

The Flood of Noah brought about the abrupt termination of the Pre-Flood Age. It also abruptly terminated the geological Altithermal Age and the Pleistocene Age. The Flood Age ushered in a new geological age called the Medithermal Age. See Figure 19-1. The Flood of Noah divides human history into the Pre-Flood and the Post Flood Ages.

Secular history has done everything possible to discount the worldwide Flood of Noah. The geological, archaeological and the anthropological sciences have all attempted to disregard, to cover up and to deny the reality of Noah's Flood. Secular humanists and Darwinian evolutionists have tried to resolve and to prove that the Biblical Garden of Eden, the Creation of Adam and Eve and the Worldwide Flood of Noah is just a myth. See Appendix D. They have replaced the Biblical record with the secular view that Man is a product of an unintelligent evolutionary process. They erroneously believe that it is possible to trace modern Man (Homo sapiens) back through the primate line to somewhere between a quarter of a million to 2 million + years into the past.

See Appendix F to gain an insight into how it is possible to identify evidences of the worldwide Flood of Noah through-out the world.

Satan's Strategy Fails

The question arises, why did the sons of God (demons) enter into a relationship with the daughters of Men? Satan strategy was to directly attack motherhood to prevent the Seed of the Woman (Jesus Christ) from ever being born. Satan's aim was to corrupt all human flesh on the Earth, so as to prevent the possibility of the Messiah from being born through woman as Savior of the world.

Just after Adam and Eve sinned, God declared war upon Satan. We read, *"I will put enmity between you (Satan) and the woman, and between your (Satan's) seed and her seed, He (The Messiah) shall bruise your head and you (Satan) shall bruise His heel."* (Genesis 3:15, NKJV). In other words, God is saying that the Seed of the Woman (Christ) would one day ultimately defeat the Seed of the Serpent. Therefore Satan knew that his time was short and his main objective from that time forward was to defeat God's pur-pose and program in providing a Redeemer and Savior for Mankind.

Satan's plan prior to the Flood was to corrupt all human flesh. The only family at the very end of this age that was exempt appears to have been that of Noah. At this point in time Satan foolishly believed that he was able to outsmart Almighty God. However, his plans were abolished by the sudden devastating, worldwide Flood of Noah. At that time all inhabitants of the earth whose flesh was corrupted by the demonic, so called Sons of God perished. Their future destination will be the Great White Throne Judgment and eternity in Hell.

Conclusion

The last 120 years before the Flood witnessed unusual and dramatic world-wide events that have left an indelible imprint upon human history. It was a time of world-wide accelerated population growth, travel, worldwide communication and megalithic and cyclopean pyramidal construction. In a certain sense, it was a time of great worldly glory, but it was also a time of great despair, hardship and inner brokenness. Noah's Flood brought this great and so called glorious Stone Age period to a dramatic close.

References for Chapter 23

1. Tim LaHaye / Jerry B. Jenkins, Are We Living in the End Times? Tyndale House Publishers, Inc. Wheaton, Illinois, p. 344.
2. M. R. De Haan, M.D., "The Days of Noah & Their Prophetic Message for Today," Zondervan Publishing House, Grand Rapids, Michigan. (1968), p. 142).
3. Ibid. p. 142.
4. Ibid. p. 142. & 5. Ibid. p.94.

Chapter 24

The Construction of a Gigantic Boat: Who was Noah?

Noah was a godly man who had religious influence and insight. He was a preacher of righteousness for we read. *"God did not spare the ancient world, but saved Noah, one of eight people a preacher of righteousness bringing in the flood on the world of the ungodly."* (2 Peter 2:5, NKJV) Noah moved with fear, not the fear of man, but the fear of God. We read *"By faith Noah, being divinely warned of things not yet seen, moved with godly fear, prepared an ark for the saving of his household, by which he condemned the world and became heir of the righteousness which is according to faith."* (Hebrews 11:7, NKJV)

The average lifespan prior to the Flood was 930 years. See Figure 12-1. Noah was 600 years old when the Flood commenced. We read in Genesis 7:6, NIV, *"Noah was six hundred years old when the floodwaters came on the earth."* However, God came to Noah 120 years prior to this time when Noah was 480 years old. We read in Genesis 6:3, NIV, "Then the LORD said, *"My Spirit will not contend with man forever, for he is mortal; his days will be a hundred and twenty years."* In other words, God is saying that there will be a period of 120 years before this old world will be destroyed. See Figure 23-1.

At the beginning of this mysterious 120 year period God gave specific instructions to Noah as to why and how he should build this gigantic boat called an Ark. The details are found in Genesis 6:9-22, (NIV) *"This is the account of Noah. Noah was a righteous man, blameless among the people of his time, and he walked with God. Noah had three sons: Shem, Ham and Japheth. Now the earth was corrupt in God's sight and was full of violence. God saw how corrupt the earth had become, for all the people on earth had corrupted their ways. So God said to Noah, "I am going to put an end to all people, for the earth is filled with violence because of them. I am surely going to destroy both them and the earth. So make yourself an ark of cypress wood; make rooms in it and coat it with pitch inside and out. This is how you are to build it: The ark is to be 450 feet long, 75 feet wide and 45 feet high. Make a roof for it and finish the ark to within 18 inches of the top. Put a door in the side of the ark and make lower, middle and upper decks. I am going to bring floodwaters on the earth to destroy all life under the heavens, every creature that has the breath of life in it. Everything on earth will perish. But I will establish my covenant with you, and you will enter the ark you and your sons and your wife and your sons' wives with you. You are to bring into the ark two of all living creatures, male and female, to keep them alive with you Two of every kind of bird, of every kind of animal and of every kind of creature that moves along the ground will come to you to be kept alive. You are to take every kind of food that is to be eaten and store it away as food for you and for them. Noah did everything just as God commanded him."*

Noah was commanded to make the Ark out of Gopher Wood which is from evergreen trees such as cypress, cedar and juniper trees, etc. Where were these trees to be found? Egyptologist Davidovits[1] verifies that all of these trees were common to Lebanon during the Neolithic Age. He says, *"The Palermo Stone, fragmentary remains of royal annals indicates that Pharaoh Sneferu of the Fourth Egyptian Dynasty, assigned a fleet of ships to import cedar from Lebanon. The trees of Egypt are not hardwood and do not yield planks of the appropriate dimensions for molds. Egypt began to import cypress, cedar, and juniper from*

Lebanon as early as the pre-dynastic epoch." This was for providing casings for pyramid building as well as for ship building. Ship building persisted throughout the Neolithic Age. Davidovits[2] also says, *"The Palermo Stone records that he (Sneferu) sent to Lebanon for cedar. He launched a fleet of forty large ships to retrieve enormous beams of cedar at the Lebanon coast."* It is interesting to note that ship building was well established among Egyptians during the Neolithic Age. There are pictures of boats, one with a steering oar from prehistoric times in Egypt. This is evidence that the Pharoah's of Egypt had boats that were capable of sailing to all parts of the world during the Neolithic Age. See Figure 20-2.

Pharoah Khufu's Boat Discovered

Another big discovery in Egypt was Pharoah Khufu's boat. Davidovitz[14] says, *"In the 1950's, an excavation of one of the pits near the Great Pyramid yielded a sacred funerary boat by Khnumu-Khufu. To the delight of archaeologists, the acclaimed artifact was preserved in perfect condition. The boat was measuring 120 feet, had a displacement capacity of over 40 tons."* Davidovitz goes on to say, *"Khufu's boat is far more seaworthy than any craft of Christopher Columbus's day. The famous mission of Thor Heyerdahl in 1970, from Morocco to Barbados in a papyrus reed boat, makes it clear that ancient Egyptian ships were capable of intercontinental travel."* How did that 120 foot boat get buried beside the Pyramids. Could that boat have been washed ashore and buried by the flood waters?

The big question arises, is there any evidence that mysterious boats may have reached America during the Neolithic Age? See the end of Chapter 22. This is an area that requires greater study. Indeed, it would appear that the last 120 years of the Neolithic Age equates to the latter part of the Pre-Flood Age. This age was equivalent in many ways to our modern Age in terms of industrial development that was taking place worldwide.

Where were the Egyptian Boats Built?

It is important to remember that the level of the ocean was about 328 feet (100m) lower than today during the Neolithic Age. See Figure 22-17. This would mean that during the Neolithic Age when the great pyramids were constructed the level pf the ocean would have been at this lower level. The big question arises where were these Egyptian ships constructed? Is it possible that all these ships were constructed someplace at a dock within the Mediterranean Sea region where the resources like timber would have been readily available? Is it possible that this ship building centre could have been located close to Lebanon where these cedar trees were abundant? Technology was rapidly advancing during the Neolithic Age similar to our present modern Age.

Where did Noah Build his Boat?

Noah was building a gigantic boat 450 feet long, 75 feet wide and 45 feet high. He may have encountered great political opposition, and ridicule or did he? As well, the cost of materials for a boat the size of Noah's would have been tremendous. One can imagine the great amount of lumber, planks, beams and other essential materials that would have been necessary to build this gigantic boat.

The big question arises, where on Earth did Noah construct this gigantic boat? Was Noah just an ordinary type of person? Did he construct this gigantic boat somewhere in Mesopotamia or Persia? Did he build this boat inland as many theologians maintain? God certainly knew that Noah was capable of constructing this huge boat. He never gives a person a responsibility that they would not be able to accomplish with His help.

Is it possible that Noah was a builder of large and small boats? Is it possible that he was the principal owner of this large Construction Company that concentrated on building Large and Small Ocean going ships and vessels in the Mediterranean region? These ships would have gone to all parts of the Earth including North and South America. He may have been involved in this type of construction prior to the 120 year period before the Nephilum became a problem.

It is very likely that Noah used tools such as axes, adzes, saws, drills made of stone and copper. Besides the axes, Early Man used the Adze (like a carpenter's plane) for smoothing beams & planks, and also had stone saws for cutting wood. In the British Museum there is a Badarian (i.e. Neolithic) flint saw which looks very efficient. It is known that in Egypt copper was used alongside stone almost back to the beginning of the Neolithic Age. The Medzamor Discovery Site in Armenia has now revealed that Early Man had already entered the iron Age during the Neolithic Age. See Chapter 21 for details.

It is said that by analyzing the Neolithic Age throughout the world, we begin to realize that these gigantic megalithic and cyclopean stone pyramids and temple structures throughout the world were all built during the Neolithic Age. They literally "blow our imagination" as to how they were constructed.

Noah's Ark was an analogous gigantic structure that was constructed under the supervision and direction of Noah. Is it possible that he also acquired his lumber from the Lebanon region? Noah's boat was constructed during the final 120 years of the Neolithic Age. This gigantic boat also "blows our imagination".

It is interesting to compare Noah's Ark with modern vessels. It was not until as recent as 1853 that the largest vessel of her type in the world was constructed. It was the P&O Liner Himalaya. This ship was 240 feet long by 35 feet wide with tonnage of 3,438. Noah's boat was 450 feet in length, 75 feet wide and 45 feet high However, it was not until 1858 that a boat was built called the Great Eastern which was 692 feet long, 83 feet wide and 30 feet high, with tonnage of 19,000. This huge ship for the first time in Post Flood history exceeded Noah's boat in size. It was five times the tonnage of any ship then afloat. In 1934 the British built the

Queen Mary which exceeded 1000 feet in length. This was followed in 1938 by the Queen Elizabeth which is 1000 feet in length. Men who are expert in shipbuilding testify to the balanced proportions of all these vessels. Modern shipbuilders still build their ships to the same general relationship of length to breadth and height as Noah did.

The Ark of Noah was 450 feet long, 75 feet wide and 45 feet high. It had a floor space of about 101,000 square feet. This was inclusive of its three story floor space. Each floor had ceilings 15 feet high. The interior volume was in excess of 1.5 million cubic feet. The boat had a dead weight of 4,140 tons. Completely empty this vessel would have floated 4.3 feet below water level. With 10,000 tons of cargo it would have floated 15 feet below water level. If we assume the weight of all the animals inside at 100 tons, and if each animal ate 20 times its own weight in food and 20 times its weight of water for a year, we should have a cargo of 4100 tons. If we add the cargo weight to the dry weight of the vessel, we arrive at a total tonnage of 8,240. This would mean that the ship's bottom would have been 12 feet below water level when it was first underway. An engineer in one of my classes worked out the above figures for me.

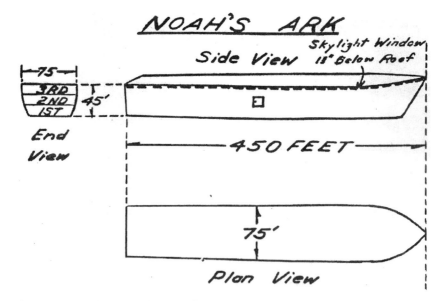

Figure 24-1: Diagram Illustrating Noah's Ark. Prepared by Don Daae.

The tonnage could be reduced somewhat by eliminating water supplies. It would be assumed that fresh drinking water would have been replenished by rainwater funneled into the Ark from the roof. The Bible is silent as to how wastes may have been removed, but we can assume that there were efficient ways of disposing garbage.

Where was Noah's Ark Built?

The big question arises as to where Noah may have built the Ark? We must remember that the level of the ocean was 328 feet (100m) lower than our present sea level during the Neolithic Age prior to Noah's Flood. See Chapter 22 and Figure 22-17 for details. It is thus necessary to examine the eastern portion of the Mediterranean Sea along the offshore region of Lebanon. This is where the Egyptian Pharaoh's used to get their high quality cedar, cypress, and juniper wood.

Clues as to the location of this offshore ship building factory may be found by mapping the offshore Mediterranean Sea bottom in detail. Then to conduct sonar, seismic and other high tech methods of detecting metal and other anomalies along the margins of the Mediterranean sea above and below the 328 foot (100m) level. This ship building factory would have been located somewhere along the shorelines of the Mediterranean Sea. Today it may be covered by certain depths of sediment. This may make its location more difficult to find.

Noah Stored Food in the Ark

God commanded Noah to stock the Ark with food for his family and the animals that would come into the Ark as follows: *"And you shall take for yourself of all food that is eaten, and you shall gather it to yourself; and it shall be food for you and for them."* (Genesis 6:21)

It is apparent that Noah and his sons would have had to bring a large amount of food aboard. Archaeologists have found that Early Egyptians as far back as the 6th Dynasty

341

(Neolithic Age) had large granaries for storing food. Many of these were 15 feet high and up to 60 feet long by 50 feet wide. These granaries were then subdivided into about seven bins, where each bin was 10 feet high. It is possible that Noah may have had similar type of storage rooms in the Ark. The Bible says that Noah built rooms in the Ark for we read, "Make *rooms in the Ark*" (Genesis 6:14). Thus, there would have been room for the many species of animals and birds as well as for the storage of food. A common scenario is that Noah would have had to store only a limited amount of food in the Ark as most of the animals would have been asleep or in a state of hibernation for most of their stay aboard. The other view states that the animals and birds would have been awake eating their daily portions of food throughout the one year and 17 days. See Figure 25-1. It is impossible to prove or disprove the above views, so we will assume a position between the two scenarios.

There has always been much controversy as to whether representatives of all land animals and birds throughout the Earth could have gotten into a boat the size of Noah's Ark. Dr. M. R. DeHaan [3] says, "*Zoologists tell us that there are less than 100 original species of quadrupeds (four footed animals), and less than 170 original species of birds. In a ship with over 100,000 square feet of floor space, it could have accommodated many times the number of original animals that entered into the Ark, and completely represented a pair of every known species, and there would be room enough for them to play, and for the birds to fly around.*"

Geology confirms that a large number of land animals became extinct at the time of Noah's Flood. Only the select land animals that are present today were brought into the Ark.

It was only necessary for one pair of each species to be in the Ark. It was not necessary for every breed, sub-species, and variety of animal to be there, but just one pair of the original species. For example, the Ark did not contain the hundreds of different breeds and varieties of dogs or cats. We know that these numerous varieties are the result of one original pair. By mutation, cross-breeding, selective mating and hybridization, an almost infinite number of varieties of dogs, cats, horses, cows and birds can be and were developed, but only one original pair was needed for the survival of the species. Thus, by the time one eliminates all the breeds, varieties, and sub-species, one is left with a surprisingly small number of original land parent species which could be comfortably accommodated in the vessel. It is also possible that God may have allowed more than one subspecies of dogs to have entered into the Ark.

Figure 23-1 shows the door of the Ark of Noah to be located on the second level. As each floor was 15 feet high, the door would have been at least 15 feet above the bottom of the boat, and thus would have been well above the level of the water on the side of the boat. The door may have been on the second or third level; however the Bible is silent as to its exact location. There was a skylight running all the way around the ship within 18 inches below the roof for we read: "*Make a roof for it and finish the ark to within 18 inches of the top. Put a door in the side of the ark and make lower, middle and upper decks* " (Genesis 6:16) The Hebrew word that is used for window is tsohar, which means light, brilliance or skylight. Filby says,[4] *"The word comes from a root meaning to mount (in the sky) mid-day, or to shine. In the 23 other occasions in the Old Testament where tsohar occurs it means noon, or mid-day. The word used here for window, Tsohar, is never again used in this sense in the Old Testament, and it is quite different from the word "challon" used in Genesis 8:6 where Noah opened the window which he had made to release the birds. It is also different from the word "arubbah" used in Genesis 7:11 for the "windows of heaven."*

It is believed that the window was a skylight or an open space running around the Ark just below the roof, which would have had a sufficient overhang to prevent rain from coming in. The skylight may have been a cubit (18 inches) in height, or the text could mean that the roof was 18 inches above the skylight. The skylight could have consisted of many rectangular windows, closed by sliding wooden panels. In Genesis 8:6 Noah opened one of the lattice type windows (challon) to let out the birds.

In the event that no glass was available for the skylight, a simple space would suffice to admit air into and out of the Ark. God made provisions for both light and air which were essential for the living creatures inside the Ark. Noah, his family, and the animals and birds may have occupied the upper levels, while the food supplies may have been stored in bins in the lower and middle decks. This would have concentrated the major weight well down in the hold of the ship.

We do not know how Noah divided each floor. It is reasonable to assume at least two long dividing walls running the length of the ship, making a central passage, possibly 15 feet wide with rooms on either side. We have no idea as to how Noah may have planned the rooms. They were probably not of equal size, but an average of 20 rooms on each floor, 30 x 45 feet each, may give some indication of space available to him. The walls of these rooms would give structural strength and support to the entire vessel.

There is no record in the Bible of any beast, bird or man being born during the one year and seven day period that they were in the Ark. All the animals went in two by two, and they came out the same way.

Entering The Ark

Noah completed the construction of the Ark during this strange 120 year period. It was at the end of this eventful 120 year period that Methuselah died, for his name means, "When he dies, judgment will come." He lived to be 969 years of age, the longest recorded life span of anyone on the Earth. His longevity reflects the long-suffering of God prior to the Flood which is recorded, "*Christ went and preached to the spirits in prison, who formerly were disobedient, when once the long-suffering of God waited in the days of Noah, while the Ark was being prepared, in which a few, that is, eight souls, were saved through water.*" (1Peter 3:19-20 NKJV)

A series of events took place towards the end of the 120 year period. The Lord God said to Noah, *"Come into the ark, you and all your household, because I have seen that you are righteous before Me in this generation. You shall take with you seven each of every clean animal, a male and his female; two each of animals that are unclean, a male and his female; also seven each of birds of the air, male and female, to keep the species alive on the face of all the earth. For after seven more days I will cause it to rain on the earth forty days and forty nights, and I will destroy from the face of the earth all living things that I have made." And Noah did according to all that the LORD commanded him. Noah was six hundred years old when the floodwaters were on the earth."* (Genesis 7:1-6, NKJV)

The first to enter the Ark was the Lord God, who would have filled the inside of the Ark with his glory, light and presence. There was no need of electric light bulbs or lanterns in the Ark, because the Lord God of Heaven and Earth was in the Ark. He is the source of all light. The Lord then invited Noah and his family to enter the Ark by saying *"Come into the Ark"* (Genesis 7:1 NKJV). Noah and his sons responded positively to the Lord's invitation by entering into the Ark.

There were five distinct groups that entered into the Ark. They were:

1. Noah and his family (8 persons).
2. Unclean beasts (2 of each species).
3. Clean beasts (14 of each species).
4. Birds of the air (14 of each species).
5. All creeping things of the Earth (2 of each species)

There were no marine animals in the Ark such as fish, amphibians, reptiles, or invertebrates. Marine animal life would have been able to look after their selves in the flood environment, being at home in water, and thus their species would have been preserved. Only the select land animal life and birds were admitted into the Ark. It is highly possible that God may have included seven unique varieties of each of the clean animal species.

God did not preserve every species and subspecies on the Earth. The Bible qualifies this in Genesis 7:16 NIV where it states, *"And they that went in, went in male and female of all flesh, **as God commanded them**."* All the land animals on the Earth today are descendants of those that were preserved in the Ark. Geology confirms that a great extinction of land animal species took place about 4,500 years ago at the end of the Pleistocene Ice Age. The saber tooth tiger, mastodon, and the mammoth are just a few of the many extinct types of species and subspecies that perished.

A Worldwide Convergence of Animals

In the providence of God there was a mysterious convergence of hundreds of animal and bird species, male and female, from different parts of the Earth to the Middle East region where the Ark was being built by Noah. There would have been kangaroos from Australia, llamas from South America, rabbits from America, elephants, lions and tigers from Africa, and so forth. This strange migration of birds, beasts, and creeping things would have reached the vicinity of the Ark at the precise moment that God's invitation to come into the Ark was given.

When the Lord God Almighty is in control there is no chaos or confusion. Often we see pictures in Bible story books of Noah and his family with long whips in their hands, directing the animals into the Ark. This concept is erroneous, and does a disservice to the scripture. Noah and his family entered the Ark prior to any of the animals. The animals came into the Ark **to Noah** under the guiding hand of the Lord for we read, *"So Noah, with his sons, his wife, and his sons' wives went into the ark because of the waters of the flood. Of clean animals, of animals that are unclean, of birds, and of everything that creeps on the earth, two by two they went into the ark **to Noah**, male and female, as God had commanded Noah." (Genesis 7;7-9, NIV)* Almighty God was in complete control.

This is further clarified in Genesis 7:13-16 NIV as follows, *"On the very same day Noah and Noah's sons, Shem, Ham,* and Japheth, and Noah's wife and the three wives of his sons with them, entered the ark— they and every beast after its kind, all cattle after their kind, every creeping thing that creeps on the earth after its kind, and every bird after its kind, every bird of every sort. And they went into the ark **to Noah**, two by two, of all flesh in which is the breath of life. So those that entered, male and female of all flesh, went in as God had commanded him; and the LORD shut him in." In other words, the Lord commanded all the specified land animals and bird life to enter the Ark, and **God shut the door** of the Ark.

There are those who say that the ungodly people would have killed the animals and birds before they would have entered the Ark. They forget that with God nothing is impossible. He could have sent legions of angels to protect these many animals and birds. It is very possible that no man or woman were even aware that these animals and birds were being directed to the Ark.

As soon as the last land animal and bird had entered into the Ark, the Lord shut the door (Genesis 7:16b). The closing of the door brought this strange 120 year period to an end.

Seven Strange Days

There was a period of seven strange days after the door of this gigantic boat had been shut and before the flood waters were upon the Earth. We read, "And it came to pass after seven days, that the waters of the flood were upon the earth." (Genesis 7:10, NIV)

This seven day period would have been a blessing to Noah and his family. They needed time to adjust to the new environment, to the animals, birds, and creeping things. It was a welcome period of relief. All those in the Ark were now in a place of perfect safety.

Outside of the Ark, the Earth was characterized by violence, crime, murder, immorality, lawlessness for we read as follows, "The Earth also was corrupt before God, and the Earth *was filled with violence, And God looked upon the Earth, and behold, it was corrupt, for all flesh had corrupted his way upon the Earth."* (Genesis 6:11-12, NIV)

It is possible that the people of the world sensed an impending judgment, and had uneasy premonitions of a coming destruction and calamity. The nations of the world were under the bondage **of the devil and his demon forces**, resulting in great evil and lawlessness.

This seven day period was indeed the darkest, blackest and strangest that our world has ever known up to this point in history. The moment the seven days ended, the Flood waters were upon the Earth, and the entire old world perished including Man, all land animals and birds, apart from marine creatures and those within the Ark. Remember, all marine and fresh water animal life were able to survive in a water environment. Geology through the science of paleontology has been able to verify the selective extinctions of many species associated with the Flood deposits. Only a select group of land animal species large and small were preserved in the Ark. Appendix F will give you a greater insight and understanding of Flood Deposits and the erosive power of Noah's Flood.

What is an Ark?

The question arises: what is an ark? There are three Arks mentioned in the Bible. They are the Ark of Noah, the Ark of Moses and the Ark of the Covenant. The question arises: what is the meaning of a Biblical Ark?

Dr. DeHaan[5] says, *"There are two words in Hebrew that are translated "Ark." Both of them mean a box or chest for safe keeping."* The Ark of Noah and the Ark of Moses is described by the Hebrew word **tebah**. It means a place of safe keeping. The Hebrew word for the Ark of the Covenant in the Tabernacle is the Hebrew word **aron** which also means a chest or box that is a place of perfect safety. All of these three arks were places of perfect safety inside, but outside of each of them, there was impending judgment, death and destruction.

348

The Ark of Noah

The Ark of Noah is described in Genesis 6:16-22. It was constructed by Noah and it was also lined with pitch. We read in Genesis 6:14-16 (NIV), "*So make yourself an ark of cypress wood; make rooms in it and **coat it with pitch inside and out**. This is how you are to build it: The ark is to be 450 feet long, 75 feet wide and 45 feet high. Make a roof for it and finish the ark to within 18 inches of the top. Put a door in the side of the ark and make lower, middle and upper decks.*"

The word pitch or bitumen is the Hebrew word "Kopher." Kopher is the same word used in the Old Testament at least 70 times. It also means blood atonement. We read, "*For the life of a creature is in the blood, and I have given it to you to make atonement for yourselves on the altar; it is the blood that makes atonement for one's life.*" (Leviticus 17:11, NIV) Dr. M. R. Dehaan[6] says, "*Now remember it is the blood that makes atonement for sin.*" It is therefore perfectly consistent to translate the phrase in Genesis 6:14 (NIV), "*make yourself an ark of cypress wood and cover it within and without with the blood of the atonement.*"

From the world's perspective Noah's ark was lined with pitch. It would have appeared as a black boat representing judgment, destruction and death. However, God saw the boat as lined with the blood of the atonement. From God's perspective the Ark was scarlet red. It was symbolic of perfect safety, protection and life for those inside.

The Ark Of Moses

The Ark of Moses is also called the Ark of Bulrushes. It came into being when the Pharaoh of Egypt made an edict that all Jewish baby boys would be cast into the river as soon as birth takes place, but every girl baby would live (Exodus 1:22).

What took place is described in Exodus 2:1-4 NIV as follows, "*Now a man of the house of Levi married a Levite woman, and she became pregnant and gave birth to a son. When* she saw that he was a fine child, she hid him for three months. But when she could hide him no longer, she got a papyrus basket for him and coated it with **tar and pitch**. Then she placed the child in it and put it among the reeds along the bank of the Nile. His sister stood at a distance to see what would happen to him." Pharaoh's daughter found baby Moses floating among the reeds. She took him to the palace and Moses was then raised in Pharaoh's Palace.

It is interesting to note that "The Ark of Bulrushes" was **lined with tar and pitch**. It was, thus, sealed to prevent the sea water from penetrating inside. In the sight of man it appeared like a black box symbolic of death. However, in the sight of God it was scarlet red. It was covered with the blood of the atonement that was symbolic of life.

We now realize that both the Ark of Moses and the Ark of Noah were both protected by the blood of the atonement. This was a fore shadow of the atoning blood that Jesus Christ shed on the Cross about 2000 years ago for the sins of the world. A part from the blood of Christ there is no hope for mankind, only impending darkness and death. To the believer, the blood of Christ brings hope, salvation, eternal life and perfect safety. Outside of Ark of Christ is death, destruction, impending judgment and banishment.

The Ark of the Covenant

The Ark of the Covenant was presented by God to Israel at Mount Sinai. It rested in the Tabernacle. It was an oblong box or chest about four feet long, about two and one half feet wide and about two and a half feet high. It was made of wood that spoke of Christ's humanity as a root out of dry ground and it was covered with gold speaking of Christ's deity. The broken Ten Commandments were in this box. As Moses came down from Mount Sinai, the children of Israel were worshipping a man made golden Calf. In anger Moses cast down the Ten Commandments and they broke in two.

Dr. M. R. DeHaan[7] says, "What a perfect picture of the incarnate Christ – perfect God and perfect man! Within this

*Ark of the Covenant was a symbol of death, judgment, and the wrath of God. This broken law demanded the death of the sinner. Like the Ark of Noah and the Ark of Moses, this ark also speaks of judgment, but God made a provision for the sinner. Over and above this broken law God ordered **a mercy seat**, a lid or cover of gold (Exodus 25). Without this cover this ark was an awful place of death and judgment condemning the sinner and consigning him to eternal banishment from the presence of God. But the mercy seat, the cover of the ark, changed all this. The high priest once a year took blood from the altar and sprinkled it above the mercy seat over the broken law. When God came down in the Shekinah Cloud into the Holy of Holies, He did not see the broken law, but only the atoning blood. The believer was therefore sheltered from the penalty of the law, and became the recipient of the grace of God."* God himself had promised: *"When I see the blood, I will pass over you"* (Exodus 12:13, KJV).

This of course points to our Lord Jesus Christ who shed His own blood on the Cross for our sins and made reconciliation for us. In Hebrews we read, *"By His blood He entered in once into the holy place, having obtained eternal redemption for us."* Hebrews 9:12, NKJV).

In Conclusion

Before we enter into the details and the mechanics of the Flood, we begin to see that the Flood of Noah brought the Old Pre-Flood World to a sudden termination. However, the Flood also links the Pre-Flood world with the post Flood world. It reveals that God's plan of salvation for pre-Flood and post Flood man hinges upon coming under the Blood for the forgiveness of their individual sins.

This plan of salvation was presented to Adam and Eve in the Garden of Eden. They received this plan for their lives. It was available to all Pre-Flood men and women who were willing to receive it. This plan carried through from Noah after the Flood to the time of Abraham and through to the crucifixion of the Man, Jesus Christ, who shed His innocent blood on the Cross for the sins of the world. The Old Testament believers looked forward to their promised Seed of the Woman. In other words, they looked forward to the Cross. Today we look back to the finished work of the Cross.

A scarlet thread of blood permeates the entire Bible from Adam and Eve to the Cross. This scarlet thread of blood continues to permeate all human life from the Cross to the present.

Jesus is truly our present day Ark of Salvation. Outside of Christ is impending death & judgment. Within Christ is peace, hope, sins forgiven and eternal life.

Today, no one has to kill a clean animal like a sheep or goat or cow and to apply the blood as a sacrifice for their sins. Today, we go directly to the foot of the Cross under the shed blood of Christ to ask the Son of God, the Lord Jesus to cleanse us of all our sins. Millions can testify to the reality of sins forgiven and an inner peace that passes all under-standing and the complete assurance of eternal life.

Just as Adam and Eve could testify of sins forgiven, so can you and I.

References for Chapter 24

1. Davidovits Joseph and Margie Morris, "The Pyramids: An Enigma Solved," Hippocrene Books, N.Y., 1989, p.31. Ibid. p. 181.
2. M. R. DeHaan, M.D. "The Days of Noah: and their pro- phetic message today." Zondervan publishing House, Grand Rapids, Michigan. p. 164.
3. Fredk A. Filby, M. Sc., PhD. (London), F.R.I.C., "The Flood Reconsidered." A review of the evidences of geology, archaeology, ancient literature and the Bible." London Pickering & Inglis Ltd., London. 1970. pp. 94-95.
4. DeHaan ibid. p.159.
5. Ibid. p. 169.
6. Ibid. p. 161.

Chapter 25

The Mechanics of Noah's Flood

It can be demonstrated that there is sufficient water today to cover the entire land areas of the Earth, including the highest mountains, by 22 feet. If this is true today, then we can certainly assume that there was sufficient water to cover the highest mountain in Noah's day. The onset of the Flood was obviously the result of a series of major earth shaking catastrophic events. The fact that God commands the heavens and the Earth does not imply that events such as the Flood are entirely supernatural. There are many natural devices God may have also employed.

The Bible gives valuable clues as to the possible Mechanics of the Flood. We read, *"And after the seven days the flood-waters came on the earth. In the six hundredth year of Noah's life, on the seventeenth day of the second month—on that day all the springs of the great deep burst forth, and the floodgates of the heavens were opened. And rain fell on the earth forty days and forty nights"* (Genesis 7:10-12, NIV).

We then read in Genesis 7:17-24 (NIIV), *"For forty days the flood kept coming on the earth, and as the waters increased they lifted the ark high above the earth. The waters rose and increased greatly on the earth, and the ark floated on the surface of the water. They rose greatly on the earth, and all the high mountains under the entire heavens were covered. The waters rose and covered the mountains to a depth of more than twenty feet. Every living thing* that moved on the earth perished—birds, livestock, wild animals, all the creatures that swarm over the earth, and all mankind. Everything on dry land that had the breath of life in its nostrils died. Every living thing on the face of the earth was wiped out; men and animals and the creatures that move along the ground and the birds of the air were wiped from the earth. Only Noah was left and those with him in the ark. The waters flooded the earth for a hundred and fifty days."

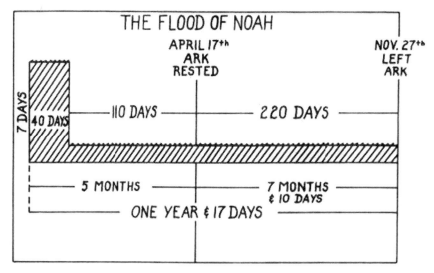

Figure 25-1: The Duration of Noah's Flood. Prepared by Don Daae. Artwork by Elaine Daae.

We read in Genesis 8: 1-2 (NKJV) "*Then God remembered Noah, and every living thing, and all the animals that were with him in the Ark. and God made a wind to pass over the earth, and the waters subsided. The fountains of the deep and the windows of heaven were also stopped, and the rain from heaven was restrained.*"

The Earth consists of three main component parts, an outer crust, an extremely hot inner mantle and an inner core. The crystalline crust is floating on extremely hot semi liquid mantle rocks. The crust is analogous in thickness to the peel of an apple. The crystalline crust is about two to four miles thick or less in ocean areas, and ranges from 15 to 30 miles thick in continental areas. The crust is never static; it is always moving, rising in certain areas and sinking in other areas. For example, the continents of North and South America are believed to be moving in a general west direction at about 2 to 4 centimetres per year overriding the thin oceanic Pacific crust which is being sub ducted under the continental crust as a large conveyor belt. The concept of plate tectonics and the drifting of the continents envisage a continual interaction between the various crustal plates.

As the crust slowly moves, great pressures of stress and tension build up, resulting in Earth movements along fault or fracture zones. This often results in earthquakes or in some cases volcanic eruptions.

These Earth shaking events may result in the production of gigantic tsunami tidal waves to sweep across oceans and continental regions. Hot liquid rock is often injected into zones of weakness within the Earth's crust. This may result in volcanism, or the intrusion of great igneous masses into the sedimentary country rock below the earth's surface.

The Bible says, *"All the fountains of the great deep were broken up"* (Genesis 7:11, NKJV). "Deep"' is the Hebrew word (tehoum). The profound deep here refers to zones below the Earth's crust where the juvenile waters are present in conjunction with hot liquid and semi-liquid mantle rocks. As the Earth's crust was ruptured during Noah's Flood, fountains of juvenile waters from below the crust were released into the oceans and atmosphere.

The technical language is very similar to the Biblical description of the "Birth of the Oceans" that took place during the First Day of Creation at the end of the Archean Age. At that early time, the Lord released water into the atmosphere which resulted in the formation of our modern oceans and the associated water cycle. Figure 3-5.

The Earth Sciences of geology and geophysics have revealed amazing information with respect to the dynamics of the Earth's interior. A special edition of Scientific American entitled, "Our Ever changing Earth," [2] gives a revealing insight into the powerful dynamics within the Earth that are continually changing, shaping and shaking our Earth.

There are those who do not realize the great amount of water that exists below the Earth's thin crust. A paper presented by Enrico Bonatti [3] in a special edition of Scientific American says, "**The water in earth's mantle could equal the amount contained in several oceans**." He goes on to say, "*Much of this water is probably primordial, captured in Earth's mantle at the time of its formation over four billion years ago.*" In other words there are still great volumes of water remaining within the Earth's interior. This water would be more mobile and readily moveable below the Earth's crust than molten rock.

At the time the Flood began, God released additional amounts of hot juvenile water into the atmosphere. The purpose was to trigger immediate rainfall. We read, "*And the windows of heaven were opened. And the rain was on the earth forty days and forty nights.*" (Genesis 7:11, 12, NKJV)

However, if great volumes of hot juvenile waters were released into the atmosphere, clouds would not condense immediately. A friend of mine Walter Nemanishen a Professional Engineer and an expert in water hydrology said to me, "*As soon as very warm, hot water begins to condense; additional BTU's of heat would be released, preventing further condensation. An outside cooling agent or catalyst is required to cause the warm waters to condense and for clouds to form and for rain to fall immediately. Without a cooling agent clouds would not form and rain would not take place. Therefore, God must have introduced such a catalyst, possibly from outer space. It could have been an extremely large comet, because the tail of a comet is extremely cold.*"

The relatively thick layer of gases and cloud comprising the Earth's atmosphere tends to act as a barrier to insulate against such intrusions. It also stores a large amount of heat, protecting the surface of the Earth against the absolute coldness of space.

If we assume the Lord God allowed the extremely cold tail of an exceptionally large giant comet to pass through the earth's atmosphere, it would act as a catalytic agent to condense the warm water into clouds causing rain to fall immediately. The Flood was an exceptional time, and the Lord may, indeed, have introduced such an exceptional giant comet to pass through the Earth's atmosphere.

It is also possible that God introduced some other trauma. For instance, the atmosphere is a relatively delicate veil against the absolute coldness of space. Should God have commanded even a small atmospheric aberration, temperatures could have fallen dramatically.

The Bible describes **a strange wind** passing over the Earth during the 40 day period, "*And God made a wind to pass over the Earth*." (Genesis 8:1, NKJV) It is possible that this "wind" was a disruption in normal atmospheric conditions made by God to temporarily reduce its ability to retain heat from solar radiation, or it **may have resulted from the passing of a giant, extremely cold comet tail.** This strange wind passed over the Earth, implying that it was not an ordinary type of wind, but was induced by an external force.

The crustal trauma that the Earth experienced at this time may be explained by the gravitational attraction of an approaching extra terrestrial object. It is here postulated that the mass within the coma of a super giant comet was sufficient to cause traumatic disruptions of the thin Earth's crust. This would have resulted in an upward swelling and rupturing of the thin oceanic crust, together with a corresponding lowering of the continental regions. This would have triggered the traumatic rupturing of the thin oceanic crust and the opening of the fountains of the deep. Isostatic re-adjustments below the earth's crust would have caused the liquid Mantle rocks to flow from the continental regions into the ocean regions to compensate for the rising of the thin ocean crust. The juvenile waters that form a significant part of the liquid magma, being more mobile, would have quickly displaced any void areas below the ocean crust.

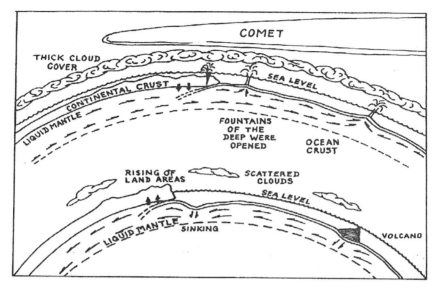

Figure 25-2: Illustrates the impact that a giant comet could have had upon the Earth's thin crystalline crust. It was Walter Nemanishen, P.Eng., a Water Hydrologist who suggested to me that God may have allowed a giant comet to pass over the Earth at this time. Prepared by Don Daae.

The Earth shaking trauma of the giant comet would have resulted in the opening of the "Fountains of the Deep" allowing hot juvenile waters to be released into the atmosphere and oceans. The traumatic breaking and shifting of the thin ocean crust in this way would have triggered giant tsunami tidal waves to sweep across continental regions in the same way that tsunami tidal waves can occur after an earthquake today.

Assuming the thin ocean crust was raised several hundreds of feet, the level of the ocean would likewise have risen by an equivalent amount. Each Earth shaking, traumatic pulse would have caused giant tidal waves to sweep across the subsiding land areas. It is here assumed that the oceanic crust was raised sufficiently high to allow the level of the ocean to rise and to cover the highest mountain peak by more than 20 feet. It must be remembered that the rising of the thin ocean crust would result in a corresponding lowering of the continental regions.

According to the New International Bible the waters completely covered the land areas and the highest mountain to a depth of more than 20 feet. We read, *"The waters rose greatly on the Earth, and all the high mountains under the entire heavens were covered. The waters rose and covered the mountains to a depth of more than twenty feet.* (Genesis 7:19-20, NIV)

All the land animals, birds and Man perished in the Flood, except for those that were preserved in the Ark. We read in Genesis 7:21-24 (NIV), *"Every living thing that moved on the earth perished—birds, livestock, wild animals, all the creatures that swarm over the earth, and all mankind. Everything on dry land that had the breath of life in its nostrils died. Every living thing on the face of the earth was wiped out; men and animals and the creatures that move along the ground and the birds of the air were wiped from the earth. Only Noah was left, and those with him in the ark."* Only land type of animal and bird life perished. All water types of life would have been able to survive for the most part.

The Bible says that it rained for 40 days and 40 nights, then God stopped the fountains of the deep and at the same instant the rain from heaven was restrained. We read, *"The fountains also of the deep and the windows of heaven were stopped, and the rain from heaven was restrained. [3] And the water returned from off the Earth continually. And after the end of the hundred and fifty days the waters were abated. [4] And the Ark rested in the seventh month, on the seventeenth day of the month, upon the mountains of Ararat. [5] And the waters decreased continually until the tenth month. In the tenth month, on the first day of the month, were the tops of the mountains seen"* Genesis 8:2-5 NIV.

This passage does not say that the rain stopped, but that it was restrained. The clouds were no longer receiving the same source of water from the fountains of the deep any longer. It is assumed that it would have taken 40 days for the tail of this comet to pass by the earth. There are giant comets that are over 50 million miles in length.

After the passing of this giant comet, the thin ocean crust would have gradually returned to "isostatic equilibrium." In other words, the earth's crust would have returned to where it was approximately prior to the Flood. This subsidence of the thin ocean crust would have also triggered a corresponding rising of the continental crust, thus allowing the waters to return off the Earth continually (Genesis 8:3). By the end of 155 days which approximates to our April 17th, the Ark came to rest on Mount Ararat (see Figure 25-1).

Mount Ararat is a 17,000 foot mountain in eastern Turkey near the border of land now occupied by Russia. At this moment in time it would appear as though Mount Ararat was higher than the nearby surrounding mountains, because it was not till the tenth month, or July, that the tops of the other nearby mountains could be seen.

Geology Confirms Noah's Flood.

Is there any geological evidence to support the dramatic lowering and rising of land areas associated with Stages 1, 2 & 3 of Noah's Flood? Skeptics will want some concrete geological evidences.

A well known British Pleistocene geologist, Professor Charlesworth, in his 1957 book, THE QUATERNARY ERA,[4] wrote: "*The Pleistocene indeed witnessed Earth-movements on a considerable, even catastrophic scale. There is evidence that it created mountains and ocean deeps of a size previously unequalled-- the Pleistocene indeed represents one of the crescendi in the earth's tectonic history. The movements affected about forty million square kilometers of the ocean floor, i.e. 70 % of the total surface of the earth. Asia was subjected to powerful and far- reaching disturbances;*

the fault troughs of the Dead Sea, Red Sea, Jordan Valley, Gulf of Aden, Persian Gulf, and Arabian Sea received their present form. Earth movements elevated the Caucasus; the amount since Mindel time (i.e. the second stage of the Ice Age) is estimated at 3,900 feet... and raised Lake Baikal region and Central Asia by 6,700 feet. Similar changes took place around the Pacific and in North China the uplift was estimated at 10,000 feet."

Dr. Lester King, Professor of geology at Natal University, South Africa, in his 1962 book, THE MORPHOLOGY OF THE EARTH [5] (p.33) stated, *"The greatest uplift has taken place in the Himalaya. The modern Andes were created by violent Pleistocene up-arching. There is, of course, much evidence of a late vertical movement of the Himalaya from Tibet into Europe, the Mountain Garland, Hindu Kish, Elbruz, and Caucasus are everywhere the product of uplifting during Pliocene to Recent times."*

Professor Charlesworth believed that the great Pleistocene Earth movements which affected 70% of the Earth's surface took place sometime after Mindel time. Geologists believe that the Mindel Age ended about 225,000 years ago. See Figure 15-1. In other words Charlesworth is saying that these dramatic Earth Movements took place sometime between the present and 225,000 years ago. Geology is now able to determine that this dramatic event took place during the Flood Age which brought the Pleistocene Ice Age to an end.

It is interesting to note that Dr. Lester King also revealed that the Andes Mountains in South America has also experienced violent Pleistocene uplift. This would explain why the several Neolithic, megalithic ruins of the ancient city of Tiauanaco in Bolivia and the many ruins high in the Andes mountains of Peru such as on the Plateau of Marcahuasi and at Machu Picchu have experienced such severe damage and breakage. This would verify that these traumatic upheavals terminated the Neolithic / Pleistocene Age worldwide.

The Gulf of Alaska Pin Points
the Time of Noah' Flood

One of many reasons why I believe these worldwide disturbances terminated the Pleistocene Age is because of the
following geological evidence. I was Manager of Exploration
and Operations of a certain Exploration Company during the
1970's and 1980's. One exploration project involved drilling
a COST well in the offshore region of the Gulf of Alaska.
About 23 major oil and gas Companies participated in the
drilling of this well.

This well was located on the flanks of a seismically defined
anticline as shown on Figure 24-3 to gain geological information in preparation for upcoming offshore lease sales.
This well was drilled to a depth of about 13,000+ feet bot-
toming in sediments of Middle Tertiary age. It encountered
4,000+ feet of Pleistocene sediments overlying sediments
of Pliocene, Miocene and Oligocene ages.

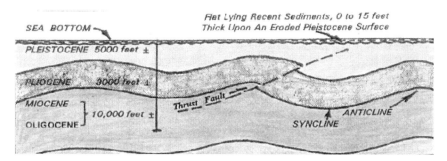

**Figure 25-3: Geology of the Gulf of Alaska offshore illustrates the
very Late Pleistocene tectonics that resulted in the formation of
anticlinal and synclinal structures. Some anticlines are partially
thrust faulted over synclines. Prepared by Don Daae.**

Seismic records revealed a thin, so called, transparent
layer about 15+feet (4.6+m) in thickness of mud and silt
of Recent Age on the sea bottom. These Recent muds are
lying undisturbed upon a pronounced unconformity. The
underlying strata had been folded into a series of anticlines
and synclines. This was due to intense compressional tectonic disruptions within the Earth's crust resulting from

Stage 1 of Noah's Flood. Many of the anticlines had even been partially thrust faulted over the synclines. The severe folding and faulting of these sediments took place after the Pleistocene sediments had been deposited. Drilling samples confirmed that the underlying 4000+feet (1,219+m) of sediments were of Pleistocene age. Seismic also confirmed that these Pleistocene sediments were increasing in thickness in a seaward direction.

Regional geology confirms that a severe compressional tectonic event took place in the Gulf of Alaska during Late Pleistocene times that resulted in the folding and faulting of the Pleistocene and the older Tertiary sediments.

It is believed that the several, severe powerful tsunami tidal waves that relate to Stage 3 of Noah's Flood were responsible for eroding and levelling this Pleistocene surface. Only detailed geological and paleontological analysis can determine how much Pleistocene sediments may have been eroded away by powerful tsunami, tidal waves. However, undisturbed mud and silty clay of Recent Age generally 5 to 15 feet (1.5 to 4.6m) in thickness were deposited above this flattened erosion surface after the termination of this severe tectonic event.

It is now possible to demonstrate on the basis of the geological evidences that the above mentioned violent Earth movements that Charlesworth and King refer to actually terminated the Pleistocene Ice Age. In other words these violent Earth movements took place about 4500 plus or minus years ago.

The Aleutian Trench confirms Noah's Flood

Another prime example of Late Pleistocene tectonic activity is found within the Aleutian Trench. During the 1960s and 1970s, the United States Government with the support of many other countries utilized the services of the dynamically positioned drill ship called the Glomar Challenger to carry out scientific expeditions throughout the oceans of the world. A large amount of geological and geophysical research was done investigating the sea bottom sedimentary section and the ocean crust at different regions throughout the world.

A geological journal called Geotimes dated October 1972, described the Project Leg 18, which concentrated its efforts along the Aleutian Deep Sea Trench as follows, "*Studies of the cores indicates that the oceanic crust now beneath the axis of the Aleutian Trench began subsiding in* **Late Pleistocene** *time, and that sediment filled the trench rapidly. The rate of tectonism and sedimentation implied by the core data are more rapid than those previously estimated. The drill cores consist of highly deformed Pleistocene sediment.*" [6]

The above article also described the flat lying undisturbed Recent (Holocene) sediments overlying the highly deformed Pleistocene formation. This is another verification of intense crustal movements taking place at the end of the Pleistocene Age. **This event equates ironically to the time of Noah's Flood.** The Flood terminated the Pleistocene and the Altithermal Ages. See Figure 19-1.

References for Chapter 25

1. Daae H. Donald, P. Geol. "Bridging the Gap: The First 6 Days." Genesis International Research Publishers, 1989. Pages 36-44. A description of the Birth of the Oceans.
2. Enrico Bonatti, PhD. "Earth's Mantle Below the Oceans." This paper is published in the Special Edition of Scientific American, September 26, 2005 edition , "Our Ever Changing Earth." Pages 65-73.
3. IBID. p.65-73.
4. Professor Charlesworth, *"The Quaternary Era,"* London,1937, p: 604-605.
5. Dr. Lester King, *"The Morphology of the Earth,"* London, *1962.* p.33.
6. Science, 1973, p.379. R.V. Challenger, Legg 23b of the Deep Sea Drilling Project aboard the RV Glomar Challenger.

Chapter 26

Noah's Calendar

Noah had a calendar that was based upon a seven day week, a 30 day month, and a 360 day year. There were 12 months in the year which in turn were based upon 12 new moons every year. Pre-Flood people were obviously keen observers of the heavens. They are the people who invented Noah's calendar.

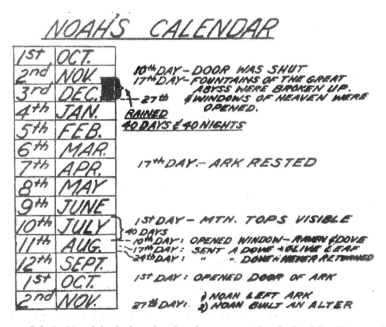

Figure 26-1: Noah's Calendar is shown on the left side. It roughly equates to our present day Gregorian Calendar on the right side. Prepared by Don Daae.

It was during the days of King Hezekiah that all the calendars throughout the world were put into a state of confusion. We read 2 Kings 20:8-11 NIV, *"Hezekiah had asked Isaiah, "What will be the sign that the LORD will heal me and that I will go up to the temple of the LORD on the third day from now?" Isaiah answered, "This is the LORD's sign to you that the LORD will do what he has promised: Shall the shadow go forward ten steps, or shall it go back ten steps?" "It is a simple matter for the shadow to go forward ten steps," said Hezekiah. "Rather, have it go back ten steps." " **Then the prophet Isaiah called upon the LORD, and the LORD made the shadow go back the ten steps it had gone down on the stairway of Ahaz**."* God answered King Hezekiah's prayer. This was about 710 B.C. Out of the confusion emerged the 365 and a quarter day year.[1] This has added a degree of confusion as to how we should relate our present day calendars to the calendar that was in use prior to the time of King Hezekiah. The 1st month of Noah's calendar roughly equates to our month of October.

The Bible does not give a name to each month, but they were listed as to the first month, second month, and so on. Biblical scholars say that the first month equates to our month of October. Thus the end of September and the beginning of October mark the end of the old year and the beginning of the New Year. In other words, October 1st was New Years Day prior to the time of King Hezekiah.

From the very beginning of human history to the present, Man has always followed a seven day week. This seven day period was also significant at the time of the Flood, because the Lord granted Noah and his wife seven days of preparation after the door of the Ark was shut. We read in Genesis 7:10-12 NIV, *"And after the seven days the floodwaters came on the earth. In the six hundredth year of Noah's life, on the seventeenth day of the second month—on that day all the springs of the great deep burst forth, and the floodgates of the heavens were opened. And rain fell on the earth forty days and forty nights." See Figure 26-2.*

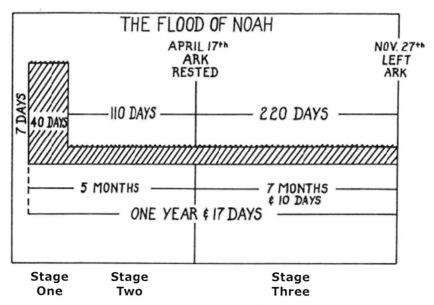

Figure 26-2: The Duration of Noah's Flood showing the Flood's three stages. Prepared by Don Daae.

Noah and his family and all the animals entered the Ark prior to the 9th day of the 2nd month. God closed the door of the Ark on the 10th Day of the 2nd month. It would appear that after the door was closed, they were all in the Ark for seven days prior to the sudden bursting of the Flood waters on the beginning of the 17th day of the 2nd month. It was on the 17th day that all the fountains of the great deep were broken up, and the windows of heaven were opened. See Figure 26-1.

Filby says, *"If all Noah's months had 30 days and we include the day on which the flood started, and also the sixteenth day of Nissan (the seventh month), but not the actual day on which the Ark rested, we shall have 14 + 30 + 30 + 30 + 30 + 16 = 150 days."* [1]

The First 40 Days

The rain was upon the Earth for 40 days to the 27th day of the 3rd month and then the fountains of the great deep and the windows of heaven were stopped. In other words the

Lord closed the doors of the great deep. We read in Genesis 7:17-20 (NIV), "*For forty days the flood kept coming on the earth, and as the waters increased they lifted the ark high above the earth. The waters rose and increased greatly on the earth, and the ark floated on the surface of the water. They rose greatly on the earth, and all the high mountains under the entire heavens were covered. The waters rose and covered the mountains to a depth of more than twenty feet.*" The Bible confirms that Almighty God was in complete control of the mechanics and all phases of the Flood.

We read in Psalm 29:10 NKJV, "**The Lord sat enthroned at the Flood, and the Lord sits as King forever.**" The Lord God Almighty was the first to enter the Ark. He sat enthroned within the Ark as King and He continues to rule as Sovereign King forever.

During this 40 day period all mankind and all land animal life and birds perished that were outside of the Ark. There was death and destruction outside of the Ark, but there was perfect peace and safety inside the Ark. We read in Genesis 7:21-23, (NIV), "*21 Every living thing that moved on the earth perished—birds, livestock, wild animals all the creatures that swarm over the earth, and all mankind.22 **Everything on dry land** that had the breath of life in its nostrils died.23 Every living thing on the face of the earth was wiped out; men and animals and the creatures **that move along the ground** and the birds of the air were wiped from the earth. Only Noah was left, and those with him in the ark.*" However, it is important to remember that marine and water life were able to survive in a water environment. There would have been plenty of food for them to eat.

It is important to realize that only the land type of animal life and birds perished. The select land animal life and birds within the Ark were the only survivors.

For those who are more curious and geologically inclined and would like to know how it is possible to identify Stage One & Stage Two Flood Deposits and the erosion effects in your area. Stage One Flood Deposits were deposited during the 40 day period of heavy rainfall that was associated with several powerful tsunami tidal waves. These sediments would consist of boulders, cobblestones and gravels of various sizes with finer grains in the matrix.

We read in Genesis 7:24 NIV, *"The waters flooded the earth for a hundred and fifty days."* After God closed the Earth's doors and after all land animal and bird life had perished, then the Earth would have experienced a strange 110 day period of relative quiescence and calm. It was during this time that the clay and finer silt particles would have settled out. The Stage two Deposits would have consisted primarily of clay with miner amounts of fine silt and volcanic ash particles. These deposits would have continued to be deposited during this mysterious 110 day period. There are particular reasons why these deposits may or may not be present in your region. See APPENDIX F.

The tops of the mountains were first seen by Noah and his family on the first day of the tenth month. Then forty days later Noah opened a lattice type window (challon in Hebrew) of the Ark and sent forth a raven and a dove (Genesis 8:5-9). The dove returned because it found no place to rest, however the raven flew to and fro and did not return. Being a scavenger, the raven would have found food in abundance.

Noah then waited another seven days, and released the dove a second time. The dove returned with an olive leaf, and Noah knew that the waters had receded to the extent that dry land was now present and a new growth of vegetation was beginning to take place (Genesis 8:10-11). Seven days later, Noah released the dove once again, and the dove never returned (Genesis 8:12). There was now sufficient new growth to provide food for this dove.

The Ark at Rest On Mount Ararat

The Ark rested on the mountains of Ararat on the 17th day of the 7th month which equates roughly to our April 17. Once the Ark came to rest, it was no longer tossed about by the wind and waves. The historical event of Noah's Ark coming to rest safely on Mount Ararat on the 17 day of the 7th month had prophetic overtones. It pointed forward to **the Exodus** and secondly to **the Resurrection of Jesus Christ.**

The Exodus: refers to the momentous day when the Children of Israel left Egypt and miraculously crossed the Gulf of Aqaba on dry land to Mount Sinai in Arabia and eventually to their land of promise in Palestine. They left Egypt on the 17 day of the 7th month. See Figure 26-1.

On the 14th day of Nisan (the 7th month) the children of Israel were commanded by God to place the blood of the lambs on the door-post of their houses, so when the death angel passed by their eldest son would be spared. God said, *"When I see the blood I will pass over you"* (Exodus 12:12). That night, all the Egyptian firstborn died. But all of the first born of Israel were spared. From that time onward, the Children of Israel were commanded by God to celebrate the Passover on the 14th Day of the 7th month. We read in Exodus 12:14,*"This is a day you are to commemorate; for the generations to come you shall celebrate it (the Passover) as a festival to the LORD as a lasting ordinance."*

The Israelites set out to cross the Great Sea, pursued by the hosts of Pharaoh. Three days later, God miraculously divided the waters to allow the Israelites to cross the Great Sea, while the host of Egyptians perished in the waters. This passing of the Great Sea occurred on the 17th day of the 7th month. This was the anniversary of the resting of Noah's Ark. However, after the children of Israel had crossed the Great Sea and were now camped at Mount Sinai, God gave them a new calendar. We read in Leviticus 23:5 *"The LORD's Passover begins at twilight on the fourteenth day of the first month."* In other words, at this time the 7th Month of Noah's Calendar became the 1st Month for Israel.

Swedish archaeologists and scientists have recently discovered the exact location where the children of Israel crossed the Great Sea. It was not the Red Sea, but it was the Gulf of Aqaba. They discovered a natural sandy crossing across the Gulf of Aqaba where the water is over a mile deep. Along this sandy crossing on the sea bottom, they discovered the remains of Egyptian chariots wheels and other debris that were encrusted with algal reef growth. They utilized a modern submersible submarine to photograph and to explore the sea bottom extending from the east coast of the Sinai Peninsula to the coastline of Arabia. They were also able to determine the exact location of Mount Sinai on the east side of the Gulf of Aqaba. This dvd is a must for people to see.[3]

The Resurrection of Jesus Christ: refers to the day when Jesus Christ rose from the grave. This date equates to the 17 day of the 7th month.

The Jewish people have celebrated the Passover ever since the Exodus. It is interesting to note that Jesus was crucified on the 14 day of Nisan (the Jewish Passover). Three days later on the 17 day of Nisan, Jesus arose from the grave. The resurrection marks the anniversary of the resting of Noah's Ark. This once again reveals the reality of Psalm 29:10, *"The Lord sat enthroned at the Flood, and the Lord sits as King forever."* He is in control of all these events.

Jesus Christ is Sovereign God

In other words, the central figure of the Old and the New Testaments is no other than the Lord Jesus Christ. Almighty God, the Father, always conducts all His work throughout the entire universe of stars, galaxies and the Earth through His Son, Jesus Christ. Jesus Christ created Adam and Eve. He was in the Ark with Noah. He met Moses on Mount Sinai and gave him the Ten Commandments. He was the one who shed His sinless Blood on the Cross for the sins of the world. Truly, Jesus Christ is the central figure of all Human History. See Figure 19-1.

Fallen Lucifer is the Prince of Darkness

However, we must be aware that the Fallen Lucifer is our real, evil enemy who is lurking behind the scenes of this world. We read in Ephesians 6:10-18 NIV, *"Finally, be strong in the Lord and in his mighty power. Put on the full armour of God so that you can take your stand against the devil's schemes. For our struggle is not against flesh and blood, but against the rulers, against the authorities, against the powers of this dark world and against the spiritual forces of evil in the heavenly realms. Therefore put on the full armour of God, so that when the day of evil comes, you may be able to stand your ground, and after you have done everything, to stand. Stand firm then, with the belt of truth buckled around your waist, with the breastplate of righteousness in place, and with your feet fitted with the readiness that comes from the gospel of peace. In addition to all this, take up the shield of faith, with which you can extinguish all the flaming arrows of the evil one. Take the helmet of salvation and the sword of the Spirit, which is the word of God. And pray in the Spirit on all occasions with all kinds of prayers and requests. With this in mind, be alert and always keep on praying for all the saints."*

It is paramount that we are aware that the Fallen Lucifer who is our arch enemy today was also the arch enemy of Pre-Flood Man. Remember, the Devil is powerful, but Jesus Christ is All Powerful.

New Years Day: Noah Opens the Door

Noah opened the door of the Ark on the 1st day of the 1st month on Noah's calendar. We read in Genesis 8:13, *"By the first day of the first month of Noah's six hundred and first year, the water had dried up from the earth. Noah then removed the covering from the ark and saw that the surface of the ground was dry."* This day had a very special meaning because it was New Years Day. What an appropriate day to open the door of the Ark. A brand new day and a brand new year was about to begin. A new world of opportunity lay before them. Noah and his family were aware that they were the only eight human survivors on the face of the Earth. It was like beginning all over again. See Figure 26-1.

However, God did not allow them or all the animals and birds to leave the Ark at this time. It is obvious that the ground was dry about the Ark; however, the water had more receding to do.

As a result, they remained in the Ark with the animals an additional one month and 27 days after Noah had opened the door.

The Mysterious Location of Noah's Ark

There is a mystery where Noah's Ark came to rest. Did it come to rest on Mount Ararat or did it come to rest on one of the smaller mountains of Ararat? The New International Version says. "And on the seventeenth day of the seventh month the ark came to rest on the mountains of Ararat." Genesis 8:4. The King James Version and the New King James and other versions say, "Then the ark rested in the seventh month, the seventeenth day of the month, on the mountains of Ararat."

The Ararat Mountains are located along the eastern border of Turkey. See Figure 28-2. Mount Ararat is a volcanic Mountain and is considerably higher than the other nearby mountains.

It is beyond the scope of this book to give an opinion as to the exact location of Noah's Ark. Over the years, many different teams of scientists and inquisitive explorers have claimed that they have found true evidence as to where Noah's Ark is located. I would advise the reader to explore the various and exciting evidences that are presently described on the Google internet.

Looking Backwards

Before we continue any further, we can begin to look Backwards with an evaluating mind to see what actually took place during the Flood Disaster Scenario called Noah's Flood. This was indeed a most dramatic tectonic and Earth shaking event that can now be documented by the science of geology.

Changes took place upon the surface of the Earth that have given clues as to where the Second Garden of Eden was located prior to the Flood and where the four major river systems were located that flowed out of this Garden.

The geological data pertaining to Noah's Flood also gives an insight into the trajectory orbit of a mysterious giant comet that has left its traces at certain places on the Earth.

The geological data pertaining to Noah's Flood also reveals the Mystery surrounding the North and South American Inca, Maya, Aztec, Toltec and other Pre-Flood Civilizations.

Let us now investigate the Mysteries of the Past that can be revealed by Noah's Flood Disaster Scenario!

References for Chapter 26

1. Filby, Fredk A. M. Sc., PhD. (London), F.R.I.C., "The Flood Reconsidered." A review of the evidences of geology, archaeology, ancient literature and the Bible." London Pickering & Inglis Ltd., London. 1970. p. 106.

2. In order to better understand the powerful erosive effects of Stage Three of Noah's Flood. See Appendix F.

3. The Exodus Revealed: Search for the Red Sea Crossing. This dvd is a must to see. For more information go to www.questar 1.com.

Chapter 27

Geological Evidences
for a Giant Comet!

We have discussed a giant comet as a plausible explanation for the great crustal disruptions during Noah's Flood. Could this scenario be powerful enough to trigger a Worldwide Flood? Are there any geological evidences that could support this thesis?

The Mysterious Red Dye Coloring

Is it possible that the red coloring in Recent Age sediments that are sometimes associated with tektites could be a clue that a major Comet may have passed through our atmosphere at the time of Noah's Flood?

Red Dye coloration in certain Flood Deposits is a worldwide phenomenon. Immanuel Velikovsky,[1] 1969 says this, "*The fossils of Choukoutien are found imbedded in a reddish loam, a mixture of clay and sand, the deposition of which belongs to the same stage as the fossils; this reddish loam occurs extensively all over northern China. Archeologists Teilhard and Young concluded that the observed coloration can neither be a quality inherited from the original material of which the loams are composed, nor a condition brought about by slow chemical processes long after their formation. The coloration of this widespread formation was believed to be of extraneous and unexplained origin, the only definite statement concerning it is that some violent change of climate, in itself not the cause of the change of color, occurred immediately before the deposition of red loams — or soon after deposition. The red loam referred to above is in reality loess."* [1]

Oceanographer H. Pettersson[2] of the Oceanographic Institute at Goteborg examined the abysmal red clay from the bottom of the Pacific. He found the red clay contained layers of ash and a high content of nickel and iron. He attributed the origin of iron and nickel to prodigious showers of meteorites. He recognized ocean bedrock lavas as of Recent Origin.

Much of Northern China is covered with a Recent layer of Loess. It is reported that Chinese scientists Ziyuan,[3] Chunlai and Dongsheng discovered microtektites in the Loess that corresponds to the Australia - Asian microtektites which had been found in deep sea sediment cores. The microtektites are amber, yellowish brown, yellowish green, light green and light brown in color. The main elemental composition of the microtektites were SiO_2, MgO, Al_2O_3 and FeO. They conclude, *"The target materials that microtektites derived from are multi-sources constituents. After impact, tektites are resulted from the various even compounded melted target materials ejecting and cooling. --- They are speculated to be the ablated drops of impacting body"*[3]

The Dictionary of Geological Terms[4] defines tektites as follows, *"A rounded pitted jet black to greenish or yellowish body of silicate glass of non volcanic origin, usually walnut-sized, found in groups in several widely separated areas of the earth's surface. Most tektites are high in silica (68-82%) and very low in water content (average 0.005%): their composition is unlike that of obsidian and more like that of shale. Tektites average a few grams in weight. They are believed to be of extraterrestrial origin or alternatively the product of large hypervelocity meteorite impacts on terrestrial rocks. Etymol: Greek tektos, "molten"."*

Our Flood Disaster Scenario envisages a super comet to have passed through the Earth's atmosphere allowing 40 days for the tail of the comet with all its fine meteoric grains to pass by the Earth.

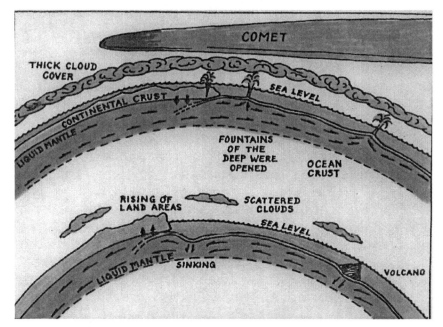

Figure 27-1: Illustrates the effect that a giant comet could have on the Earth's thin crystalline crust. Artwork by Don Daae.

The fallout of fine meteoric grains into the atmosphere and to the Earth could account for the microtektites and tektites that are characteristic of this age. It would also account for the reddish coloration of the deep sea clays and other sediments as well as the reddish stain that is sometimes present on pebbles and boulders of this age in different places throughout the Earth.

A second verification is the sudden freezing of the woolly mammoths in northern Siberia. The extreme coldness of the comet tail would be sufficient to instantly freeze the carcasses. It would also have cooled the climate sufficiently to allow the carcasses to have remained frozen to the present day.

More exploratory work is necessary to ascertain the regions of the Earth that have similar aged sediments with similar characteristics. This may also give evidence as to the direction that this proposed comet may have travelled as it passed over the Earth. The Bible says, "*God made a wind to pass over the earth.*" (Genesis 8:1, NIV) The implication in this verse is that this wind was an extraterrestrial wind. It could have been the wind generated by the tail of a giant comet. Some super comets are believed to be many millions of miles in length. This could explain why the northern portions of the Earth remained cold following the Flood of Noah.

Frozen Mammoths in Northern Siberia

Is it possible that the mysterious graveyards of pre-Flood woolly mammoths in Northern Siberia can be explained by the passing of the above mentioned extremely cold giant comet? I believe the evidence points to this conclusion.

Geological evidences for Noah's Flood are found in Northern Siberian sediments that are post Pleistocene and pre-Recent in age. Encased in the frozen tundra, are several grave-yards of prehistoric animals such as the woolly mammoth.

The body of a mammoth was first discovered in 1797 with fresh frozen flesh, skin, and hair. The flesh was edible and wolves and sledge dogs fed on it without harm. Gath[5] says, "*A Russian hunter, Liakhov, discovered the Liakhov Islands in the Arctic Ocean region just north of the Northern Siberian mainland. He brought back a report that such was the enormous quantity of mammoth remains that it seemed that the island was actually composed of the bones and tusks of elephants, cemented together by icy sand.*"

Gath[6] also reports, "*The New Siberian Islands discovered in 1805 and 1806, as well as the islands of Stolbovoi and Belkov to the west present the same picture. The soil of these desolate islands is packed full of the bones of elephants and rhinoceroses in astonishing numbers.*"

James D. Dana,[7] a leading American geologist wrote, "*The encasing in ice of huge elephants, and the perfect preservation of the flesh, shows that the cold finally became suddenly extreme, as of a single winters night, and knew no relenting afterward.*" It is possible that the presence of a giant comet could explain why these mammoths were instantly frozen. Secondly, the fact that they have remained frozen would indicate that the climate in this particular region of the Arctic has remained cold to the present day. The powerful tsunami tidal waves associated with Noah's Flood can explain how these mammoths were swept to this remote burial place in Northern Siberia.

Whitley[8] says, "*It is recorded in the literature that "the contents of the stomachs have been carefully examined, they reveal the undigested food, leaves of trees now found in southern Siberia, but a long way from the existing deposits of ivory. Microscopic examination of the skin showed red blood corpuscles, which was a proof not only of sudden death, but that the death was due to suffocation either by gases or water, evidently the latter in this case. But the puzzle remained to account for the sudden freezing up of this large mass of flesh so as to preserve it for future ages*"

I believe that Gath Whitley is correct in saying that these mammoths were feeding on the lush vegetation of southern Siberia. They were suddenly swept northward by powerful tidal waves to their resting place at the time of Noah's Flood into the far north regions of Siberia. The extremely cold tail of the Giant Comet would have frozen them almost instantly. The continuing Arctic cold has apparently been sufficient to preserve them in their original state to the present day.

It is possible that the Sovereign intervention by God in sending the Flood and by cooling the climate by means of a giant comet is a logical explanation for the quick deep freeze of these mammals. It would have taken 40 days and 40 nights for the tail of the comet to pass over the Earth. It is obvious that the climate has continued to remain cold and Arctic like to this day.

When Hedenstrom and Sannikov discovered the New Siberian Islands in 1906, they found the remains of enormous petrified forests which extended for tens of miles. The trunks of the trees were partly standing upright and partly lying buried in the frozen soil. Wrangell says,[9] "*On *the southern coast of New Siberia are found the remarkable wood hills [piles of trunks]. They are 30 fathoms (180 feet high), and consist of horizontal strata of sandstone, alternating with strata of bituminous beams or trunks of trees. On ascending these hills, fossilized charcoal is everywhere met with, covered with ashes, but, on closer examination, this ash is also found to be a petrification, and so hard that it can scarcely be scraped off with a knife."*

Today, dogs can eat the flesh of these mammoths without getting sick. This indicates that they have remained frozen since the time they were deposited. Thus from this time forward the climate has remained in a deep freeze state. Whether the climate was arctic prior to this time is not really known. It would appear that the flood waters were responsible for transporting these mammoths as well as the trees from a warmer and more temperate climate from the south to their present resting place in the north.

The secular world denies or will not admit that Noah's Flood was responsible for the above deposits. Also there are Christian geo-scientists who do not believe or will not admit that Noah's Flood was global. They believe the Flood was restricted to the Middle East region. They will not even want to believe that these deposits are the result of Noah's Flood. They will not even believe that Noah's Flood could have been the major event that brought the Pleistocene Age to a dramatic close. See Figure 19-1. Young Earth Creation Science people believe this event occurred sometime after Noah's Flood. They do not have an explanation as to how these extinct animals got to their resting place.

There is much disagreement among Christians as to whether Noah's Flood was universal or only local throughout the world. Of course, secular scientists continue to deny the very occurrence of Noah's Flood. But their defense is becoming less and less credible. See APPENDIX F.

References for Chapter 27

1. Immanuel Velikovsky, *Earth In Upheaval*, Dell Publ. Co. N.Y., 1969, p.67. The scientific community is always very critical of anyone who dares to quote any portion of Velikowsky's books. This is unfortunate indeed. I do not agree with everything that he has written, but this is just one quotation from the great amount of research that he has done.

2. H. Petterson, *Chronology of the Deep Ocean Bed*, Tellus: Quarterly Journal of Geophysics, 1949.

3. Ouyang Ziyuan, Li Chunlai, An Zhisheng, *A Discovery and Study of Microtektites in Loess*, in Progress In geology of China (1989- 1992), Papers to 29th IGC, Geological Publishing house, Beijing, China, 1992.

4. Dictionary of Geological Terms.

5. Ziyuan, Chunlai and Dongsheng Chinese Scientists.

6. Dictionary of Geological Terms[4]

7. Ouyang Ziyuan, Li Chunlai, An Zhisheng, *A Discovery and Study of Microtektites in Loess*, in Progress In geology of China (1989- 1992), Papers to 29th IGC, Geological Publishing house, Beijing, China, 1992.

8. *The Dictionary of Geological terms*, 3rd edition, prepared by the American Geological Institute, edited by R. L. Bates, & Julia A. Jackson 1984.

9. Gath, Whitley D. "The Ivory Islands in the Arctic Ocean." Journal of Philosophical Society of Great Britain, xii, 1910, p. 36, also see p. 255.

10. Gath, p. 42.

11. Dana James D., Manual of Geology, 1894. p. 1007. Check at Library?

12. Whitley Gath, p. 56.

13. Wrangell, F.P. "Narrative of an Expedition to Siberia and the Polar Sea". Place, Publisher, p.173. check this at library

Chapter 28

The Caspian Sea: The Most Likely Location for Eden

Much mystery and speculation surrounds the precise location of the Second Garden of Eden. Most Bible scholars seem to place its location in the vicinity of the fertile crescent of Mesopotamia, or in the general vicinity of Asia Minor or even as far west as the Black Sea region. It is interesting to note, that not any of the areas that have been suggested as the Garden of Eden have ever been backed or supported by the geological evidences.

The most likely location for the Garden of Eden is to the east of the Caucasus / Talish Mountains and to the north of the Elburz / Shaw Jaman Mountains in the vicinity of the Caspian Sea region. Under this scenario, the Caspian Sea would have been the dynamic large headwater lake that would have been the source for the four major river systems that flowed out from Eden. The beautiful Garden of Eden would have been to the east of this lake, for we read, *"Now the Lord God had planted a garden IN THE EAST, in Eden; and there He put the man that He had formed"* (Genesis 2:8). How is this possible?

Critics would be quick to point out that this would be an impossible location for the Garden of Eden. They would emphasize that the present day Caspian Sea is a low lying, land locked, salty inland sea and the adjacent area to the east is dry, desert like and relatively barren. They will say that the area to the south and east of the Caspian Sea is barely above sea level. They will point out that the level of the water in the Caspian Sea is 28 meters (92 feet) below sea level. Rivers from all directions flow into it and it does not have an outlet.

Figure 28-1: Map Showing the Caspian Sea region with the Greater Caucasus and the Talish Mountains to the west; the Elburz and the Shah Jaman Mountains to the south and southeast. This Caspian Sea region is rich in oil and gas. Interpretation by Don Daae.

The Caspian Sea is presently the largest inland body of water in the world. It extends about 1207 km (750 miles) in a north-south direction and varies in width from 209km to 435km (130 to 270 miles). It has a mean depth of approximately 168 meters (550 feet) with extremes ranging from 8 meters (26 feet) in the north to about 975 meters (3200 feet) in the south. Today all rivers flow into the Caspian Sea.

In order to reconcile the apparent paradox of what the Garden of Eden was prior to Noah's Flood and what it is today, it is necessary to find the answer in the geological history of this region.

The Geology of the Caucasus, Elbruz, Hindu Kish Mountains

A well known British Pleistocene geologist, Professor Charlesworth, in his 1957 book, THE QUATERNARY ERA,[1] wrote: "*The Pleistocene indeed witnessed Earth-movements on a considerable, even catastrophic scale. There is evidence that it created mountains and ocean deeps of a size previously unequalled-- the Pleistocene indeed represents one of the crescendi in the earth's tectonic history. The movements affected about forty million square kilometers of the ocean floor, i.e. 70 % of the total surface of the Earth. Asia was subjected to powerful and far- reaching disturbances; the fault troughs of the Dead Sea, Red Sea, Jordan Valley, Gulf of Aden, Persian Gulf, and Arabian Sea received their present form. Earth movements elevated the Caucasus; the amount since Mindel time (i.e. the second stage of the Ice Age) is estimated at 3,900 feet (1,189 m) and raised Lake Baikal region and Central Asia by 6,700 feet (2,042 m). Similar changes took place around the Pacific and in North China the uplift was estimated at 10,000 feet (3,040 m).*"

Dr. Lester King, Professor of geology at Natal University, South Africa, in his 1962 book, THE MORPHOLOGY OF THE EARTH [2] (p.33) stated, "*The greatest uplift has taken place in the Himalaya. The modern Andes were created by violent Pleistocene up-arching. There is, of course, much evidence of a late vertical movement of the Himalaya from Tibet into Europe, the Mountain Garland, Hindu Kish, Elburz, and Caucasus are everywhere the product of uplifting during Pliocene to Recent times.*"

Professor Charlesworth believed that the great Pleistocene Earth movements which affected 70% of the Earth's surface took place sometime **after Mindel time,** which also relates to **the Kansan time** on Figure 15-1. Geologists believe that the Mindel Age ended about 225,000 years ago. The questions arise; when during the past 225,000 years did these great Earth movements take place? Bear in mind that geologists believe the Pleistocene was about 2.5 million years in length. See Figure 19-2. The big question arises, what took place after Kansan time?

Secular evolutionary archaeologists maintain it is possible to trace modern Man (Homo sapiens) in Europe back to about 225,000+ years. However, on the basis of the geological, archaeological and anthropological sciences, it is now possible to confirm that Man has been on the Earth for only about 6,000+ years. See figures 19-1 & 19-2.

It is now possible to demonstrate on the basis of the geological evidences that the above mentioned violent Earth movements that Charlesworth and King refer to actually terminated the Pleistocene Ice Age. In other words these violent Earth movements took place at the time of Noah's Flood about 4500 years ago. How is this possible? The answer is found in and through the science of geology.

The Caspian Sea Basin

The Caspian Sea Basin is framed on the south and east by a mountain garland of the Caucasus, Elburz, Shah Jaman Mountains that are joined eastward with the Hindu Kish and the Himalaya Mountains (Figure 28-1). The Caspian Sea is an excellent example of a half-graben structural basin that is bounded by a near vertical normal fault along its southern and eastern boundaries. See Figure 28-2.

Today the Caspian Sea Basin is a prolific oil and gas bearing basin. There are numerous prolific gas and oil fields within and to the east of the Caspian Sea. See Figure 28-1. It must be remembered that there would be many structural features within this basin.

The Origin of the Caspian Sea Basin

The Caspian Sea Basin began to form when the southern Gondwanaland tectonic plate, namely Northern Africa and

India began moving northward impacting Asia and Europe. This all began during Late Triassic and Early Jurassic time. See Figure 3-5. Therefore, the sediments in the lower portion of the Caspian Sea Basin would be of Jurassic Age.

The Caucasus/ Elburz Mountains have been progressively forming over a period of many millions of years coincident with the progressive subsidence of the Caspian Sea Half-Graben Basin (Figure 28-2). Sediments of Jurassic, Cretaceous and Tertiary age would be present. The total thickness of these sediments may be in the vicinity of 30,000 feet (9,144 meters) plus or minus. These sediments are possibly underlain by portions of older sediments of Early Mesozoic, Paleozoic and by Pre-Cambrian aged rock. The thickness of these older rock layers, if present, would be more regional to this area.

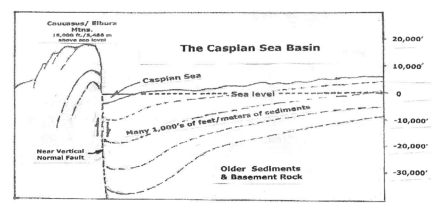

Figure 28-2: A schematic SW-NE structural cross section along the south western portion of the Caspian Sea Half Graben Structural Basin. It shows the near vertical normal fault that separates the Caucasus/Elburz Mountains from the Caspian Sea Basin. This is based upon detailed work that Don has done in analyzing similar basins in other places throughout the world. See references 3 & 4. He has also analyzed the Lancaster Sound Basin in Northern Canada. He has also gained knowledge of similar basins such as the Anadarko Basin in the USA as well as the Persian Gulf Basin. He has compared these basins to the Niger Basin in Africa. Interpretation and artwork by Don Daae, P.Geol.

The science of geology confirms that when certain areas undergo pronounced vertical uplift, the adjacent subsiding area will experience dramatic subsidence. The Caspian Sea is an excellent example of a half-graben structural basin that is bounded by a near vertical normal fault along its western and southern boundaries. By comparing similar geological basins throughout the world, it is found that the basin subsidence is always much greater than the uplift of the adjacent Mountains.

Late Pleistocene Orogeny

Dr. Charlesworth estimated that the Caucasus Mountains were elevated by about 3900 feet (1189 m) during the latter part of the Pleistocene Ice Age. We are now able to confirm that this earth shaking event actually took place about 4,500 years before the present at the end of the Pleistocene Age.

The Caspian Sea Basin would have experienced simultaneous subsidence to the east and north of the near vertical normal fault that would be greatly in excess of 3900 feet (1189 m). According to the science of geology the Caspian Sea Basin could very well have subsided somewhere between 6,000 to 8,000 feet (1524 to 2438 m) at the time of Noah's flood.

This dramatic tectonic event is definitely related to the great worldwide crustal movements to which Dr. Charlesworth and Dr. Lester King are referring. This is the geological event that brought the Pleistocene Ice Age to a dramatic termination. It also relates directly, time wise, to the world wide Flood of Noah that took place about 4,500 years ago. See Figure 19-1.

A Description of the Second Garden of Eden

On the basis of the Bible record, the Second Garden of Eden was a most magnificent and beautiful garden. It was decked with abundant varieties of fruit trees, shrubs and vegetables that supplied food for Adam and Eve.

It was indeed a magnificent oasis in the midst of the surrounding sin cursed Earth with its millions of varieties of plant, animal and bird life. It was the closest place to Paradise on Earth because God was present in this Garden.

On the basis of regional geology, the Second Garden of Eden was located to the east side of the Caucasus & north of the Elburz Mountains. It would have included the entire Caspian Sea region and would have extended a certain distance eastward of the Caspian Sea. We read in Genesis 2:8-22 NIV, "*Now the LORD God had planted a garden in the east, in Eden; and there he put the man he had formed.*"

On the basis of geology and prior to Noah's Flood, the second Garden of Eden would have been located at an altitude of about 6,000 to 8,000 feet (1829-2,438m) higher than it is today. It is estimated that the surrounding garland of mountains, namely the Caucasus, Talish, Elburz/ Shaw Jaman Mountains to the east and south would have towered at least 3,000 to 6,000 feet (914-1,829 m) above this elevated Garden area.

There would have been numerous rivers flowing from the mountains into this Pre-Flood Caspian Sea. There was another river flowing through the Garden of Eden into the Caspian Sea. We read in Genesis 2:10 NIV, "*A river watering the garden flowed from Eden from there it was separated into four headwaters.*" We also read in Genesis 2:5c and 6, NIV, "*And there was no man to work the ground, but streams came up from the earth and watered the whole surface of the ground.*" The King James version says in Genesis 2:6, "*but a mist went up and watered the whole face of the ground.*" There is a certain mystery surrounding this Garden called Eden. However, we can conclude that this Garden of Eden was a most beautiful place with lush vegetation containing fruit and vegetables of every kind that were food for Man. God also created within this most beautiful Garden the first domestic animals such as cattle, sheep, goats, dogs, cats, chickens etc. that are described in Chapter Seven.

The Second Garden of Eden was indeed a magnificent oasis in the midst of the surrounding sin cursed Earth with its millions of varieties of plant, animal and bird life. It was the closest place to Paradise on Earth, except for one major factor. This was the presence of the Tree of Good and Evil. In other words, **evil was lurking in this garden ready to happen**. The fallen Lucifer was also there as an accident ready to happen. **Thus, God gave Adam and Eve a choice either to follow Him or to reject Him and to follow Satan**. This is the same choice you and I must make today.

References for Chapter 28

1. Professor Charlesworth, *The Quaternary Era, Vol.1,* p: 604-605/

2. Dr. Lester King, Professor of Geology at Natal University, South Africa, in his 1962 book, "The Morphology of the Earth."

3. Daae, H.D., P.Geol. & A.T.C. Rutgers PhD, 1975, "Geological History of the Northwest Passage." Bull. Can. Petrol. Geol., Vol. 23, No.1. The north–south cross section across Lancaster Sound is not all that different from Figure 27-2. High mountains are also present on Devon Island to the north of Lancaster Sound.

4. Daae, H.D., P.Geol. 1983, "The Geological History and Evaluation of the Lancaster Sound Basin, NWT., with Specific Reference to the Dundas Structure." This was one of the Resource Management Support Documents that was submitted to the Federal Government.

Chapter 29

Four Major Rivers flowed out of Eden

It is obvious from the Biblical description of the Garden of Eden that it must have been located in a high plateau region bordered by lofty mountains. There had to be a large headwater lake within the garden that was fed by smaller rivers that had its source higher up in the nearby mountains. There were also four major rivers that flowed out of this lake and away from Eden. This would indicate that a major headwater lake within Eden acted as a highly charged dynamic watershed providing abundant water to feed four major rivers systems that flowed away from the garden area to four distinct parts of the Earth.

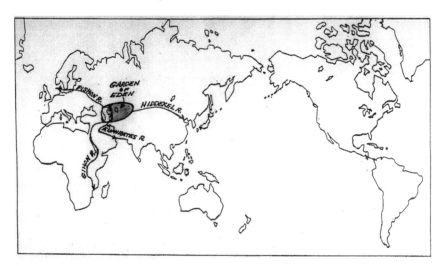

Figure 29-1: The figure shows the proposed location for the specific area called the Garden of Eden and the Four Major River Systems that flowed out of Eden.

The First River is believed to have flowed in a northwesterly direction into western Asia and into northern Europe. It possibly emptied into the North Sea, for we read: *"The name of the first is Pishon; it is the one which encompasses the whole land of Havilah, where there is gold. And the gold of that land is good. Bedellium and the onyx stone are there"* (Genesis 2:11-12). It is hereby assumed that this Pishon River flowed in a northwest direction. This river would have provided an access for Early Man to migrate northwestward into Europe and Western Asia. In other words, the descendents of Adam and Eve were the first Early Men and Women to inhabit this portion of the Earth.

The Second River flowed southwestward through the land of Canaan along the Jordan River Rift Valley, through the Gulf of Aqabah and the Red Sea Rift Valley. It would have then flowed into the East African Rift Valley through Ethiopia, Kenya, Tansania. It would have eventually emptied into the Indian Ocean in the vicinity of Beira, Mozambique. We read as follows, *"The name of the second river is Gihon; it is the one which encompasses the whole Land of Cush"* (Genesis 2:13). Cush is the ancient name for Ethiopia. The question arises how a river could possibly flow into this region of Africa, because it would be physically impossible for this to happen today? See Figure 29-1.

How is it possible to resolve this apparent mystery? It becomes obvious that physical changes have taken place in the region.

The answer is found in the findings of the Legg 23B[1] of the Deep Sea Drilling Project aboard the R.V. Glomar Challenger drill ship. This project was devoted to scientific drilling in the central and southern Red Sea region. Drilling revealed that the Red Sea Rift Valley is underlain by Late Miocene evaporates including rock salt, at relatively shallow depths throughout most of its extent. However, **these evaporates are absent** in the central rift valley zone that is underlain by recent igneous basaltic rock. It was reported in Science Magazine[1] *"that there were rocks as old as or older than the late Miocene (about 5 million years) within one or two*

*miles of a supposedly active spreading centre. One inter-
pretation of the magnetic anomaly pattern from this area
indicates that rocks no older than about 2 million years
should be present. This was based on the assumption that
a continuous Tertiary spreading history exists for the Red
Sea. A more reasonable interpretation is that **spreading
resumed only recently** in the Red Sea region following
a period of quiescence that extended back into the early
Miocene.*" In other words, Pleistocene, Pliocene, Middle and
Upper Miocene sediments are all absent in the central region of the Red Sea Rift Valley. Only Late Miocene sediments
are present along the flanks. **According to the survey,
the spreading (rifting or separating) of the Red Sea
appears to be Recent. In other words, the geological term Recent would indicate that the rifting or the
separation took place at the end of the Pleistocene
Age.** This coincides with the termination of the Altithermal
Age. This would have been the precise time when Noah's
Flood took place. See Figure 19-1.

The central portion of the north-south trending Red Sea
Rift Zone contains heavy metal rich black shale deposits
and basalt igneous rocks, similar to deep ocean tholelitic
basalts. The temperatures along the rift zone are today
unusually high, and the zone is characterized by hot brine
occurrences. This would indicate that there is today a continual escape of hot juvenile waters from below the Earth's
crust along the central portion of the Red Sea Rift Valley
into the waters of the Red Sea.

It is also important to realize that the history of the Red
Sea Rift Valley extends back into the Late Pleistocene time.
This is evidenced by the fact that the Gihon River flowed
into the land of Ethiopia prior to Noah's Flood. However,
it has remained fairly stable in this particular region until
this recent traumatic event took place at the end of the
Altithermal Age.

The central portion of the Red Sea is obviously very young.
This is confirmed by the warmer waters above the bottom (igneous tholelitic) basalts within the central portion

of the Red Sea Rift Valley. It would thus appear that the recent separation or reactivation of the Red Sea spreading center took place at the close of the Pleistocene Age. This was about 4,500 years ago. It is important to notice that Geophysical studies have revealed and confirmed a "very recent" opening (separation) of the Red Sea region.

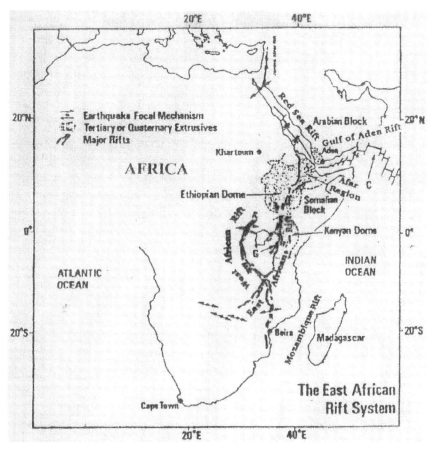

Figure 29-2: This map shows the path that the Gihon River would have followed from the Garden of Eden southward through the Jordon River Rift Valley, the Gulf of Aqabah, through the Red Sea into the East African Rift Valley system and eventually emptying into the Indian Ocean at Beira, Mozambique. Prepared by Don Daae. It was revised after E. Ronald Oxburgh, 1978.[2]

According to the science of geology, this type of structure is called a "Triple Junction Structure." It has three arms that are positioned at 120 degrees to each other. The East African Rift Valley is the failed 3rd arm. It has experienced dramatic sinking, but no significant separation. The Red Sea Rift and the Gulf of Aden Rift Valley have both experienced complete separation that have been in filled with hot igneous basalts from deep down.

The West African Rift Valley is also the failed third arm of a Triple Junction Structure. See Figure 29-2. It began to form when Madagascar began to break away from Africa at Beira, leaving a 120 degree angle. Further geological work will determine the geological timing of this Triple Junction structure.

I have had the privilege of working the geology and geophysics of the Lancaster Sound Rift Valley Basin in the NWT of Canada. This basin is the failed 3rd Arm of a Triple Junction Structure that formed when Greenland separated from Canada leaving a 120 degree angle with Devon and Baffin Islands. However, this separation is much older and is believed to have taken place about Early Jurassic time. Figure 3-5.

Prior to Noah's Flood, Africa was joined more closely to Saudi Arabia. It is believed that the S.E. Corner of Arabia was attached close enough to Ethiopia, prior to 4500 years ago, to prevent the Gihon River from flowing southward into the Gulf of Aden and then into the Indian Ocean as it does today. Instead, this second river system from the Garden of Eden flowed southward along the topographically low rift valley region that extends through the land of Canaan. It would have followed the Jordan River through the Gulf of Aqabah into the Red Sea region. It would have then entered into the East African Rift Valley through the land of Ethiopia and southward through Kenya, Tanzania and eventually emptying eventually into the Indian Ocean at Beira, Mozambique. See Figures 29-2.

This Second Gihon River would have provided an excellent access or water highway for Early Man that is the early descendants of Adam and Eve to migrate into Africa. These people would have been the early Pre-Flood people who manufactured the stone tools that archaeologists have classified as the Paleolithic (Oldowan and Acheulian) stone tool cultures. This would also explain the gradual development of technology and the presence of more advanced pre-Flood Mesolithic and Neolithic Cultural remains that are also present in this part of East Africa.

The Third River flowed eastward from Eden. It possibly passed through the interior part of Asia, perhaps through the Gobi Desert region, emptying eventually into the Pacific Ocean, for we read: *"The name of the third river is Hiddekal; **it is the one which goes toward the east** of Assyria"* (Genesis 2:14). This Hiddekal River provided an access for early Pre-Flood Man to migrate eastward into China, Mongolia, Australia and North and South America.

The Fourth River flowed southeasterly through the Fertile Crescent region of Mesopotamia, emptying into the Persian Gulf. It was known as the Euphrates River, for we read: *"The fourth river is the Euphrates"* (Genesis 2:14). It is generally accepted that this refers to the river known as the Euphrates today. It would seem that Adam and Eve may very well have journeyed southeastward from the Garden of Eden along this Euphrates River. They would have settled in the rich area of the Fertile Crescent region of Mesopotamia.

It is also interesting to note that the ancient home of Noah is believed to be just north of the present Persian Gulf. This is also where Post Flood Modern History began.

It will remain for geologists and geo-morphologists to identify and map the above mentioned four river systems. Many of these channels would probably now be infilled with gravels and sands resulting from Noah's Flood. Local and regional Late Pleistocene movements at the time of Noah's flood would also make their identification more difficult to observe.

References for Chapter 29

1. Science, 1973, p.379. R.V. Challenger, Legg 23b of the Deep Sea Drilling Project aboard the RV Glomar Challenger.
2. Oxborough E. Ronald, 1978, "Rifting in East Africa and Large Scale Tectonic Processes." In Symposium Volume, "Geological Background to Fossil Man: Recent Research in the Gregory Rift Valley, East Africa." Edited by Walter Bishop, Geological Society of London, University of Toronto Press.

Chapter 30

What Happened to the Pleistocene Ice?

One of the big mysteries with respect to the Pleistocene Ice Age is what happened to all the continental Ice? Did this vast amount of ice just slowly melt away or is there a plausible alternative explanation?

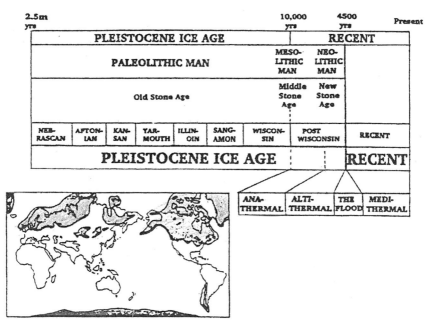

Figure 30-1: Illustrates the long duration of the Pleistocene Epoch or Ice Age extending back to about 2.5 million years into the past. The map at the base shows the regions of the Earth that were covered by Ice. Prepared by Don Daae.

The Pleistocene Glaciation is the last of five major Ice Ages that have been geologically identified throughout the geological history of the Earth. They are as follows:

1. The Pleistocene Ice Age.
2. The Lower Permian Ice Age.
3. The Upper Ordovician Ice Age.
4. The Upper Proterozoic Ice Age.
5. The Gowganda Ice Age of Lower Proterozoic Age.

The magnitude of these five glaciations or major Ice Ages are briefly described in my book.[1] "Bridging the Gap:The First 6 Days." Also see when they took place in Figure 3-5. They were all major Ice Ages that left an indelible imprint within the geological history of the Earth. However, the intervening geological ages have been free of ice and relatively mild. The only other time to my knowledge that minor evidences of ice have been identified was during the Cambrian Age in the Northern Yukon Territories. However, this did not appear to be a dominant regional or worldwide event.

My personal belief is that God allowed these periods of glaciations to cleanse and to revitalize the Earth's environment in preparation for new developments and new creations of plant and animal life.

The Pleistocene Epoch

The term Pleistocene was first defined by Charles Lyell in 1833 from a Tertiary succession of sediments in Sicily. He said, "*The criterion for separating the Pleistocene beds from the underlying Pliocene beds was the greater similarity of the fauna of the upper beds with modern fauna.*"[1] (Clarke & Stern, p.380) In other words, the many animal fauna like the now extinct woolly mammoth, mastodon, saber tooth tiger, giant sloth, giant beaver and many more all characterize the fauna of the Pleistocene Epoch.

Today as we look back in time, we realize that all these many species of Pleistocene fauna were present throughout the world until very recent times. What happened to them? Another big question is this: what happened to the massive sheets of ice that still covered large portions of the Earth at the time these fauna disappeared?

There was a sudden extinction of these animal fauna. We are now able to determine that these Pleistocene fauna became extinct at the end of the Altithermal Age. This in turn relates to the termination of the Pleistocene Epoch or Age and the beginning of the Recent Age. See Figure 30-1. In order to understand the magnitude of the Pleistocene Epoch, it is necessary to give the reader a glimpse into this age. Maybe we will be able to understand more clearly: what happened to the Pleistocene Ice?

The Pleistocene Age (Epoch) is estimated to cover a time span of about 2.5 million years. It can be subdivided into four colder glacial advance periods referred to in North America as the Nebraskan, Kansan, Illinois and Wisconsin glaciations with three intervening warmer periods when the ice edge melted back a certain distance. In the Old World of Europe and Asia, these sub divisions have different names. See Figure 15-1. These different transgressive and regressive stages of the Pleistocene Ice Age have revealed that the main core of glacial ice remained in place. In other words, the regions in Figure 30-1 remained covered by ice except along the southern edges. In Europe and Asia and in North America, the southern edges have been well documented by various geological studies.

It is believed that the maximum limits of the ice were achieved during the last advance called the Wisconsin Glaciation. Then, about 10,000 years before the present, the climate throughout the Earth entered into a period of pronounced warming. This new age from 10,000 years to about 4,500 years before the present is often classified as the Post Wisconsin Age. It can also be subdivided into the Anathermal and the Altithermal ages. See Figure 30-1. All of these now extinct fauna were still present throughout the world in great numbers during this time.

The term Pleistocene Epoch terminates at the end of the Post Wisconsin Age. This also equates to the end of the

Altithermal Age. See 19-1. Let us now investigate the magnitude of the Pleistocene Ice Age.

The Extent of Glacial Ice in Canada

There was more than one center of ice accumulation. One such centre of ice accumulation was in the Hudson Bay region where it is estimated that the ice had attained thicknesses in the order of 14,000 to 18,000 feet (4267m to 5,286m) in thickness. It was believed that this thick Ice mass extended in a north, northwest direction into the NWT of Canada. From this region of much accumulation, the ice moved by a series of long linear lobes eastward, southward and westward. Of course the thickness of glacial ice between the lobes would have been thinner.

I was extremely interested in ice movement because I had the privilege of being raised on a farm in southeastern Saskatchewan near the USA border. My three older brothers and I spent many hours picking the many glacial rocks and boulders that had been carried by glacial ice into this region. These rocks would be put into large rock piles. As a child, I often wondered how these strange rocks ever got into my dad's fields. Some of these rocks were up to 6 feet in length. They sure gave us a lot of hard work to do.

I had the privilege of spending four months on a geological Field Party in northern Saskatchewan in the Churchill and Reindeer River region. One of our senior geologists was very knowledgeable of the Pleistocene Ice Age. He taught me a great deal about this Age. On traverses, we would encounter certain Precambrian granite outcrops where we would observe the glacial striations. We would run our fingers along the striations to determine the direction of ice movement. The striations were smooth in one direction and rough in the other direction. We could thus determine that the ice had moved in a southwest direction. We also had regional topographic maps and aerial photographs. They gave evidence and confirmation to the linear SW direction of ice movement. It was believed that the ice from this particular region would have flowed into the southwestern portion of Saskatchewan and possibly into the Cypress Hills region.

The Cyprus Hills in the SW portion of Saskatchewan is a high topographic region. Its summit is in the vicinity of 4,816 feet (1468m) above sea level. It has become a benchmark for attempting to determine the relative thickness of the Pleistocene Ice throughout Saskatchewan and at its thickest source in Northern Manitoba and the Hudson Bay region.

The Cypress Hills is much higher than the regions to the north and south that are generally in the range of about 2,000 feet (610m) above sea level. By projecting the thickness of the glacial ice that at one time surrounded the Cypress Hills one can roughly project the progressive thickening of the continental ice in a north and northeast direction. It is thus estimated that the glacial ice in the region of the Hudson Bay was possibly in the range of 14,000 to 18,000 feet (4267m to 5,286m) in thickness.

The Pleistocene glacial Ice completely surrounded the Cypress Hills. However, the upper central portion of the Cypress Hills was never covered by ice. Thus, this region came to be considered a biologists paradise to investigate animal and plant life of an earlier time that continued to survive and were still living in these hills.

There were obvious lobes of ice flowing from the central ice core region in Canada to the east, south and west. Later I had the privilege of doing reconnaissance geological field work on Devon Island and Baffin Island in the North West Territories of Canada. I also supervised a geological Field Party on Bylot Island just south of Lancaster Sound. Our Company had the privilege of participating in the drilling of 24 wells with Panarctic Oil Limited in the in the High Arctic Sverdrup Basin region of Canada and one well with Elfex Oil Company on Banks Island and a second on Prince Patrick Island in the Western Arctic.

The company I was employed with was the Operator of the Magnorth Project where we conducted over 23,000 miles of geophysical seismic lines throughout the Northwest Passage from McClure Strait in the west to Lancaster Sound in the east and also into the Baffin Bay region. We were able to determine that the sea bottom of Lancaster Sound, which is located between Devon and Baffin Islands, had been scoured by Pleistocene Glacial Ice that had moved in an eastward direction into Baffin Bay. This also indicated that the Pleistocene Ice source region to the west had to be of much greater thickness. This also indicated that the greater thickness of ice was to the west of Lancaster Sound. This thicker portion would also have been connected with the thick ice pack to the south in the Hudson Bay Region.

Coincident with the buildup of glacial ice in Central Canada was a similar build up of glacial Ice along the Rocky Mountain region in western Alberta. Similar thicknesses of ice were also present in the Interior and Coastal Mountain Ranges of British Columbia as shown on Figure 30-1 and 30-2. This thick ice pack would have extended northward into the Yukon Territories and portions of Alaska.

It is believed that the northwest trending Ice Corridor that existed between these two ice packs may have been inter-mittently filled with ice at different times during the long history of the Pleistocene Epoch. The glacial ice would have also extended southward various distances into the north-ern portions of the USA.

It is interesting to note that the surface glacial erratics east of Calgary, Alberta exhibit an Archean Pre-Cambrian sig-nature, whereas the erratics to the west of Calgary have a signature reflecting the rock types in the mountain regions to the west of Calgary.

The Anathermal Age

It was not until about 10,000 years ago that the climate throughout the Earth became pleasantly warm. This marks the beginning of the Anathermal Age. It was during this Age that an ice corridor began to form in a northwest direction from Calgary, Alberta and into the Yukon Territories and through the central regions of Alaska. This was a natural place for the Ice corridor to form between these two major regions of ice development.

It must also be realized that the level of the ocean during the Anathermal and the Altithermal Ages was about 328 feet (100 m) lower than today. See Figure 22-17 and associated text. This lower shoreline made it possible for Early Man to have travelled from Mongolia through Eastern Russia across the present Bering Sea region on dry land.

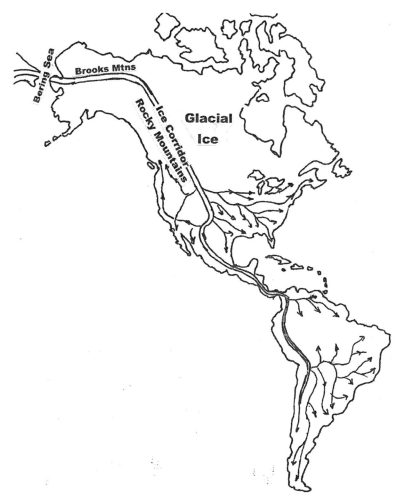

Figure 30-2: Map showing the Migratory routes of Early Man from Asia to North and South America. This Figure was prepared by Don Daae after Sauer[2] 1944 & MacGowan & Hester[3] 1962.

The Altithermal Age

According to the science of archaeology and anthropology only the Neanderthal man occupied North & South America during the Anathermal Age. See Chapter 19.

The Neanderthal men and their families would have travelled along this ice corridor through central Alaska and the Yukon Territories down through central Alberta and into the USA, Mexico and eventually into South America.

Figure 30-2 reveals that the Early Neanderthal Men and their families only settled and inhabited the regions to the south of the Pleistocene Ice edge in America. Thus, it becomes evident that the main portion of the Pleistocene Ice was still present in Canada during the entire Altithermal Age. This is verified by the many archaeological sites of the Neanderthal Men to the south of the ice edge.

It is also interesting to note that there are several locations in southern Saskatchewan where artifacts of Early Neanderthal Man have been found to the north of the ice edge. It is believed that the glacial ice was much thinner between the thicker lobes of Pleistocene Ice. This enabled the Neanderthal explorers to explore certain regions where the ice was thinner or even absent into the southern portions of Saskatchewan, Manitoba and Ontario.

One must remember that there are many archaeological sites of the North American Indians throughout Canada and the United States. The Indians are classified as Modern Man because they are Post Flood people, whereas the Neanderthal Man is known as Pre-Flood people or Early Man.

How is it possible to bridge the gap between these two groups of mankind, namely the Neanderthal Man and the North American Indian? Is it possible that the sciences of geology, archaeology and anthropology can unlock this mystery?

On my dad's farm in southeast Saskatchewan, there were many North American Indian projectile artifacts. My one uncle had a large number of North American Indian artifacts that he cherished. A neighbour who farmed a short distance to the west by the name of Stanley Durr found a "Folsom" Projectile point. Now what is so special about a Folsom artefact? This artefact relates to Early Man who lived according to Archaeological dating between 9000-8500 years ago. This projectile point was made by the Neanderthal Man. See figure 19-4. See www. Saskatchewan Archaeology near Estevan.

Modern day Archaeology reveals a great gap of about 3,000 years separating the North American Indians and Early Man as shown on Figure 19-4. However, they fail to explain why there was such a long gap in time.

How is it possible to relate Early Man throughout Europe, Asia, Africa and Australia to Modern Day Man? This manuscript reveals how it is possible to bridge the gap between Early Man and Modern Man in a reasonable logical way.

The Mysterious Northern Michigan Copper Mines

There was a mysterious pre-Flood, copper mining operation in the northern peninsula of Michigan that is dated by modern archaeologists as ranging in age from 5,000 to 3,200 years BP. It is estimated that a minimum of half a billion pounds of the world's highest grade copper was excavated from this mysterious site. This site is described in Chapter 22 where it is estimated that it would have required 10,000 men 1,000 years to develop this extensive mining operation throughout this region. In other words many thousands of Neanderthal people would have been involved with this massive mining operation.

There is a paper entitled "Wisconsin's Ancient Copper Miners" by Herbert Wagner. It was originally published in the Wisconsin Outdoor Journal. Also see Google at Wisconsin's Ancient Copper Miners.

Herbert Wagner says, "*That prehistoric copper mining took place in Michigan's Upper Peninsula and on Isle Royale is an established fact. Whether or not a similar if smaller industry existed in northwest Wisconsin is more problematic as the evidence is sparse and largely anecdotal. While the aforementioned accounts all point to ancient mining activity in northwest Wisconsin before the settlement period, they are often little more than folk legend or gleaned from old newspaper accounts that are notorious for being tinged with boosterism, stock jobbing, and incipient "copper fever." Critics will express doubt and demand harder evidence, because without scientific proof these old claims are little more than mirages and no more credible than Carver's claim was to practical 19th century mining men."*

This would have been a flourishing site where many thousands of Neanderthal people were living and working at this mining site prior to Noah's Flood.

It is therefore believed that many of these Neanderthal persons would have explored many of the regions of Canada where the ice was less thick or had melted back during the warmer weather of the Anathermal and the Altithermal ages.

The big question is this: what happened to the Pleistocene Ice and to the Neanderthal man? What happened to the great numbers of prehistoric animal species such as the woolly mammoth, the mastodon, the saber tooth tiger, the great herds of camel and the list could go on and on? They all mysteriously disappeared at the end of the Altithermal Age.

Noah's Flood is the Answer

It becomes obvious that Noah's Flood was responsible for terminating the Altithermal Age. See Figure 19-1. It also was responsible for removing the Pleistocene Ice throughout the entire Earth except in the mountain regions. Ice is lighter than water. Once the Flood waters had reached its highest point which was 120 feet above the highest mountain, the lighter blocks of Pleistocene ice would have begun to lift and float away.

However, wherever there were high mountains the ice would not have been free to float away. This is why the mountain regions have retained large portions of thick ice up to the present day.

Today, there is a floating Polar Ice Pack that is present in the Beaufort Sea region of Canada. The southern edge of this Polar Ice Pack moves northward in the warmer summer months and southward during the colder winter months. The southern edge of this Polar Ice Pack can be traced eastward from the Beaufort Sea region. It roughly passes through the central portion of the North West Territories in the vicinity of the North West Passage. It then can be traced into the Baffin Bay region and then to the southern tip of Greenland.

As a result, the Canadian North West Passage is free of ice for only 1 to 4 months of the year. When our Company was running seismic surveys throughout this passage, there was only one summer that we were able to enter into the McClure Straight region with our seismic ship. The McClure Straight is located in the western portion of the Northwest Passage. Even then, we needed the help of a Canadian Ice Breaker in order to run seismic lines.

Lancaster Sound is located in the eastern portion of the Northwest Passage. Along the north shore of Lancaster Sound is Devon Island. The eastern portion of Devon Island is mountainous and is covered with thick glacial ice. These mountains were obviously high enough to prevent the glacial Ice from lifting up and floating away. This glacial ice field continues for a certain distance to the west of the high mountain region.

I have had the privilege of flying in a twin engine Otter aircraft just above this ice field more than once. However, the western half of Devon Island is free of ice. Obviously all the ice to the west was lifted up and floated away by Flood waters. The ice to the east remained in place because of its nearness to the high mountains.

There will be many who will strongly oppose this view. Some will be in strong denial that Noah's Flood ever took place. There are others who will say that the ice just melted away normally. There are some Christians who believe that Noah's Flood was local only to the Middle East region. The Creation Science (Young Earth) people believe Noah's Flood took place prior to the Pleistocene Ice Age. Thus, there are so many conflicting views.

To the people who believe that the Ice just melted away normally, they will have to wrestle with a certain question. Why is there an absence of large bodies or blocks of thick ice throughout the northern regions of Canada where the temperatures have remained cooler and where melting would have taken place more slowly?

I have had the privilege of visiting various places in the northern mainland of Canada and into the High Arctic Islands of Canada. Where are the remnant blocks of thick ice that have not melted as yet? They are not present. Sure there is ice, but only what one would expect to find under normal conditions. This is why the Inuit were able to occupy the northern regions of Canada that were covered with thick continental sheets of ice prior to Noah's Flood..

References for Chapter 30

1. Clarke & Stern, p.380
2. Sauer[2] 1944 &
3. MacGowan & Hester,[3] " 1962

Chapter 31

The Origin of Modern Man

The origin of Modern Man began the very moment Noah and his family stepped out of the Ark onto dry land on one of the mountains of Ararat in eastern Turkey. This was the moment that Noah and his family began a new life. It was a time of beginning all over again for the human race.

It was also at this time when Earth's <u>New Golden Age</u> began. God spoke to Noah saying, "*Go out of the Ark, you and your wife, and your sons and your son's wives with you. So Noah went out, and his sons and his wife, and his son's wives with him. Every beast, every creeping thing, every bird, and whatever creeps on the Earth, according to their families, went out of the Ark.* (Genesis 8:15, 16, 18-19). It was a time of beginning again.

One can imagine the strong emotional feelings that must have flooded the minds of Noah and his family as they stepped out of the Ark on to dry land. They knew that they were the only surviving human beings upon the Earth. A new world of opportunity lay before them. This was truly a time of beginning again for the human race.

Noah's Alter & Worship to Almighty God

The very first thing that Noah did when he left the Ark was to build an altar to the Lord. The Bible says: "*He took of every clean animal and of every clean bird and offered burnt offerings on the altar*" (Genesis 8:20). This act of worship was in keeping with the plan of redemption that God had presented to Adam and Eve in Genesis 3:21 which says, *"The LORD God made garments of skin for Adam and his wife and clothed them"*. This act by God involved the shedding of blood of a clean type of animal such as a lamb. This death of a lamb acted as a substitute for the future true Lamb of God who would one day shed His sinless blood on the Cross for the sins of the world. Through this act of worship, Noah was appropriating the shed blood of the animals as a covering for their sins. They were also giving honor, glory, thanks and praise to the Lord God of Heaven and Earth who miraculously saved their lives.

At this sacred ceremony upon the altar, which was possibly just outside of the Ark, the Lord God Almighty honoured Noah's act of worship, for we read, *"And the Lord smelled a soothing aroma"* (Genesis 8:21). It was at this sacred ceremony that God gave Noah and his family a revelation into the future where He reveals to Noah that he will never again destroy the world a second time with water. However, He does imply to Noah that the evil imagination of Man's heart will, however, lead to a second judgment. Until then, or as long as the Earth remains, everything will continue in a relatively uniform manner. We read, *"While the Earth remains, seedtime and harvest, cold and heat, and winter and summer, and day and night shall not cease"* (Genesis 8:22).

God's Instructions for Post Flood Mankind

At the sacred ceremony on Mount Ararat, God gave Noah instructions concerning Man's responsibilities and conduct in this new age. These instructions are binding upon Post Flood Man, and will continue as long as the present world shall last. These instructions are not to be confused with the Moral Law which is the Ten Commandments that were later given to Moses on Mount Sinai, even though the two are entirely complimentary.

God instructed Noah *and his three sons and their wives as follows, "be fruitful and multiply, and fill (populate) the*

Earth." (Genesis 9:1, NKJV) This was identical to the instruction given to Adam and Eve in Genesis 1:28. The Earth has undergone two major worldwide human migrations to fulfill this instruction. The first worldwide migration of Mankind was at the very dawn of human history. These were the descendants of Adam and Eve who populated the entire Earth during the Pre-Flood days. The second major worldwide human migration took place after the Flood. These were the descendants of Noah, his three sons, and their wives. This was truly a time of beginning again.

God instructed Noah and his family as to what they could eat, *"And the fear of you and the dread of you shall be on every beast of the Earth, on every bird of the air, on all that move on the Earth, and on all fish of the sea. They are given into your hand. Every moving thing that lives shall be food for you. I have given you all things, even as the green herbs"* (Genesis 9:2-3). Mankind was now free to eat the meat of all animal flesh on the earth, the birds of the air and the fish of the sea, as well as all plant food. This instruction differs from that given to Adam and Eve, as they were to be strict vegetarians. The instruction to Noah applies to fallen man, whereas the instruction to Adam & Eve was to sinless Man before the Fall.

God instructed man never to eat or drink blood *"But you shall not eat flesh with its life, that is, its blood"* (Genesis 9:4, NKJV). In this passage, God qualifies the one thing that Man is not allowed to eat. He is able to eat the flesh of animals, but he must never eat or drink their blood, because blood is sacred in the eyes of God. Leviticus 17:14 (NIV) says, *"You must not eat the blood of any creature, because the life of every creature is in its blood."*

God instructed Man as to capital punishment in Genesis 9:5-6 (NIV) `Surely for your lifeblood I will demand *a reckoning;* from the hand of every beast I will require it, and from the hand of man. From the hand of every man's brother I will require the life of man. Whoever sheds man's blood, by man his blood shall be shed; for in the image of God He made man." In this passage God is saying to Man that if an animal such as a bear, dog, or lion kills a man that this particular animal must be put to death, so as to prevent any further killings. Likewise if a man should kill another man, then the murderer is to be put to death by man. This is to prevent further killings.

Later, in the Bible God reconfirms capital punishment with the Nation of Israel for pre-meditated murder. However, if the killing was not pre-meditated, then there were cities of refuge where the person who committed the killing could go for protection.

The Rainbow Covenant

After God had given these four basic instructions, he established a covenant with Man. A covenant is a solemn promise to do or not to do a certain thing. The Rainbow Covenant states that God will never destroy all flesh on the Earth ever again by means of a world wide flood. This covenant was between God and Noah, his descendants and every living creature and to the birds, cattle and beasts of the Earth that went out of the Ark. A rainbow in the cloud was made as a sign, that whenever one would see the rainbow, it would be a remembrance of this everlasting covenant.

Noah and His Family Return Home

Upon leaving the Ark on Mount Ararat or upon one of the mountains of Ararat, it is believed that Noah and his family worked their way homeward to the Fertile Crescent region of Mesopotamia. See Figure 26-3. It is possible that they worked their way eastward to the present Euphrates River system that would have led them to the fertile Crescent region of Mesopotamia which is just to the north of the Persian Gulf region of today. See Figures 29-1 and 15-9.

Babylonian literature says that Noah had loaded the Ark with supplies, silver and gold. It is highly probable that Noah and his family preserved valuable cooking utensils, clothing, tools, knives, hammers, saws, grinding stones, pottery, and so forth, in the Ark, that would have assisted them in the new age after the Flood.

It can be assumed that Noah and his family would have spent a certain time in the region of Mount Ararat, prior to returning to their homeland. They would have gathered all their supplies together, bringing cattle, sheep, goats, camels, horses, dogs, cats, and chickens with them to their homeland in the land of Shinar.

Noah and his family had a distinct advantage over Adam and Eve, in that they could benefit from the great amount of knowledge, wisdom, history, technology, and cultural advances of pre-Flood days. They were able to take advantage of this great knowledge base and to build upon it. They were also able to pass this information on to their descendants. During the first 120 years after the Flood, there was only one race and one nation of people, who spoke only one language.

The Bible implies that Noah and his family first settled to the east of Shinar, where they probably began to raise their families. As the waters of the Flood receded, they then moved from the east into the fertile land of Shinar, which is described as follows, *"Now the whole Earth had one language and one speech. And it came to pass, as they journeyed from the east, that they found a plain in the land of Shinar, and they dwelt there."* (Genesis 11:1 & 2, (NKJV).

The Animals and Birds Return Home

It is likely that the Lord allowed the various animals and birds to abide near the region of the Middle East for a time, to have new families. The Lord would then have guided each species of animals and birds back to their homelands. He would have led the marsupial kangaroos and koala bears to Australia, the llamas, certain species of monkeys, and tapir to South America, gophers, deer, rabbits, and moose to North America, zebras, tigers, and elephants to Africa, and so on.

The Great thicknesses of glacial Ice that covered Canada prior to Noah's Flood was now gone. The animals were now free to migrate freely southward through Canada and southward. See Chapter 30 and Figures 30-1 and 30-2.

A question naturally arises in the minds of men as to how animals could cross the sea to Australia, and North America, and the many islands of the oceans. There is now scientific evidence to indicate that the level of the ocean was lowered to 180 feet (54.9m) below the present sea level after Noah's Flood.

Dr. Robert Dill from the Oceanographic Survey at Long Beach California gave an interesting movie presentation to the Canadian Society of Petroleum Geologists in Calgary, Alberta in the late 1960's. He presented the research results performed with the submersible Deep Star Submarine along the continental slope offshore California. In the filmstrips, a powerful search light was focused on the sea bottom and one could see many species of sea life on or just above the sea floor.

At the 180 foot depth, one could see in the film strips numerous tree trunks standing erect on an old submerged shore line. Specimens of wood were dated by carbon-14 and were found to be about 5000 plus or minus years old. Similar observations were made by the Deep Star Semi-Submersible in various parts of the world, such as in other parts of America, Europe, and Africa etc. He said that where ever they went, they were able to detect this older shoreline at about 180 feet (54.9m) below sea level.

At that time, I was working the geology for a major Oil Company in the northern Yukon Territories and along the North Slope region of Alaska. It was shortly after the big Prudhoe Bay oil and gas discovery. I checked through all the bathymetric maps and discovered that there was a slight tightening of the bathymetric contours at the 180 foot depth along the northern slope of the Yukon and Alaska that was indicative of a shoreline development. I also discovered that the water depth in the Bering Sea region is shallower than 180 feet (54.9m). This indicated to me that Russia and Alaska were connected by a land bridge at this particular time.

I had the privilege later to meet with a certain geologist in Hawaii; he verified that there was an old shoreline at the 180 foot (54.9m) subsea level in Hawaii. He also took me to the university and showed me areal photographs throughout Southeast Asia. One could see the numerous dendritic branching forms of rivers and streams that were now submerged under sea water. We discussed the possibility that those river channels could have been formed about the same time as the 180 foot shoreline was formed. This would give added confirmation that this lower shoreline would have been Post Flood in age. See Figure 22-6.

According to Dr. Lester King[1] of Natal University, a large extension of Southeast Asia has recently sunk beneath the sea, until only islands and peninsulas remain visible where formerly land was continuous. If the sea level was 180 feet lower than the present, then Australia would have been joined to Southeast Asia by a land bridge. This would have facilitated the migration of the different species of animal life back to their homelands into North and South America, Australia and to other parts of the Earth. The English Channel is also less than 180 feet (54.9m) in depth. The British Isles would have been attached to France by an extensive land bridge. The lower sea level would have also facilitated the migration of animals to certain islands of the sea via land bridges that today are separated from the mainland by sea water.

Conclusion

The Flood of Noah was a short lived catastrophic event that completely destroyed all Mankind; all land animals, and all birds, except for Noah, his family of eight persons, and the birds and land animals that were preserved in the Ark. However, representations of all water type of animal life and all land and water plant life would have survived for the most part.

References for Chapter 31

1. Dr. Lester King, professor of geology at Natal University, South Africa in his book, "The Morphology of the Earth." p. 33.

Chapter 32

Earth's New Golden Age: What Went Wrong?

The first 115 plus or minus years after Noah's Flood equates to the early emergence of a new civilization in the land of Sumer. This age can be referred to as "Earth's Golden Age." This new world age began the moment Noah and his family stepped out of the Ark on Mount Ararat.

It was in the region of Sumer at a place that was first called Babel and later became known as Babylon that a very interesting Stone Tower was being constructed. This age ended abruptly when the construction of the Tower of Babel was terminated by Almighty God. The people were scattered to select parts of all the Earth. See Figure 15-6.

During this time there was an unusual camaraderie among the people, in that they were of one race and one language. Every person could trace their ancestry back to Noah and his three sons. There was only one nation of people on the Earth. We read in Genesis 11:1 (NKJV), "*Now the whole Earth had one language and one speech.*"

The Emerging Civilization of Sumer

A powerful leader emerged at this time by the name of Nimrod. The Bible traces his ancestry through the line of Ham. He was the youngest son of Cush. The Bible describes him with these words, "*He [Nimrod] began to be a mighty one in the Earth. He was a mighty hunter before the Lord"* (Genesis 10:8-9, NKJV). His fame as a hunter spread among the people. Archaeologists say that Nimrod, who today is synonymous with the secular god Marduk, is represented on Babylonian and Assyrian seals and reliefs in victorious combat with a bull and a lion. Hislop[1] has this to say, *"In the woodent referred to, first we find the Assyrian Hercules, that is Nimrod the giant, as he is called in the Septuagint version of Genesis, without club, spear, or weapons of any kind, attacking a bull. Having overcome the bull, he sets the bull's horns on his head as a trophy of victory and a symbol of power; and thenceforth the hero is represented, not only with the horns and hoop above, but from the middle downward with the legs and cloven feet of the bull. Thus equipped he is represented as turning next to encounter a lion."*[1]

Nimrod arose as the dominant leader of the Post Flood Age. He was able to provide protection and to unify all people under one powerful political and religious system. As a political leader he founded the cities of Babylon, Erech, Accad and Calneh in the land of Shinar. He brought all these early cities under one Kingdom, called the Kingdom of Babel. See Figure 33-1. The Bible says, *"And the beginning of his kingdom was Babel, Erech, Accad and Calneh, in the land of Shinar* (Genesis 10:10, (NKJV).

Nimrod was an empire builder. The cities and the population of his kingdom at this time were very small, but it was the beginning of Imperialism. We read, *"From the land he went to Assyria and built Ninevah, Rehoboth, Calah, and Resin between Ninevah and Calah.* (Genesis 10:11, NKJV)

For many centuries after the Flood, Ninevah and Babylon were the two leading cities of the world. According to Halley[2], cuneiform inscriptions state that Ninevah was colonized from Babylon. This is an archaeological confirmation of the Bible record.

The fertility of the land in southern Mesopotamia, and commerce along the Euphrates and Tigris River systems, allowed the attainment of a high degree of culture among the

Sumerians. Pfeiffer[3] has this to say, "*They developed the cuneiform writing, introduced the wheel, the arch, and the vault, produced a calendar and a system of mathematics based on the number 60.*" Mathematically the system was duodecimal, or base-12. Our modern time-keeping is based on Babylonian duodecimal mathematics. For example 60 seconds per minute, 60 minutes per hour, the 12 hour clock. Pfeiffer[4] says, "*They contributed much to the rise of civilization in this part of the world. Learning how to irrigate the lower reaches of the valley, they built city-states for the growing population of the area.*"

Pfeiffer[5] had this to say about their commerce and business, "*Our oldest law codes, those of Eshnunns (in Akkadian), Lipit Ishtar and Ur-Nammu (in Sumerian), are Sumerian in origin. Business life in ancient Sumer was developed to the point where standard weights and measures were employed.*" Nimrod was also a religious leader. After his death he was deified as a god of Babylon. Halley[6] says: "*Babylonia was long known as the land of Nimrod. He was afterward deified, as god of Babylon, his name being identified with Merodach*" (Halley, p. 81).

Nimrod subtly drew people away from the true faith practiced by Noah and Shem. He instituted a man-made type of religious system. At first it may have been difficult to discern whether his religion was true or false, for Nimrod was probably a very upright type of man. However as time passed by the true nature of Nimrod was revealed.

Religious apostasy is always difficult to discern at first. Many true believers realize that there is something wrong taking place, but often seem helpless to deter it. The pressure and influence of so called more enlightened men and women eventually takes over. This is the beginning process of religious apostasy. Soon the true religion that was proclaimed by Noah and his followers was replaced by a worldly secular type of religion. This is Satan's deceptive way of destroying God's true religion throughout the world.

References Chapter 32

1. Alexander Hislop, The Two Babylons, Neptune NJ, Loizeau, 1959, p.33-34.
2. H. H. Halley, "Halley's Handbook." Zondervan Publishing House, 1965, p.82.
3. Pfeiffer, Charles, "Baker's Bible Atlas." Baker Book House, 1977, p.47.
4. Pfeifer, ibid. p.47.
5. Pfeifer, p.46.
6. Halley. p.81.

Chapter 33

The Tower Of Babel

Nimrod's aim was to build a political and religious system that would be like Heaven on Earth. He set out to build a great city called Babel (Babylon), with a high tower whose top would reach up to Heaven. He began to build a pyramid shaped building that would have a sacred alter at the top. Once people could climb to the top of this magnificent structure, then it was conceived they would be closer to their god and would be able to better worship him. This again is Satan's trick of getting man and woman to worship himself rather than Almighty God. This basically is a religion of works, where people are fooled into thinking that it is possible to work their way into heaven and to be closer to God by their hard earned religious works.

The Tower of Babel was designed very similar to the great megalithic pyramids and other smaller stone structures that characterize the 120 year period prior to Noah's Flood. Many of these structures also had a place to worship their "serpent god" at the top. It is obvious that Noah and his sons had relayed to their family members about the cyclopean and megalithic pyramids and stone structures that were constructed prior to the Flood. Now history began repeating itself once again.

This again is Satan's trick of diverting attention from the True and Living God to himself. Man ends up worshipping the Devil, who is no other than the Fallen Lucifer himself.

We read, "*Then they said to one another, Come, let us make bricks and bake them thoroughly. They had brick for stone, and they had asphalt for mortar and they said, Come, let us build ourselves a city and a tower whose top is in the heavens; let us make a name for ourselves lest we be scattered abroad over the face of the whole Earth.*"' (Genesis 11:3-4, NKJV).

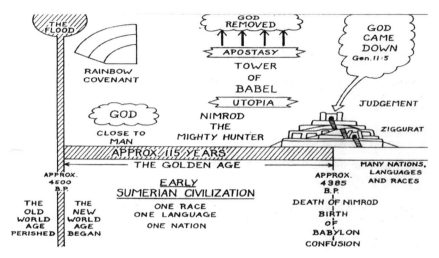

Figure 33-1: Beginning Again: Earth's Golden Age! This diagram illustrates the history of Noah and his family from the Flood to the Tower of Babel. It began with the closeness of God with Man. Man chose to remove God by the worship of a false god. By Don Daae.

Nimrod inspired the people to build a so called utopian state, a place where Man could live and worship in a heavenly surrounding. These were lofty ambitions. The people were given the opportunity of trying to reach heaven by their good and hard work, but they were doing it the wrong way. Their aim was to make a name for themselves.

As time progressed God was being overshadowed by a false apostate type of religion. It was based entirely upon Man's efforts to reach God by their good works. The majority of the people had no place for Almighty God in their lives, and God was removed from their presence and their thinking. Nimrod turned people away from the true and living God to worship a false man-made god. He sought to build a tower which would bring them closer to heaven and to their god who was no other than Satan, the Fallen Lucifer.

The Tower of Babel was built with baked bricks and asphalt for mortar. The Biblical description of this tower is similar to a ziggurat. A ziggurat was a pyramidal, stepped, temple tower most commonly built in the major cities of Mesopotamia from about 2200 until 500 BC. About 25 ziggurats are known. They are about equally divided among Sumer, Babylonia, and Assyria, the three ancient centers of power in Mesopotamia. Ziggurats were built with a solid core of sun dried bricks and faced with kiln baked bricks. They are square or rectangular averaging 170 square feet in height and being about 125 feet (38.1m) by 170 feet (51.8m) at the base. Not any are preserved to its original height. Ascent to many ziggurats is by an exterior triple stairway. In one case there is a spiral ramp.

The Babylonians often built a five staged tower, or ziggurat, in the vicinity of the temple. It was built with a solid core of sun dried bricks and faced with kiln baked bricks. It consisted apparently of two stories and a tower of five superimposed stages crowned by a sacred shrine at the summit. The Greek historian Herodotus described the ziggurat at Babylon as an eight staged tower surrounded by a ramp and having a sanctuary on the topmost stage. The temple on it according to Herodotus contained a couch and a golden table, but not a statue of the god, since it was thought that the god himself came to this divine house on the mountain.

God Came Down

Almighty God was not pleased with the political, religious system that Nimrod and his followers were creating for themselves. The Lord God came down to the Earth, which means in Biblical terms that something dramatic was going to take place. We read, "*But the Lord came down to see the city and the tower which the sons of men had built. And the Lord said, Indeed the people are one and they all have one*

428

language, and this is what they begin to do, now nothing that they propose to do will be withheld from them. Come let us go down and there confuse their language, that they may not understand one another's speech" Genesis 11:5-7, NKJV.

The Lord God saw that the people were all of one nation; they had one language, and were under the rule of one powerful man, Nimrod. The Lord knew that nothing that they would proceed to do to fulfill their false religious ambitions would be withheld from them, or as the Bible says, *"Now nothing will be restrained from them which they have imagined to do"* (Genesis 11:6, NKJV).

The people were ignoring Almighty God's instructions to Noah; in particular that they were to go out and populate the entire Earth. The people under Nimrod did not want to travel or to be dispersed to all parts of the Earth. They wanted to *"make a name for themselves, lest we be scattered over the face of the whole Earth"* (Genesis 11:4, NKJV). In order to break up this close-knit nation of people, the Lord came down and confused their language, so that they were not able to understand one another's speech.

In reality, God came down and terminated the Tower of Babel Apostasy Age. The first thing God did was to put a stop to their pyramid building. They were guilty of bringing in a repeat of the Pyramid Age that God had terminated at the time of Noah's Flood. Secondly, He brought this religious apostasy to an abrupt end. He then made man aware of the fact that the followers of Noah were to populate the entire Earth.

The Second World-wide Migration Of Man Begins

The Lord directed people groups to all parts of the Earth. We read, *"So the Lord scattered them abroad from there over the face of all the Earth, and they ceased building the city. Therefore its name is called Babel, because there the Lord scattered them abroad over the face of all the Earth, and they ceased building the city."* (Genesis 11:8, NKJV).

We then read in Genesis 11:9, NKJV, "*Therefore its name is called Babel, because there the LORD confused the language of all the earth; and from there the LORD scattered them abroad over the face of all the earth.*"

In this way the Bible describes how the multiple races, languages and nations of the Earth originated. Nimrod had succeeded in bringing the entire known world under one powerful, political, and religious system. This culminated in God commanding a second great world-wide migration of Man. One of the commands that God had given to Noah was that his descendents were to populate the entire Earth. This was the same instruction that God gave to Adam and Eve.

The exact time after the Flood when the Tower of Babel dispersion took place is not known. However the Bible gives a general idea as to when it occurred for we read, "*To Eber was born two sons: the name of one was Peleg, for in his days the earth was divided; and his brother's name was Joktan*" (Genesis 10:25, NKJV). We, thus, conclude that the Lord divided the people abroad over the face of all the Earth sometime during the lifespan of Peleg. Peleg lived on the Earth for 209 years and had sons and daughters (Genesis 11:19). We can calculate that Peleg was born 101 years after the Flood, based upon the genealogical record presented in Genesis 11, verses 10 to 32. We also know that the Tower of Babel dispersion took place before Peleg had any sons. If we assume that Reu was Peleg's first son, then the dispersion took place sometime between 101 and 131 years after the Flood. This book assumes that God brought Nimrod's kingdom to an end about 115 years after the Flood. See Figure 33-1.

Chapter 34

The Origin of Modern Nations

At the Tower of Babel dispersion, the Lord God established 70 new racial groups of people, each with a different, unique language, each becoming a distinct nation. Each nation of people were directed to a certain pre-appointed geographic location on the Earth. We read, "*Therefore its name is called Babel, because there the Lord confused the language of all the Earth; and from there the Lord scattered them abroad over the face of all the Earth*" (Genesis 11:9, NKJV).

When studying the Table of Nations in Genesis 10, the reader must remember that the exact location of these nations today is in many cases indefinite and conjectural. However, every race of people and nation throughout the Earth today can trace their ancestry back to one of the 70 sons of Japheth, Ham and Shem. The reader is suggested to pursue texts such as "The Pentateuch and Haftorahs", edited by Dr. J.H. Hertz,[1] or "Bakers Bible Atlas" by Charles F. Pfeiffer[2]. This will enable you to get a more in-depth insight into the possible locations of the different nations. There are also many other good books and papers that have been written by persons who have made an in-depth study of the Post Flood Anthropology of Man.

How Did it All Happen?

How did the Inuit people get to Mongolia, Alaska and the Northern Territories of Canada? How did the Indian people get to Canada, the United States, and Central America and to all parts of South America? What happened to the many thousands of feet (meters) of Glacial Ice that had covered all parts of Canada prior to Noah's Flood? The North American Indians and the Inuit were able to occupy all parts of Canada because the glacial ice was now gone. See Chapter 30.

How did the aboriginal people get to Australia? How did the various racial groups pf people get to all parts of Africa, Europe, Asia, India, China, and Southeast Asia and to the Islands of the Sea?

Within a few hundred years after Noah's Flood, the entire Earth became inhabited by 70 new ethnic groups of people. Each ethnic group had their specific and unique ethnic qualities, characteristics and languages. God also gave them a unique place or location on the Earth to occupy. Thus for many centuries each ethnic group remained relatively isolated from each other. This explains why every geographic region on Earth are occupied by certain people who have distinct physical and linguistic characteristics. We read in Acts 17:26, *"And He has made from one blood every nation of men to dwell on the face of the Earth, and has determined their reappointed times and the boundaries of their habitation."* It is also important to note that all ethnic groups of people have the same blood types. This reveals that they are all directly related to Noah and his wife. It also means that they were all able to marry cross culturally and to have children. Their children had characteristics of both ethnic groups. As time progressed the individual characteristics of the original groups became more indistinct.

The details of how this all took place is beyond the scope of this book. However, there are books that have been written by Post Flood Anthropologists that give various insights into the various parts of the world where the different language and racial groups of people have migrated. This discussion is beyond the scope of this manuscript.

References for Chapter 34

1. Dr. J.H. Hertz, The Pentateuch and Haftorahs," Oxford University Press, London, 1929.
2. Pfeiffer, Charles, "Baker's Bible Atlas." Baker Book House, 1977.

Chapter 35

Legends of the Flood

The object of gaining information about the Flood of Noah through legends is to trace the migrations of the human race from the Middle East to all parts of the Earth. It is interesting to discover that people from most nations and races throughout the Earth have a "Flood Story" within their legends. The fact that these Flood legends are so universal and widespread gives strong credence and support to the Biblical account, which states that all nations and races of people living in the world today can trace their ancestry back to Noah's three sons Japheth, Ham and Shem and more specifically to the 70 sons of Shem, Japheth and Ham.

Babylonian Legend

The Babylonian story of the Flood is possibly the best known and the most detailed account. It is called the Epic of Gilgamesh. Gilgamesh was the 5th King of the Erech Dynasty, which was one of the first dynasties after Noah's Flood. This epic gives the story of his adventures, one of which was a visit to the island abode of Utnapishtim, the Babylonian Noah. This was in search of the secret of eternal life which Utnapishtim was supposed to possess. This visit is depicted on a seal that was found at Tell Billa near Nineveh. In his reply to Gilgamesh, Utnapishtim (Noah) relates the story of the Flood and his escape from it. His story is contained on many different tablets, with variations.

Halley[1] briefly described it as follows, "*The assembly of the gods decided to send a Deluge. They said, on the sinner let his sin rest. O man of Shuruppak, build a ship, save your life. Construct it with six stories, each with seven parts. Smear it with bitumen inside and outside. Launch it upon the ocean. Take into the ship seed of life of every kind. I built it. With all that I had I loaded it, with silver, gold and living things that I had. I embarked upon the ship with my family and kindred. I closed the door. The appointed time arrived. I observed the appearance of the day. It was terrible. All light was returned to darkness. The rains poured down. The storm raged; like a battle charge on Mankind. The boat trembled. The gods wept. I looked out upon the sea. All Mankind was turned to clay, like logs floating about. The tempest ceased. The Flood was over. The ship grounded on Mt. Nazir. On the seventh day I sent out a dove; it returned. I sent out a swallow; it returned. I sent out a raven, it alighted, it waded about; it croaked; it did not return. I disembarked. I appointed a sacrifice. The gods smelled the sweet savor. They said, let it be done no more.*"

The above mentioned narrative was found by George Smith of the British Museum in 1872 in tablets from the library of Assur-banipal at Ninevah. It was copied from tablets dating back to the Dynasty of Ur, a period about midway between the Flood and Abraham. Later, many of these ancient tablets were found. Expressions repeatedly occur in these tablets such as the "flood," and "the age before the flood," or "the inscription of the time before the flood." The clay prism gives the names of the 10 long-lived pre-Flood kings. It says, "After the 10th king, then the flood overthrew the land." There have been alterations of these legends over time.

Other Legends

Filby alludes to the fact that the story of the Flood seems to have been so well known that it became one of the popular books in the ancient cuneiform libraries in the Middle East and fragments of a number of slightly differing texts are known.

Filby[2] describes one text as follows, "*One broken fragment from Sumeria speaks of the Flood sweeping over the land and tossing the huge boat about. It tells how Ziusudra the king, the Preserver of the seed of mankind .. . opened a window of the huge boat. Several similar fragments were referred to by Prof. Kramer and in two of these we are told the flood wiped out everything. Yet another ancient fragment tells how the god Ea commanded Atra-khasis to enter the ship, close its door, bring in grain, live-stock and possessions, as well as wife, kinsfolk and craftsmen*" The region of Sumeria was in reality the land of Sumer. See Figure 15-9.

Early Phoenicians had recollections of the Flood. Filby[3] says, "*Bronze models of ships of Phoenician production, showing various kinds of animals standing in them, going back to the seventh century bc, have been found in Italy and in Sicily. The Phoenicians also believed that Sydyk and his seven sons (making eight persons) were builders of the first ship.*"

Halley[4] relates a number of other traditions of the Flood, "*The Egyptians had a legend that the gods at one time purified the Earth by a great Flood, from which only a few shepherds escaped in a mountain. Greek tradition has it that Deucalion, warned that the gods were going to bring a flood upon the Earth for its great wickedness, built an Ark, which rested on Mt. Parnassus. A dove was sent out twice. Hindu tradition says Manu, warned, built a ship, in which he alone escaped from a Deluge which destroyed all creatures. Chinese tradition tells the story of Fah-He, founder of Chinese civilization, represented as having escaped from a flood sent because Man had rebelled against heaven, with his wife, 3 sons and 3 daughters. England Druids had a legend that the world had been re-peopled from a righteous patriarch who had been saved in a strong ship from a flood sent by the Supreme Being to destroy Man for his wickedness. Polynesians have stories of a flood from which 8 escaped in a canoe. Mexicans have a legend that one man, his wife and children, were saved in a ship from a flood which overwhelmed the Earth. Peruvians have legend that one man and one woman were saved in a box that floated on the flood waters. American Indians have various legends in which 1, 3, or 8 persons were saved in a Boat above the waters on a high mountain. Greenland have a legend that the Earth once tilted over, and all men were drowned, except one man and one woman, who re-peopled the Earth."*

See Filby[5] for additional details of these flood stories.

Conclusion

In conclusion, almost every race and nation of people throughout the world have traditions of a great flood that destroyed all Mankind. This tradition has been impressed indelibly upon the memory of the ancestors of Japheth, Ham and Shem before they even departed from the Middle East region of Sumer. It has been transmitted from generation to generation to the present day.

Halley[6] said, *"All these myths are intelligible only on the supposition that some such event did actually occur. Such a universal belief, not springing from some instinctive principle of our nature, must be based on an Historical Fact."*

References for Chapter 35

1. H. H. Halley, "Halley's Handbook." Zondervan Publishing House, 1965, p.76.
2. Filby Fredk. A. M.Sc., PhD., "The Flood Reconsidered." Pickering & Inglis
3. Ltd., 1970. p. 41.
4. Filby, p.45-46.
5. Halley, p. 75.
6. Filby Fredk. Ibid. pp. 48-57.
7. Halley, p. 75.

APPENDIX A

The Dating of Human History

There is controversy and disagreement among Christian Theologians as to the possible time when Noah's Flood took place, when Adam and Eve were created and when the prophesied return of Jesus Christ would take place. There are theologians who favour the Massoretic Text (MT) over the Septuagint Text (LXX). These are the two major texts used for dating human history back to the Flood and to Adam and Eve.

Figure A-1 compares the Massoretic Text (MT) and the Septuagint Text (LXX). The year 2000 AD is, herein, used as the reference date. For example, the birth of Christ is 2000 years before the present (B.P.). The Exodus is dated at 1446 years B.C. or 3446 years B.P. The date when Jacob arrived in Egypt to visit his son Joseph is dated at 1576 B.C. or 3576 years B.P. Beyond this point the two texts begin to differ.

The Massoretic Text (MT) is that from which the King James Bible was translated into English. It is a direct product of a Hebrew Text which was incorporated by 100 AD into what is now known as the Massoretic Text (MT).

The Septuagint Text (LXX) goes back in time to about 5654 BC. It is an ancient translation of a very early Hebrew Text and was known and used extensively by writers of the New Testament. As an example, Luke, who wrote Luke's Gospel, includes Cainan, the son of Arphaxad, in his genealogy. This is considered evidence that he had access to the Septuagint LXX Text. The Massoretic text does not mention Cainan in Genesis Chapter 11. This is sited as verification that this represents a gap in the Massoretic Text. This may argue for an acceptance of the Septuagint Text or does it?

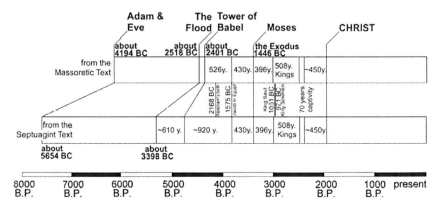

Figure A-1: This diagram illustrates the relationship between the Massoretic text (MT) and the Septuagint Text (LXX). It assumes that the year 2000 AD is the reference point for dating Early Man. This was computer generated by petroleum geologist Warren Clendining.

Teachout[1] expresses the following warning, "*It has not been suggested that the text of the Septuagint is to be generally accepted in preference to the text that the Massoretes preserved. The question has been concerning the numbers in Genesis 5 and 11. There is much disagreement among Bible scholars who strongly feel that the LXX rarely, if ever, preserves a text which is superior (closer to the original) to the MT. Many other writers, usually those who would reject the inerrancy of the scriptures, go much farther in the other direction and use almost any pretext to change and amend the Hebrew text. This approach does not foster or even allow for any degree of confidence in the tremendous accuracy and integrity of the Masseretic Text.*" P.11.

Teachout [2] then says."*There are many fine Bible scholars who take a much more careful approach to scripture and apply valid scholarship and research to all available sources of the Bible times in attempting to solve every problem in understanding and interpreting God's inerrant Word. I believe that this is the proper approach. A Christian must start out with the absolute confidence that God has preserved His Word and that it has been well preserved in the Massoretic text and in reputable translation of it. Only when there is concrete evidence, in the form of very early sources, should another source, such as the LXX, be considered to be of value in search for a more valuable text."* [2]

In Figure 10-1, I have chosen to date the Creation of Adam & Eve at about 6,000 plus years BP and the Flood at about 4,500 years plus or minus before the present. This is also based upon the Egyptian Type Section where many Egyptologists are beginning to date the termination of the Old Kingdom Age at about 2500 BC or about 4500 years BP. There are other theologians who believe the date of the Flood should be around 4350 to 4400 years BP. This is based upon an earlier birth date for Abraham at about 100 to 150 years closer to the present.

In Figure 19-1, I have chosen to date the creation of Adam and Eve at 6,175 + years before the present. This is based upon the date of the Flood at 4,500 years before the present plus the genealogical date of 1656 years from the Flood to Adam as shown on Figure 12-1.

There is a mystery surrounding the exact date when God created Adam and Eve. There is also a certain mystery surrounding the exact date for the birth of Abraham. Thus, it is impossible for anyone to predict the exact date of Noah's Flood or when Jesus Christ will return.

There are many Christian people who believe in the imminent return of Christ and so they should. I believe, many of us can remember that many prominent Christian Theologians believed the return of Christ would take place at about the year 2000 AD. Of course they were wrong, because no man will ever know the exact time. I have conservatively referred to Noah's Flood at about 4500 years BP and the creation of Adam and Eve to be about 6,000+ years BP. We are now beyond 6,000 years BP and counting and this is my intension. See Figure 7-1.

Jesus said in Mathew 24:39-37, "No one knows about that day or hour, not even the angels in heaven, nor the Son, but only the Father. As it was in the days of Noah, so it will be at the coming of the Son of Man. And in Mathew 24: 44 Jesus said, *"So you also must be ready, because the Son of Man will come at an hour when you do not expect him."*

According to the Messianic Genealogy of Adam through Seth to Noah's Flood, the time interval is about 1656 years. If we assume Noah's Flood occurred at about 4500 years, then Adam and Eve would have been created about 6,156 BP. However, if we used a different date for the Flood at 4350 years, then 6,000+ years would be in order. This is the reason I prefer to be on the safe side. Naturally others will disagree.

I would like to end this discussion with this little story. I do not know its source. There was a certain Pastor who asked the men of his congregation this question, "Do you believe Jesus could come today? The men said, "We think not." Then he went to a group of women and said, "Do you think Jesus could come today. They said, "We think not." So he went to a group of children and said, "Do you think that Jesus could come today, and they said, "We think not." Then the Pastor quoted Mathew 24:44 (the Scofield Reference Bible), *"Therefore. Be ye also ready: for in such an hour as ye think not the Son of man cometh."* In other words the return of Jesus Christ is always imminent.

We should stop trying to prove by Biblical chronology and historical dates that Christ is coming today. Rather, keep striving to fulfill the plan that Almighty God has given to you and I to complete on this Earth. Every person has been created for a purpose. Strive to complete that purpose. In other words, continue to pursue your dream. Prepare for further studies to acquire the skills necessary to fulfill your dreams. Continue to make plans for one hundred years for you, your family and your grandchildren. But at the same time, live each day as though Jesus could come today.

Jesus said in Luke 19:13 (KIV), "Occupy till I come." In other words we are to continue doing what the Lord wants us to do until He comes.

References For Appendix A

1. Teachout, Richard A. "Noah's Flood 3398 BC; A new case for Biblical Chronology," Caldwell, Idaho: Bible Science Association Inc., 1971. P.11.
2. Ibid. p.11.

APPENDIX B

What is Flood Geology?

Flood Geology is the belief that the Earth was created about 6000+ years ago and that the worldwide catastrophic Flood of Noah is responsible for depositing the great volumes of water laid sedimentary rock throughout the Earth about 4350 to 4500 years ago. Many of the Creation Science people are now saying the Earth could be about 10,000 years old. If that is the case, then Noah's Flood would have taken place sometime before the Septuagint age of 5398 BP years ago. Figure A-1.

What is the Origin of Flood Geology?

Ellen G. White, the prophetess and founder of the Seventh Day Adventist Movement, was the earliest proponent of Flood Geology. She maintained that God had given her a divine revelation that there were no deaths on Earth until after the Creation Week when Adam and Eve sinned. Their sin, which resulted in their impending death, was passed on to all Mankind and to all animal and plant life. She thus maintained that the Earth could be no older than about 6,000 years.

In 1923, geologist Dr. George McCready Price (1870-1963)[1], a member of the Seventh Day Adventist Movement, wrote a College textbook, "Evolutionary Geology and the New Catastrophism," that embraced Ellen White's vision. It featured the Genesis Flood as the central geological event in the history of the Earth.

In 1961, Whitcomb & Morris[2] wrote a book entitled, "The Genesis Flood." It expanded upon the work of Dr. Price. This theory was rapidly popularized among fundamental and evangelical Christians in the United States, Canada and other parts of the world. "The Genesis Flood" became the basis for the Theory of Catastrophic Flood Geology and Creation Science. Its proponents consider this theory as representing absolute truth based upon strict hermeneutic exegesis.

Today, anyone who dares criticize this approach is accused of promoting Biblical heresy and promoting Theistic Evolution. Because, so many Christians have accepted Flood Geology and Creation Science as Biblical Truth, it is important to expose the root of its error.

Flood Geology is also endorsed by a systematic theologian Bible College Professor James Oliver Buswell.[3] He discusses the Works of God in Creation with respect to the origin of angels. He said, "*So far as the teaching of the scriptures is concerned, the creation of the angels may have taken place at any time prior to the end of the sixth day, but that the fall of Satan and the evil angels took place after God's pronouncement that "everything he had made" was "all very good" "Gen.1:31)."* He then qualifies his conclusion by saying, "*The fall of Satan must have taken place between the end of the sixth day and the temptation of man in the Garden of Eden.*" Buswell is in complete agreement with Whitcomb & Morris that the Fall of Man took place soon after the Fall of Lucifer and his angels and that the Fall of Man resulted in death being passed upon all animal and plant life. He also believes that Adam and Eve's sin is responsible for the death of all animal, plant and human life. This is the doctrine of "**The Edenic Curse**.

Henry Morris[4] says, "*At the end of the six days of creation, and for an indefinite time after that, there was apparently no evil in the entire universe.*" He maintains that it was after the Fall of Man that death fell upon all plant, animal and human life. Prior to this moment in time there were no deaths of plant, animal or human life. The proof of this is verified by the phrase in Genesis 1:31, "*Then God saw everything that He had made and indeed* ***it was very good***." He maintains that God could never have said that it was very good if sin was already present. On the basis of this statement, he believes that the Earth can only be about 6,000+ years old. Any person who dares to believe that the Earth could be older on the basis of the geological record of the Earth is guilty of advocating the False Doctrine of **Uniformitarian Geology**. How does one respond to these great Theologians who are advocates of Flood Geology? What is Uniformitarianism?

We will be assessing and answering these questions as we progress in Appendix C.

References For Appendix B

1. George McCready Price, PhD., "Evolutionary Geology and the New Catastrophism," Mountain View, California, Pacific Press Publishing Association. 1926.
2. John C. Whitcombe, Jr., Th.D. and Henry M. Morris, PhD and are the authors of, "*The Genesis Flood*," the Presbyterian and Reformed Publishing Company, Philadelphia, Pennsylvania, 1967. pages 454-473.
3. James Oliver Buswell, Jr., Ph.D., "A Systematic Theology of the Christain Religion, Volume One, Zondervan Publishing House of the Zondervan Corporation, Grand Rapids, Michigan 49506. p. 131, ninth printing 1975. This book is commonly used as a textbook in Christian Colleges since its first printing in 1962. Whitcomb and Morris's Genesis Flood has also been a key reference and textbook in Christian Colleges..
4. Morris M. Henry, "The Beginning of the World," Accent Books, Denver, CO, 1981, p.55.

APPENDIX C

The Edenic Curse according to Flood Geology

It is important to note that Flood Geology only acknowledges The Edenic Curse, but not the Adamic Curse. See Chapters 4 for a new definition of the Edenic Curse & see Chapter 10 for an explanation of the Adamic Curse.

Whitcomb & Morris[1] are the authors of, "The Genesis Flood." They are considered by many to be the Fathers of Flood Geology. They strongly maintain that the only object created during the First Day of Creation was the Earth. They also strongly contend that the vast universe of stars and galaxies were created during the 4th Day of Creation. They contend that the Universe and the Earth were created about 6,000+ years ago during a six 24 hour Creation Week. The reason for believing this is based upon their interpretation of the Edenic Curse. Flood Geology persons are of the belief that God has only given Mankind one record and that is the **Record of the Holy Scriptures**. They completely ignore the second record which is the **Record of Geology & Paleontology**. Their teachings of the Edenic Curse is totally based upon the record of the Bible.

They believe the Edenic Curse began at the very moment Adam and Eve disobeyed Almighty God and partook of the forbidden fruit. As a result, their sin was transmitted to all of their descendants. However, they went one step further to say that Adam and Eve's sin resulted in the death of all plant and animal life and that it affected the entire universe. In other words, the "Edenic Curse" was also transmitted to all plant and animal life as well as to the entire physical universe of stars and galaxies.

The Doctrine of Uniformitarianism

Flood Geology maintains there were no deaths of animal or plant life on the Earth prior to the Fall of Adam and Eve. They maintain that all plant and animal life that ever existed on Earth were created by God in the Garden of Eden during the Creation Week about 6,000+ years ago. They, thus, conclude that the Earth can only be about 6,000+ years old. They also believe that the catastrophic Flood of Noah was responsible for depositing the thousands of feet of geological sedimentary strata throughout the Earth. They believe that **the entire fossil record is a result of Noah's Flood**. If a person should dare to believe that the record of geology and paleontology (the fossil record) can be trusted, then that person is branded as a Theistic Evolutionist who believes in the false doctrine of Uniformitarianism.

Their reasoning is based upon the false premise that God created all plant life during the 3rd Creation Day. He created all animal life during the 5th & 6th Days of creation. Therefore, each Creation Day had to be only 24 hours in duration and not millions of years. They contend plant life could never have survived for millions of years because the sun, moon and stars were not created till the 4th Day of Creation. Without the sun, the plant and animal life could never have survived beyond a few days. This, therefore, proves that the long geological ages of millions of years is false and is based upon evolutionary teaching.

After discussing the pros and cons of the Edenic curse, Whitcomb amd Morris[1] say, "*In conclusion, we find ourselves faced with an important alternative. We must accept either the current theories of palaeontology, with an inconceivably vast time-scale for fossils before the appearance of man on the earth, or we must accept the order of events as set forth so clearly in the Word of God. Both views cannot be true at* *the same time, any more than can a Biblical anthropology and an evolutionary anthropology be true at the same time. But if the "bondage of corruption," with all that such a term implies for the animal kingdom, had its source in the Edenic curse, then the fossil strata, which are filled with evidences of violent death, must have been laid down since Adam. And if this be true, then the **uniformitarian** time-table of modern palaeontology must be rejected as totally erroneous; and a Biblical catastrophism (centering in the year-long, universal Deluge) must be substituted for it as the only possible solution to the enigma of the fossil strata."*

Where is the error in their reasoning? Since their book was written in 1961, they have been able to indoctrinate and convince a majority of Christians and Christian Colleges and Denominations to believe that the Earth is only about 6,000+ years old. Any one who opposes this view are considered to be perpetuating Biblical error and Theistic Evolution. Theistic evolution in this case is compromising the Bible record with an evolutionary Old Earth concept that is based upon the traditional science of geology & the fossil record.

We in Genesis International Research believe in an old Earth. We believe that God has given Mankind two specific records. They are "**The Record of the Bible**," and "**The Record of the Earth**." Both of these records are available for Man to discover and to explore within the boundaries of the Earth. We are able to demonstrate that these two records are amazingly compatible. In view of the fact that we do not believe in Theistic Evolution, we are also branded in the same category as all the other so called Old Earth Creationists.

Let us look at Whitcomb and Morris's reasoning more specifically:

First, they say that the current theories of palaeontology and geology can not be trusted because of the vast time scale for fossils. Is this a logical premise? After studying and working with regional geology and palaeontology over the past many years, I have come to the conclusion that both of these sciences can be trusted. There is a remarkable compatibility that exists between the record of the Bible, the record of geology and the fossil record. See figures 10-1, 3-5 & 3-1 as well as my book, "Bridging The Gap: The First 6 Days."[2]

Second, they say that the only alternative to an old Earth is to accept the order of events as set forth so clearly in the Word of God. This sounds like very correct theology. But let us look into their logic a little deeper. In their concept of the Edenic Curse, they are accusing Adam and Eve of being responsible for all the evil, heartbreak, violence and death in this world. **Not once does Whitcomb or Morris mention the Fall of Lucifer as being the cause of the Edenic curse. They don't consider Lucifer who is now called Satan and the Devil to be the blame for anything.** Where do they err in their reasoning?

What is the Error of Young Earth, Flood Geology?

The error in their reasoning is simply this: **they do not acknowledge, or are they willing to literally interpret, the Second Tree in the Garden of Eden, the Tree of the Knowledge of Good and Evil**. Rather, Morris and Whitcomb strongly maintain that at the end of the six days of creation, and for an indefinite time after that, there was apparently no evil in the entire universe. At the same time, they maintain that they always interpret all passages of the Bible literally. However, they fail to literally interpret the most important tree in the Garden of Eden, "**The Tree of the Knowledge of Good and Evil.**" They don't even mention or attempt to literally interpret this tree. Because, if they would dare to literally interpret this tree, then they would have to admit the Earth is old.

Why are they ignoring the **Tree of the Knowledge of Good & Evil?** After God created Adam, one of the first things God did was to take Adam to the two trees in the garden. The Lord God commanded the man saying, "*of every tree of the garden you may freely eat; but of the tree* *of the knowledge of **good** and **evil** you shall not eat, for in the day that you eat of it **you shall surely die**"*[3] (Genesis 2:16-17). This was a test of Adam's obedience to the Lord. God was speaking a language that Adam could understand. This event took place before Adam was asked to name the animals and before Eve was created.

There is a **Rule of First Mention** that theologians apply when they interpret scripture. It is stated as follows, *"When a word or phrase is first mentioned in the Bible, it will give a clue as to its meaning in later portions of scripture where its meaning may not be too clear."* The first mention of **evil and death** are both found in Genesis 2:15-17 (NIV) which says, *"The LORD God took the man and put him in the Garden of Eden to work it and take care of it.* [16] *And the LORD God commanded the man, "You are free to eat from any tree in the garden;* [17] *but you must not eat from the tree of the knowledge of good and **evil**, for when you eat of it you will surely **die**."* If we apply the Rule of First Mention, we can demonstrate that evil and death originated with the Fall of Lucifer, not with the Fall of Adam and Eve. See Chapters 2, 3, and 4.

If we are willing to literally interpret this portion of scripture, then we must conclude that the Fall of Lucifer had already taken place prior to the first mention of evil and death and prior to the Creation of Adam and Eve and prior to the end of the Sixth Day of Creation. The question arises how long before the creation of Adam and Eve did Lucifer Fall? We can find the answer to this question from the Bible and from the science of geology. See Chapters 1 to 13.

Why have Whitcomb and Morris not recognized and literally interpreted the Second Tree of the Knowledge of Good and Evil? Why have later Young Earth Creationists who endorse Flood Geology failed to recognize the Biblical fact that evil and death were present in the Garden of Eden prior to the end of the Sixth Day and prior to the creation of Adam and Eve? This is a mystery! If they would acknowledge and literally interpret this tree, they would lose their credibility.

God said it was Good: What does this Mean?

Much controversy surrounds the phrase, "God said it was good" when pertaining to the Creation Week in Genesis Chapter One. Each Creation day is followed by the statement, God said it was good, except the Second Day. Then God said that the Sixth Day was very good. Why should there be controversy over these statements by Almighty God.

Creation Science "Flood Geology" people are saying there is no mention of evil throughout the entire universe until after the 6th Day of Creation. Let us now examine these Six Creation Days to see if there are clues that Lucifer may have fallen prior to the early part of the 7th Day.

Our GIRA Interpretation

I will now present our GIRA Interpretation. It is based upon the premise that God has given Mankind two records. They are the Bible Record and The Record of Geology which is the record of the Earth's history. We will now examine each Creation Day to see whether these two records are compatible.

The First Creation Day

Figure 3-5 relates the record of geology to the First Day of Creation. We read, "*In the beginning God created the heavens and the earth. Now the earth was formless and empty,* **darkness** *was over the surface of the deep, and the Spirit of God was hovering over the waters.*" NIV Genesis 1:1-2. This **darkness** is the first clue that Lucifer had already fallen during the early part of the First Day of Creation. We read, "*God is light; in Him there is no darkness at all.*" NIV 1John 1:5. Darkness is always associated with the Fallen Lucifer. We then read, "*And God said, "Let there be light," and there was light.* ⁴ **God saw that the light was good,** *and He separated the light from the* **darkness***.* ⁵*God called the light "day," and the darkness he called "night." And there was evening, and there was morning—the first day.*" NIV Genesis 1:1. What is important to notice in this passage

454

is that **God could only call the light good**, because the darkness was symbolic of evil resulting from Lucifer's Fall. On the basis of the Rule of First Mention, this is the first clue that the Fall of Lucifer had already taken place during the First Creation Day.

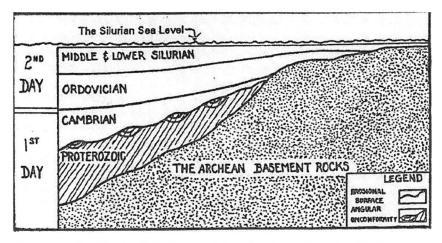

Figure C-1: West of Calgary, Alberta Canada, the Proterozoic sediments at Lake Louise are about 20,000 feet (6,096m) thick. This unit increases to about 30,000 feet (9,144) in thickness to the west of Golden B.C. The overlying Cambrian sediments are about 10,000 feet (3,048m) in thickness around Lake Louise increasing to about 13,000 feet (3,962m) at Mount Robson near the town of Jasper. Figure by Don Daae.

Figures 3-5 & C-1 relate the record of geology to the First Day of Creation. The science of geology has verified that the Proterozoic water laid sediments of the First Day are often up to 20,000 to 30,000 feet (6,096-9,144 m) in thickness in the great basin regions on Earth. Where ever these sediments have not experienced diagenetic destruction resulting from great heat generated due to mountain building processes fossil life is present from bottom to top. Many species of algae and bacteria have been identified. Towards the upper portion of the Proterozoic, scientists have also found a distinct species of a jelly fish, a sponge and traces of worm burrowing. This is indicative of the first created animal life on Earth. The overlying Cambrian Age sediments are often up to 10,000+ feet (3,048+m) in thickness. Is it

455

possible that these great thicknesses of sediment were deposited by Noah's Flood?

The Cambrian Explosion of Animal life

It was during the Lower Cambrian Age that the dramatic Cambrian Explosion of animal life took place. This event changed our planet overnight. Many leading scientists are saying that 40 to 47 disparate architectural body plans (phyla) of new animal life came into existence in what is often referred to as a geological instant. At the end of the Cambrian Age, the first major worldwide extinction of animal life took place. In this, extra-ordinary event, the 40 to 47 animal phyla (body plans) were reduced to about 35 animal phyla (body plans). These 35 animal phyla have continued to the present. See Figures 3-1, 3-5 and of course Figure 8-4.

These 35 animal phyla or body plans were all that God has required in order to create all the multi thousands of micro and macro animal species in later geological ages. For instance, when God created Adam and Eve about 6,000+ years ago, He placed them into the chordate phyla. This phylum is characteristic of all species that have a vertebral column with a notochord. This had nothing to do with evolution, but it has everything to do with God's plan for this Earth. It was another act of special creation by our all powerful, Creator God. It was also the final act of creation by God prior to the termination of the 6th Day of Creation. See Figure 3-5.

From the time of the Cambrian Explosion of animal life to the present, God has only created new species of animal life. He has never to our knowledge created one additional phylum. This is why, the dramatic Cambrian Explosion of Animal life is so vitally important to observe.

Is it possible to believe that all these Proterozoic and Cambrian sediments that contain fossil life from bottom to top are the product of Noah's Flood as Young Earth Creationists believe? Definitely not. Is this all the product of evolution? Definitely not. Evolution is not smart enough to create new species because it is based upon a non intelligent, undirected evolutionary process. But, God is. These sediments of Day One are found on every continent of the Earth. See Figure C-1.

These many animal species lived and died. They have been preserved within the sediments of the Earth by Almighty God for you and I to observe. This once again verifies the fact that death was present and the Fall of Lucifer had taken place prior to the Proterozoic Age. Figure 3-5.

The Second Creation Day

We read, *"And God said, "Let there be an expanse between the waters to separate water from water." ⁷So God made the expanse and separated the water under the expanse from the water above it. And it was so. ⁸God called the expanse "sky." And there was evening, and there was morning—the second day."* NIV Genesis 1:6-8.

During the Second Day, the phrase, it was good is omitted for the reason given in Chapter 6. However, the science of geology reveals that the sediments of Ordovician and Silurian ages were widely distributed throughout the continental regions of the Earth. I have had the great privilege of mapping these sediments throughout western Canada including the Arctic Islands, throughout central Alaska and portions of the northern United States. See Figure C-2. These sediments are often in the 2,000+ to 20,000 foot (609.6+ to 6,096m) range of thickness. The coral reefs of this age are of giant proportions. On Banks Island in the NWT there are pinnacle reefs up to 4,000+ feet in height. Our company had the privilege of participating in the drilling of this well. Also see my book called, "Bridging the Gap: The First 6 Days." This book relates the amazing compatibility that exists between the record of Geology and the record of the Bible. Is this the product of Noah's Flood? Definitely not. Is this the product of Evolution. Definitely not. Evolution isn't smart enough to accomplish this amazing task and to deposit these sediment in such an orderly and mappable manner. But, God is. This reveals God's mighty creative power and acts. This gives an insight into His creative plan for this Creation Day. Sediments of this age are found on every continent throughout the Earth.

THE BIBLICAL RECORD		THE GEOLOGICAL RECORD			INTERPERTATION
		Period	Evidence	Stratigraphy	
The 3rd Day	*"Let the dry land appear":* Gen. 1:9	Silurian U 400M yr.	Caledonian Orogoney	Regional Erosion & Uplift	
The 2nd Day	*"God made the firmament and divided the water above from the waters below."* Gen. 1:6 cloud cover Greenhouse established	Silurian — L U Ordo- M vician — L 500M yr.	Support for Greenhouse Ice Age --?-- Support for Greenhouse		There were many separate acts of Special Creation throughout the 2nd Day
The 1st Day		U Camb- M rian L		Shelf Basinal Carbonates Shales	

Figure C-2: The sediments of the 2nd Day of Creation are shown as they relate to the Arctic Islands region and to northern Yukon and Alaska. These sediments are present in many other places throughout the Earth. Figure by Don Daae.

The Third Creation Day

We read, *"And God said, "Let the water under the sky be gathered to one place, and let dry ground appear." And it was so. 10 God called the dry ground "land," and the gathered waters he called "seas." And God saw that it was good. 11 Then God said, "Let the land produce vegetation: seed-bearing plants and trees on the land that bear fruit with seed in it, according to their various kinds." And it was so. 12The land produced vegetation: plants bearing seed according to their kinds and trees bearing fruit with seed in it according to their kinds. And **God saw that it was good.** 13 And there was evening, and there was morning—the third day."* What did God create that was good? He created ferns, trees, corals, and many species of invertebrate animal life.

These sediments are often 8,000 feet+ (2,438m+) in thickness. They are present in the Rocky Mountain region west of Calgary Alberta, Canada. The impressive Rundle and Banff Formations of Pennsylvanian and Mississippian ages and the Palliser and other Devonian Formations are all of this age. These formations are also present throughout Alberta, Saskatchewan and into Manitoba of Western Canada. The various ages of Devonian reefs produce great quantities of oil and gas throughout Western Canada. These rock units extend southward throughout central USA and northward into the NWT. Are these sediments the product of Noah's Flood? Definitely not. Are they the product of Evolution. Definitely Not. Evolution isn't smart enough to create all these new species of life and to deposit these great thicknesses of sediments in such an orderly and mappable manner, but God is. Is this a product of Uniformitarianism? Definitely not. This once again gives an insight into God's creative plan for this Creation Day. Sediments of this age are found on every continent throughout the Earth.

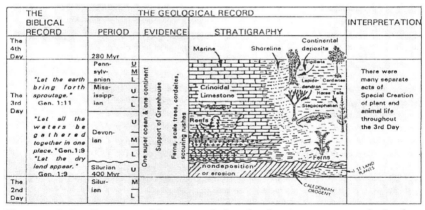

Figure C-3: Some evidence of land plants appeared during the Upper Silurian Age. By Middle Devonian a considerable diversity of land plants and trees had spread over land areas. The Pennsylvanian anthracite coals are considered to be of highest quality. The Greenhouse effect that was established during the 2nd Day continued throughout the 3rd Day. Figure by Don Daae.

The Fourth Creation Day

We read, "And God said, "*Let there be lights in the expanse of the sky to separate the day from the night, and let them serve as signs to mark seasons and days and years,* [15] *and let them be lights in the expanse of the sky to give light on the earth." And it was so.* [16] *God made two great lights—the greater light to govern the day and the lesser light to govern the night. He also made the stars.* [17] *God set them in the expanse of the sky to give light on the earth,* [18] *to govern the day and the night, and to separate light from darkness. And God saw that* **it was good**. [19] *And there was evening, and there was morning—the fourth day."* Genesis 1:14-19 NIV.

There appears to be a contradiction, because God created (bara) the sun, moon and stars during the First Day of Creation. The Hebrew word bara means original creation. It means God created the vast universe of stars and galaxies during the First Day of Creation out of no previous existing material. However, during the 4th Day, God made (asah) the sun, moon, and stars. The Hebrew word asah does not mean original creation. See Figures 8-1 & 8-2 & C-4. Asah implies that the sun, moon and stars were given a new appointment. They were to serve for seasons, days and years. The greenhouse effect that encompassed the Earth during the 2nd and 3rd Days was now broken. The sun, moon and stars were now free to shine directly upon the Earth allowing for season, days and years. It is interesting to note that trees prior to the Permian Age lacked seasonal rings, whereas trees from this age to the present have definite seasonal rings. This once again verifies the complete accuracy of the Bible record. It gives us a great insight into God's plan for this Earth.

Regional geology reveals that North and South America were still attached to Europe, Asia and Africa during Permian time. However, long linear Permian rift valleys developed causing thick sediments to be deposited in these valleys. It was not until the beginning of Jurassic time that North and South America had completely separated from Europe and Africa. See Figure 3-5. Details are given in my book, "Bridging the Gap: The First 6 Days." Some of the details are illustrated on Figure C-4.

THE BIBLICAL RECORD		THE GEOLOGICAL RECORD			INTERPRETATION
		PERIOD	EVIDENCE	STRATIGRAPHY	
The 5th Day		Triassic 225 m.yrs		Marine Shoreline Continental deposits	
The 4th Day	"Let them be for signs, seasons, days and years" Gen. 1:14 "God made the [sun, moon & stars}--- He set them in the firmament to give light upon the Earth." Gen.1:16,17	P E R M I A N 280 m.yrs	U L	Seasons Established Warm, arid conditions locally moist A major Ice Age (cool) Worldwide changes in climate	Mass Extinction of Paleozoic Life	There were many separate acts of Special Creation of plant and animal life throughout the 4th Day
The 3rd Day		Pennsyl- vanian			

Figure C-4: The sediments of the 4th Day are up to 8,000+ feet (2,438+m) in thickness along the Dave Lord Ridge in the Northern Yukon Territories of Canada. There were mass extinctions of animal life at the termination of the Permian Age. Figure by Don Daae.

The 4th Day ended with massive extinctions of animal and plant life. It is conjectured that possibly 99% of all invertebrate animal life became extinct. 75% of amphibian groups, 80% of reptile groups became extinct. Many species of plant life came to a sudden end which included the large scale lepidodendron and sigillaria trees. Many species of plant and animal life were replaced with new species of plant and animal life that gave a new face to the animal and plant world. Evolution was not smart enough to do this, but God was. This was the work of the Almighty Architect and Creator of the Universe who brought the 4th Day to a dramatic close and ushered in a new age that the Bible refers to as the 5th Day. Were these sediments deposited by Noah's Flood? Definitely not. They were all deposited in a normal, mappable manner. The question is this: can the geological formations that we have just described be classified under the banner of Uniformitarianism? Definitely not. Can evolution explain the phenomenal changes, creations of new life and mass extinctions of life and the dramatic changes of climate? Definitely not.

The Fifth Creation Day

We read, *"And God said, "Let the water teem with living creatures, and let birds fly above the earth across the expanse of the sky."*[21] *So God created the great creatures of the sea and every living and moving thing with which the water teems, according to their kinds, and every winged bird according to its kind. And God saw that* **it was good**. *[22]God blessed them and said, "Be fruitful and increase in number and fill the water in the seas, and let the birds increase on the earth.* [23]And there was evening, and there was morning—the **fifth day**." Genesis 1:20-23 NIV.

The 5th Day relates basically to the **age of the dinosaurs and birds**. Also entire new species of all invertebrate animal life were created. Today, there are 16 groups of modern birds and 14 of these groups had their beginnings during Cretaceous times. Modern turtles and tortoises first appeared during the Late Triassic.

THE BIBLICAL RECORD		THE GEOLOGICAL RECORD			INTERPRETATION
		PERIOD	EVIDENCE	STRATIGRAPHY	
The 6th Day		Tertiary 65myr.		Marine Shoreline Continental deposits	
The 5th Day	God Created: 1. Great Water Monsters 2. Every living (water) creature that moves. 3. Winged things that fly. Gen. 1:21	CRETA-CEOUS U Albian L JUR-ASSIC TRIASSIC 225m.yrs	1.Dino-saurs 2. Marine Reptiles -plesiosaurs -ichthyo-saurs -mosasaurs also -lizards -snakes -turtles -frogs 3. Birds & pterosaurs	Mass extinctions of dinosaurs, marine reptiles & pterosaurs Ducks Angiosperms grebes FIRST FLOWERING PLANTS gulls pelicans PTEROSAURS ginkos archaeopteryx DINOSAURS PLESIOSAURS cycads conifers ferns Protoavis (early Bird) THECODONTS	There were many separate & successive acts of Special Creation of plant and animal life throughout the 5th Day
The 4rd Day		Permian			

Figure C-5: The sediments of the 5th Day are generally several thousand feet thick. In the great basin regions they are up to 20,000 + feet (4,572m) in thickness. Figure by Don Daae.

Crocodiles and alligators first appeared in Mid Jurassic time. Lizards were abundant during this time. Snakes can be traced back to the Upper Cretaceous. The modern frogs, newts and salamanders appeared during the Jurassic Age.

The sudden appearance of the angiosperms (flowering plants) took place during the upper part of the Albian Epoch. By the beginning of the Upper Cretaceous the forests were essentially modern. This included such trees as beeches, birches, maple, oak, walnut, palm, tulip, Sweet gum, Breadfruit, ebony and many more. These sediments are generally rich in oil and gas. Are these sediments the result of Noah's Flood as Creation Science people maintain? Definitely not. Are they the product of blind evolution? Definitely not. Evolution isn't smart enough, but God is.

The 5th Day ended with the sudden and radical worldwide extinctions of the dinosaurs, marine reptiles, pterosaurs and the selective extinctions of other species.

The Sixth Creation Day

And God said, *"Let the land produce living creatures according to their kinds: livestock, creatures that move along the ground, and wild animals, each according to its kind." And it was so.* [25] *God made the* **wild animals** *according to their kinds, the* **livestock** *according to their kinds, and all the creatures that move along the ground according to their kinds. And God saw that* **it was good**.*"* Genesis 1:24-25 NIV.

God made wild animals and domestic animals during the 6th Day. See Figures 3-5 & C-6. We know that domestic animals are warm blooded and according to the science of palaeontology all the new species of wild animals of the Cenozoic Era are all warm blooded mammals.

A mystery surrounds the demise of the dinosaurs. However, the birds, the earliest mammals such as the insectivores & the marsupials, the turtles, tortoises, crocodiles, alligators, snakes, lizards, frogs, toads, newts, and salamanders survived the 5th Day and continued to flourish during the 6th Day. This once again reveals the complete accuracy of the scriptures.

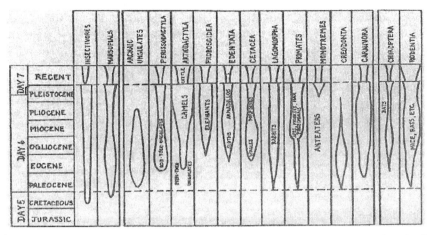

Figure C-6: This diagram shows the 15 Groups of warm blooded animals that God created and established during the 6ᵗʰ Day of Creation. Each group had morphological similarities that were characteristic of that group. God placed Man in the Primate Group. Day 7 began towards the end of the Pleistocene Age. Prepared by Don Daae.

The sudden dramatic extinction of the dinosaurs marks the end of the 5ᵗʰ Day and the beginning of the 6ᵗʰ Day of Creation. This also marks the beginning of the Age of the Warm Blooded Mammals. See Figures C-6. About 99% plus of all warm blooded mammals were created after the dinosaurs became extinct. It may be interesting to note that the famous beautiful Rocky Mountains in Canada and the USA also began to form after the dinosaurs became extinct.

Palaeontologists have identified 15 Groups (Orders) of warm blooded animals that are classified as chordates during the 6ᵗʰ Day. A chordate is a vertebrate animal that has a vertebral column with a notochord. Geology has confirmed that each Mammal Group contains many unique species that were created at many different time intervals. Darwinists always try to prove that every new species must have evolved from a previous species. They still have not come forth with the proof.

Each new mammal species can be related directly to the chordate phyla (body plan) that God created and established at the Cambrian Explosion of animal life during the First Creation Day. See Figures 3-1 & 3-5. This has nothing to do with evolution, but it has everything to do with God's creative plan.

The first one or two species of the Insectivore and Marsupial Groups have been found within the sediments of the 5th Day. See Figure C-6. However, all new species within these two Groups were created during the 6th Day.

There were thousands of new creations of animal species that relate directly to the other thirteen mammal groups.

The end of the Pleistocene witnessed the mass extinctions of many hundreds of species. These extinctions resulted from Noah's Flood about 4500 years ago. See Figures 10-1 and 14-1.

The accumulated thickness of the 6th Day sediments in the basin regions of the Earth range from 1000 feet (305m) to 30,000+ feet (9,144m+) in thickness. In the continental regions, the thicknesses are less. Are these sediments the product of Noah's Flood? Definitely not. They were all deposited in an orderly mappable manner. See Figures 3-5 & 7-1.

Man was the final act of creation

We read, "Then God said, "Let us make man in our image, in our likeness, and let them rule over the fish of the sea and the birds of the air, over the livestock, over all the earth and over all the creatures that move along the ground." 27So God created man in his own image, in the image of God he created him; male and female he created them. 28 God blessed them and said to them, "Be fruitful and increase in number; fill the earth and subdue it. Rule over the fish of the sea and the birds of the air and over every living creature that moves on the ground." 29Then God said, "I give you every seed-bearing plant on the face of the whole earth and every tree that has fruit with seed in it. They will be yours for food. 30And to all the beasts of the earth and all the birds of the air and all the creatures that move on the ground—everything that has the breath of life in it—I give every green plant for food." And it was so. ³¹*God saw all that he had made, **and it was very good**. And there was evening, and there was morning—the sixth day."* Genesis 1:24-31 NIV. See Figure 3-5.

It is interesting to note that modern Man first appeared on Earth towards the end of the Pleistocene Ice Age. Man and woman were God's crowning act of creation.

As I have pointed out before, whatever God creates is always good. God had just completed everything that He had planned, formed, created and made from the First Day to the end of the Sixth Day. This also included his final act of creating Man & Woman. God could now truly say, "**It was very Good**." This phrase has nothing to do about whether evil was present or not present as Creation Science people maintain. The fact that death was present during each Creation Day confirms that the Fall of Lucifer and his angels had already taken place prior to the Proterozoic Age. See Chapters 1 to 8.

The moment Eve ate of the forbidden fruit in disobedience to God, the 6th Day came to a sudden termination and the 7th Day began.

The Seventh Day

The Seventh Day is not a Creation Day. No new plant or animal species have been created since the end of the 6th Day. God rested on the 7th Day from all His work. This rest has been continuing for about 6,000+ years. See Figure 3-5.

Concluding Remarks

Creation Science or Young Earth Creationists maintain that the Earth is only about 6,000+ years old. They contend that all of the sediments that are described above are only about 4,500 years old and were all deposited by Noah's Flood.

I have been accused time and time again of bringing forth theistic evolution and promoting scriptural error. I have been accused of being a Theistic Uniformitarian. The attacks have often been vicious because this is what students have been taught at Bible Colleges, Christian schools and churches by Creation Science people.

The reason why I have written this Appendices C is to make clear to the reader that it is possible to show the complete compatibility that exists between the record of the Bible with the record of geology, archaeology, anthropology, palaeontology and palynology. Other scientists have shown that a remarkable compatibility also exists between the record of biology, micro-biology, astronomy and all the other natural sciences with the record of the Bible. Let us now march forward with the scientific evidences that reveal the bigness and the greatness of Almighty God.

We are all aware that we are under attack by the Fallen Lucifer, the Prince of the air and of the darkness, who has been and still is blinding the eyes of men, women and children to believe THE LIE that God does not exist. See chapters 1 to 6.

References for Appendix C

1. Henry M. Morris, PhD and John C. Whitcomb, Jr., Th.D. are the authors of, "*The Genesis Flood*," Pages 454-473. It is in these pages that Morris & Whitcomb say, "*At the end of the six days of creation, and for an indefinite time after that, there was apparently no evil in the entire universe.*"

2. Daae H. D., P.Geol., "Bridging the Gap: The First 6 Days." Genesis International Research Publishers, Calgary, Alberta Canada, 1989. This book is in the process of being revised.

APPENDIX D
The Meaning of Evolution

Atheist and Evolutionist Richard Bozarth wrote an article in "The American Atheist", September 1978 entitled, "The Meaning of Evolution." The gist of the article describes a battle between two ideologies, Christianity and Atheistic Evolution.

Bozath clearly states that the purpose of Atheistic Evolution is to scientifically prove that Adam and Eve never existed, that the Fall of Man never took place, that there is no such thing as original sin.

This is how Bozarth[1] describes the battle, "*Christianity has fought, still fights, and will continue to fight science to the desperate end over evolution, because evolution destroys utterly and finally the very reason Jesus' earthly life was supposedly made necessary. Destroy Adam and Eve and the original sin, and in the rubble you will find the sorry remains of the son of god. Take away the meaning of Jesus death, then Christianity is nothing! What this all means is that Christianity cannot lose the Genesis account of creation for Christianity is fighting for its life.*" Then he goes on to say, "*And it must surely lose, just as it has lost every battle it has fought against science, since modern science got its start in the 16th Century. The day will come when the evidence constantly accumulating around the evolutionary theory becomes so massively persuasive that even the last and most fundamental Christian warriors will have to lay down their arms and surrender unconditionally. I believe that day will end Christianity."*

He then says, *"And into the void - what? Another religion? I would say yes, for this has been the pattern of history, were it not for what we are building today in the American Atheists. Atheism is the philosophy, both moral and ethical, most perfectly suited for a scientific civilization. If we work for the American Atheists today, Atheism will be ready to fill the void of Christianity's demise when science and evolution triumph."*

My Comments

Today, we are deceptively told that Atheistic Evolution is not religious, that we must free science from religion. Who is kidding who? Bozarth is admitting that evolution is a religion. However, Bozarth is gravely mistaken. Christianity isn't fighting for its life. Christianity throughout the world is stronger today than ever before. It is the religion of Atheistic naturalism that is fighting for its life.

This has been demonstrated in Eastern Europe and Russia where religious Atheism dominated the Eastern Block of Communist countries for 70 years. During 1989, Communism, which is based upon Atheistic Scientific Naturalism, came crashing down. No one could have predicted this sudden demise.

The next wall that will soon come crashing down is the religion of Atheistic Scientific Naturalism that has gained control of our science curriculum throughout the world.

I am pleased to report that Genesis International Research can scientifically address all of Bozarth's claims. First, we have demonstrated that there is a remarkable compatibility between the Geological and the Biblical records (See Don Daae's[2] book. "Bridging The Gap: The First 6 Days"). Second, we have demonstrated that the science of geology has provided a scientifically sound framework for the dating of Adam and Eve at about 6,000+ years ago. This verifies the Bible record as being true. See Figures 3-5 and 10-1. Third, the Fall of Man and the Origin of Sin are primarily a theological issue. However, we have shown how the science of geology provides strong evidence to support this thesis.

The Bible says that death is a direct result of sin. Geology, through the fossil record, verifies that the fossil record is a record of life and of death. This pinpoints the origin of sin to a time prior to the first appearance of life and death on the Earth, which is at the beginning of the geological age called the Proterozoic. See Figure 3-1 and 3-5.

All the succeeding geological ages from the Proterozoic onward contain evidences of life and death. Fourth, Geology, likewise, gives scientific evidence for the fall of Adam and Eve at the end of the Anathermal Age. See Figure 10-1. Genesis 3:17 says *"Cursed is the ground because of you, through painful toil you will eat of it all the days of your life. It will produce thorns and thistles."* Thorns and thistles implies drier weather conditions on Earth. Geology confirms that the Adamic Curse was responsible for the eventual death of all mankind, but it also revealed the curse that God placed upon the Earth. This Adamic curse resulted in progressive drier climate conditions that characterize the geological Altithermal Age. This resulted in the incipient growth of modern desert areas throughout the world and the drying out of the great inland lakes. Also the fossil remains of Early Man throughout the Altithermal Age confirms the deaths of Man resulting from the curse that God imposed upon Adam's sin. See Figure 10-1. This curse has also continued throughout the Medithermal Age to the present.

In conclusion: The Edenic Curse brought death to all plant and animal life, whereas the Adamic Curse brought death to all mankind. The Bible says in 1 Corinthians 15:26 NIV, *"The last enemy to be destroyed is death."* This will take place in the future at the termination of the 7th Day.

Many of my peers in geology have said, *"I cannot accept the Bible as being true, because there is no way that the science of geology and the Bible can agree.*" We now have a message to present to the geological profession, that they can, with the confidence of the geological record, believe that the Bible record is true. See www.gira.ca

References for Appendix D

1. Atheist and Evolutionist Richard Bozarth wrote an article in "The American Atheist", September 1978 entitled, "The meaning of Evolution." The gist of the article describes a battle between two ideologies, Christianity and Atheistic Evolution.
2. Daae H. Donald, "Bridging The Gap: The First 6 Days." Genesis International Research Publishers, Calgary, Alberta. See www.gira.ca.

APPENDIX E

The Length of a Creation Day

Each of the Six Biblical Creation Days ends with this significant phrase, "**The Evening & the Morning**." What does this phrase mean? In Israel, each day always began in the evening at sunset. The Israelites would plan in the evening, what they would do in the morning. After a good night rest, at sunrise, they would commence the work necessary to complete the plan conceived the evening before. The work would continue throughout the daylight hours.

In like manner, when Man constructs a large building all the conceivable plans would have to be put into place before construction begins. He will have an Architect draw the details or the plan of every aspect of this building. This is the "Planning Stage." Once the large building has been constructed according to the architectural plan, then the "Working Stage" becomes complete.

The evening of each day represents a time when God the Father, the Great Divine Architect of the Universe conceived a plan for each Creation Day. It was in the morning of each Creation Day that God the Son, the Great Divine Creator, would have commenced the work necessary to carry out the perfect will of His Father by creating and forming all things according to that architectural plan. By the commencement of night time all the work for that particular day would have been completed. The night time would represent a time of rest.

God's Plan for the First Creation Day: We read in Genesis 1:3a, "Let there be light." This is a plan. God the Father planned a universe of light. The commencement of this plan marks the beginning of the First Day of Creation.

God's finished work of the First Creation Day: Genesis 1:3b says, "And there was light." God the Son, the Great Divine Creator created, formed and made a universe of light which in reality included the entire Universe of stars and galaxies. This implies the completion of God's plan for the First Day of Creation.

Likewise, each of the following Days of Creation can be divided into an evening (planning stage) and a morning (working stage). Each stage may have involved much time in terms of multi millions of earth years when measured in the perspective of eternity past.

The Hebrew word for Day is "**Yom.**" It has the following 3 basic meanings.

1. **Period of daylight:** This is always a variable length of time.
2. **Period of time:** This is always a variable length of time.
3. **A 24 hour day:** This is a fixed period of time.

Exodus 20: 8-11 compares the Work Week to the Creation Week as follows,

"Remember the Sabbath day by keeping it holy. [9] *Six days you shall labor and do all your work,* [10] *but the seventh day is a Sabbath to the LORD your God. On it you shall not do any work, neither you, nor your son or daughter, nor your manservant or maidservant, nor your animals, nor the alien within your gates.* [11] *For in six days the LORD made the heavens and the earth, the sea, and all that is in them, but* **he rested on the seventh day.** *Therefore the LORD blessed the Sabbath day and made it holy."* On the basis of this portion of scripture, many theologians believe that the length of each work week is the same as the length of the creation week.

We can all agree upon the following:

a. **The Work week:** consists of 7 days (six days of work, one day of rest).
b. **The Creation week:** consists of 7 days (six days of work, one day of rest).

However, by comparing scripture with scripture, we find that:

a. **The Work Week:** Relates to the 3rd meaning of the Hebrew word for yom. It always relates to or equates to a 24 hour day.
b. **The Creation Week:** Relates to the 1st & 2nd meanings of yom. It never equates to a 24 hour day, but to a period of time that could be millions of years in duration. Thus, we are beginning to see a difference in time span between the Work week and the Creation week.

The Creation Week:

1. **Law of first reference** says that the first time a word, phrase or incident occurs in the Bible it gives a key to its meaning elsewhere in the Bible where its meaning may be in doubt. The first mention of day (yom) is found in Genesis 1:5 (NIV) which says, "God called the light "day," and the darkness he called "night." And there was evening, and there was morning—the first day."
2. **In Genesis 1:5**, the Hebrew word day is yom. It refers to a period of daylight, which is always variable in length. For instance, a period of daylight at the north pole can range from 24 hours in the summer to near zero minutes in the mid of winter. Between the north and south poles, we always experience a variance in the length of daylight. We also find that each of the Six Days of Creation ends with this interesting phrase, "And there was evening, and there was morning the 2nd Day, the 3rd Day, the 4th Day, the 5th Day and the 6th Day. It was during the evening of each Creation Day that God the Father brought forth a plan for that day. It was in the morning of each day that God the Son, the Great Divine Creator commenced to create all things for that day according to His Father's plan. See Figures 8-1 and 8-2.

3. **Hebrews 4: 1-9**: The 7th Day (yom) equates to the last 6,000+ years of Earth's history. It began the moment Eve was created. Just as God, entered into His rest on the 7th Day of Creation, He wants you and I to enter into the rest that is found in Jesus Christ which is a continuing rest. See Figure 10-1.
4. **2 Peter 3:8 & Psalms 90: 4:** One day is as a 1,000 years (period of time).
5. **2 Peter 3:10:** The day of the Lord relates to an event. He will come in the twinkling of the eye.
6. **Job 18: 20:** The day of Job relates to the time of Job's sufferings. It was a period of time).
7. **Psalm 137:7:** The Day of Jerusalem equates to 70 years of captivity in Babylon. This was a period of time.
8. **Psalm 95: 8:** The Day in the wilderness equates to 40 years. This was a period of time.

G. Conclusion: The 7th Day has been continuing for 6,000 plus years since the Fall of Adam and Eve. Each of the 6 Days of Creation represent periods of (variable) time. Geology would suggest the First Day was the longest. See Figure 3-5. The **History of the Earth** chart suggests the First Day began 4.6+ billion Earth years into the past. It ended about 510 to 520 million years ago. Only the Lord God of Heaven and Earth knows the exact age of the Earth in terms of Earth years. However, he has placed certain time clocks into the rocks of the Earth.

These time clocks are revealed through the various "Radiometric Dating Methods" that are used for dating the age of the Earth as described by Dr. Roger C. Wiens. See his remarks at the end of Chapter 3. Also see Figure 3-5.

APPENDIX F

The Calgary Type Section
&
How to Identify Evidences of
Noah's Flood Worldwide

In geology, it is common to have a standard Type Section for each geological formation. This is based upon it being the best representative section within a geological region. When a new well is drilled, the equivalent formations can be compared with the Type Section to see if there are any variations that may be significant. A geological formation is a mappable unit of sediments that have similar characteristics within a certain region. The Canadian Society of Petroleum Geologists has published geological type sections for all geological "Formations" in all regions of Canada. It is called, "The Lexicon of Canadian Stratigraphy."

In view of the fact that Noah's Flood was global and that three definite stages of the Flood are present throughout the world, we believe that the "Calgary Type Section" has representations of all three stages. This qualifies two separate sites in Calgary, Alberta as being "Typical Type Sections" that can be compared to Flood stages and associated deposits throughout the world. They are "The Fish Creek Mazama Type Section" and "The Shouldice Mazama Type Section."

To my knowledge, no one has even suggested that similar stages of Noah's Flood could be present and identified on a world wide basis. Let us examine what we mean by Stage One, Stage Two and Stage Three of Noah's Flood.

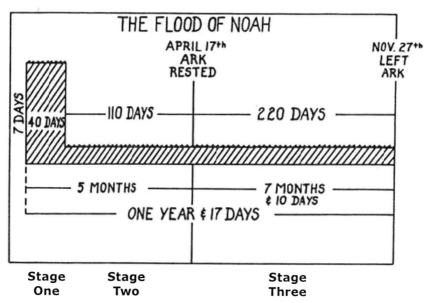

Stage
One

Stage
Two

Stage
Three

Figure F-1: The duration of Noah's Flood revealing its three Stages. Figure by Don Daae.

Stage One represents sediments that were deposited during the first 40 days of Noah's Flood. During this stage several powerful tsunami tidal waves would have swept across all the continents of the Earth causing severe erosion and redeposition in other areas. Chapter 24 details the mechanics of the Flood. It describes the continual heavy rainfall and the severe crustal adjustments that the Earth experienced throughout this 40-day interval. One would expect these deposits to consist of large and small well reworked boulders, cobblestones and conglomerates. In other places they would consist of gravels mixed with mucky clays and bones of pre-Flood animal life and artifacts of Early Man. There would also be in situ, remnant locations of Early Man below the gravels and boulders. There would also be places where the large and small stone structures of Early Man would have been partially or even completely covered by sediments.

Stage Two represents sediments that were deposited during the next 110-day period when the flood waters increased to at least 120 feet above the highest mountain on Earth. During this stage the Earth's surface would have experienced a period of quiescence with very little or no erosive activity taking place. Only the finer clay and some fine silt particles would have settled out forming a layer primarily of clay. One would not expect to find artifacts in sediments of this age.

Stage Three relates to the final 220 day period of Noah's Flood. During this time the Earth's crust returned step by step by several crustal re-adjustments to isostatic equilibrium. See Figure 24-2. This process resulted in dramatically changing the surface landscape throughout the Earth.

There would have been several still stand periods when the sea level would have remained constant for a limited time. This would have allowed shorelines to develop at different elevations above our present sea level. Elevated shorelines have been documented throughout the Earth in geological literature and other books and writings. Authors often tend to believe that each of these shorelines relate to different geological events separated by great time intervals. Many do not believe that each elevated shoreline could very well relate to different phases of Stage Three of Noah's Flood.

Some of these shorelines are several thousand feet above our present sea level. I will give one illustration. During the summer of 1956, I had the privilege of being on a Geological Structural Field Party in the Canadian Rocky Mountains between Jasper and Banff. We began at the Pocahontas Cabins along the Athabasca River which is located to the east of the town of Jasper. On this Field Party, we had four geologists, twenty four horses, a packer, a wrangler and a cook.

We worked our way in a southward direction between the first and second ranges of the Rocky Mountains. We moved to a new camp every three days. At each camp site, we would study and analyze the structure of the geological formations along the first and second ranges. This involved a team of two geologists climbing to the top of a prominent mountain and analyzing the structure of the different formations on either side. As we worked our way southward, we went into the foothills to examine the geology at Limestone Mountain. As we were journeying back to the Rocky Mountains on horseback, we saw what appeared to be a distinct shoreline on a mountain to our left. We wondered how it got there. It was evident that for that shore line to form, the sea level had to have been several hundreds of feet (meters) higher than the Foothills region to the east. It would then have been several thousand feet (meters) higher than the plains of Western Canada. Many similar mysterious shorelines have been found in the British Isles, Scandinavia, Europe, Asia, South America and many other places.

During Stage Three of Noah's Flood, there would have been a series of isostatic readjustments of the thin ocean crust. Several powerful tsunami waves would have swept over the Earth following each dramatic crustal adjustment. A new shore line would always be formed at each intervening level of still stand.

During this 220 day period of Noah's Flood, there would have been several isostatic readjustments taking place allowing the sea level to eventually reach its eventual well documented level of about 180 feet (55m) below our present sea level. See Figure 29-17. This lower sea level was raised to our present sea level at a later date. See Chapter 29 and Figure 29-17 for more information.

The Calgary Fish Creek
Mazama Type Section

Introduction:
The Calgary Fish Creek Mazama Site is shown on Figure F-2. It consists of a Lower and an Upper Unit. The Lower Rock Unit is about 4 feet (1.2 m) plus in thickness. It is overlain by about 5 feet (1.5m) of whitish grey clay. The Lower Unit is lying upon a pronounced erosion surface of Pleistocene Ice Age sediments.

Stage two: Upper Unit
Stage One: Lower Unit

Pleistocene Glacial Lake Sediments.

Pleistocene Boulder Clay.

Figure F-2: The Fish Creek Mazama Site: The total Mazama Formation is 9 feet+ (2.7m+) in thickness. It rests upon an eroded Pleistocene surface. The Lower Mazama Boulder Unit is up to 4 feet (1.2m) plus in thickness. The Upper Mazama Clay Unit is about 5 feet (1.5m) thick. Interpretation by Don Daae. Photo by Don Daae.

The Pleistocene Sediments:

The Pleistocene sediments in this particular region range in thickness from 150 to 200 feet (45.7-60.9m) in thickness. The upper 30+ feet (9.1m) in places consists of light grey glacial lake sediments that are underlain by dark gray boulder clay. The reason why this lower portion is called boulder clay is because the Glacial Ice has reworked and distributed large and small irregular shaped blocks of Paskapoo Sandstone throughout portions of this Pleistocene clay unit.

The Pleistocene sediments are underlain by the Paskapoo Sandstone of an older age. The Paskapoo is several hundred feet in thickness. It is, in turn, underlain by over 14,000 feet (4,267+m) of older sediments.

Figures F-3 & F-4: The definite boundary between the Lower and upper units are seen on the left and right photos. Geologist Mike Gilders examines a thin white layer that is rich in white Volcanic Ash within the Upper Clay Unit. Photos by Don Daae.

The Lower Mazama Boulder Rock Unit:

This Lower Mazama Boulder Rock Unit is resting upon an eroded Pleistocene surface. It is up to 4+feet (1.2m+) in thickness. It consists of whitish sub-rounded boulders, cobblestones, conglomerates that are all mixed together. Some of the boulders are more angular. The boulders vary in size from 2.5+ feet (.76m) in diameter to smaller sizes. They are all completely coated with a whitish volcanic ash coating mixed with a calcareous precipitate. 10% HCL acid will effervesce strongly when applied. This boulder unit is widespread throughout the Calgary region. These whitish boulders are used for ornamental purposes along driveways and at residential and shopping centres throughout the city of Calgary.

The Upper Mazama Clay Unit: is about 5 feet+ (1.5m+) in thickness. It consists of soft whitish grey clay with occasional thin white layers that have been identified as being rich in volcanic ash. White volcanic ash is distributed throughout this unit giving it a whitish grey coloration. There is a pronounced break that separates the Upper and Lower unit as is shown on Figures F-3 & F-4.

The Shouldice Park Mazama Type Section

The Shouldice Park Mazama Site in west Calgary along the north bank of the Bow River is shown on Photos F-5, 6 & 7. These photos show the same Lower and Upper Units that are present at the Fish Creek Mazama Type Section.

Figures F-5 & F-6: The Shouldice Site in west Calgary along the north shore of the Bow River. The White Upper Mazama Clay unit is about 5 feet (1.8m) in thickness. The Lower Mazama Boulder unit is only exposed at the base of photo to the right. It is 4+ feet (1.2m) more or less in thickness. Photos by Don Daae.

The Lower Boulder Rock Mazama Unit is resting upon an eroded Pleistocene surface. The only portion of this unit that is exposed is shown at the lower right portion of photo F-6. There is a sharp break separating this Lower Boulder

Rock Unit from the above Clay Unit. These Rocks are coated with a white volcanic ash and a calcareous precipitate which effervesces strongly when 10% acid is applied. These boulders have been steadily eroding into the Bow River Valley. This is evidenced on photo F-7. These rocks consist mainly of quartzite and quartz sandstones. They vary in size from 2 feet in diameter to cobblestone and gravel size.

The Upper Mazama Clay Unit is resting unconformably upon the Lower Boulder Unit. It consists of whitish grey clay mixed with varying amounts of volcanic ash. See Figures F-5 & F-6.

Figure F-7 is a view of the Shouldice Park Mazama Site looking eastward along the Bow River Valley. The many white boulders along the northern bank of the Bow River have been eroded away from the Lower Mazama Boulder Rock Unit.

Figure F-7: The Upper White Clay Unit outcrops along the northern bank of the Bow River. It consists of about 5 feet (1.5 meters) of whitish grey Mazama clay. The eroded boulders, cobblestones and conglomerates have been eroded down along the flanks of the Bow River Valley from the Lower Boulder Unit. The view is to the east. Photo by Don Daae.

The question arises, how is it possible to relate the Shouldice Park Mazama Site and the Fish Creek Mazama Site to Noah's Flood?

Geological Evidences for Noah's Flood in Calgary

The Fish Creek Masama Site in south Calgary and the Shouldice Park Masama Site in west Calgary can both be directly related to Noah's Flood. They both reveal all aspects of the three stages of Noah's Flood.

The first reason for believing these two sites can be related directly to Noah's Flood is because both the Lower and Upper Units at both sites are coated with a white volcanic ash deposit. They are often called the "Mazama Deposits."

This name is derived from a volcano in the State of Oregon, USA called Mount Mazama. This volcano erupted about 6,600 years before the present according to geological dating. This is a tentative, not an absolute date. It is based upon the carbon-14 dating of organic matter that is present within the Masama deposits. A slight correction to the carbon-14 dating of this organic matter could change this date to anywhere from 6600 to 4500 years before the present without doing injustice to the dating method. *See www.Mazama Ash.*

The www.mazama website says, *"The eruption was a cataclysmic event dated at about 6,600 years ago. Great thicknesses of pumice were deposited on the flanks of Mount Mazama, while finer material was blown over great distances by the winds.The widespread distribution of the Mazama Ash has made it useful in archaeological studies as a horizon, or time, marker. Studies of sediments formed in relation to the ash deposits suggest that the ash formed at a time when generally drier climates prevailed in the regions in which the ash occurs. The mineralogical composition of the ash is distinctive and allows it to be distinguished from other volcanic ash deposits."* The Mazama Volcanic Ash is a major constituent of this Calgary Mazama deposits at both of the above mentioned sites.

Geologists are able to trace this whitish ash from Mount Mazama in an eastward direction through northern USA into portions of southern British Columbia in Canada and into the Ice corridor region of central Alberta. This ash can be traced eastward throughout much of the State of Montana and as far eastward as North Dakota. This ash layer is a useful geological and archaeological time marker through-out this entire region. The definite identification factor of the Mazama Ash is its chemical composition and the refractive index of the volcanic glass.

The Second Reason to believe the Mazama deposits in the city of Calgary are directly related to Noah's Flood is because they have all the characteristics of a Pluvial (Flood) Deposit.

The Boulders, cobblestones and conglomerates are all coated with a white Mazama volcanic ash on all sides. This indicates they were being continually carried along and ro-tated by powerful water action. Some of the sub-rounded boulders are over 2.5 feet (0.76m) in diameter and would have required powerful tsunami type of water flow to trans-port them to their destinations.

The Third Reason to believe these deposits are related directly to Noah's Flood is because of its timing. They are Post Pleistocene in age. See Figure 19-1 & 19-2. On this basis and together with the record of geology worldwide, I am dating this Mazama deposit at about 4,500 years before the present. The base of this unit marks the termination of the Pleistocene Ice Age and the beginning of the Flood Age. Prior to this event a glacial Lake was present throughout much of the Calgary region. In some places the glacial Lake sediments are up to 60 feet (18.28 m) in thickness. This indicates that this lake was in existence for a considerable time prior to this sudden pluvial event. It also marks an abrupt termination of the Pleistocene Ice Age because the Lower Boulder Rock Unit rests upon an eroded Pleistocene surface.

The Three Stages of Noah's Flood

The Calgary Masama deposits can be subdivided into two major units. The Lower Boulder Rock Unit relates directly to "Stage One" of Noah's Flood and the Upper Clay Unit relates to "Stage Two" of Noah's Flood. See Figure F-1. The results of "Stage Three" are evidenced by the severe erosion that has taken place following the deposition of the Upper Clay unit. See Figures F-2 & F-7.

Stage One of Noah's Flood in Calgary

Stage One relates to the first 40 day period of Noah's Flood. See Figure F-1. During this stage the Earth experienced several traumatic, tsunami tidal waves that would have swept across all continents of the Earth coincident with heavy rainfall. See Chapter 24 for a description of the mechanics of Noah's Flood.

Stage One deposits in the Calgary region would have taken place during the first 40 Days of Noah's Flood. It is interesting to note that continuous, heavy rainfall characterizes the differences between Stage One, Two and Three deposits of Noah's Flood not only in Calgary, but also throughout the world. Geologically speaking, these large boulders would have required extremely high water energy conditions in order to transport them along the north-south trending Ice Corridor to their resting places within the city region of Calgary. This is evidenced at the Fish Creek Site and the Shouldice Site in Calgary Alberta. See Figures F-2 and the F-7 sites.

It must be remembered that during Stage One continental ice up to several thousand feet (meters) in thickness was still present to the east of Calgary extending into the province of Saskatchewan and eastward in Canada. Thick glacial Ice was also present to the west of Calgary within the Rocky Mountains and the interior Mountain Ranges of British Columbia. See maps in Figures 30-1 & 30-3.

Figure F-8: These Whitish Mazama rocks are used for ornamental purposes throughout the city of Calgary, Alberta Canada. They are Stage One rocks. Don Daae refers to these rocks as NOAH'S ROCKS. Photo by Don Daae.

It must also be remembered that these Mazama boulders would not be present everywhere throughout the northwest trending Ice Corridor that extended northward into the Yukon and throughout central Alaska. In a lateral direction the nature and character of Stage One deposits may be quite different. The boulders would not have volcanic ash coatings outside of the region where the volcanic ash was present. There are many places where one would expect to find deposits of this age mixed with the artifacts of Early

Man and with the remains of many species of Pre-Flood animal life such as the woolly mammoth, the mastodon, saber toothed tiger, camel and many more.

Figure F-9: The white Mazama rocks are used for ornamental purposes at the Shawnessy Shopping Centre in South Calgary. They relate to Stage One of Noah's Flood.

Figure 10-10: This is another photo within the Shawnessy Shopping Centre in Calgary, Alberta where the white ornamental Mazama boulders are attractively displayed. Little do people realize that these boulders represent Stage One deposits of Noah's Flood. Photos by Don Daae.

Stage Two of Noah's Flood

Stage Two of Noah's Flood is characterized by the pronounced rising of the flood waters. It relates to the following 110 Day Period of Noah's Flood. See Figure F-1. It was during this time that a period of relative quiescence took place throughout the Earth when the Flood waters increased in depth and finally reached their maximum elevation. During this time only the finer fraction of clays and also some fine silt particles would have been deposited. These deposits are classified as Mazama Deposits only if they are in the vicinity where the volcanic ash from Mount Mazama is present. In the Calgary region the soft clay contains a mixture of whitish volcanic ash.

What Happened to the Pleistocene Ice?

At the time of Noah's Flood great thicknesses of Pleistocene Ice still covered the region to the east of the northwest trending Ice Corridor. See Figure 30-3. Being that ice is lighter than water, these great sheets of ice would have risen with the Flood waters during Stage Two of Noah's Flood. They would have floated away.

However, the ice to the west of the Ice corridor in the high mountain regions of the Rocky Mountains and the high Interior Mountain Regions of British Columbia would have remained in place. The ice in the lower regions of British Columbia and the northern USA would have also floated away.

The removal of continental ice would have also taken place in northern Europe and Asia at this time. The high mountain regions would have retained the glacial ice.

Stage Three of Noah's Flood

Stage Three of Noah's Flood witnessed the greatest and most dramatic erosive damage throughout the Earth that characterizes the Earth's surface today. This stage relates to the final 220 day period of Noah's Flood. See Figure E-1. As the Flood Waters began to decrease, there were various stages of still stand where shorelines were formed at various elevations. For instance in Europe, Asia and in America geologists have described various mysterious shorelines several hundreds and even thousands of feet above sea level. These shorelines have been described in all areas of the world. Each time great crustal adjustments took place in ocean regions, powerful tsunami waves would have swept across the Earth causing much erosion at each still stand horizon.

Stage Three at the Two Calgary Sites

During Stage Three numerous powerful tsunami tidal waves carved extensive deep and shallow river channels in the Calgary region. These valley systems were at that time filled with rushing water. Most of the Stage One and Stage Two Flood Deposits were in most places completely eroded away and were re-deposited within the newly carved "Stage Three Channels." It is, indeed, amazing that any of the Stage One & Two deposits were ever preserved, because of the extensive and dramatic erosion that resulted during Stage Three.

This erosive channelling becomes very noticeable when we observe the way Stage One & Two deposits have been truncated by deep river valleys at the Fish Creek and the Shouldice Sites. See Figures F-2, 3, 4, 5, 6 & 7. It is obvious that these two lower units were originally deposited as a blanket over wide regions of the City of Calgary and surrounding areas. When a person examines the intervening regions between these two Sites one finds a continuation of these Mazama deposits in many places.

Stage Three Mysteries

Within Calgary many of the reworked boulders and gravels within the Stage Three valleys are remnants of Unit One. However, many of the boulders and smaller rocks and gravels infilling these channels do not always have a volcanic coating but were brought in from other sources. Some of them may have a characteristic slight reddish stain. This reddish stain is also a regional and worldwide phenomenon of significant importance. (see Chapter 26.)

If geologists do not acknowledge the reality of Noah's Flood, then they must explain where the large amounts of high-energy water came from to deposit these sediments and to cause the subsequent deep and widespread erosion of younger valleys and river systems to form throughout Western Canada and throughout America. This all occurred after the great thicknesses of ice had been removed and after the Pleistocene Ice Age had come to a dramatic termination. Today these large and small river valley systems have a small little river or creek meandering within.

The powerful tsunami waves that can be related to the Third Stage of Noah's Flood were responsible for carving and re-carving the landscape not only in Canada but throughout the entire Earth.

How to Identify Flood deposits Worldwide

In order to identify Noah's Flood deposits worldwide it is necessary to have Type Sections as reference points. The Fish Creek and the Shouldice Type Sections in Calgary Alberta are only two places among many. The science of geology always requires a recognition of type sections in order to relate similar aged geological units from place to place.

The Egyptian Type Section is discussed in Chapter 20. It unlocks the mystery of Early Man throughout the Earth. It also reveals when Noah's Flood took place. It is indeed one of the most complete and important type sections in the world. It can also help to verify the Calgary Mazama Type Sections as to the time when this deposit was made. However, more detailed work must still be done in Egypt to differentiate the First, Second and Third Stages of Noah's Flood. As we walked around the Pyramids, the tour guide showed us the great amount of sedimentary sands and gravel that had previously in filled the surrounding temple structures. This all took place after the termination of the Old Kingdom Age. See Figure 20-2.

The Mas d'Azil Cave Site in France and the Ninevah, Ur and Fara Sites in the Persian Gulf region are also excellent Type Sections. See Figure 15-4.

The Santa Lagoa Site of Early Man in Brazil is a known archaeological Type Section. However, more detailed work should be done to identify the Three Stages of Noah's Flood. Chapter 19 describes various sites of Early Man in North and South America. Many of these sites could be considered excellent Type Sections.

The Olduvai Gorge Section in East Africa is another very good Type Section. See Figure 16-2. At Olduvai, units 1, 11, 111 and 1V are all Stage One deposits because they contain the remains of now extinct animal life and the washed in Acheulian artifacts of Early Paleolithic Man that characterize the Pre-Flood Altithermal Age. Unit 1 is lying upon a pronounced Pleistocene erosion surface where Mary Leakey has found 18 Pre-Flood archaeological sites of Early Man of Paleolithic Age.

Stage Three of Noah's Flood at Olduvai is evidenced by the east-west Olduvai Gorge. This Gorge cuts through and exposes the entire 300 feet (91.4m) of section referred to as beds 1, 11,111, 1V. The big mystery confronting archaeologists and anthropologists is: where did the powerful pluvial waters come from to erode such a deep channel. Our GIRA Interpretation explains where the water came from. It envisages several Stage Three powerful tsunami waves that swept over this region of Africa causing the present carving of Africa with multiple channels large and small. Today only a small little creek or river is flowing through these wide valleys.

The Mazama Type Section is only one of several Mazama Type Sections that could be established between Mount Mazama in the State of Oregon and Calgary Alberta Canada. The www.mazama website says, *"The eruption was a cataclysmic event dated at about 6,600 years ago. Great thicknesses of pumice were deposited on the flanks of Mount Mazama, while finer material was blown over great distances by the winds. The widespread distribution of the Mazama Ash has made it useful in archaeological studies as a horizon, or time, marker."* Leon Dennison, a United States geologist, has done extensive research of the Mazama and other Recent field studies in the Western USA. He relayed to me about a site in the State of Oregon where the Mazama sediments separate the archaeological artifacts of Early Man below the Mazama layer. They have found the artifacts of the North American Indian above the Mazama layer. See Figure 19-4 for greater clarification. Truly more intensive geological studies must be done.

The www.gira.ca website will also be providing additional information on the archaeological significance of the Mazama deposits.

Noah's Flood: A Big Hidden Secret

The big hidden secret throughout the world is acknowledging the authenticity of Noah's Flood on the basis of geology, archaeology and anthropology. The reason for this hidden secret is because a "Big Problem" exists.

Creation Science (Young Earth) Creationists have convinced many within the Christian community that Noah's Flood took place prior to the Pleistocene Ice Age. They claim that the entire geological column from the Archean basement to the beginning of the Pleistocene Ice Age is a direct product of Noah's Flood. See Figure 3-5. This consists of tens of thousands of feet (meters) of sediments. Thus, the above described three Stages of Noah's Flood **is not on their radar screen.**

The Scientific Affiliation of Christian Scientists in the USA is the largest Old Earth Creation organization today. I was a member of this organization for several years. They do not acknowledge that Noah's Flood was universal, but generally believe it was a local Flood restricted more or less to the Middle East region. Thus, the above mentioned sediments that relate to the three Stages of **Noah's Flood in America is not on their radar screen.**

The Darwinian Secular World View considers Noah's Flood as a myth. Thus, geological evidences regarding **Noah's Flood is not on their radar screen.** Darwinists

have gained control of the curricula of our secular universities, colleges, and now our high school and elementary
school curricula. Their ultimate aim is to eradicate all mention of God from all aspects of our educational system.
They have no apparent fear of Almighty God. In their short
sightedness, they do not seem to realize that their efforts
are soon going to come crashing down as they will face an
eventual lost eternity. See Appendix D. Jesus so wisely said,
*"For what is a man profited if he gains the whole world, but
loses his own soul."* (Mathew 16:26, NKJV)

Note: Further pertinent information will be posted on the
www.gira.ca website. For instance how can a person explain
the presence of the gigantic Okotoks erratic at Okotoks,
Alberta, Canada? How does it fit into the Flood scenario?
This will soon be explained on our website. It has a very
logical explanation.